BUILDING THE MODERN CHUP

Ashgate Studies in Architecture Series

SERIES EDITOR: EAMONN CANNIFFE, MANCHESTER SCHOOL OF ARCHITECTURE, MANCHESTER METROPOLITAN UNIVERSITY, UK

The discipline of Architecture is undergoing subtle transformation as design awareness permeates our visually dominated culture. Technological change, the search for sustainability and debates around the value of place and meaning of the architectural gesture are aspects which will affect the cities we inhabit. This series seeks to address such topics, both theoretically and in practice, through the publication of high quality original research, written and visual.

Other titles in this series

The Challenge of Emulation in Art and Architecture
Between Imitation and Invention
David Mayernik
ISBN 978 1 4094 5767 1

Building Transatlantic Italy
Architectural Dialogues with Postwar America
Paolo Scrivano
ISBN 978 1 4724 1483 0

The Architectural Capriccio
Memory, Fantasy and Invention
Edited by Lucien Steil
ISBN 978 1 4094 3191 6

Forthcoming titles in this series

The Architecture of Luxury
Annette Condello
ISBN 978 1 4094 3321 7

Shoah Presence: Architectural Representations of the Holocaust
Eran Neuman
ISBN 978 1 4094 2923 4

Reconstructing Italy
The Ina-Casa Neighborhoods of the Postwar Era
Stephanie Zeier Pilat
ISBN 978 1 4094 6580 5

Building the Modern Church

Roman Catholic Church Architecture in Britain,
1955 to 1975

Robert Proctor
Glasgow School of Art, UK

Routledge
Taylor & Francis Group

LONDON AND NEW YORK

First published 2014 by Ashgate Publishing

Published 2016 by Routledge
2 Park Square, Milton Park, Abingdon, Oxfordshire OX14 4RN
711 Third Avenue, New York, NY 10017, USA

First issued in paperback 2016

Routledge is an imprint of the Taylor & Francis Group, an informa business

British Library Cataloguing in Publication Data
A catalogue record for this book is available from the British Library.

The Library of Congress has cataloged the printed edition as follows:
Proctor, Robert, 1973– author.
    Building the modern church : Roman Catholic Church architecture in Britain, 1955 to 1975 / by Robert Proctor.
        pages cm. – (Ashgate studies in architecture)
    Includes bibliographical references and index.
    ISBN 978-1-4094-4915-7 (hardback : alk. paper) – ISBN 978-1-4094-4916-4 (ebook) – ISBN 978-1-4724-0644-6 (epub)
    1. Church architecture – Great Britain – History – 20th century. 2. Catholic church buildings – Great Britain – History – 20th century. I. Title.

    NA5468.P76 2014
    726.50941–dc23
                                                                    2013043683

ISBN 13: 978-1-138-24611-9 (pbk)
ISBN 13: 978-1-4094-4915-7 (hbk)

To Mariadele and Nicholas

Contents

List of Illustrations   *ix*
Acknowledgements   *xxiii*

1   Introduction   1

2   Tradition   15

3   Modern Church Architecture   47

4   Forms of Modernism   69

5   Modern Church Art   109

6   Modernism and the Liturgical Movement   133

7   Liturgical Change   173

8   Devotion   219

9   Ritual and Community   251

10 The Church and the World   277

11 Conclusion   325

Plans   329

Bibliography   *337*
Index   *357*

Illustrations

The author has made every effort to contact copyright holders and would be pleased to correct any errors or omissions that are brought to his attention, in subsequent editions.

BLACK AND WHITE FIGURES

1.1   St Gregory, South Ruislip, London, by Gerard Goalen, 1965–67. View of nave looking towards sanctuary: sanctuary stained glass by Patrick Reyntiens, © Patrick Reyntiens, all rights reserved, DACS, London, 2013; clerestory stained glass by Charles Norris, added c.1987. Photo: Robert Proctor, 2010

1.2   St Gregory, South Ruislip, London, by Gerard Goalen, 1965–67. View from street: lintel sculpture by Steven Sykes. Photo: Robert Proctor, 2010

1.3   St Gregory, South Ruislip, London, by Gerard Goalen, 1965–67. View into baptistery: statue of St Gregory by Willi Soukop; font lettering by Ralph Beyer; stained glass by Patrick Reyntiens, © Patrick Reyntiens, all rights reserved, DACS, London, 2013. Photo: Robert Proctor, 2010

2.1   Trinity Congregational church, Lansbury Estate, London, by Cecil Handisyde and D. Rogers Stark, 1949–51. Photo: John Pantlin. Source: Architectural Press Archive / RIBA Library Photographs Collection

2.2   Sts Mary and Joseph, Poplar, London, by Adrian Gilbert Scott, 1951–54. Photo: Stewart Bale Ltd, 1956. Source: parish archive

2.3   Westminster Cathedral, London, by J. F. Bentley, 1895–1903. Nave photographed in 1953 before addition of marble cladding. Photo: Reginald Hugo de Burgh Galwey. Source: Architectural Press Archive / RIBA Library Photographs Collection

2.4   St Patrick, Leicester, by Reynolds & Scott, 1957–59. Photo: Robert Proctor, 2009

2.5   St Joseph, Wembley, London, by Reynolds & Scott, 1956–58. Photo: Robert Proctor, 2010

2.6   St Bernard, Burnage, Manchester, by Reynolds & Scott, 1957–59. Photo: Entwistle, Thorpe & Co. Ltd, c.1959.

2.7   Ratcliffe College Chapel, Leicester, by Ernest Bower Norris, 1957–59. Sculpture and *dalle de verre* windows by Jonah Jones. Photo: Robert Proctor, 2009

2.8   St John Fisher, West Heath, Birmingham, by Sandy & Norris, 1963–64. Photo: Robert Proctor, 2009

2.9   St Raphael, Stalybridge, by Massey & Massey, 1960–63. *Dalle de verre* by Pierre Fourmaintraux of Whitefriars Studios; Stations of the Cross in ceramic by Alan Boyson and Neal French. By permission of Alan Boyson and Neal French. Photo: Richard Brook, *c.*2000

2.10   Our Lady of the Rosary, Marylebone, London, by H. S. Goodhart-Rendel and D. A. Reid of F. G. Broadbent & Partners, 1958–64. Main entrance facade. Photo: Robert Proctor, 2009

2.11   Our Lady of the Rosary, Marylebone, London, by H. S. Goodhart-Rendel and D. A. Reid of F. G. Broadbent & Partners, 1958–64. Interior. Photo: Robert Proctor, 2009

2.12   Holy Cross, Birkenhead, by F. X. Velarde, 1959. Photo: Stewart Bale Ltd., *c.*1959. Source: Shrewsbury Diocesan Archives, Birkenhead

2.13   St Alexander, Bootle, Liverpool, by F. X. Velarde, 1957. Photographer unknown, *c.*1960. Source: Bryan Little, *Catholic Churches Since 1623* (London: Robert Hale, 1966), pl. 37

2.14   St Luke, Pinner, London, by F. X. Velarde, 1958. Main facade with relief sculpture of the Virgin and St Luke by David John. Photo: Robert Proctor, 2010

2.15   Our Lady of Mount Carmel and St Simon Stock, Kensington, London, by Giles Gilbert Scott, 1960. Photo: Robert Proctor, 2009

2.16   Christ the King, Plymouth, by Giles Gilbert Scott, 1960–62. Photo: Steve Cadman, 2011

2.17   Our Lady of Lourdes, Hackenthorpe, Sheffield, by Reynolds & Scott, 1957. Photo: Robert Proctor, 2009

2.18   Our Lady and St Joseph, Hanwell, London, by Reynolds & Scott, 1962–67. Photo: Robert Proctor, 2010

2.19   Our Lady and St Joseph, Hanwell, London, by Reynolds & Scott, 1962–67. View towards choir gallery. Photo: Robert Proctor, 2010

3.1   St Paul, Glenrothes, by Gillespie, Kidd & Coia, 1956–58. Photo: William Toomey. Source: Architectural Press Archive / RIBA Library Photographs Collection

3.2   St Patrick, Kilsyth, by Gillespie, Kidd & Coia, 1964. Photo: Robert Proctor, 2010

3.3   Hopwood Hall Chapel, De La Salle Training College, Middleton, Manchester, by Frederick Gibberd and Reynolds & Scott, 1961–65. Photo: John Mills, *c.*1965. Source: RIBA Library Photographs Collection

3.4   Frederick Gibberd, competition-winning plan for Liverpool Metropolitan Cathedral, 1960. Source: RIBA Library Photographs Collection. Courtesy of the Gibberd Garden Trust and Frederick Gibberd Partnership

3.5   Metropolitan Cathedral of Christ the King, Liverpool, by Frederick Gibberd, 1960–67. Bell tower sculpture by William Mitchell. Photo: Elsam, Mann & Cooper. Source: Architectural Press Archive / RIBA Library Photographs Collection

3.6   Our Lady of Victories, Kensington, London, by Adrian Gilbert Scott, 1952–59. Perspective of first design, drawn by J. D. M. Harvey, 1954. Source: parish archive. Courtesy of the parish of Our Lady of Victories, Kensington

3.7   Our Lady of Victories, Kensington, by Adrian Gilbert Scott, 1952–59. The sculpture of the Risen Christ by Michael Clark replaced a crucifix in the 1980s. By permission of Joseph Lindsey-Clark. Photo: Robert Proctor, 2009

3.8   Our Lady of the Visitation, Greenford, London, by David Stokes & Partners,

1956–60. Photo: Colin Westwood, c.1960. Source: RIBA Library Photographs Collection

3.9   Our Lady Help of Christians, Tile Cross, Birmingham, by Richard Gilbert Scott, 1965–67. Photo: Robert Proctor, 2009

4.1   St Columba, Bolton, by Greenhalgh & Williams, 1956. Photo: Robert Proctor, 2008

4.2   St Columba, Bolton, by Greenhalgh & Williams, 1956. Interior view towards sanctuary; furnishings reordered since construction. Photo: Robert Proctor, 2008

4.3   Our Lady of Lourdes, Farnworth, Bolton, by Greenhalgh & Williams, 1957. Photo: Ambrose Gillick, 2012

4.4   Our Lady of Lourdes, Farnworth, Bolton, by Greenhalgh & Williams, 1957. Photo: Robert Proctor, 2008

4.5   St Patrick, Walsall, by Harrison & Cox, 1964. Photo: Robert Proctor, 2009

4.6   St Patrick, Walsall, by Harrison & Cox, 1964. View from sanctuary towards main entrance. Photo: Robert Proctor, 2009

4.7   St Thomas of Canterbury, Rainham, Kent, by E. G. Dodds and K. C. White, 1959. Exterior with ceramic panel of St Thomas of Canterbury by Adam Kossowski. Photo: Robert Proctor, 2010

4.8   St Charles Borromeo, Kelvinside, Glasgow, by Gillespie, Kidd & Coia, 1956–60. Photographer unknown, c.1960. Source: Glasgow School of Art

4.9   Our Lady of the Visitation, Greenford, London, by David Stokes & Partners, 1956–60. View towards entrance before completion. Photo: Colin Westwood, c.1960. Source: RIBA Library Photographs Collection

4.10   St Agnes, Huyton, Liverpool, by Lionel A. G. Prichard & Son, 1959–65. Interior view towards choir gallery. Photo: Ambrose Gillick, 2011

4.11   St Agnes, Huyton, Liverpool, by Lionel A. G. Prichard & Son, 1959–65. Photo: Robert Proctor, 2008

4.12   St Mary, Denton, Manchester, by Walter Stirrup & Son, 1961–63. Photo: Robert Proctor, 2008

4.13   Holy Family, Southampton, by Liam McCormick, 1966. Photo: Robert Proctor, 2010

4.14   St Bride, East Kilbride, by Gillespie, Kidd & Coia, 1957–64. Interior viewed from side gallery, c.1964. Photo: Sam Lambert. Source: Architectural Press Archive / RIBA Library Photographs Collection

4.15   St Patrick, Rochdale, by Desmond Williams, 1964–69. Perspective drawing of early design, c.1964: the design was subsequently much reduced and simplified, and a circular drum added over the centre. Courtesy of Desmond Williams. Source: parish archive

4.16   St Patrick, Rochdale, by Desmond Williams, 1964–69. Photo: Robert Proctor, 2013

4.17   St Patrick, St Helens, by F. X. Velarde Partnership, 1962–65. Photo: Elsam, Mann & Cooper, c.1965. Source: RIBA Library Photographs Collection

4.18   St Patrick, St Helens, by F. X. Velarde Partnership, 1962–65. Baptistery. Photo: Robert Proctor, 2008

4.19   St Paul, Bow Common, by Robert Maguire and Keith Murray, 1958–60. Photo: Reginald Hugo de Burgh Galwey. Source: Architectural Press Archive / RIBA Library Photographs Collection

4.20   Our Lady of the Rosary, Donnington, by Richard O'Mahony & Partners, 1965–67. Photo: Elsam, Mann & Cooper, c.1967. Source: archive of OMF Derek Cox Architects, Liverpool

4.21   Sts Peter and Paul, Lichfield, by Gwilliam & Armstrong, 1967. Photo: Ambrose Gillick, 2012

4.22   St Peter, Dumbarton, by Garner, Preston & Strebel, 1971. Photo: Robert Proctor, 2010

4.23   St Michael & All Angels, Wombwell, Barnsley, by Weightman & Bullen, 1867–68. Photo: Robert Proctor, 2009

4.24   Our Lady of Walsingham, Bootle, by Lanner Ltd, 1973. Interior view towards main entrance. Carved frieze of the Last Judgement by Eric Carr, c.1976. Photo: Robert Proctor, 2008

5.1   Église du Sacré-Coeur, Audincourt, by Maurice Novarina, 1951. View of baptistery with glass by Jean Bazaine. © ADAGP, Paris, and DACS, London, 2013. Photo: Denis Mathieu, 2013

5.2   St Aidan, East Acton, London, by Burles & Newton, 1959–61. View of nave: frieze of the Stations of the Cross by Arthur Fleischmann; painting of the Crucifixion by Graham Sutherland, c.1964. Courtesy of the Estate of Graham Sutherland. Photo: Robert Proctor, 2009

5.3   St Bernadette, Lancaster, by Tom Mellor, 1958. Reredos painting by John Piper. Courtesy of the Estate of John Piper. Photographer unknown, c.1958. Source: parish archive

5.4   Madonna and Child by Jacob Epstein at Convent of the Holy Child Jesus, Cavendish Square, London, 1951–53. Photo: Steve Cadman, 2011

5.5   St Charles Borromeo, Kelvinside, Glasgow, by Gillespie, Kidd & Coia, 1956–60. Stations of the Cross by Benno Schotz, RSA. Courtesy of the Trustees of the late Benno Schotz, RSA. Photo: Robert Proctor, 2010

5.6   St Paul, Glenrothes, by Gillespie, Kidd & Coia, 1956–58. Crucifixion by Benno Schotz, RSA. Courtesy of the Trustees of the late Benno Schotz, RSA. Photographer unknown, c.1958. Source: Glasgow School of Art

5.7   Metropolitan Cathedral of Christ the King, Liverpool, by Frederick Gibberd, 1960–67. Lady chapel: Madonna and Child by Robert Brumby; stained glass by Margaret Traherne. By permission of Robert Brumby and the Dean of the Metropolitan Cathedral of Christ the King. Photo: Robert Proctor, 2012

5.8   Metropolitan Cathedral of Christ the King, Liverpool, by Frederick Gibberd, 1960–67. Blessed Sacrament chapel: painting, tabernacle and stained glass design by Ceri Richards, © Estate of Ceri Richards, all rights reserved, DACS, London, 2013; stained glass executed by Patrick Reyntiens, © Patrick Reyntiens, all rights reserved, DACS, London, 2013. By permission of the Dean of the Metropolitan Cathedral of Christ the King. Photo: Henk Snoek. Source: Architectural Press Archive / RIBA Library Photographs Collection

5.9   Metropolitan Cathedral of Christ the King, Liverpool, by Frederick Gibberd, 1960–67. Crucifix by Elisabeth Frink, © Estate of Elisabeth Frink, all rights reserved, DACS, London, 2013; stained glass behind by John Piper and Patrick Reyntiens, © Patrick Reyntiens, all rights reserved, DACS, London, 2013. By permission of the Dean of the Metropolitan Cathedral of Christ the King. Photo: Robert Proctor, 2012

5.10   St Mary, Leyland, by Weightman & Bullen, 1960–64. Suspended crucifix in ceramic by Adam Kossowski. Sculpture of the Virgin and Child by Ian Stuart. Blessed Sacrament chapel tapestry of the Crucifixion by Jerzy Faczynski, made by the Edinburgh Tapestry Company; stained glass by Patrick Reyntiens, © Patrick Reyntiens, all rights reserved, DACS, London, 2013. Photo: Elsam, Mann & Cooper, c.1964. Source: parish archive

5.11   St Mary, Leyland, by Weightman & Bullen, 1960–64. Stations of the Cross by Arthur Dooley (Veronica's veil); stained glass behind by Patrick Reyntiens,

© Patrick Reyntiens, all rights reserved, DACS, London, 2013. Photo: Robert Proctor, 2010

5.12   St Bernadette, Lancaster, by Tom Mellor, 1958. Stations of the Cross by Peter Watts (Nailing of Christ to the Cross). By permission of Richard Watts. Photo: Robert Proctor, 2011

5.13   St Mary Magdalene, Cudworth, by John Rochford, 1960–61. Stations of the Cross by David John. By permission of David John. Photo: Robert Proctor, 2009

6.1   St Christophorus, Niehl, Cologne, by Rudolf Schwarz, 1958–60. Stained glass and painting of the Risen Christ by Georg Meistermann, © DACS, London, 2013. Photographer unknown. Source: © Rheinisches Bildarchiv Köln

6.2   St Paul, Bow Common, London, by Robert Maguire and Keith Murray, 1958–60. Photograph taken on completion c.1960 but before installation of the ciborium. Photo: Eric de Maré. Source: Architectural Press Archive / RIBA Library Photographs Collection

6.3   Our Lady and the First Martyrs, Bradford, by J. H. Langtry-Langton, 1935. The interior has been reordered twice, most recently in 1971 by Peter Langtry-Langton to restore aspects of its original arrangement. Photo: Robert Proctor, 2009

6.4   J. D. Crichton, 'A Dream-Church', *Music and Liturgy* (June 1943), 73. Plan drawn by 'Mr Leighton Bishop'. Courtesy of the Trustees of the Society of St Gregory

6.5   Holy Redeemer, Pershore, by Hugh Bankart, 1957–59. Photographer unknown, c.1960. Source: parish archive

6.6   Our Lady of Fatima, Harlow, by Gerard Goalen, 1954–60. View showing original liturgical arrangements: stained glass by Charles Norris. Photo: John McCann, c.1960. Source: John McCann / RIBA Library Photographs Collection.

6.7   Chapel of the Priory of St Louis and St Mary, Missouri, by Hellmuth, Obata & Kassabaum, c.1959–62. Photo: G. E. Kidder Smith, mid-1960s. Source: © Massachusetts Institute of Technology. Courtesy of MIT Libraries, Rotch Visual Collections

6.8   St Ambrose, Speke, Liverpool, by Weightman & Bullen, 1958–61. Photo: Ambrose Gillick, 2012

6.9   St Catherine, Lowton, by Weightman & Bullen, 1957–59. Photo: Robert Proctor, 2008

6.10   St Columba, Cupar, by Peter Whiston, 1964. Photo: Robert Proctor, 2012

6.11   Metropolitan Cathedral of Christ the King, Liverpool, by Frederick Gibberd, 1960–67. View from side gallery: entrance on the left; Blessed Sacrament chapel on the right; stained glass by John Piper and Patrick Reyntiens, © Patrick Reyntiens, all rights reserved, DACS, London, 2013. By permission of the Dean of the Metropolitan Cathedral of Christ the King. Photo: Robert Proctor, 2012

6.12   Metropolitan Cathedral of Christ the King, Liverpool. Unexecuted competition design by Denys Lasdun, 1960. Source: RIBA Library Drawings and Archives Collections

6.13   Metropolitan Cathedral of Christ the King, Liverpool. Unexecuted competition design by Gerard Goalen, 1960. Courtesy of Martin Goalen

6.14   St Margaret of Scotland, Twickenham, London, by Williams & Winkley, 1964–69. View from sanctuary to font: stained glass behind by Patrick Reyntiens, © Patrick Reyntiens, all rights reserved, DACS 2013. Photo: © Richard Einzig, c.1969 / arcaidimages.com. Source: archive of Austin Winkley & Associates, London, www.austinwinkley.co.uk

6.15   St Margaret of Scotland, Twickenham, London, by Williams & Winkley, 1964–69.

Exterior. Photo: © Richard Einzig, c.1969 / arcaidimages.com. Source: archive of Austin Winkley & Associates, London, www.austinwinkley.co.uk

6.16   St Margaret of Scotland, Twickenham, London, by Williams & Winkley, 1964–69. Sanctuary in use, c.1969: stained glass by Patrick Reyntiens, © Patrick Reyntiens, all rights reserved, DACS, London, 2013. Photo: Norbert Galea. Source: archive of Austin Winkley & Associates, London, www.austinwinkley.co.uk

6.17   Cathedral of Sts Peter and Paul, Clifton, Bristol, by Percy Thomas Partnership, 1965–73. Architects' sketch of the liturgical entrance procession, 1965. Source: Clifton Diocesan Archives. Courtesy of Ronald Weeks and the Trustees of the Diocese of Clifton

6.18   Clifton Cathedral, Bristol, by Percy Thomas Partnership, 1965–73. Architects' studies for the nave, 1966. Source: Clifton Diocesan Archives. Courtesy of Ronald Weeks and the Trustees of the Diocese of Clifton

6.19   Clifton Cathedral, Bristol, by Percy Thomas Partnership, 1965–73. Architects' summary of design studies, 'Relationships of Basic Elements', 1966. Source: Clifton Diocesan Archives. Courtesy of Ronald Weeks and the Trustees of the Diocese of Clifton

6.20   Clifton Cathedral, Bristol, by Percy Thomas Partnership, 1965–73. View of consecration ceremony, 1973, showing Blessed Sacrament chapel with sanctuary and nave visible behind through openings. Photo: Brian Middlehurst, 1973

6.21   Clifton Cathedral, Bristol, by Percy Thomas Partnership, 1965–73. Stained glass by Henry Haig. Photo: Brian Middlehurst, c.1973

7.1   St Mary, Dunstable, by Desmond Williams, 1961–64. The altar position has not changed since completion, but it was

originally furnished with the tabernacle and six candlesticks along its rear edge. Photo: Robert Proctor, 2013

7.2   St Catherine of Siena, Horsefair, Birmingham, by Harrison & Cox, 1961–65. Undated photograph of Mass shortly after completion of the church. Photographer unknown. Source: parish archive. Courtesy of the Birmingham Roman Catholic Diocesan Trustees

7.3   Sacred Heart, Gorton, Manchester, by Reynolds & Scott, 1958–62. Photo: Robert Proctor, 2013

7.4   St Stephen, Droylsdon, Manchester, by Greenhalgh & Williams, 1958–59. Photo: Robert Proctor, 2012

7.5   St Paul, Glenrothes, by Gillespie, Kidd & Coia, 1956–58. Photo: William Toomey, c.1958. Courtesy of Architectural Press Archive / RIBA Library Photographs Collection. Source: Glasgow School of Art

7.6   St Joseph, Faifley, Glasgow, by Gillespie, Kidd & Coia, 1960–63. View after early reordering, c.1965, when the tabernacle was moved to an altar behind the sanctuary. Photographer unknown. Source: Glasgow School of Art

7.7   St Peter's College, Cardross, by Gillespie, Kidd & Coia, 1959–67. The ground-floor chapel was located at the end of the left-hand block, embraced by side chapels in towers. Photo: Thomson of Uddingston, c.1967. Source: Glasgow School of Art

7.8   Immaculate Heart of Mary, Hayes, London, by Burles, Newton & Partners, 1958–62. View towards choir gallery over entrance: Stations of the Cross by Arthur Fleischmann. Photo: Robert Proctor, 2010

7.9   Our Lady, Queen of the Apostles, Heston, London, by Burles, Newton & Partners, 1961–64. Photo: Robert Proctor, 2010

7.10   St Francis de Sales, Hampton Hill, London, by Burles, Newton & Partners, 1964–67. Nave windows by Jerzy Faczynski and J. O'Neill & Sons; chapel on the right with stained glass by Gilbert Sheedy. Photo: Robert Proctor, 2010

7.11   St William of York, Stanmore, London, by Hector O. Corfiato & Partners, 1960–61. Photo: Robert Proctor, 2010

7.12   St Teresa, Newtown, St Helens, by William & J. B. Ellis, 1964–65. Photo: Robert Proctor, 2008

7.13   Sacred Heart, Cumbernauld, by Gillespie, Kidd & Coia, 1961–64. Stations of the Cross in *dalle de verre* by Sadie McLellan. Photo: Robert Proctor, 2011

7.14   St Nicholas, Gipton, Leeds, by Weightman & Bullen, 1960. Altar and communion rails: the sanctuary has been partly reordered since completion. Photo: Robert Proctor, 2009

7.15   St Theresa of Lisieux, Borehamwood, London, by F. X. Velarde Partnership, 1961–62. Photo: Elsam, Mann & Cooper, *c*.1962. Source: archive of OMF Derek Cox Architects, Liverpool

7.16   Good Shepherd, Nottingham, by Gerard Goalen, 1961–64. Stained glass by Patrick Reyntiens, © Patrick Reyntiens, all rights reserved, DACS, London, 2013. Photo: Henk Snoek, *c*.1964. Source: RIBA Library Photographs Collection

7.17   St Bride, East Kilbride, by Gillespie, Kidd & Coia, 1957–64. View of rear of nave showing font. Photo: Sam Lambert, *c*.1964. Source: Architectural Press Archive / RIBA Library Photographs Collection

7.18   Our Lady of Good Counsel, Dennistoun, by Gillespie, Kidd & Coia, 1962–65. View from entrance towards font. Photo: Studio Brett, *c*.1965. Source: RIBA Library Photographs Collection

7.19   Our Lady Help of Christians, Tile Cross, Birmingham, by Sir Giles Scott, Son &

Partner, 1962–67. Sketch proposals by Richard Gilbert Scott for a double altar, 1965. Source: Archives of the Roman Catholic Archdiocese of Birmingham. Courtesy of Richard Gilbert Scott

7.20   Our Lady Help of Christians, Tile Cross, Birmingham, by Sir Giles Scott, Son & Partner, 1962–67. Sketch proposals by Richard Gilbert Scott for sanctuary arrangement, 1965. Source: Archives of the Roman Catholic Archdiocese of Birmingham. Courtesy of Richard Gilbert Scott

7.21   Our Lady Help of Christians, Tile Cross, Birmingham, by Sir Giles Scott, Son & Partner, 1962–67. View from transept: stained glass by John Chrestien. Photo: Robert Proctor, 2009

7.22   Our Lady of Good Counsel, Dennistoun, Glasgow, by Gillespie, Kidd & Coia, 1962–65. Photo: Studio Brett, *c*.1965. Source: RIBA Library Photographs Collection

7.23   St Aidan, Coulsdon, London, by Burles, Newton & Partners, 1966. Photo: Robert Proctor, 2010

7.24   St Michael, Wolverhampton, by Desmond Williams, 1965–67. The liturgical furnishings, including font, are mostly original: reredos, tabernacle, candlesticks, altar and font inserts by Robert Brumby. By permission of Robert Brumby. Photo: Robert Proctor, 2009

7.25   St Elphege, Wallington, London, by Williams & Winkley, 1969–72. The font is visible beyond the altar, next to the main entrance door. Photo: Robert Proctor, 2010

7.26   St Thérèse, Port Talbot, by F. R. Bates, Son & Price, *c*.1969. The tabernacle was originally housed in a chapel to the left of the sanctuary. Photo: Robert Proctor, 2012

7.27   St Joseph, Hunslet, by J. H. Langtry-Langton & Partners, 1968–71. Diagram of plan by Peter Langtry-Langton, *c*.1971.

By permission of Peter Langtry-Langton.
Source: souvenir booklet accompanying
church opening, 1971, Leeds Diocesan
Archives

7.28   Our Lady and St Peter, Wimbledon,
London, by Tomei, Mackley & Pound, 1970–
73. The tabernacle was originally placed
in the chapel to the right of the sanctuary.
Photo: Robert Proctor, 2010

7.29   St Thomas More, Manor House,
London, by Burles, Newton & Partners,
c.1974. View of the chapel. Photo: Robert
Proctor, 2010

8.1   St Aidan, Coulsdon, London, by Burles,
Newton & Partners, 1966. Sculpture of the
Virgin and Child by Xaver Ruckstuhl. Photo:
Robert Proctor, 2010

8.2   St Clare, Blackley, Manchester, by
Weightman & Bullen, 1956–58. Mosaic of
St Clare by George Mayer Martin; Stations of
the Cross by David John. By permission of
David John. Photo: Ambrose Gillick, 2012

8.3   Holy Family, Pontefract, Leeds, by
Derek Walker, 1964. Reredos of Christ
in Majesty, candlesticks, altar sculpture
and tabernacle by Robert Brumby. By
permission of Robert Brumby. Photo:
J. Roberts & Co., 1964. Source: Leeds
Diocesan Archives

8.4   St Mary, Failsworth, Manchester, by
Greenhalgh & Williams, 1961–64. Reredos
mosaic of Our Lady of All Graces designed
by B. Nolan. Photo: Robert Proctor, 2012

8.5   St Mary, Failsworth, Manchester, by
Greenhalgh & Williams, 1961–64. External
sculpture of the Immaculate Conception
and Mysteries of the Rosary by E. & J.
Blackwell. Photo: Robert Proctor, 2012

8.6   St Stephen, Droylsden, Manchester,
by Greenhalgh & Williams, 1958–59. May
devotions, 1960s. Photographer unknown.
Source: parish archive. Courtesy of the
Diocese of Salford

8.7   St Catherine of Siena, Birmingham, by
Harrison & Cox, 1961–65. May devotions,
1960s. Photographer unknown. Source:
parish archive. Courtesy of the Birmingham
Roman Catholic Diocesan Trustees

8.8   St Bernadette, Lancaster, by Tom
Mellor, 1958. Perspective by the architect
dated 1955. Courtesy of David Mellor.
Source: parish archive

8.9   Votive Shrine of Our Lady of Lourdes,
Blackpool, by F. X. Velarde, 1955–57. Integral
sculpture by David John. Photo: Robert
Proctor, 2011

8.10   Our Lady of Fatima, Harlow New
Town, by Gerard Goalen, 1954–60. Stations
of the Cross by Irene Foord-Kelcey. By
permission of Christopher Foord-Kelcey.
Photo: Robert Proctor, 2010

8.11   St Paul, Wood Green, London, by
John Rochford, 1967–72. Stations of the
Cross by Michael Clark. By permission
of Joseph Lindsey-Clark. Photo: Robert
Proctor, 2010

8.12   St Martin, Castlemilk, Glasgow, by
Gillespie, Kidd & Coia, 1957–61. Photo:
Robert Proctor, 2010

8.13   Clifton Cathedral, Bristol, by Percy
Thomas Partnership, 1965–73. Stations of
the Cross by William Mitchell. By permission
of William Mitchell. Photo: Robert Proctor,
2013

8.14   Aylesford Priory, Kent, by Adrian
Gilbert Scott, 1954–64. Central sculpture
of the Virgin Mary by Michael Clark. Photo:
Robert Proctor, 2010

8.15   Aylesford Priory, Kent, by Adrian
Gilbert Scott, 1954–64. Chapel of the Forty
Martyrs of England and Wales: ceramics by
Adam Kossowski; dalle de verre windows by
Charles Norris. Photo: Robert Proctor, 2010

8.16   Aylesford Priory, Kent, by Adrian
Gilbert Scott, 1954–64. Reliquary of St
Simon Stock by Adam Kossowski; dalle de

verre windows by Charles Norris. Photo: Robert Proctor, 2010

8.17   'Shrines of Our Lady', from *Catholic Herald* (4 Dec. 1953), 7. Drawn by Tim Madden. Courtesy of the *Catholic Herald*, catholicherald.co.uk

8.18   Pilgrimage of Our Lady of the Taper, Cardigan. Undated photograph, appearing to show installation of new statue in 1956. Photographer unknown. Source: Menevia Diocesan Archives. Courtesy of the Diocese of Menevia and Canon Seamus Cunnane

8.19   Our Lady of the Taper, Cardigan, by Weightman & Bullen, 1970. View from courtyard: statue-shrine to the left; church in the centre; presbytery forming wall to the right. Photo: Robert Proctor, 2010

9.1   Basil Spence, design for St Martin and St Ninian, Whithorn, 1951. Photograph of model. Source: © Courtesy of the Royal Commission on the Ancient and Historical Monuments of Scotland, Spence, Glover and Ferguson Collection. Licensor, www.rcahms.gov.uk

9.2   St Martin and St Ninian, Whithorn, by H. S. Goodhart-Rendel, 1955–60. Photo: Ambrose Gillick, 2012

9.3   Tyburn Convent, London, by F. G. Broadbent & Partners, 1960–63. Photo: Robert Proctor, 2010

9.4   Plaque at Marble Arch, London, commemorating the site of the Tyburn gallows, laid in 1964. Photo: Robert Proctor, 2010

9.5   Sts Mary and Joseph, Poplar, London, by Adrian Gilbert Scott, 1951–54. Statue of St Patrick; one of the Stations of the Cross by Peter Watts is also visible. Photo: Robert Proctor, 2010

9.6   St Patrick, Coventry, by Desmond Williams, 1967–71. Stained glass depicting St Patrick in the vestibule, artist unknown. Photo: Robert Proctor, 2009

9.7   Sacred Heart, Camberwell, London, by D. Plaskett Marshall, 1959. Connemara marble cladding added to piers later. Photo: Robert Proctor, 2010

9.8   St Raphael, Yeading, London, by Justin Alleyn, 1961. Reredos of Connemara marble; Lady chapel and Sacred Heart chapel also showing use of marble; *dalle de verre* windows by Pierre Fourmaintraux of Whitefriars Studios. Photo: Robert Proctor, 2010

9.9   Sts Mary and Joseph, Poplar, London, by Adrian Gilbert Scott, 1951–55. Stained glass by William Wilson. Photo: Robert Proctor, 2010

9.10   St Joseph, Wolverhampton, by Jennings, Homer & Lynch, 1967. Connemara marble in the sanctuary on the wall behind the altar and for the altar and communion rails; stained glass of Sts Peter and Paul by Hardman & Co. Photo: Robert Proctor, 2009

9.11   St Joseph, Wolverhampton, by Jennings, Homer & Lynch, 1967. View to rear of church: stained glass of St Patrick by Hardman & Co. Photo: Robert Proctor, 2009

9.12   St Anthony Bobola Polish Church, London, 1961 onwards, alterations by Aleksander Klecki. Sculpture and stained glass by Aleksander Klecki. Photo: Robert Proctor, 2013

9.13   Church of St Anne, Fawley Court, Buckinghamshire, by Crabtree & Jarosz, 1973. Photographer unknown. Source: archive of George W. T. Jarosz, London

9.14   Notre Dame de France, London, by Hector O. Corfiato, 1955. Tapestry by Dom Robert, Tabard Workshop, Aubusson, 1955; chapel with fresco by Jean Cocteau of 1960 visible in the centre of the photograph; fresco © ADAGP, Paris, and DACS, London, 2013. By permission of the Rector and Trustees of Notre Dame de France. Photo: Robert Proctor, 2010

9.15   St Paul, Wood Green, London, by John Rochford, 1965–72. Vestibule passageway containing stained glass from former church of 1904. Photo: Robert Proctor, 2010

9.16   St Mary, Leyland. Procession at opening ceremony, 1964. Photo: Tony Hart. Source: parish archive

10.1   St Anthony of Padua, Preston, by Giles Gilbert Scott, 1958–59. Photo: Robert Proctor, 2013

10.2   St Theresa, Sheffield, by John Rochford, 1959–60. External sculpture by Philip Lindsey Clark. Photo: Robert Proctor, 2009

10.3   St Anthony, Wythenshawe, by Adrian Gilbert Scott, 1957–60. The Portway runs alongside the church; its junction with Rudpark Road is at the centre of the photograph. Photo: Robert Proctor, 2013

10.4   Our Lady of the Assumption, Langley, near Manchester, by W. & J. B. Ellis, 1956–61. Initial design proposal of 1956. Courtesy of Ellis Williams Architects. Source: parish archive

10.5   Our Lady of the Assumption, Langley, near Manchester, by W. & J. B. Ellis, 1956–61. In the final design the church's orientation was rotated by 90°, and its tower moved to the road junction; also visible here are a convent on the left and the presbytery on the right. Photo: Robert Proctor, 2013

10.6   St Michael and All Angels, Woodchurch, Birkenhead, by F. X. Velarde Partnership, 1962–65. Photographer unknown, c.1965. Source: Architectural Press Archive / RIBA Library Photographs Collection

10.7   St Michael and All Angels, Woodchurch, Birkenhead, by F. X. Velarde Partnership, 1962–65. Sculpture of the Virgin and Child by Norman Dilworth. By permission of Norman Dilworth. Photographer unknown, c.1965. Source: Architectural Press Archive / RIBA Library Photographs Collection

10.8   Glenrothes New Town Outline Plan, by the Glenrothes New Town Development Corporation Architects' Office under Peter Tinto, 1952, showing sites for churches. By permission of Fife Council Archive Centre, Glenrothes

10.9   St Bride, East Kilbride, by Gillespie, Kidd & Coia, 1957–64. Photo: G. Forrest Wilson, c.1964. Source: Glasgow School of Art

10.10   Anglican church of St Paul, Harlow New Town, by Humphrys & Hurst, 1957–59. Photo: Robert Proctor, 2010

10.11   Our Lady of Fatima, Harlow New Town, by Gerard Goalen, 1954–60. Photo: Ray Stebbings, c.1960. Source: reproduced by courtesy of Essex Record Office, Chelmsford

10.12   Our Lady of Fatima, Harlow New Town, by Gerard Goalen, 1954–60. Photo: Robert Proctor, 2010

10.13   St Catherine of Siena, Horsefair, Birmingham, by Harrison & Cox, 1961–65. Photo: Robert Proctor, 2009

10.14   Cathedral of St Mary, Edinburgh. Sketch proposal for rebuilding the cathedral by T. Harley Haddow & Partners, 1966. Perspective by Alexander Duncan Bell showing view from Leith Walk. Source: Scottish Catholic Archives, Edinburgh

10.15   St Gregory, Alresford, by Melhuish, Wright & Evans, 1968. Photo: Robert Proctor, 2010

10.16   St Gregory, Alresford, by Melhuish, Wright & Evans, 1968. Interior during Mass, as published in Architectural Review (1970). Photo: Peter Baistow, 1970. Source: Architectural Press Archive / RIBA Library Photographs Collection

10.17   St Bernadette, Bristol, by Kenneth Nealon, Tanner & Partners, 1966–68. Photo: Robert Proctor, 2013

10.18   Our Lady of the Wayside, Shirley, near Birmingham, by Rush, Granelli &

Partners, 1965–67. Interior viewed from within main entrance: lady chapel in centre; sculpture of the Risen Christ by Elisabeth Frink, left, © Estate of Elisabeth Frink, all rights reserved, DACS, London, 2013. Photo: Robert Proctor, 2009

10.19   Our Lady of the Wayside, Shirley, near Birmingham, by Rush, Granelli & Partners, 1965–67. Sculpture of Our Lady of the Wayside in wood by Walter Ritchie. Photo: Robert Proctor, 2009

10.20   St Thomas More, Sheffield, by John Rochford & Partners, 1964–69. Exterior viewed from main road. Photo: Anthony Tranmer, c.1969

10.21   St Thomas More, Sheffield, by John Rochford & Partners, 1964–69. View of nave: stained-glass crucifix by Patrick Feeny Photo: Anthony Tranmer, c.1969

10.22   St Thomas More, Sheffield, by John Rochford & Partners, 1964–69. View of hall, open to corridor at the left and the nave partitions beyond. Photo: Anthony Tranmer, c.1969

10.23   St Helen's Parochial Centre, Crosby, by Weightman & Bullen, 1973–74. Interior viewed from social room, arranged for Sunday liturgy. Photo: Robert Proctor, 2008

10.24   St Helen's Parochial Centre, Crosby, by Weightman & Bullen, 1973–74. Photo: Robert Proctor, 2008

10.25   St John Stone, Woodvale, Southport, by Richard O'Mahony & Partners, 1970–71. Interior in use at time of opening. Photo: James Hunter, c.1971. Source: archive of OMF Derek Cox Architects, Liverpool

10.26   Cathedral of St Mary and St Helen, Brentwood, alteration and extension of church of 1861, by Burles, Newton & Partners, 1974. View from sanctuary showing partitions. Photographer unknown. Source: Brentwood Diocesan Archive

10.27   Cathedral of St Mary and St Helen, Brentwood, alteration and extension of church of 1861, by Burles, Newton & Partners, 1974. View towards new entrance with original spire behind. Photographer unknown. Source: Brentwood Diocesan Archive

10.28   Lancaster University Chaplaincy Centre, Lancaster, by Cassidy & Ashton, 1966–69. View of central concourse towards Roman Catholic chapel with screens opened. Photo: Robert Proctor, 2011

10.29   Lancaster University Chaplaincy Centre, Lancaster, by Cassidy & Ashton, 1966–69. Photo: Robert Proctor, 2011

10.30   St George's Chapel, Heathrow Airport, London, by Frederick Gibberd & Partners, 1964–68. View from Anglican apse towards Roman Catholic apse. Photographer unknown, c.1968. Source: Architectural Press Archive / RIBA Library Photographs Collection

10.31   St Andrew, Cippenham, Slough, by Michael Hattrell, 1968–70. View from social areas towards worship space: font in timber and perspex at opening. Photo: Colin Westwood, c.1970. Source: RIBA Library Photographs Collection

10.32   St Andrew, Cippenham, Slough, by Michael Hattrell, 1968–70. View of worship space: partitions and liturgical furnishings mostly not original. Photo: Robert Proctor, 2010

10.33   St Andrew, Cippenham, Slough, by Michael Hattrell, 1968–70. Photo: Colin Westwood, c.1970. Source: RIBA Library Photographs Collection.

10.34   All Saints, Pin Green, Stevenage New Town, by Stevenage Development Corporation Architects' Department, 1970–74. Exterior viewed from within neighbourhood centre. Photo: Robert Proctor, 2013

10.35   All Saints, Pin Green, Stevenage New Town, by Stevenage Development Corporation Architects' Department, 1970–74. Design plan for church and community centre, 1970. Source: parish archive

10.36   All Saints, Pin Green, Stevenage New Town, by Stevenage Development Corporation Architects' Department, 1970–74. Photo: Robert Proctor, 2013

COLOUR PLATES

1   St John Fisher, West Heath, Birmingham, by Sandy & Norris, 1963–64. *Dalle de verre* windows by Jonah Jones. Photo: Robert Proctor, 2009

2   Holy Trinity, Dockhead, London, by H. S. Goodhart-Rendel, 1958–60. Photo: Matt Clayton, 2013

3   St Luke, Pinner, London, by F. X. Velarde, 1958. Interior with Crucifixion by David John. By permission of David John. The original sanctuary fittings have been altered. Photo: Robert Proctor, 2010

4   St Augustine, Manchester, by Desmond Williams, 1965–68. Reredos sculpture, altar, crucifix and candlesticks by Robert Brumby; *dalle de verre* slot windows by Pierre Fourmaintraux of Whitefriars Studios. By permission of Robert Brumby. Photo: Robert Proctor, 2012

5   St Aidan, East Acton, London, by Burles & Newton, 1959–61. Sanctuary artworks: six of the Forty Martyrs in *dalle de verre* by Pierre Fourmaintraux of Whitefriars Studios and painting of the Crucifixion by Graham Sutherland, *c*.1964. Courtesy of the Estate of Graham Sutherland. Photo: Robert Proctor, 2009

6   St Bernadette, Lancaster, by Tom Mellor, 1958. Reredos painting by John Piper. Courtesy of the Estate of John Piper. Photo: Robert Proctor, 2011

7   Metropolitan Cathedral of Christ the King, Liverpool, by Frederick Gibberd, 1960–67. Stained glass by John Piper and Patrick Reyntiens. © Patrick Reyntiens, all rights reserved, DACS, London, 2013. Photo: Robert Proctor, 2012

8   St Mary, Leyland, by Weightman & Bullen, 1960–64. Frieze of the Last Judgement in ceramic by Adam Kossowski. Photo: Robert Proctor, 2010

9   Cathedral of Sts Peter and Paul, Clifton, Bristol, by Percy Thomas Partnership, 1965–73. The original doors by William Mitchell have been replaced. Photo: Robert Proctor, 2013

10   Good Shepherd, Nottingham, by Gerard Goalen, 1961–64. Stained glass, 'Tree of the Cross', in *dalle de verre* by Patrick Reyntiens. © Patrick Reyntiens, all rights reserved, DACS, London, 2013. Photo: Robert Proctor, 2009

11   St Paul, Wood Green, London, by John Rochford, 1967–72. Sculpture by Michael Clark; stained glass by Moira Forsyth; resin and fibreglass painting in nave of the Seven Sacraments by Carmel Cauchi, added *c*.1980. By permission of Joseph Lindsey-Clark and Carmel Cauchi. Photo: Matt Clayton, 2012

12   Our Lady of Fatima, Harlow New Town, by Gerard Goalen, 1954–60. Stained glass by Charles Norris showing the Mysteries of the Rosary (transepts), Tree of Jesse and Our Lady of Fatima (nave). Photo: Robert Proctor, 2010

13   Votive Shrine of Our Lady of Lourdes, Blackpool, by F. X. Velarde, 1955–57. Sculpture by David John. By permission of David John. Photo: Robert Proctor, 2011

14   English Martyrs, Horley, by Justin Alleyn, 1959–62. Stations of the Cross in *dalle de verre* by Pierre Fourmaintraux of Whitefriars Studios. Photo: Robert Proctor, 2010

15   St Francis of Assisi, Cardiff, F. R. Bates, Son & Price, 1960. Stations of the Cross in sgraffito and ceramic by Adam Kossowski. Photo: Robert Proctor, 2010

16   Cathedral of St Mary, Edinburgh. Sketch proposal for rebuilding the cathedral by T. Harley Haddow & Partners, 1966. Perspective by Alexander Duncan Bell showing view from within the St James Centre. By permission of Alexander Duncan Bell and Harley Haddow. Source: Scottish Catholic Archives, Edinburgh

PLANS

All plans are by Ambrose Gillick, 2012–13, and depict the buildings as completed and with liturgical arrangements at the time of opening, as far as can be deduced.

1a   St Joseph, Wembley, London, by Reynolds & Scott, 1956–58

1b   Holy Trinity, Dockhead, London, by H. S. Goodhart-Rendel, 1958–60

1c   St Bernard, Burnage, Manchester, by Reynolds & Scott, 1957–59

1d   St Luke, Pinner, London, by F. X. Velarde, 1958. By permission of OMF Derek Cox Architects, Liverpool

2a   St Bride, East Kilbride, by Andy MacMillan and Isi Metzstein of Gillespie, Kidd & Coia, 1957–64

2b   St Paul, Glenrothes, by Andy MacMillan and Isi Metzstein of Gillespie, Kidd & Coia, 1956–58

2c   St Joseph, Faifley, Glasgow, by Andy MacMillan and Isi Metzstein of Gillespie, Kidd & Coia, 1960–63

2d   St Margaret, Clydebank, Glasgow, by Andy MacMillan and Isi Metzstein of Gillespie, Kidd & Coia, 1970–72

3a   St Mary, Leyland, by Weightman & Bullen, 1960–64. Courtesy of the Trustees of the Roman Catholic Archdiocese of Liverpool and Weightman & Bullen Architects

3b   St Ambrose, Speke, Liverpool, by Weightman & Bullen, 1958–61. Courtesy of the Trustees of the Roman Catholic Archdiocese of Liverpool and Weightman & Bullen Architects

3c   St Agnes, Huyton, Liverpool, by Lionel A. G. Prichard & Son, 1959–65

4a   Our Lady of Fatima, Harlow, by Gerard Goalen, 1954–60

4b   St Gregory, South Ruislip, London, by Gerard Goalen, 1965–67

4c   St Michael and All Angels, Woodchurch, Birkenhead, by F. X. Velarde Partnership, 1962–65. Courtesy of OMF Derek Cox Architects, Liverpool

4d   Holy Redeemer, Pershore, by Hugh Bankart, 1957–59

5a   Cathedral of Sts Peter and Paul, Clifton, Bristol, by Percy Thomas Partnership, 1965–73

5b   St Margaret, Twickenham, London, by Williams & Winkley, 1964–69. Courtesy of Austin Winkley & Associates, London

6a   St Thomas More, Sheffield, by John Rochford & Partners, 1964–69

6b   St Andrew, Cippenham, Slough, by Michael Hattrell, 1968–70

6c   Lancaster University Chaplaincy Centre, Lancaster, by Cassidy & Ashton, 1966–69. © Cassidy + Ashton, Preston

7a   St Bride, East Kilbride, by Andy MacMillan and Isi Metzstein of Gillespie, Kidd & Coia, 1957–64. Map reproduced by permission of Ordnance Survey on behalf of HMSO. © Crown Copyright 2013. All rights reserved. Ordnance Survey licence number 100013973

7b   St Michael and All Angels, Woodchurch, Birkenhead, by F. X. Velarde Partnership, 1962–65. Map reproduced

Acknowledgements

Inevitably, this book's production has been a collaborative endeavour, and there are many people I need to thank for their involvement in the project. Most importantly, Ambrose Gillick was a project research assistant for two years, and many of the most crucial parts of this history resulted from his work. He also created many of the illustrations and obtained permissions for many more. Much of my thinking has benefited from his work and thought on the project, and his commitment and energy spurred me on.

The project was funded from several sources. The Arts and Humanities Research Council awarded me a substantial Early-Career Research Grant for the final stages of work to complete the book. In the early stages, the Paul Mellon Centre for the Study of British Art funded several research trips through smaller grants and more recently awarded Ashgate a publication grant towards the cost of producing the book. Throughout, my employer, the Glasgow School of Art, provided funding for research and time to carry it out. I am grateful to all of them and also to those individuals who helped along the way, notably Damian Sutton, Diana Periton, Florian Urban, Ken Neil, Julie Ramage, Tim Sharpe, Andrew Saint, Gavin Stamp, Alan Powers, Judi Loach, Richard Brook, Kathleen James-Chakraborty, Livia Hurley, Libby Horner, Christopher Marsden, Elaine Martini and Paul Walker. Thanks are also due to those who have given opportunities to present and publish work in progress on the project, helping to develop the ideas in this book, including Judi Loach, Raymond Quek, Monica Penick, Vladimir Kulić, Timothy Parker, Andrew Crompton, Trevor Kilgore, Claire O'Mahony, Jan De Maeyer, Sophie Andreae, Peter Brownhill, Andrea Longhi, Carsten Hermann and Clive Fenton, as well as Valerie Rose for accepting this book for Ashgate.

Many archivists and librarians have kindly shared their material, and I have especially to thank Canon J. A. Harding, Meg Whittle, Father David Lannon, Susannah Waters, Justine Sambrook, Jonathan Makepeace, Andrew Nicoll, Caroline Cradock, Robert Finnigan, David Buri, Nancy Young, Father John Sharp, Father Nicholas Schofield, Chris Fanning, Father Paul Harrison, Father Peter Phillips, Father Stewart Foster, Patrick Pike and Alan Randall. Many parish priests and parishioners have also taken time and interest to open their churches and share their parish histories and archives – sadly far too many to list or remember, but I would like in particular to thank Paul Andersson, Father Jonathan Cotton, Canon Seamus Cunnane, Monsignor James Curry, Bernard Harrison, Father Jeremy Trood, Father John McKeown, Andrzej Suchcitz, Father Dennis Touw and Sister Anthony Wilson. I am grateful to numerous architects, artists and priests and their descendants (and practices) for graciously according interviews, furnishing documentary information and allowing me to reproduce original material, in particular Alexander Duncan Bell, Patricia Brown, David Brown, Robert Brumby, Norman Dilworth, Neil Fozzard, Martin Goalen, Tim Gough, Dennis Hepworth, George Jarosz, David John, Peter Langtry-Langton, Brian Mooney, Gerald Murphy, Barbara Powell, Jonathon Prichard, Andy MacMillan, William Mitchell, Joy Mitchell, Richard O'Mahony, Tony Tranmer, Richard Gilbert Scott, Giles Velarde, Ronald Weeks, Desmond Williams, Iain Quayle and Austin Winkley. If there are errors of interpretation or significant omissions in my discussions of their work they are my own, and I ask their forbearance.

1

Introduction

On the evening of Wednesday 16 September 1959, the Roman Catholic parishioners of St Gregory the Great at South Ruislip in London gathered in their local primary school hall to hear their parish priest, Philip Dayer, describe his plans for the parish. Dayer's speech provides an insight into the thoughts of a priest charged with founding a new parish.[1] He had been appointed the year before by the archbishop of Westminster, William Godfrey, and had converted the garage of the house he acquired into a chapel.[2] Dayer insisted that the primary aim of the fledgling parish was to build a church.

> For thousands of years, the PARISH has been the unit within the Catholic Church by means of which its great mission of applying the fruits of Christ's redemption is brought about. A parish should have its Church – the focal point of worship where the sacrifice of Calvary is renewed day by day. It should have its font which gives birth to new children of God. The parish is a social unit, a family with a Father, it shows itself visibly as an entity. … Until we have built our own Church we will not have reached our highest goal.[3]

In this short statement of the vital connection between the church building and the institutional Church lies the central argument of this book.

The church building presents an image of the institutional Church, and, at the same time, when a congregation gathers within it for worship, it also constitutes the reality and local manifestation of that institution. This is not a new interpretation: it was an important idea in the mid-twentieth century when the churches in this book were built.[4] The church building is therefore a physical space which is also the social space of an institution, where that institution takes shape. Dayer's speech to his parishioners in South Ruislip emphasised this conjunction: worship, he said, is the 'focal point' of the parish and takes place in the church; the font, a designed object within the building, 'gives birth' to new members of the parish, reproducing and sustaining the Church; the 'family' of the parish, the 'unit' of the Church, 'shows itself' in the building.

The parish not only shows itself in the building, however, it is also constructed with it. The church is a social space produced by human reason and activity. The purpose of Dayer's speech, after all, was to urge his parishioners to give money and time towards the construction of both the social and physical fabric of this unit of the Church. In this book I accept the premise that '(social) space is a (social) product', constructed by people for the purpose of maintaining a model of social relations; space is not a neutral container, but 'a tool of thought and of action'.[5] As a tool, it is made. Social spaces are produced by many varied agents and influences. The institutional Church is produced in a new context, by different people, and therefore in distinctive forms each time a church building is constructed.

SOCIAL AND URBAN CONTEXTS

The wider context for the church of St Gregory explains its presence and form. Before Dayer was sent to South Ruislip in 1958, Roman Catholics in the area attended a pre-war church in Eastcote, half an hour's walk away. After the Second World War, a scout hut was adopted as a chapel for South Ruislip, served by a priest from Eastcote.[6] The reason for this new foundation was a significant expansion of the population southwards into formerly rural South Ruislip as new housing developments continued throughout the 1930s and into the 1950s. Most was private suburban development, but there was also a local authority housing scheme. In Ruislip as a whole, the population rose from 16,000 in 1931 to 68,000 in 1951 and continued to grow.[7] The new parish therefore met a pressing need to serve a substantial new population. This was a period of massive population shifts overseen by the state, including vast new suburban housing estates surrounding cities, radical inner-city developments and the planning of entirely new towns. The Church followed and responded to these movements with programmes of new building.

The demand for new churches also resulted from the social context of the Church in Britain. Catholicism in Britain was largely a result of immigration, above all from Ireland, beginning in the nineteenth century and continuing throughout the twentieth. The decade of the 1950s was a period of peak immigration from Ireland and Europe as the post-war welfare state and recovering industries demanded labour.[8] Meanwhile earlier generations of Irish immigrants had settled and established themselves in British society. Amongst Roman Catholics the rate of church attendance was extremely high, much higher than in other denominations, and the numbers attending church were increasing, peaking around 1960.[9] Since it was not until the 1970s that a serious decline in religious practice set in, the period leading up to this point, explored in this book, was one of enthusiastic optimism within the Church and apparent fervour amongst a burgeoning faithful.

Like other parishes that built new churches in the 1950s and 1960s, the parish of St Gregory was created because of population flows, themselves produced by cultural, economic and political circumstances, movements at a national scale that were particularly visible in parishes located in new areas of rapidly changing and expanding cities. As city authorities channelled and shaped this population movement, urban planning became an important factor in the production of the space of the church. The Roman Catholic church building was therefore tied to the development of a modern Britain.

CHURCH AS INSTITUTION

Following the parishioners' meeting in 1959, the parish priest of St Gregory organised its campaign for a new church. Soon they were ready to build, commissioning architect Gerard Goalen to provide plans and a model in 1965. The Archdiocese of Westminster had to give approval to these plans before they could proceed. The Roman Catholic Church itself was therefore another agent in this production of the space of the church, in two ways: firstly, in its practical organisation and provision of the means for building churches, as a patron; and secondly, in the effects of its changing principles, through an institutional discourse. The Church combined a centralised authority in the Vatican with local levels of power. The Vatican supplied both universal regulations and more general guidance, regulating the forms that churches could take. The hierarchy of bishops served a national area: England and Wales were combined and Scotland had its own bishops' conference; Ireland and Northern Ireland, not covered by this book, were governed by a single separate hierarchy.[10] The parish formed the smallest unit administered by the priest and his assistants, or curates. Both the founding of a parish and the building of a church were initiated by the parish priest and decided by the diocese. At South Ruislip, the Archdiocese of Westminster monitored the progress of the new church of St Gregory. At a meeting in 1965, Goalen arrived to present his plans for the church, and they were referred to the archbishop of Westminster for his personal approval.[11] While the diocese and the bishop authorised the building, members of the parish had to pay for it themselves. This is why Dayer was so keen to rally his flock and encourage their efforts.

One reason that South Ruislip could begin building in 1965 was that it did not have to pay for it all at once. To raise support for the building, Dayer issued a leaflet to his parish with an encouraging preface from Archbishop John C. Heenan explaining in detail how the building would be funded and proposing that every family commit to a weekly offering.[12] Around half the estimated cost of £55,000 was to be met with a loan. Like many parishes and dioceses at this time, South Ruislip benefited from the general prosperity of this period, when credit was relatively easy to obtain. From the end of the Second World War until the mid-1950s, it had been difficult to build new churches because all building was strictly rationed by the government: building licences ensured that scarce materials and labour were reserved for the highest priority buildings, while churches were low on the scale, classed with 'sports and entertainments'.[13] Restrictions finally eased in the mid-1950s, and Catholics grasped the opportunity, with hundreds – probably well over a thousand – new church buildings undertaken in the period considered here: one clergyman estimated that in the 1960s in England and Wales alone, 600 new Catholic churches had been built.[14] By the late 1960s and early 1970s, new building slowed and existing projects stalled as interest rates rose. Credit was squeezed in the late 1960s, and one of the worst financial crises of the twentieth century ensued as the 1970s began. The later part of the period was inevitably marked by a lull in church building. The period of two decades until that time witnessed a boom in the construction of new churches, stimulated by loans and absorbing substantial capital from across the Church.

The Roman Catholic Church influenced the form of its church buildings through its written teachings and the wide-ranging discourse of commentary that surrounded them. New ideas in theology were so rapidly disseminated that within a few years they could have an impact on the experiences of a churchgoer in a London suburb. One of the most important reasons for examining the period ten years either side of 1965 is that this year marked the closing of the Second Vatican Council. The council consisted of a series of gatherings in Rome, beginning in 1962, at which all the bishops of the world revised and approved documents that had been prepared by committees of theologians. These documents summarised the doctrine of the Church in a way that was meant to be relevant to the modern world, responding to new theological ideas and liturgical practices that had developed in the century or so before. Many of the council's statements in such important areas as the liturgical rites and the nature of the Church marked an acceptance of new theological tendencies and had striking implications for how the Church's members should conduct themselves and understand their role. The ideas behind the documents of Vatican II were not new, and their impact had already been felt. Yet the effects of the council were swift and highly visible, above all as a radical reform of liturgy took place in the years immediately after it, transforming the daily practices of the faithful.

This reform principally concerned the Mass. The Church wanted to encourage the 'active participation' of the congregation in liturgy, as the Mass was increasingly interpreted as the communal worship of the Church rather than a ritual performed mainly by a priest. Before about 1960, the Mass was said throughout the Roman Catholic Church in the West predominantly in Latin, the congregation's role largely one of devout attention from the pews. The priest stood at the altar facing away from the people towards the back of the sanctuary, even for the readings, and had to say parts of the Mass inaudibly. The Mass as it was said in Britain in the 1950s had remained little changed since the Council of Trent, which had set down a version of the liturgy for near-uniform use across the Church in 1570. Slowly, however, the 'dialogue Mass' was introduced to Britain from Europe, involving congregational responses. In the new liturgy, developed in stages from the mid-1960s until 1970, the Mass was increasingly said in the local language and entirely so in its final phase. Then the priest would stand behind the altar facing the people; the congregation would join in with responses and singing, some giving readings from the sanctuary and forming an offertory procession; and the rites were radically simplified in texts and gestures. This shift in the forms of worship changed what the Church required from its buildings. The shape of the church and its congregation had to relate to the conception of the liturgy as a communal action; increased movement of both congregation and celebrants required new spatial forms; the sanctuary had to be designed afresh. Other rites were also reformed with further implications for the design of the church, most notably baptism.

In South Ruislip, Dayer and Goalen established their plans for the sanctuary layout in 1965 in direct response to the liturgical reforms emanating from the Vatican. The simple table-like stone altar was placed well forward in the oval sanctuary so that the priest could stand behind it to say Mass facing the people, and the tabernacle was placed in a broad niche on the wall behind it, an arrangement that served the new forms and conceptions of the liturgy just then enshrined at the council (Figure 1.1). Cardinal Heenan approved the plans himself shortly before setting out for Rome to attend the final session of the council.[15] The Church's reforms of liturgy and its approval of new theology thus had immediate effects on church architecture even in this suburban parish.

1.1   St Gregory, South Ruislip, London, by Gerard Goalen, 1965–67. View of nave looking towards sanctuary: sanctuary stained glass by Patrick Reyntiens, © Patrick Reyntiens, all rights reserved, DACS, London, 2013; clerestory stained glass by Charles Norris, added c.1987. Photo: Robert Proctor, 2010

CHURCH AND ARCHITECT

Roman Catholic church buildings were also produced by their architects, and most were also members of the Church. At the time of his design for the church at South Ruislip, the architect Gerard Goalen gave his own talk to the parishioners. He began with a discussion of the Second Vatican Council, its 'Constitution on the Sacred Liturgy' of 1963, and the liturgical movement, the combined theological and architectural developments that led to the council's reforms. Goalen explained this movement's notion of the liturgy as a corporate action, a form of worship undertaken by all the people present, not just the priest. He went on to explain how this idea had motivated his oval plan for the church of St Gregory, a free-standing altar opposite the entrance surrounded by arcs of seating (Plan 4b). The seating, curving around three sides of the altar and sloping gently towards it, and the absence of any heavy barrier between sanctuary and congregation would help to ensure that the faithful had a good view of the liturgy and could be closely involved in it.[16]

Goalen was designing not as a liturgist, however, but primarily as a modern architect. He explained that two principles of modern architecture had informed his work: the design of spaces according to function and the 'honest employment of modern methods of building'.[17] The church would be constructed with a reinforced concrete frame and brick walls, all exposed to view. More importantly, the novelty of its plan was a result of thinking from first principles, ignoring centuries of precedents for church architecture. 'The church I have been privileged to design for this parish', he said, 'may not look like a conventional solution to the church-building problem. It is the product of a reconsideration of the purposes of *your* parish church and a reconsideration of the ways in which a building can provide for those purposes'.[18] As the architect, proposing his own 'reconsideration' of the church, Goalen was perhaps the most obvious agent in the production of this space. The contributions of artists in stained glass, sculpture and other media, usually under the direction of architects, were also significant in producing the space of the church.

Another reason for choosing to look at the post-war period from 1955 to 1975 is therefore to examine how modern architecture affected church design. By 1955 modern architecture had become generally accepted in Britain, partly as a result of the constraints of limited materials and urgent building needs after the war.[19] The establishment of modernism in church architecture, however, was slower. Though perhaps first marked with Basil Spence's competition winning design for the Anglican Coventry Cathedral in 1951, it only seems to have reached a mainstream of practice in the Roman Catholic Church in Britain around the time that Frederick Gibberd won the competition for Liverpool Metropolitan Cathedral the following decade in 1960. Before this date, Catholic church architecture in Britain was predominantly eclectic, using historical styles including Gothic and Romanesque or an uncontroversial modern style more typical of the 1930s. In the 1960s, the majority of church designs attempted a deliberate expression of new building materials, and, as at South Ruislip, often questioned the conventions of the building type. Post-war modernism in architecture, however, was very diverse.

St Gregory, opened in 1967, demonstrates the interests of its architect, Gerard Goalen, interests that existed in symbiosis with those of the Church. The visible roof structure of deep concrete beams followed Arne Jacobsen's dining hall at St Catherine's College, Oxford, a building that had a great influence on British architects in its severely geometric and rational use of reinforced concrete. The importance to Jacobsen of designing every element of the building and its furnishing and of commissioning original artworks in sympathy with it are also features of Goalen's church, with its custom-made benches with fine concrete supports and its expressive modern statues in bronze by Willi Soukop, a well-established artist. Such a cohesive approach to design had long been an important principle of modern architecture in Britain.

Goalen's internal ring of delicate reinforced concrete columns, their surfaces revealing the traces of their wooden shuttering, were likely to have been inspired by the early twentieth-century French architect, Auguste Perret, whose best-known building was a church with similarly made concrete columns, Notre Dame du Raincy near Paris of 1922. This church was well known by the 1960s because it had been included in histories of modern architecture as a pioneer of the expressive use of reinforced concrete, and had been praised in publications on modern church architecture as one amongst a canon of exemplary buildings.[20] Meanwhile the use of exposed hook-shaped bricks on the interior walls at St Gregory, which give a rich expressive texture as well as acoustic dispersion, the brick and quarry tile paving and the exposed concrete structure further link Goalen to the younger generation of British architects who had come into practice in the mid-1950s, those such as Colin St John Wilson, James Stirling and James Gowan who had drawn on Le Corbusier's post-war architecture to create a style of rough, untreated materials broadly known as brutalism. Brutalism, however, began with prolific theoretical writing by architects such as Alison Smithson and Peter Smithson in the 1950s, demanding a strict approach to the design of a building according to its 'programme' and careful thought for the social implications of architectural forms and, in that sense, had a close similarity of purpose to the liturgical movement, an important connection I will examine shortly. This post-war modernist approach had become typical in architecture by the 1960s, and, as Goalen explained in his talk, led to his oval plan.

The church of St Gregory, like all the others studied in this book, can therefore be positioned in its period in terms of the contemporary context of architectural discourse and design practice. Crucially, it is the way architectural decisions related to the aims of the Church in its local contexts that is important here. The selection of a modern architect for St Gregory suggests that this parish was anxious to address the modern world and show its contemporary relevance. The parish evidently wanted a building that would confer upon it a high cultural status, since it chose an architect who had previously built Catholic churches that had been well received by the architectural profession.[21] The parishioners also demonstrated an interest in modern art. Goalen commissioned Steven Sykes to make a bold sculptural lintel in bronze over the entrance (Figure 1.2). Sykes was best known by then for his design in 1959 of the Gethsemane Chapel at Coventry Cathedral.[22] Patrick Reyntiens, who made the stained glass at St Gregory, and Ralph Beyer, who carved inscriptions there, had both also worked at Coventry (Figure 1.3). Their commissioning at South Ruislip therefore suggests a desire for an avant-garde image, and yet also for an uncontroversial acceptance within the modern British cultural mainstream. Positioned on the side of a main road through Ruislip, the church and its sculpture were prominent in the neighbourhood in an overt declaration of a Catholic culture that accepted modernity. Goalen's oval plan not only demonstrates his own acceptance of liturgical reform, but also the allegiance of the parish to new liturgical thinking. The building, as Dayer himself said, is an expressive statement about this particular parish and its ideas about the Church.

1.2   St Gregory, South Ruislip, London, by Gerard Goalen, 1965–67. View from street: lintel sculpture by Steven Sykes. Photo: Robert Proctor, 2010

These three primary agents in the production of the Roman Catholic church – the architect as designer, the Church as institutional framework and discursive field, and the city as social and spatial influence – can be distinguished in the creation of modern church architecture. Church architects were generally members of the Church, acting as expert laymen. They were also often involved in city planning and participated in a discourse of modern architecture in which urbanism was a central aspect. Each field underwent vital transformations in the two decades between 1955 and 1975, with important consequences for church architecture. The Roman Catholic church building in Britain, in the radical shifts in forms which it underwent during the period from 1955 to 1975, was a socially constructed artefact, its architecture making manifest the diverse and changing conceptions of the institutional Church held by its members. The architecture of the church, considered in its broadest sense, was produced only in part by architects; it was also the product of negotiation between architects, their patrons and their wider context.

WRITING A HISTORY OF CHURCH ARCHITECTURE

One of the most difficult tasks in writing this book has been to select from the profusion of churches built at this time a smaller number for detailed study. My selections of case studies have been based on several criteria. Firstly, this book is chiefly focused on the parish church, and so monastic, convent, school and seminary buildings have been only rarely included in favour of this primary subject area.

1.3   St Gregory, South Ruislip, London, by Gerard Goalen, 1965–67. View into baptistery: statue of St Gregory by Willi Soukop; font lettering by Ralph Beyer; stained glass by Patrick Reyntiens, © Patrick Reyntiens, all rights reserved, DACS, London, 2013. Photo: Robert Proctor, 2010

Secondly, I have chosen buildings which seemed architecturally good or those that have been generally agreed to be of high quality and interest (especially during the period in question and also through more recent heritage designation). While 'quality' is an arbitrary value, and I have not sought to be specific about it, it tends to encompass buildings of comparatively large scale, high expense and architectural innovation. The danger of selecting in this way is that it can skew analysis towards exceptional buildings and validate a narrative of progress by over-emphasising the avant-garde. Therefore I have also aimed to choose typical buildings of different types, representative buildings of different architectural firms, and examples of liturgically interesting buildings regardless of apparent architectural quality; moreover, I have focused on buildings that still exist without substantial alteration, those for which there is archival material available for research and those in urban areas. Throughout, my selection has of course been motivated by what I have wanted to examine: the move from eclectic to modern architecture and from pre- to post-conciliar conceptions of liturgy and the Church; the parish church in a changing urban and social context; and special forms of church, notably the pilgrimage shrine. Inevitably, therefore, many buildings, and many that would be considered by some readers as important, are absent from this book and must be left for others to study.

Roman Catholic church architecture of the post-war period in Britain has barely yet been written about.[23] The book by Bryan Little, *Catholic Churches Since 1623*, remains the standard work on Roman Catholic churches built since the Reformation, ending at its point of publication in 1966 with the anticipation of some significant future buildings.[24] This and the few other published studies of the subject tend to be descriptive rather than interpretive, concerned with documenting architectural features, at their best selecting and arranging buildings typologically; some accounts are biographical; but few give any substantial analysis of their architectural, religious and social conditions.[25] There is little yet written even on twentieth-century British church architecture in general: Elain Harwood's article of 1998 remains definitive.[26] There are, however, significant recent studies of the social history of the Church, most notably by Michael Hornsby-Smith, on which I have drawn.[27] The most serious exception to the piecemeal approach to modern Catholic church architecture in Britain is an unpublished PhD dissertation by Paul Walker, completed in 1985 at the University of Sheffield and discovered towards the end of research on this book.[28] Walker's thesis differs substantially in its approach to mine: writing close to the time of the buildings he was studying and as one involved in the post-war movement towards a modern church architecture, he was less inclined to view the subject as a historian, instead taking a theoretical and theological approach. Yet many of his sources coincide with mine, and some of his original research has been incorporated here.

This book makes some use of theory, although it is deliberately kept light in touch to avoid overpowering its subject matter. Theory is used more as a framework for selecting and juxtaposing particular sources, for reading them in certain ways and for an analysis of architecture. Henri Lefebvre's *Production of Space* informs the overall organisation and theme of the book, considering the church space as actively produced rather than divinely given, naturally arising, developed through tradition or conjured by architectural genius.[29] Sources such as anthropology, sociology, geography and theology have seemed necessary to understand certain subjects. This remains, however, a work of architectural history, and I take no particular stance on theological or philosophical questions which others are better suited to answer.

One characteristic of much that has so far been written on modern church architecture is a polemical stance in a debate over modernism and tradition that has raised passionate opinions.[30] The purpose of this book is not polemic, even though it works by deploying arguments. I would not claim an impossible objectivity, but I have nevertheless attempted a few steps of academic detachment: I have sympathy for all the subjects of this book – the conservative and traditional as much as the modern and experimental.

NOTES

1   Philip Dayer, 'General Parish Meeting, Deanesfield School Hall' (16 Sept. 1959) (parish archive, St Gregory, South Ruislip, London).

2   Ibid.; see also Peter Dayer, 'Philip Richard Dayer, 1912–2005: A Tribute by his Brother' (2005), St Gregory the Great, South Ruislip, http://stgregory.all-catholic.net/philipdayer.html (accessed 29 June 2011).

3   Dayer, 'General Parish Meeting'.

4   See Yves M. J. Congar, *Lay People in the Church: A Study for a Theology of Laity*, trans. Donald Attwater (London: Geoffrey Chapman, 1963), 325, 435.

5   Henri Lefebvre, *The Production of Space*, trans. Donald Nicholson-Smith (Oxford: Blackwell, 2001), 26.

6   Diane K. Bolton et al., *A History of the County of Middlesex*, vol. 4: *Harmondsworth, Hayes, Norwood with Southall, Hillingdon with Uxbridge, Ickenham, Northolt, Perivale, Ruislip, Edgware, Harrow with Pinner*, ed. T. F. T. Baker, J. S. Cockburn and R. B. Pugh, Victoria County History (London: Oxford University Press, 1971), 144–5, British History Online, http://www.british-history.ac.uk/report.aspx?compid=22447#n2 (accessed 29 June 2011).

7   Ibid. 127–34.

8   See for example John Archer Jackson, *The Irish in Britain* (London: Routledge and Kegan Paul, 1963), 9–19, 85–105; Michael P. Hornsby-Smith, 'A Transformed Church', in Michael P. Hornsby-Smith (ed.), *Catholics in England, 1950–2000: Historical and Sociological Perspectives* (London: Cassell, 1999), 3–25 (8–9).

9   Callum G. Brown, *Religion and Society in Twentieth-Century Britain* (Harlow: Pearson, 2006), 25–6, 183.

10   Irish church architecture of this period, in contrast to that of Britain, has been quite well studied already (including Northern Ireland). See Richard Hurley and Wilfrid Cantwell, *Contemporary Irish Church Architecture* (Dublin: Gill & Macmillan, 1985); Richard Hurley, *Irish Church Architecture in the Era of Vatican II* (Dublin: Dominican Publications, 2001); Ellen Rowley, 'Transitional Modernism: The Case of 1950s Church Architecture in Dublin', in Edwina Keown and Carol Taffe (eds), *Irish Modernism: Origins, Contexts, Publics* (Bern: Peter Lang, 2009), 195–216; Paul Larmour and Shane O'Toole (eds),

North by Northwest: The Life and Work of Liam McCormick (Kinsale: Gandon Editions, 2008).

11   Minutes of meeting of the Council of Administration, Archdiocese of Westminster (26 May; 16 June 1965) (Westminster Diocesan Archives, London [WDA], He1/C23(a)).

12   Philip Dayer, 'A Personal Message to Every Catholic in the Parish of St Gregory, South Ruislip' (1965) (parish archive).

13   A. E. Holder, 'Extract from the White Paper on Capital Investment in 1948. Ministry of Works Civil Licence' and commentary; Ministry of Works (H. W. Clark) to A. E. Holder (15 Dec. 1947); Church of Scotland Building Licences Advisory Committee, Edinburgh (R. F. R., secretary) to James R. Lyons (solicitor) (5 Dec. 1947) (Glasgow Roman Catholic Archdiocesan Archives, Glasgow [GRCAA], PP/40/6).

14   Joseph Gray (auxiliary bishop of Liverpool), 'Modern Church Building', *Catholic Building Review*, northern edn [*CBRN*] (1970), 273–6.

15   Minutes of meeting of the Council of Administration, Archdiocese of Westminster (26 May 1965) (WDA, He1/C23(a)).

16   [Gerard Goalen], 'St Gregory the Great, South Ruislip' (n.d.) (parish archive). The design can be dated by its entry in the *Catholic Building Review*, southern edn [*CBRS*] (1965), 44–5; minutes of meeting of the Council of Administration, Archdiocese of Westminster (26 May 1965) (WDA, He1/C23(a)).

17   [Goalen], 'St Gregory'.

18   Ibid. On Goalen's work, see Cordula Zeidler, 'Die Einheit des Raumes: Kirchenbauten des britischen Architekten Gerard Goalen', *Kunst und Kirche* 3 (2003), 136–8.

19   Nicholas Bullock, *Building the Post-War World: Modern Architecture and Reconstruction in Britain* (London: Routledge, 2002), xi.

20   For example Peter Collins, *Concrete: The Vision of a New Architecture: A Study of Auguste Perret and His Precursors* (London: Faber & Faber, 1959); Henry Russell Hitchcock, *Architecture: Nineteenth and Twentieth Centuries* (New Haven: Yale University Press, 1977), 424–6; Albert Christ-Janer and Mary Mix Foley, *Modern Church Architecture: A Guide to the Form and Spirit of 20th Century Religious Buildings* (New York: McGraw-Hill, 1962), 5–6; Robert Maguire and Keith Murray, *Modern Churches of the World* (London: Studio Vista, 1965), 15–16.

21   A copy of an architectural journal with an article on a previous church by Goalen, the Good Shepherd, Nottingham, is in the parish archive, suggesting that the magazine was consulted as part of the decision over commissioning an architect ('Church, Nottingham', *Architect and Building News* [23 Sept. 1964]: 583–9; see also 'Church of St Gregory the Great', *Building* [Mar. 1968]: 95–8; 'Some New Ecclesiastical Structures', *Concrete and Constructional Engineering* [Jan. 1964]: 38–9).

22   Tanya Harrod, 'Obituary: Steven Sykes', *The Independent* (24 Feb. 1999), http://www.independent.co.uk/arts-entertainment/obituary-steven-sykes-1072852.html (accessed 11 July 2011).

23   In contrast to modern churches more widely: see for example n. 11 above for Ireland; Hugo Schnell, *Twentieth Century Church Architecture in Germany* (Munich: Schnell & Steiner, 1974); Suzanne Robin, *Églises modernes: Évolution des édifices religieux en France* (Paris: Hermann, 1980); G. E. Kidder Smith, *The New Churches of Europe* (London: Architectural Press, 1964); Christ-Janer and Foley, *Modern Church Architecture*; Wolfgang Jean Stock, *European Church Architecture, 1950–2000* (Munich: Prestel, 2002); Andrea Longhi and Carlo Tosco, *Architettura, chiesa e società in Italia (1948–1978)* (Rome: Edizioni Studium, 2010);

Jay M. Price, *Temples for a Modern God: Religious Architecture in Postwar America* (New York: Oxford University Press, 2013).

24   Bryan Little, *Catholic Churches Since 1623: A Study of Roman Catholic Churches in England and Wales from Penal Times to the Present Decade* (London: Hale, 1966).

25   For example Denis Evinson, *Catholic Churches of London* (Sheffield: Sheffield Academic Press, 1998); Christopher Martin and Alex Ramsay, *A Glimpse of Heaven: Catholic Churches of England and Wales* (Swindon: English Heritage, 2009); Paul D. Walker, 'Liturgy and Architecture: Catholic Church Building in the Twentieth Century', *Ecclesiology Today* 38 (2007), 43–51; Alan Powers, *Francis Pollen: Architect, 1926–1987* (Oxford: Robert Dugdale, 1999); id. (ed.), *H. S. Goodhart-Rendel, 1887–1959* (London: Architectural Association, 1987); Gavin Stamp, '"A Catholic Church in Which Everything is Genuine and Good": The Roman Catholic Parish Churches of Sir Giles Gilbert Scott', *Ecclesiology Today* 38 (2007), 63–80; Fiona Ward, 'Merseyside Churches in a Modern Idiom: Francis Xavier Velarde and Bernard Miller', *Twentieth Century Architecture* 3: *The Twentieth Century Church* (1998), 95–102; Robert Proctor, 'Churches for a Changing Liturgy: Gillespie, Kidd & Coia and the Second Vatican Council', *Architectural History* 48 (2005), 291–322; Diane Watters, *Cardross Seminary: Gillespie, Kidd & Coia and the Architecture of Postwar Catholicism* (Edinburgh: Royal Commission on the Ancient and Historical Monuments of Scotland, 1997); id., 'Post-War Church Patronage in the West of Scotland: The Ecclesiastical Architecture of Gillespie, Kidd & Coia', *Journal of the Scottish Society for Art History* 3 (1998), 44–51; Johnny Rodger (ed.), *Gillespie, Kidd & Coia: Architecture, 1956–1987* (Glasgow: Lighthouse, 2007).

26   Elain Harwood, 'Liturgy and Architecture: The Development of the Centralised Eucharistic Space', *Twentieth Century Architecture* 3: *The Twentieth Century Church* (1998), 51–74; see also Peter Pace, *The Architecture of George G. Pace, 1915–75* (London: Batsford, 1990).

27   Hornsby-Smith (ed.), *Catholics in England*; id., *The Changing Parish: A Study of Parishes, Priests and Parishioners after Vatican II* (London: Routledge, 1989); id., *Roman Catholics in England: Studies in Social Structure Since the Second World War* (Cambridge: Cambridge University Press, 1987).

28   Paul D. Walker, 'Developments in Catholic Churchbuilding in the British Isles, 1945–1980' (PhD diss., University of Sheffield, 1985).

29   Similarly, my thinking has been informed by Janet Wolff, *The Social Production of Art* (London: Macmillan, 1981); Pierre Bourdieu, *Outline of a Theory of Practice*, trans. Richard Nice (Cambridge: Cambridge University Press, 1977); id., *Distinction: A Social Critique of the Judgement of Taste* (London: Routledge, 1984); Michel Foucault, *Archaeology of Knowledge*, trans. A. M. Sheridan Smith (London: Routledge, 2002).

30   Recent books arguing against modern church architecture include Michael Rose, *Ugly as Sin: Why They Changed our Churches from Sacred Places to Meeting Spaces, and How We Can Change them Back Again* (Manchester, NH: Sophia Institute Press, 2001); Moyra Doorly, *No Place for God: The Denial of the Transcendent in Modern Church Architecture* (San Francisco: Ignatius Press, 2007); and, with greater subtlety, Stephen J. Schloeder, *Architecture in Communion: Implementing the Second Vatican Council Through Liturgy and Architecture* (San Francisco: Ignatius Press, 1998).

2

Tradition

By 1955, modern architecture had reached such widespread acceptance that it had become the prevailing mode of design for many building types, from housing and schools to offices. There were also several notable modernist church buildings: on the Lansbury Estate at Poplar in east London, Trinity Congregational church by Cecil Handisyde and D. Rogers Stark had been completed as a showpiece of the Festival of Britain's architecture programme in 1951 (Figure 2.1), and that year Basil Spence won the competition for Coventry Cathedral, arousing enormous public interest in modern architecture. Roman Catholics in Britain would eventually also accede to this movement; yet at first, their predominant reactions were compromise or stoic resistance in defence of a perceived tradition of church architecture.

A short walk from the strikingly modern concrete Congregational church, at the heart of the experimental housing estate of Lansbury, planned by Frederick Gibberd, stands the huge brick bulk of the Catholic church of Sts Mary and Joseph, Poplar, designed by Adrian Gilbert Scott (Figure 2.2). This church's foundations were just being laid while visitors to the Festival of Britain toured the estate in 1951, and the church was eventually completed in 1954. Its exterior is a strange mixture of parabolic arches in squat brick walls with patterned parapets and a copper-roofed central tower. It was seen – and intended – as a rejection of the modernity of its surroundings in favour of an expression of a lasting Catholic tradition. Architectural critic Ian Nairn derided its 'sprawling, lumpish mass' and dominating scale, its aggressively but superficially 'traditional' approach insensitive to real historical precedent, and its antagonism towards its surroundings.[1] While Scott claimed that he had designed the church to complement the neighbouring houses, also of brick, he deliberately eschewed Lansbury's progressive modernism for an architecture that declared a conception of the parish church as a bastion of enduring values in a transient world. Scott had 'intended', he stated, 'to follow the Catholic tradition of ecclesiastical architecture'.[2] Architects, he later wrote, had to respect 'the general demand that our churches should look like churches'; the Congregational church, 'locally known as the laundry', showed that modernism was unsuitable for sacred use.[3] Many Catholic architects and clergy agreed.

2.1   Trinity Congregational church, Lansbury Estate, London, by Cecil Handisyde and D. Rogers Stark, 1949–51. Photo: John Pantlin. Source: Architectural Press Archive / RIBA Library Photographs Collection

Following the controversy over this building, the archbishop of Westminster, Cardinal William Godfrey, wrote several pieces for the *Catholic Building Review* addressed to architects and clergy promoting tradition in church architecture in balance with the needs of modern times, advising against an excessive modernism:

> There is a happy mean. Our aim ought to be to preserve all that is precious in traditional art while keeping in mind the needs of the age in which we live. … It would seem that some of the buildings today have departed too much from the traditional style of architecture.[4]

Churches, he insisted, had to maintain an 'ecclesiastical character':

> One would not like to see the spire, campanile, belfry or tower disappear from the landscape. For centuries these have told us of the sacred character of our buildings and have led us to the house of God. A church should be recognisable as a church by the wayfarer, even from afar.[5]

As the tide began to turn towards modernism even amongst his own clergy and architects in 1960, he maintained his position:

It is said that we must build for our own time. True: but our own time can accept a lack of decorum which is not according to the mind of the Church. The old should not be set aside simply because it is old. The heritage of sacred art bequeathed by our forbears is precious. The barn-like church has nothing sacred or symbolic to commend it. It does not lift the mind to God.[6]

2.2   Sts Mary and Joseph, Poplar, London, by Adrian Gilbert Scott, 1951–54. Photo: Stewart Bale Ltd, 1956. Source: parish archive

In arguing for a tradition-minded church architecture, Godfrey articulated the official position of the Roman Catholic Church.

The Vatican repeatedly reinforced the importance of 'tradition' in sacred art and architecture. Canon law stated that bishops 'are to take care that in the building or repair of churches the forms received from Christian tradition are preserved'.[7] Joseph O'Connell, a parish priest and writer on canon law and liturgy, summarised the Church's position in a widely distributed and popular book, *Church Building and Furnishing: The Church's Way* of 1955. The Church, he said, did permit modern art and architecture, but only when tempered by tradition and remaining recognisably sacred. O'Connell cited the Council of Trent: 'that nothing disordered may meet the eye, nothing distorted and confused in execution, nothing profane and unbecoming, since sanctity befits the house of God'.[8] Pius XII's encyclical letter of 1947, *Mediator Dei*, advised that 'these modern arts, architecture, sculpture, painting, steer a middle course between an excessive naturalism on the one hand and an exaggerated symbolism on the other', interpreted as a balance between historicism and modernism in architecture.[9] In 1952, in reaction to a controversy over modern church art and architecture in France after the completion of the church of Notre Dame de Toute Grâce at Assy, filled with modern art, the Vatican issued a widely published 'Instruction on Sacred Art' reinforcing the appeal to tradition in canon law, insisting that church architecture 'must not in any way be equated with profane building'.[10] Equating modern architecture with secular building types was exactly how Adrian Gilbert Scott defended his preference for tradition at Poplar: modern architecture, many felt, was intrinsically profane.

O'Connell, like Scott and Godfrey, evoked a tradition of church architecture:

> There is a certain traditional idea of a church, based on its purpose and its needs, which has gradually taken shape and been handed down. It is quite a general idea – a broad concept – of certain fundamental features or characteristics which are common to all Catholic churches, whatever the material or style in which they are built.[11]

It was an idea that had potential to justify modern architecture as the style of the twentieth century, yet in the 1950s the majority of architects of British Catholic parishes sought more literally to build this 'traditional idea of a church' through familiar forms of Catholic architecture.

Continuity of form underlying variable local appearances was also seen as a quality of the institutional Church: the Church, universal and divine, had stable doctrinal principles, but over time it showed gradual development in their expression, an argument that originated with nineteenth-century British theologian and later cardinal, John Henry Newman.[12] The concept of tradition therefore permitted change and adaptation to modern circumstances. Unlike modernism in architecture, however, this change was incremental rather than revolutionary. It was only because of the threat of revolution posed by modern architecture that the idea of tradition in church architecture had to be articulated at all. As Eric Hobsbawm argues, the concept of tradition presupposes a break in continuity against which its proponents set themselves.[13] Modernism's defining characteristic was its rejection of tradition as an objective authority. Catholic church architects in the 1950s, meanwhile, invented and sustained an idea of tradition in opposition to modernism while accepting some aspects of modernity.[14]

A BRITISH CATHOLIC TRADITION: THE BYZANTINE-ROMANESQUE REVIVAL

Scott's church at Poplar has been described as 'Jazz-Modern Byzantine' in style, with its centralised Greek-cross plan and ascending volumes, zig-zag patterns in its internal stonework and Scott's characteristic parabolic arches mixing Byzantine elements with motifs from pre-war art deco and expressionist church architecture.[15] The church was also described as 'Romanesque', its plain brick walls and 'Lombard band' parapet detailing distantly reminiscent of early medieval churches in Italy.[16] Byzantine and Romanesque styles of architecture were often conflated in architects' interpretations: the eastern Byzantine was thought to have led directly to the western Romanesque, especially at the point where they met in Ravenna. In the nineteenth century, when this chronology originated, the two terms had been used entirely interchangeably. In the later nineteenth century, early Christian, Byzantine and Romanesque revival architecture began to be identified with Roman Catholicism, as Protestants viewed its art as primitive and idolatrous and its architecture as European rather than English.[17] The culmination of the Victorian Byzantine revival was the Roman Catholic Cathedral at Westminster in London, designed around 1895 by J. F. Bentley and opened, still incomplete, in 1903 (Figure 2.3). It was the most important Catholic building project of its age and had a long-lasting effect on subsequent Catholic church architecture throughout Britain. At Poplar 50 years later, its influence can still be seen in Scott's monumental ciborium, with its columns of the same yellow marble.

In the first half of the twentieth century, an amalgam of Byzantine and Romanesque styles gradually became fashionable for Roman Catholic churches. There were several reasons why the Byzantine-Romanesque appealed. At Westminster, Bentley had argued that the churches of Constantinople, Ravenna and Venice represented the 'first phase' of Christian architecture, and this style was therefore viewed as a more primitive and authentic tradition of church architecture than the Gothic.[18] By the twentieth century, it began to be seen as a style that could effectively combine tradition with modernity. Westminster Cathedral was vaulted in concrete, but perhaps its most endearing quality to twentieth-century architects was its incompleteness: its vast wall surfaces of brick were intended to be covered in marble and mosaic like St Mark's Cathedral in Venice, a programme that was only beginning in the 1950s, but the sublimity of Bentley's brickwork had its own aesthetic merit. In the 1920s, Charles Reilly, head of the Liverpool School of Architecture, wrote that Westminster's 'lofty plain wall surfaces, even of common stock brick, were more important in giving the idea of remoteness and seclusion from the world than the richest clustered Gothic columns', an enthusiasm that he instilled in his students – amongst them Francis Xavier Velarde, who would become one of the most thoughtful exponents of Byzantine-Romanesque Catholic church architecture in Britain.[19]

In the simplicity and structural honesty of plain brick walls lay the potential for this style to reconcile tradition and modernity: it did not need ornament to look good and complete, though it could be ornamented later. Because it was an architecture of brick it was cheaper than the stone-built Gothic, while still 'rational' in expressing its cheaper construction 'in the frankest and fullest manner', as William Lethaby wrote in a classic study of Hagia Sophia.[20] Byzantine-Romanesque was also seen as an appropriate style to accommodate more innovative forms of structure, particularly in reinforced concrete.

2.3 Westminster Cathedral, London, by J. F. Bentley, 1895–1903. Nave photographed in 1953 before addition of marble cladding. Photo: Reginald Hugo de Burgh Galwey. Source: Architectural Press Archive / RIBA Library Photographs Collection

MANCHESTER ROMANESQUE, MIDLANDS BYZANTINE

Most of the architects who embraced tradition in the 1950s belonged to the generation that entered practice before the Second World War. Velarde and Scott had both acquired Catholic church commissions in the 1930s. So, too, had Reynolds & Scott of Manchester, one of the most prolific of post-war church architecture practices, and the related firm of Sandy & Norris in Stoke-on-Trent. Francis Reynolds and William Scott had trained at the Manchester University School of Architecture in the 1920s, and both obtained travel scholarships to Italy in 1929.[21] Reynolds went to work for the Manchester firm of Hill, Sandy & Norris, designing a small number of basilican churches in the 1930s in a Byzantine-Romanesque style that his employers had developed in the previous decade, adding modern touches in the form of art deco ornament, most notably at St Bernadette, Liverpool.[22] After the war, Reynolds took over the office in Manchester, joined by Scott, while Sandy & Norris, of whom Ernest Bower Norris was principal designer, moved to Stafford to cater for the firm's largely Catholic clients in the Midlands. Reynolds & Scott became the more successful practice with dozens of church commissions, besides many schools and colleges, in Manchester, the Wirral, the East Midlands and London.

Both firms maintained continuity with their earlier practice. Indeed some of their churches were so similar that they must have derived from churches they had already built together: Norris's churches of St Joseph the Worker at Sutton-in-Ashfield, Nottinghamshire, 'in the style of modern Romanesque', and of the Blessed Sacrament at Braunstone in Leicester were almost identical to Reynolds & Scott's church of St Patrick, Leicester (Figure 2.4); St Patrick, in turn, was a variation on its architects' church of St Joseph at Wembley in London (Figure 2.5, Plan 1a); their church of St Bernard at Burnage in Manchester was a further variant (Figure 2.6, Plan 1c), while Norris's St John Vianney, Blackpool, resembled St Joseph, Wembley.[23] Between them these architects not only sustained a tradition of English Catholic Byzantine-Romanesque church architecture, but also developed an architectural kit to be assembled according to each parish's needs, creating buildings with a family resemblance but with enough variety to allow the architects some creative freedom and the parishes a sense of individuality. All were built in brick (rusty red in Leicester, honey brown in London, grey-brown and red in Manchester). Most had the same simplified Romanesque columns in cast stone screening passage aisles, omitted in cheaper versions. St Patrick and St Joseph had plaster saucer domes suspended from steel roofs, imitating Westminster Cathedral, while St Bernard had a handsomely proportioned barrel vault. Gabled transepts projected more or less deeply to accommodate side chapels.[24] St Joseph had a neo-Georgian west front; St Patrick had a more Italianate Romanesque appearance with campanile; St Bernard had a gabled front with deep arched portal.

Reynolds & Scott and many other architects who saw themselves as traditional wrote little to explain these churches. The architects' statement in the souvenir opening booklet for St Bernard, Burnage, was typical in giving more attention to the sanctuary's marble cladding (itself an aspect of the Byzantine revival) than to any explanation of the church's architecture. One theme was continuity between exterior and interior: the exterior revealed the interior form, external columns repeated those inside. Another important theme was the view to the sanctuary:

passage aisles meant that sightlines were unobstructed and the repeated arches drew attention to the altar, 'the focus of the whole church'. The exterior had the 'character of dignity and solidity', the interior one of 'spaciousness'.[25] Reynolds & Scott did not need to explain or defend tradition since they had no shortage of clients who wanted their brand of church. Indeed they were equally prepared to build modern Gothic revival churches when asked to do so: their priority was to give clients what they wanted and to do it well.

Though Norris's churches were often indistinguishable from those of Reynolds & Scott, he was especially fascinated by the Byzantine domed Greek-cross form of church. He had first explored this type in the 1920s at St John the Baptist in Rochdale, modelled after Hagia Sophia and later decorated with sumptuous mosaics by the firm of Ludwig Oppenheimer. Even then Norris had been interested in the potential of the Byzantine style to accommodate aspects of modern architecture, since this building was constructed largely of reinforced concrete.[26] After the war he had several opportunities to explore this version of the Byzantine revival further. His first was for Ratcliffe College, Leicester, where he designed a new chapel around 1957 (Figure 2.7). Norris travelled with the college's president to northern France to look at contemporary church buildings there, but remained seemingly more influenced by his previous work in Rochdale than by anything he saw abroad.[27] Like his church at Rochdale, the Ratcliffe College chapel, 'in the modern trend with a basic Byzantine feeling', as Norris put it, was constructed in reinforced concrete clad in brick, a dome floating over a clerestory, while vertical slot windows in the transepts gave it a modern look.[28] A few years later, Norris designed St John Fisher at West Heath in Birmingham, a simple brick building described by the architect as 'a modern interpretation of the Romanesque style' with a Greek cross plan, though it was intended to extend the nave at a later date (Figure 2.8).[29] Without the budget for a dome, this church was economically roofed in timber with an octagonal clerestoried tower.

In both churches, a modern innovation in church architecture was interpreted as Byzantine in order to reconcile it with tradition. Artist Jonah Jones was commissioned for decorative work at Leicester and West Heath, and for their windows he chose a technique that had been developed in France in the 1930s known as *dalle de verre* ('glass slab'), in which the glazing was made of small thick chunks of coloured glass set in heavy, often concrete, frames, forming rough, stylised images with dazzling colours. Norris undoubtedly saw this technique in France. It was described as 'transparent mosaic' by Eugène Auguste Roulin, a French Benedictine monk who had settled at Ampleforth Abbey in Yorkshire, who illustrated distinctly Byzantine figures in windows by Jean Gaudin in his book *Modern Church Architecture* of 1947.[30] Jones described his own windows at West Heath as 'a sort of compound of Byzantine, Romanesque, and possibly early French mediaeval influences', claiming to have revived 'the spirit, if not the actual style, of Byzantine Christianity' and citing the mosaics of Ravenna as an inspiration. The abstraction of the figures that resulted from this technique was, he thought, a modern parallel of a Byzantine rejection of sentimental imagery. Norris's plain but expansive architecture was a suitably 'unproclaiming and noble frame' for his work.[31] The disconcerting modern appearance of Jones's windows, his figures fragmented into vivid patches of colour, was therefore justified as a development within an existing tradition.

2.4   St Patrick, Leicester, by Reynolds & Scott, 1957–59. Photo: Robert Proctor, 2009

2.5   St Joseph, Wembley, London, by Reynolds & Scott, 1956–58. Photo: Robert Proctor, 2010

2.6   St Bernard, Burnage, Manchester, by Reynolds & Scott, 1957–59. Photo: Entwistle, Thorpe & Co. Ltd, *c.*1959

2.7   Ratcliffe College Chapel, Leicester, by Ernest Bower Norris, 1957–59. Sculpture
and *dalle de verre* windows by Jonah Jones. Photo: Robert Proctor, 2009

2.8 St John Fisher, West Heath, Birmingham, by Sandy & Norris, 1963–64. Photo: Robert Proctor, 2009

So, too, was another feature of these two churches' interiors, the ciborium, made popular by Westminster Cathedral's revival of this substantial element of sanctuary furnishing. At both Leicester and West Heath, Norris reinterpreted the conventional columned canopy in modern forms and metal structures: at Ratcliffe College with pencil-like shafts and a wavy canopy like a fragment of the Festival of Britain; at St John Fisher, in a sleek and entirely modern design, hinting perhaps at the local car industry (Plate 1).[32] While the ciborium was an ancient feature revived in twentieth-century Catholic church architecture, it was reinterpreted here through modern means. At Leicester, however, Jones decorated the canopy with an allegorical scene based on Byzantine mosaics, accentuating an allegiance to the past.

Historical allusions were reassuring. Priest and bishop could be sure that the building would demonstrate continuity with the historical Church while also conveying a distinctive image identified in modern British cities with twentieth-century Catholicism. The Romanesque was also practically reassuring, suggesting the solidity of traditional construction and the economies of a plain architecture. In many cases architects were specifically asked to design in Romanesque by their clerical clients.[33] Yet the Romanesque and Byzantine styles could easily be given a more modern appearance, built with modern techniques, decorated with modern artworks and furnishings, and adapted to new kinds of plan. It was an enormously successful approach. Reynolds & Scott built all over England, and many other architects built in a similar manner: Harrison & Cox in Birmingham, Archard & Partners in London, Wilfrid Mangan in Preston and London, R. S. Ronchetti and Arthur Farebrother in Yorkshire, to name only the largest firms. St Teresa in Filton, Bristol by O'Brien, Morris & McCullough combined Byzantine and Romanesque associations with reference to early Christian basilicas: a 'traditional style' but, like modernist architecture, 'strictly functional' and with 'little or no decoration', as its architects wrote.[34]

The Byzantine was such a prevalent style that even modernist architects could be drawn to it. St Raphael's, Stalybridge, designed by Edward J. Massey of Warrington and opened in 1963, was entirely modern in style, with a reinforced concrete frame combining cylindrical piers and segmental vaults, perhaps following Chamberlin, Powell & Bon's Golden Lane housing in London (Figure 2.9). This gave a lightness and openness at odds with the Byzantine architecture of walls and volumes: here walls were merely infill panels of brick. Yet a Byzantine allegiance at Stalybridge was signalled by a low reinforced concrete dome over the sanctuary with a clerestory around its base. The dome was off-centre from the rectangular plan, so that most of the seating occupied a nave, though the transepts were broad to accommodate congregational seating, arranged on three sides of the sanctuary in response to the developing understanding of the liturgy in the 1960s. Galleries at each side could be used by a choir, suggestive of Byzantine church galleries.[35]

Perhaps the most striking feature of this church was a frieze of stained-glass across the ground floor in *dalle de verre*, made by Pierre Fourmaintraux of Whitefriars Studios in London.[36] Fourmaintraux pioneered the technique in Britain and made many windows in both Catholic and non-Catholic churches throughout the country, as well as undertaking secular commissions.[37] His windows at

2.9   St Raphael, Stalybridge, by Massey & Massey, 1960–63. *Dalle de verre* by Pierre Fourmaintraux of Whitefriars Studios; Stations of the Cross in ceramic by Alan Boyson and Neal French. By permission of Alan Boyson and Neal French. Photo: Richard Brook, *c.*2000

St Raphael give a figurative, narrative depiction of the Old Testament story of Tobias and Raphael using this chunky technique that imposed a degree of abstraction. If Jones could appeal to the Byzantine in his use of *dalle de verre*, its use to create a broad enclosing surface at St Raphael's made it even more evocative of mosaic. Yet this technique also had Gothic associations: the architect intended this panel to be visible outside when the church's lights were on, and elsewhere – at St Richard, Chichester, for example, where Gabriel Loire's windows filled the spaces in a reinforced concrete frame – this method was also interpreted as a modern version of medieval stained glass.[38] At St Raphael's, Stalybridge, however, Massey seems to have used it as part of a coherent reworking of twentieth-century (and particularly perhaps Lancastrian) Catholic Byzantine architecture into a more progressive and liturgically innovative church architecture. It may have been an exceptional building, but, like its more conservative counterparts, it represented a dual allegiance both to modern conditions and to a conception of a continuing tradition.

ROMANESQUE REINTERPRETED IN LIVERPOOL AND LONDON

While Reynolds & Scott and Sandy & Norris produced churches that met their clerical clients' expectations, drawing on stock features they had established before the Second World War, several architects took a more original and personal approach to an explicitly anti-modern church design, also based on the Romanesque.

Francis Xavier Velarde and Harry Stuart Goodhart-Rendel both wrote in opposition to the modern movement; indeed Goodhart-Rendel had been forced to resign from his position as Director of Education at the Architectural Association in 1938 because of his anti-modern stance. In a booklet on church architecture published shortly after the war, Goodhart-Rendel presented his ideas on 'commonsense churchplanning'. Churches, he insisted, had to be permanent, and so he argued against untested modern materials such as steel and reinforced concrete. In a clear rejection of modernism, he wrote that the architect had to suppress his ego, avoiding anything 'sensational, revolutionary, or pretentious'.[39] Goodhart-Rendel instead studied and admired Victorian architects including William Butterfield, Temple Moore and Bentley, seeing his own work as continuing in their path.[40] Following Jacques Maritain's *Art and Scholasticism*, he saw the architect as an intellectual, an inspired artist, whose intense application to design through the creative exploration of the rules and techniques of his art would combine with his personal devotion to imbue his work with a Christian spirit.[41]

Velarde, also influenced by Maritain, wrote that tradition had to be accepted but modified through the artist's creativity:

> If art somehow cuts itself off from tradition, if somehow it fails to give expression to it, then it cuts itself off from life and ceases to be human; it does not even begin to be great art. … The true artist … must be in some degree a creator; he can never be a mere copyist, plagiarist, or skilful selector from the creative work of the past. It is his function to combine tradition and creativeness, which are not opposed but, rightly understood, are complementary and even integral to each other.[42]

Creativity would lead the artist forward, inspiring a modern church architecture in continuity with the past; but it should also look inwards, drawing on familiar memories of churches to inspire an emotional sympathy in the viewer. It was important for the architect to emphasise 'the specifically Catholic character' of the church building, and perhaps for that reason Velarde's post-war churches were personal reinterpretations of the Byzantine and Romanesque.[43]

Goodhart-Rendel's most important post-war Roman Catholic churches in London, Holy Trinity, Dockhead, and Our Lady of the Rosary, Marylebone, were both Romanesque in inspiration, and each was an original take on the style. Holy Trinity's monumental symmetry, sheer brown brick walls patterned with coloured brickwork and twin thick-set towers connected by a high arch over the severe west window, followed German Romanesque rather than Italian precedent, especially the influential early twentieth-century church at Ulm by Theodor Fischer.[44] Dockhead's vaulted nave had passage aisles running through internal buttresses, a system that had interested Victorian architects (Plan 1b). Goodhart-Rendel's polychrome brickwork and the ungainly character of this church owed much to his interest in Butterfield, on whom he had lectured in 1934, and who was then also being popularised by John Summerson, who praised the intelligent 'ugliness' of Butterfield's church architecture.[45] At Dockhead, Goodhart-Rendel applied a contemporary analysis of the Victorian architect's approach to materials and composition to the Catholic twentieth-century neo-Romanesque tradition in church architecture (Plate 2).

2.10   Our Lady of the Rosary, Marylebone, London, by H. S. Goodhart-Rendel and D. A. Reid of F. G. Broadbent & Partners, 1958–64. Main entrance facade. Photo: Robert Proctor, 2009

Our Lady of the Rosary, completed after the architect's death by his practice, has a family resemblance to Holy Trinity, with a similar interest in broad brick surfaces and polychrome decoration (Figure 2.10). 'Romanesque in feeling', though of no particular style, as Goodhart-Rendel's practice partner Francis Broadbent wrote, with more influence this time from both southern French and Italian Romanesque precedent, this church was altogether lighter, with a pink and red brick bell tower over the entrance and pointed transverse arches over the nave conferring more delicacy than sublimity (Figure 2.11).[46] The differences between these two London churches, similar in conception but of varied characters, might be explained in part by their architect's emphasis on 'good manners' in architecture, the notion that buildings should look in keeping with their neighbours.[47] Holy Trinity's dark cragginess suited the surrounding warehouses of London's East End and its imposing towers confronted a major traffic route, while the Rosary church in affluent Marylebone huddled amongst residential and commercial blocks and stepped back from its terraced neighbours alongside the main road. The architect's individualism in his approach to precedent was a means of producing the most fitting building for its purpose and place.

For Goodhart-Rendel, style was a starting point rather than an aim, and he transformed the Romanesque through personal vision rather than by accommodating modern circumstances. Modernity was evidently not important beyond the acceptance of contemporary requirements of worship; for economic reasons, however, he did accept reinforced concrete, commissioning engineer Felix Samuely for the vaults at Dockhead and using this necessity as a spur to further

creativity.[48] Velarde, too, developed a distinctive language of church architecture broadly based on the Romanesque and accommodating new techniques with only limited effects on form: modern techniques, he argued, had to be 'traditionalized'.[49] His pre-war Catholic churches in Liverpool, St Matthew, Clubmoor, and St Monica, Bootle, combined art deco design with the Byzantine, inspired especially by German church architecture of the 1920s.[50] By the 1950s, Velarde's churches became simpler reinventions of the Byzantine and Romanesque. St Teresa, Upholland, was plain and barn-like in red brick articulated with groups of Romanesque windows. Two round chancel arches defined the deep sanctuary, and its single aisle was framed with thick-set columns covered in golden mosaic supporting round arches. Its tower was topped with open round-headed arches and a big copper pyramid.[51] Velarde's architecture relied on broad masses, exposed brick and simple repeated motifs.

2.11 Our Lady of the Rosary, Marylebone, London, by H. S. Goodhart-Rendel and D. A. Reid of F. G. Broadbent & Partners, 1958–64. Interior. Photo: Robert Proctor, 2009

English Martyrs, Wallasey, and Holy Cross, Birkenhead, had stark brick exteriors
giving way to colourful interiors with vivid painted ceilings and mosaic-clad
aisle piers, a pairing of austere Romanesque forms with modern decoration that
characterised his post-war churches (Figure 2.12). St Alexander, Bootle, was a
similarly large church with a twin-towered west front (Figure 2.13). Its forms were
reduced to essential cubic masses pierced by rounded openings for the three great
doors and open towers, like a child's drawing of a church.

By the 1950s, Velarde began to receive commissions in London, and there his
assistants, including Richard O'Mahony and Janet Gnosspelius and his son Julian
Velarde took his architecture some way towards modernism. At St Luke, Pinner,
historical references were abstracted further: the cut-out forms of St Alexander
remained, but the aisle windows were made with precast concrete frames in a simple
pattern, and the small square clerestory windows gave this church some affinity
with contemporary Scandinavian-influenced modernism (Figure 2.14, Plan 1d).[52] The
interior was spartan, enlivened with highlights of rich decoration: the ceiling was
formed with blue-painted timber coffers, forming a strip over the nave and descending
to a reredos with a large crucifixion sculpture by David John (Plate 3). The nave
columns were covered in gold mosaic and given simple alternating capitals, a memory
of the Byzantine style. St Luke was Byzantine and Romanesque in spirit, if no longer
in style, and modern in design and detail.[53] Smaller and similar churches in London
followed, including St Theresa of Lisieux, Borehamwood, where Velarde's assistants
completed the church with segmental arches and an especially severe exterior.[54]
In this post-war period, Velarde's reinterpretation of Romanesque architecture
can be viewed as the result of his own hermetic development as an architect:

2.13   St Alexander, Bootle, Liverpool by F. X. Velarde, 1957. Photographer unknown, c.1960.
Source: Bryan Little, *Catholic Churches Since 1623* (London: Robert Hale, 1966), pl. 37

2.14   St Luke, Pinner, London, by F. X. Velarde, 1958. Main facade with relief sculpture
of the Virgin and St Luke by David John. Photo: Robert Proctor, 2010

some stylistic aspects from contemporary architecture were worked into his approach, partly through the involvement of younger assistants; yet, while his churches frequently incorporated modern stylistic elements, the radical new approaches of modern architects were rejected in favour of incremental changes to traditional forms.

MODERN GOTHIC

While Byzantine and Romanesque were the most popular historical references in Catholic church architecture after the Second World War, the memory of the nineteenth-century Gothic revival and A. W. N. Pugin's campaign to associate it with Catholicism remained strong. While neo-Romanesque architecture could lead to a simplification that approached a modern style and adopted some elements of modern architecture, Gothic had potential to lead more directly to modernism through its supposedly rational expression of structure – an interpretation that Pugin himself had made and which became especially important in French architecture through Viollet-le-Duc, taken up in modern church architecture most famously by Auguste Perret at Le Raincy. Yet many architects of post-war churches in Britain ignored this potential in favour of a continuing development of a Gothic revival tradition in church architecture adapted to the more limited means of the mid-twentieth century.

The distant successor of Pugin's own firm even remained in practice in the 1950s, when Charles Purcell led the firm of Pugin & Pugin, then based in Liverpool. He had taken over the firm from his cousin, Pugin's grandson Sebastian Pugin Powell, in 1949.[55] The firm had been popular in Glasgow under Archbishop Charles Eyre in the late nineteenth century and continued to build there after the Second World War. Purcell's church of St Ninian in Knightswood (completed after his death by S. Stevenson-Jones in 1958) was a modest building of brick with precise Early English tracery in stone, simplified mouldings and a deep apse behind a chancel arch, hardly distinguishable from a church of the nineteenth century, though as Purcell had had to resort to concealing a steel structure by disguising it as timber, there was little left but the image of the Gothic.[56] Purcell had no reason to change with the times, since he continued to receive commissions for a Puginian style of church.

Meanwhile, many of the post-war Roman Catholic churches of Sir Giles Gilbert Scott, Adrian's brother, were also Gothic, following his work for the Church of England at Liverpool Cathedral, designed in 1903 and still far from complete at the time of his death in 1960. Scott's Catholic churches included the Carmelite priory church of Our Lady of Mount Carmel and St Simon Stock in Kensington, London, and Christ the King, Plymouth, completed by his practice in 1962.[57] While these churches were designed in different forms of Gothic, neither could be mistaken for anything but the work of a twentieth-century architect. Kensington, a replacement for a bombed church, had an affinity with the work of Goodhart-Rendel, a wide nave roofed with transverse arches supporting a high clerestory, passage aisles cut through at ground level, the Gothic represented rather than recreated through the pointed forms of the arches and an elaborate reredos (Figure 2.15).

Partly for economy and partly for a modernised aesthetic, complex mouldings were eliminated, while the exterior employed plain brick surfaces with stone detailing confined to windows and doorways. The absence of more complex features made the building austere – a form of Gothic without medieval precedent, a personal development of the Gothic revival in parallel with Goodhart-Rendel's development of the Romanesque. Scott's church in Plymouth was less innovative, with masonry piers forming arcaded aisles and a deep chancel, yet the piers, diagonal in section, had no mouldings or capitals, and the exterior was a plain brick box and tower (Figure 2.16). Scott's original design made use of parabolic arches, but the parish priest had pressed him for a more conventional Gothic church: selected because of his reputation for this style, Scott could hardly move towards modernism; but he nevertheless designed in a decidedly contemporary form of the Gothic revival.[58]

A decade before, this approach to church architecture had been summarised by John Summerson, with Edward Maufe's Anglican Cathedral at Guildford in mind:

> The obvious, elementary way [of designing churches] is to grab at the disappearing tail of the Gothic Revival. … This means leaving out all the expensive and technically difficult parts of Gothic, streamlining the silhouette, keeping everything plain (say two cusps for every twenty in a 14th century equivalent) and relying on charming materials and a little sculpture on the safe side of Eric Gill. That way has the very substantial merit of being instantly acceptable to the majority of church-goers. Well done, it is completely unobjectionable; modesty and orthodoxy commend it.[59]

This was faint praise from a critic promoting modern architecture, but accurately conveyed the intentions of architects such as Scott: to accept the limitations of cost that made archaeologically accurate Gothic impossible and therefore to build modestly, adapting the Gothic for modern conditions while accepting an obligation to satisfy the client's desire for a recognisable church. It was an approach that was especially employed for the restorations and extensions of earlier Gothic revival churches of this period, including Scott's continuing work at Ampleforth Abbey church, the reconstruction after bombing of Pugin's St George's Cathedral at Southwark in London by Romilly Craze and the reconstruction and extension by Stanley Kerr Bate of the Benedictine Abbey church at Ealing in London, a bombed late-Victorian church by F. A. Walters.[60]

Other architects attempted to achieve the impression of Gothic with less concern for authenticity and a more hybrid and pragmatic approach open to the expressive use of new materials. Reynolds & Scott, though better known for the Romanesque, frequently turned their hands to this mode of design in the 1950s and early 1960s, explicitly attempting to reconcile aspects of modern architecture with traditional conceptions of the church. At the Sacred Heart, Moreton, near Birkenhead, a west tower in red brick and red sandstone looked convincingly like that of a medieval village church, but the windows were simple cheap lancets punched into the plain brick walls without tracery or mouldings. The interior was essentially similar to their Romanesque churches in form, with pointed transverse arches and a timber reredos merely suggestive of a Gothic style. This building perhaps confirms that, though it may have been desired in certain cases, Gothic architecture was normally impossible to build by then.

2.15   Our Lady of Mount Carmel and St Simon Stock, Kensington, London,
by Giles Gilbert Scott, 1960. Photo: Robert Proctor, 2009

2.16   Christ the King, Plymouth, by Giles Gilbert Scott, 1960–62. Photo: Steve Cadman, 2011

2.17   Our Lady
of Lourdes,
Hackenthorpe,
Sheffield, by
Reynolds & Scott,
1957. Photo: Robert
Proctor, 2009

Our Lady of Lourdes at Hackenthorpe in Sheffield was built at the same time, but veered further towards modernism: 'this church', the architects wrote, 'whilst modern in general has nevertheless an echo of tradition of the Perpendicular style'.[61] Externally it gave little indication of any style: it was a brick box with tall slot windows and a west tower, more art deco than Gothic, based loosely on the influential 1930s church of St Saviour at Eltham in London by Welch & Lander and N. F. Cachemaille-Day. Hackenthorpe's windows were tall rectangular slots in stone surrounds, suggestive of late Gothic verticality but evading literal comparisons. In many other modern churches of this kind, including Reynolds & Scott's Holy Cross in Hucknall, Nottingham, such slot windows were given triangular heads, allowing them to retain enough of the style to ensure its recognisability. The interior at Hackenthorpe was a conventional passage-aisle plan, but was constructed with reinforced concrete portal frames tapered inwards towards the top forming shallow pointed arches (Figure 2.17). The nave may have been suggestive of Perpendicular Gothic, but it was achieved in a construction method derived from warehouses and aircraft hangars.[62] It was clearly important that this modern method should be visible in itself: the tapering of the concrete arches, the plain purlins supporting the ceiling, and the absence of any kind of decorative treatment belonged to the architectural vocabulary of the portal frame. Yet it was equally important that the historical reference should be perceived: the nave arches 'recall vault construction', wrote the architects, the half-frames forming the apse 'giving interesting architectural effect and emphasising the altar and sanctuary'.[63]

2.18   Our Lady
and St Joseph,
Hanwell, London,
by Reynolds & Scott,
1962–67. Photo:
Robert Proctor, 2010

Many architects began to minimise overt Gothic characteristics further, leaving only the expression of structure to imply medieval precedent and the conventional basilican plan to provide a reassurance of continuity, a route that could end in forms of modernism. Reynolds & Scott took this direction in the 1960s: at Our Lady and St Joseph in Hanwell, London, concrete portal frames with V-shaped arms suggested vaulting ribs, the concrete treated and coloured as a modern equivalent of Gothic mouldings, while a broad tower marked the entrance: yet though traditional forms were suggested, there was nothing left of historical style (Figures 2.18, 2.19).[64] By then, however, this architecture was criticised as not radical enough. If it was a modern church architecture, it was not the revolutionary modernism of the younger generation but an approach to architecture that emerged out of an explicit concern with tradition. Because Reynolds & Scott accepted the Church's

2.19   Our Lady and St
Joseph, Hanwell, London, by
Reynolds & Scott, 1962–67.
View towards choir gallery.
Photo: Robert Proctor, 2010

demand that tradition be maintained, and did so by catering to the preconceptions of clergy and faithful rather than challenging them, they became the most prolific firm of Roman Catholic church architects in Britain.

TWENTIETH-CENTURY TRADITION

The Romanesque and Byzantine revival styles were viewed by architects and clergy as a continuing tradition of twentieth-century Catholic church architecture, while the Gothic was sometimes favoured as a more generic tradition of Christianity in Britain.

Such a notion of what constituted tradition was invented anew by each architect on every occasion these forms were used. The word arose frequently in architects' statements about their buildings: 'it was felt that the Church should be traditional in character, and its design is based upon the Romanesque style', wrote Arthur Farebrother on St Catherine, Didsbury; Norris's church of the Assumption in Blackpool was 'in the style of the traditional "Romanesque" with the elimination of all unnecessary trimmings'.[65] Meanwhile the church of Our Lady of Lourdes at Birkdale by Lionel Prichard, a simplified neo-Romanesque with the addition of a steel-columned porch, could be described as 'a building which, though relying to some extent on traditional forms and construction, is thoroughly modern in essence'.[66] Architects sometimes defended themselves by ascribing their approach to the preferences of the clergy: Archard & Partners' rebuilt church of St John, Hackney, in London, for example, was 'traditional in character in accordance with the wishes of the Ecclesiastical Authorities, but contemporary techniques have been employed which are expressed in the elevational treatment'.[67] Just as often, however, architects articulated a defence of tradition, as another Catholic church architect, J. S. Comper, explained: 'I don't believe for a moment that traditional building – particularly as regards religious buildings – is played out. Real architecture has always been a matter of very slow development through the centuries'.[68] Architects worked alongside clergy to construct a distinctive image of the Church, through each new church building: as a beacon of stability and continuity, linked to the universal Church of the past, refusing to accept all the values of the modern world while at the same time claiming a place within it.

If the traditional approach could incorporate some aspects of modern conditions, it was by definition 'anti-modernism': it existed in parallel with modernism, which it rejected, not simply before it.[69] Goodhart-Rendel, for example, thought modern European church architecture 'queer', 'experimental', 'ferocious' or 'whimsical' and praised the work of Velarde; Velarde objected to the 'repellant', 'odd' or 'inscrutable' in church art.[70] Tradition was advocated predominantly by the generation that began in practice before the Second World War, architects who had grown up with modern materials and techniques and witnessed the rise of modern architecture. As this generation gave way to younger architects, modernism gained ground in church architecture. Goodhart-Rendel died in 1959, his practice taken up by his assistants to become Broadbent, Hastings, Reid & Todd, designing in a soft Scandinavian modernism in the 1960s. Velarde died in 1960 and was succeeded by Richard O'Mahony, who accepted all the implications of the modern movement in a series of important churches in the new decade. Giles Gilbert Scott died that year and Adrian Gilbert Scott in 1963, their practices inherited by Giles's son Richard Gilbert Scott, who designed several decidedly modern churches. Reynolds died in 1967, his assistant Brian Mooney then partnering Scott to give even this firm a wholly modern approach. The elder architects' insistences on tradition were a direct challenge to modern architects, who were about to transform the image of the church as a building, and therefore also as an institution, far beyond familiar forms.

NOTES

1   Ian Nairn, 'Criticism: Lansbury Centrepiece', *Architectural Review* (Oct. 1954), 263–4; Hermione Hobhouse and Stephen Porter (eds.) *Survey of London*, vol. 43: *Poplar, Blackwall and Isle of Dogs* (London: Athlone, 1994), 223–39, British History Online, http://www.british-history.ac.uk/report.aspx?compid=46491 (accessed 3 May 2013).

2   'Lansbury Neighbourhood', *Architects' Journal* (15 June 1950), 737–51 (749); Little, *Catholic Churches*, 135.

3   Adrian Gilbert Scott, letter to the editor, *The Tablet* (4 Dec. 1954), 558.

4   William Godfrey, foreword to *CBRS* (1957), 33.

5   Ibid.

6   Ibid.

7   Canon 1164, quoted in J. B. O'Connell, *Church Building and Furnishing: The Church's Way* (London: Burns & Oates, 1955), 28.

8   Council of Trent, Session XXV, ibid. 32–3.

9   Pius XII, '*Mediator Dei*: On the Sacred Liturgy' (1947), 195, http://www.vatican.va/holy_father/pius_xii/encyclicals/documents/hf_p-xii_enc_20111947_mediator-dei_en.html (accessed 19 July 2012).

10 'Instruction of the Holy Office on Sacred Art', 1952, in O'Connell, *Church Building and Furnishing*, 41.

11 Ibid.

12 John Henry Newman, *An Essay on the Development of Christian Doctrine* (London: James Toovey, 1845).

13 Eric Hobsbawm, 'Introduction: Inventing Traditions', in Eric Hobsbawm and Terence Ranger (eds), *The Invention of Tradition* (Cambridge: Cambridge University Press, 1983), 1–14 (7–8).

14 Sarah Williams Goldhagen, 'Coda: Reconceptualizing the Modern', in Sarah Williams Goldhagen and Réjean Legault (eds), *Anxious Modernisms: Experimentation in Postwar Architectural Culture* (Cambridge, MA: MIT Press, 2000), 301–23 (303, 317–18).

15 Gavin Stamp, 'Adrian Gilbert Scott', in Geoffrey Fisher, Gavin Stamp and Joanna Heseltine, *Catalogue of the Drawings Collection of the Royal Institute of British Architects*, vol. 14: *The Scott Family* (Amersham: Gregg, 1981), 185.

16 'The New Church at Poplar', *The Tablet* (31 July 1954), 118.

17 J. B. Bullen, *Byzantium Rediscovered: The Byzantine Revival in Europe and America* (Oxford: Phaidon, 2003), 158–60, 163.

18 Peter Howell, 'Letters from J. F. Bentley to Charles Hadfield: Part II', *Architectural History* 25 (1982), 65–97, 156–61 (80–81); J. A. Hilton, *The Artifice of Eternity: The Byzantine-Romanesque Revival in Catholic Lancashire* (Wigan: North West Catholic History Society, 2008), 28–9.

19 C. H. Reilly, *Some Architectural Problems of To-Day* (London: Hodder & Stoughton, 1924), 39, cited in Ward, 'Merseyside Churches', 95–6.

20 W. R. Lethaby and Harold Swainson, *The Church of Sancta Sophia, Constantinople: A Study of Byzantine Building* (London: Macmillan, 1894), 198–9, cited in Hilton, *The Artifice of Eternity*, 25.

21 Royal Institute of British Architects nomination papers for Francis Maurice Reynolds (fellowship, 1946) and William Scott (fellowship, 1947) (Royal Institute of British Architects Library, London [RIBA], Manuscripts Collection).

22 Richard Pollard, Nikolaus Pevsner and Joseph Sharples, *Lancashire: Liverpool and the South West* (London: Yale University Press, 2006), 387.

23 *CBRS* (1956), 44–5 (Wembley), 98–9 (Braunstone); (1957), 116–17 (Leicester); (1958), 46–7 (Wembley); (1959), 166–9 (Sutton-in-Ashfield), 173–5 (Leicester); (1961), 172–3 (Sutton-in-Ashfield); *CBRN* (1957), 94–5; (1959), 73–8 (Burnage); (1958), 141–2 (Blackpool). A likely candidate for the combined firm's original church might be St Dunstan, Manchester, 1937 (Clare Hartwell, Matthew Hyde and Nikolaus Pevsner, *Lancashire: Manchester and the South-East* [London: Yale University Press, 2004], 88).

24 Pre-war precedents for these features include Reynolds & Scott's St Willibrord, Clayton, Manchester, and Walter Tapper's Our Lady and St Thomas, Gorton, Manchester, of 1927 (see Hartwell, Hyde and Pevsner, *Lancashire*, 363, 371–2; Nikolaus Pevsner, *Lancashire: The Industrial and Commercial South*, Buildings of England [Harmondsworth: Penguin, 1969], 337; on passage aisles, see Little, *Catholic Churches*, 160–62).

25 St Bernard's, Burnage, *Souvenir Book of the Opening of the New Church* (Manchester: n.p., 1959) (parish archive).

26 'The New Church of St. John, Rochdale, Lancs.', *Architects' Journal* (29 July 1925), 162–9; Walker, 'Developments in Catholic Churchbuilding', 329–30.

27 [Claude Leetham], 'The Genesis of the New Chapel', *Ratcliffian* 30 (1961–62), 144 (Ratcliffe College Archive, Leicester); *CBRS* (1958), 148. They may have been especially interested in Jean-Baptiste Hourlier's church of Saint-Louis, Lorient, Brittany, which had a similar plan and dome, though with more overt use of concrete (Franck Pilloton [ed.], *Églises de France reconstruites* [Paris: Musée d'Art Moderne, 1956], 47–8).

28 *CBRS* (1961), 170; [Leetham], 'The Genesis of the New Chapel', 144; *CBRS* (1957), 109–11; (1958), 148–9; (1960), 162–3; (1962), 213.

29 *CBRS* (1964), 114; Philip Smith (parish priest, St John Fisher, West Heath) to Francis Grimshaw (archbishop of Birmingham) (n.d.) (Archives of the Roman Catholic Archdiocese of Birmingham [ARCAB], P55/T); *CBRS* (1963), 132–4.

30 E. Roulin, *Modern Church Architecture*, trans. C. Cornelia Craigie and John A. Southwell (St Louis and London: B. Herder, 1947), 487–9.

31 The Church of St John Fisher, West Heath, *Souvenir Brochure* (Birmingham: n.p., 1964) (ARCAB, P55/T); Peter Jones, *Jonah Jones: An Artist's Life* (Bridgend: Seren, 2011), 109–12.

32 Illustrated in *Ratcliffian* 30 (1961–62), unnumbered plates (Ratcliffe College Archive); *CBRS* (1961), 170–71.

33 For example Harrison & Cox at Our Lady of the Assumption, Birmingham (*CBRS* [1958], 128); Sebastian Comper at Christ the King, Bedford (*CBRS* [1960], 150); even Gillespie, Kidd & Coia were initially asked to use Romanesque at St Benedict, Drumchapel (Proctor, 'Churches for a Changing Litany', 300); J. B. Moriarty (parish priest, St Benedict, Drumchapel) to Jack Coia (Gillespie, Kidd & Coia) (8 Feb. 1960) (Glasgow School of Art Archives [GSAA], GKC/CHDU/1/1/221).

34 *CBRS* (1959), 196; (1960), 196–7.

35 *CBRN* (1960), 98.

36 *CBRN* (1961), 118.

37 Brian Thomas and Eileen Richardson (ed.), *Directory of Master Glass-Painters* (London: Oriel Press, 1972), 113–14.

38   *CBRN* (1963), 66.

39   H. S. Goodhart-Rendel, *Commonsense Churchplanning* (London: Incorporated Church Building Society, n.d.), 18.

40   Gavin Stamp, 'Victorian Survival of Revival? The Case of H. S. Goodhart-Rendel', *AA Files* 15 (1987), 60–66.

41   Powers, *H. S. Goodhart-Rendel*, 17–20; Jacques Maritain, *Art and Scholasticism, with Other Essays*, trans. J. F. Scanlan (London: Sheed & Ward, 1930).

42   R. Velarde and F. X. Velarde, 'Modern Church Architecture and Some of its Problems', *Clergy Review* 38 (1953), 513–26 (516).

43   Ibid. 517.

44   Powers, *H. S. Goodhart-Rendel*, 44.

45   H. S. Goodhart-Rendel, *English Architecture Since the Regency: An Interpretation* (London: Constable, 1953), 126–35; John Summerson, 'William Butterfield: Or, the Glory of Ugliness', in *Heavenly Mansions* (London: Cresset, 1949), 159–76; Powers, *H. S. Goodhart-Rendel*, 10–12.

46   *CBRS* (1962), 62; 'From Our Notebook', *The Tablet* (16 Sept. 1961), 879.

47   Goodhart-Rendel, *Commonsense Churchplanning*, 18–19, citing Arthur Trystan Edwards, *Good and Bad Manners in Architecture* (London: P. Allan, 1924).

48   Powers, *H. S. Goodhart-Rendel*, 44; *CBRS* (1958), 57–9.

49   Velarde and Velarde, 'Modern Church Architecture', 515.

50   Pollard, Pevsner and Sharples, *Lancashire*, 156–7; Walker, 'Developments in Catholic Churchbuilding', 358, 362.

51   Pollard, Pevsner and Sharples, *Lancashire*, 598–9.

52   *CBRS* (1958), 50–51.

53   Ibid.; Bernard A. Harrison, *St Luke's Catholic Church, Pinner: The Story of a Parish* (London: n.p., 2007), 42–4.

54   *CBRS* (1961), 72–3; (1962), 57–9; (1963), 34–7.

55   John Sanders, 'Pugin & Pugin and the Diocese of Glasgow', *Architectural Heritage* 8 (1997), 89–107 (103).

56   *CBRN* (1958), 188–9; Walker, 'Developments in Catholic Churchbuilding', 352.

57   Stamp, ' "A Catholic Church" ', 76–7.

58   Ibid. 79; *CBRS* (1962), 215–17.

59   John Summerson, 'Coventry Cathedral', *New Statesman* (8 Sept. 1951), 253–4, quoted in Bullock, *Building the Post-War World*, 77.

60   Walker, 'Developments in Catholic Churchbuilding', 338, 341–4; Little, *Catholic Churches*, 178, 205; *CBRS* (1956), 33–5; (1958), 35–9, 69; (1961), 40–43; (1962), 51–3.

61   *CBRS* (1957), 102.

62   Walker, 'Developments in Catholic Churchbuilding', 354.

63   *CBRS* (1957), 102.

64   *CBRS* (1962), 60–61; (1965), 53–4; (1967), 44–7.

65 *CBRN* (1956), 58; (1959), 170.

66 *CBRN* (1956), 42.

67 *CBRS* (1956), 38.

68 *CBRS* (1964), 134.

69 Goldhagen, 'Coda', 308.

70 Goodhart-Rendel, *English Architecture*, 280–81; Velarde and Velarde, 'Modern Church Architecture', 518.

3

Modern Church Architecture

While architects who adhered to tradition could claim the support of Church documents and the clergy, modernism was advocated and practised by many Roman Catholic church architects and increasingly welcomed by the clergy after 1955. This chapter examines some of the reasons behind this turn towards modernism, while the following chapters explore in more detail the variety of ways in which modern architects approached church design. Modernism could bring to the Church the promise of an institution that was part of the modern world and relevant to the needs of its inhabitants, a different vision of the institution to that proposed by architects such as Velarde or Goodhart-Rendel. This was a world characterised by rapid change, by the vast movements of people rehoused in new towns and estates, by new and exciting products and materials and, above all, by a feeling of optimism for the future as war and its aftermath of economic struggle became a memory. The Catholic Church was not hermetically sealed from this general cultural climate; on the contrary, its members were inhabitants of the modern world, wished to understand the Church in its terms and hoped to present a public face of the Church that would be well regarded by modern society. Modern architecture offered potential to achieve these aims.

Modernism was characterised by the ready acceptance and expression of modern conditions in architecture in relation to the contemporary technological, social and cultural world. Architects eagerly employed the latest building techniques and materials, from steel and reinforced concrete to industrial prefabrication. Rejecting the conventions of tradition and the past, they wanted to analyse the functions required of their buildings to see if people's lives could be better accommodated in new ways. This implied not just the scrutiny of existing functional programmes but also the working out of new programmes and the rejection of conventional ideas about building types.[1] The new conditions of the city were an important aspect of social and technological modernity with which architecture had to engage, so architects aimed to participate in urbanism even through the design of individual buildings. Architects also shared in a wider artistic culture that included modern artists and craftsmen, drawing on their ideas and commissioning their work for new buildings. Within these broad principles, any one architect or writer might emphasise some intentions over others, so that modernism became extremely diverse in its concerns and in the forms of buildings that resulted, particularly as younger generations of modern architects brought further complexity to modernist architectural discourse and design from the 1950s.[2]

The modernist attitude in architecture of thinking in detail about the functions of a building and planning it without recourse to convention to meet its social needs was the most fundamental and revolutionary principle of this movement. In church architecture, however, it could also be the most problematic, because it threatened to upset not only the way churches looked but also how they were used. The most radical modernism found its ally in the liturgical movement, as a rethinking of the conventions of buildings coincided with the work of clergy who were advocating a similar approach to liturgy – an analysis of its purpose and a revision of the forms of its rites and settings. In adapting modern architecture from different sources to their practice of church design, modern architects contributed to the production of the spaces of the institutional Church in its local manifestations.

MODERNISM IN ARCHITECTURAL PRACTICE

One principal reason for the turn towards modernism in church architecture was that by 1955 the architectural profession and its journals had long since moved decidedly in that direction.[3] While members of the older generation running small practices as principal designers could resist the wider influence of the profession, larger firms gave more work to younger employees who had trained in a different atmosphere. For most architects churches were a small proportion of their business, often modest in recompense compared to more important post-war projects associated with the welfare state such as schools, housing and hospitals and the increasing quantity of work available from commercial clients. Architects' ideals were therefore formed in a larger arena than church architecture, in work where modernism was virtually a necessity given the economic and planning constraints established by the state, particularly for schools.[4] Church projects were frequently given to younger architects, many of whom had studied in schools of architecture where modern methods or at least precedents were taught; and, inevitably, given the nature of practice just after the war, their apprenticeships had involved work on modern secular projects, especially schools and housing.

The Church tended to trust the architects it knew. A few young architects, such as Gerard Goalen, established their own practices by obtaining commissions from Catholic dioceses for the first time in the 1950s. Yet when architects established new practices they had usually come from firms with an existing relationship with the Church: Austin Winkley, trained at the Architectural Association School of Architecture, had worked for the Bolton firm of Greenhalgh & Williams, which had a longstanding relationship with Roman Catholic clergy throughout England; Desmond Williams of Manchester had been in partnership with Arthur Farebrother; others, such as Francis Prichard in Liverpool, Richard Gilbert Scott and Peter Langtry-Langton took over the family firm, the latter after having worked for Basil Spence.[5] Perhaps the majority of modern Catholic churches in post-war Britain were designed by relatively large practices with an established reputation with the Church, notably Weightman & Bullen of Liverpool, working throughout England and Wales, and Gillespie, Kidd & Coia of Glasgow, who built churches across Scotland.

The organisational structure of Gillespie, Kidd & Coia was fairly typical of architectural firms of this period, and the ample evidence for the firm allows a detailed picture to be drawn of the workings of an architectural practice specialising in churches. In 1969, eccentric Glasgow architect Jack Coia, famous by then for a substantial body of Roman Catholic churches, was awarded the annual Gold Medal of the Royal Institute of British Architects. Invited to speak on receiving the award, he made his two partners in the practice – Isi Metzstein and Andy MacMillan – walk up to the podium to give speeches of their own. They in turn praised the firm's architectural assistants, including Charles MacCallum and Robert Walkinshaw.[6] Together, they had been responsible for some of the most extraordinary modern churches in Britain. In the 1950s, the practice had made a sudden transition into a youthful avant-garde form of modern architecture for which Coia himself could obviously not have been responsible. Coia had become a partner in the older Glasgow firm of Gillespie & Kidd in 1927, but the two senior partners both died in the 1920s.[7] As a Catholic child of Italian parents in a sectarian city at the height of a depression, Coia struggled to obtain clients and turned to the archbishop of Glasgow, Donald Mackintosh, for help. He received several commissions for new churches, which he designed in styles ranging from eclectic Romanesque and Renaissance at St Anne's in Dennistoun to International Style modernism for a Catholic pavilion at the British Empire Exhibition in Glasgow of 1938, a work significantly intended to highlight the Catholic Church's role in modern Britain.[8] By this period, however, his work was already influenced by his assistants, especially T. Warnett Kennedy, who cultivated an active interest in European modernism. In the 1950s (after Kennedy's departure), Coia returned to a modern-traditional approach similar to that of Velarde, for example at St Paul in Shettleston.

Gradually, however, he relinquished much of the design work to younger members of his firm while remaining its figurehead. In that role, he nurtured the modernist enthusiasms of this new generation of architects. Metzstein, who had escaped Berlin as a child and served his apprenticeship with Coia while studying at the Glasgow School of Architecture, was joined in 1954 by fellow student MacMillan, who had been working for the East Kilbride Development Corporation. Within a few years they were designing largely on their own. The firm's churches of this period ranged from modest Scandinavian-style modernism at St Paul's, Glenrothes, designed in 1956 (Figure 3.1), to a more monumental approach inspired by Le Corbusier, Louis Kahn and English brutalism at churches such as St Patrick's, Kilsyth (Figure 3.2).[9] Like many other firms, the name of Gillespie, Kidd & Coia represents a changing group of architects transforming the approach to church design after the war, while the apparent continuity of practice offered by the senior partner allowed the architects to maintain a special relationship with the Catholic Church and a continuing specialism in church building.

3.1   St Paul, Glenrothes, by Gillespie, Kidd & Coia, 1956–58. Photo: William Toomey.
Source: Architectural Press Archive / RIBA Library Photographs Collection

3.2   St Patrick, Kilsyth, by Gillespie, Kidd & Coia, 1964. Photo: Robert Proctor, 2010

In the 1950s, Coia would present his assistants' designs to dioceses, persuading and reassuring bishops and financial secretaries alongside the parish priests who had selected him specifically to build modern churches.[10] The same was true of Weightman & Bullen in Liverpool, where the ageing Alfred Bullen, brother of two priests in the archdiocese, attended the Sites and Buildings Commission in the 1950s on behalf of his assistants, several of whom were young Polish immigrants.[11]

While for most architects churches were one aspect of a wider range of output, church design nevertheless remained distinctly outside the mainstream of architectural practice. It allowed aesthetic experimentation with greater freedom than was possible in the rationalised projects of housing and schools, which had government guidelines for planning and strict limits on cost. Church projects gave architects opportunities to work closely with artists, to whose professional sphere they often felt close, occasions that were otherwise rare. Churches often came with expectations from both client and architect of a different kind of modern architecture, one that was more permanent, more grounded in historical precedent and convention, even if these could be radically reinterpreted, and carried an assumption of sacredness at odds with the expediency and efficiency demanded in other areas of architectural practice. These assumptions lent themselves well to certain forms of modernism, especially the more expressive and artistic forms emerging with the advent of the New Brutalism in the 1950s. Churches were much less often discussed in the architectural press than before – indeed in 1960 the magazine *Church Buildings Today* (later retitled *Churchbuilding*) was started to cater for this neglect. Church architects read specialist periodicals such as the French magazine *L'Art sacré*, begun in 1936 and edited by Dominicans Marie-Alain Couturier and Pie-Raymond Régamey, responsible for pioneering modern art and architecture in the Catholic Church, and *L'Art d'église*, a similar Belgian journal edited by Frédéric Debuyst, a Benedictine, from 1959. The former was always available in Coia's office; the latter was read by Richard O'Mahony and Austin Winkley amongst others.

One reason why churches were regarded almost as a parallel branch of modernist practice is that modernist principles often excluded aesthetic wilfulness in a discourse of functionalist derivation of form from programme. Architects had been encouraged from the heart of the modern movement to integrate art into their work and cater for the emotional needs of society in a debate on the 'New Monumentality' instigated by Siegfried Giedion in the 1940s, yet in Britain a more strict approach to programme often remained in architectural discourse.[12] When Gillespie, Kidd & Coia's churches were discussed in the architectural press, they were always praised, but hints of criticism implied they might be straying outside the modern movement: the *Architects' Journal*, confidently describing their church of St Paul at Glenrothes as 'probably the most successful modern church to be built on this side of the English Channel', qualified this statement by noting 'certain mannerisms', including a design detail for which there was 'no apparent reason', while an article in the Scottish journal *Architectural Prospect* on St Bride at East Kilbride cagily described its use of brick as a 'return to tradition'.[13] Church architecture carried a risk for modern architects that they might be seen as betraying the movement's principles, a criticism that was made even of Le Corbusier when he astonished architects with his chapel of Notre Dame du Haut at Ronchamp.[14]

This problem was decisively resolved when the influence of the liturgical movement transformed the debate on church architecture in Britain around 1960, reconciling the building type with the principles of modern architecture. Yet even when there was greater consensus over the principles of a modern church architecture, the forms in which those principles were expressed could vary widely: there were many different strands of modernism, and each could embody the institution of the Church in a different way.

MODERN ARCHITECTS AND THE CHURCH

While church architects had their own reasons for adopting modern architecture, the clergy gave them patronage knowing and accepting their approaches, though often with much debate. Most architects of post-war Roman Catholic churches were trusted firms and individuals with longstanding relationships with the Church, and most were also Catholic. Though few of Coia's assistants were Catholics, it was his prominent Catholicism that brought Gillespie, Kidd & Coia repeated commissions from the Church. Meanwhile other firms often did favour Catholics, although by no means exclusively. Non-Catholic architects were occasionally employed on exceptional commissions. After the Nonconformist Frederick Gibberd won the Liverpool Metropolitan Cathedral competition in 1960, for example, he was asked to design a chapel for the De La Salle order's teacher training college at Middleton, near Manchester, supplanting the college's existing architects, Reynolds & Scott, who were relegated to the status of draughtsmen (see Figure 3.3); later, Gibberd was invited to work for the Benedictine Douai Abbey in Berkshire.[15] Occasionally a project seemed too prestigious for the smaller scale of Catholic firms: hence Clifton Cathedral in Bristol was designed, following advice from the RIBA, by Sir Percy Thomas & Son.

Most architects of post-war Roman Catholic churches had developed relationships with dioceses before the Second World War, and so, like Gillespie, Kidd & Coia, while their design approaches changed, their work existed in institutional continuity with the past. A few dioceses maintained lists of approved architects and recommended them to parish priests – in Menevia, for instance, the diocese covering southern Wales, Weightman & Bullen of Liverpool had almost the status of official diocesan architects, though other firms occasionally found work.[16] This was unusual, however; in most cases there was little or no official control over the choice of architect. The Archdiocese of St Andrews and Edinburgh, responding to Peter Whiston after the architect complained of being overlooked for work, assured him that 'it has been diocesan policy, as far as possible to leave parish Priests free to choose their own architects'.[17] Similarly, in Westminster, an artist approached Cardinal Heenan to ask for work in the diocese, only to be told: 'I never interfere with the choice of priests when they employ artists and architects. I think that the only way of securing commissions is through personal recommendations.'[18] Patronage networks ran across dioceses: the church-building career of John Rochford, for example, began and remained most fruitful in his native Sheffield in the diocese of Leeds in the 1950s, gradually extending southwards with work in Nottingham

in the early 1960s, and culminating with several important commissions in London later in the decade. Architects sometimes artfully cultivated the clergy: Reynolds & Scott occupied an office overlooking Albert Square, where every year a procession of Catholic parishes from across Manchester converged; after the event, the architects would invite the clergy inside for a drink with a view of the dispersing crowds.[19] Coia, too, moved his practice strategically to Park Circus, next to the Glasgow archdiocesan office.[20] It was generally left to the parish priest to select his own architect, but he would rely on recommendations from colleagues and the bishop to choose one who could be trusted for Catholic work.

In most areas, there was a choice of several Catholic architects, a choice which could also therefore be a stylistic one on the part of the priest. Coia and his partners faced competition from several other architects in the three dioceses in which they worked. In Glasgow, Thomas Cordiner had, like Coia, been well established since the 1930s, but tended to produce less daringly modern churches than Coia after the war. Another architect of the older generation, Alexander McAnally, similarly continued to design churches in the city in Gothic and Romanesque revival modes well into the 1960s. Cordiner may have been, as Metzstein put it, 'Jack Coia's *bête-noir*', but when a parish priest chose Coia it was often specifically because he wanted a modern church.[21] Similar choices were available to parish

3.3   Hopwood Hall Chapel, De La Salle Training College, Middleton, Manchester, by Frederick Gibberd and Reynolds & Scott, 1961–65. Photo: John Mills, c.1965. Source: RIBA Library Photographs Collection

priests in London, Liverpool, Manchester, Leeds and elsewhere. The competition between firms, though limited, therefore allowed the parish to choose an architect according to the image of the church it desired for itself, while architects satisfied the diversity of their clients' visions by occupying well-defined areas of current architectural practice. Priests and parishes who wanted a modern church building chose architects they trusted specifically to accomplish this task.

MODERNISM AND THE CHURCH

The Roman Catholic Church came to accept and embrace modern design because of what it could bring to the visual expression of the institutional Church, but it made this acceptance on its own terms, qualifying it with numerous conditions and colouring it with its own ideals and demands. The documents that O'Connell cited in advocating a middle course between the extremes of modern and historical styles could also be interpreted as permitting modernism. While *Mediator Dei* and the 'Instruction on Sacred Art' condemned excessive and controversial novelty and abstraction, they also said that modern art and architecture were not to be prohibited, since the Church had never promoted or advocated any particular style. O'Connell gave the opinion of Cardinal Celso Costantini, a Vatican official and commentator on modern church art:

> Nowadays one can see churches whose construction was inspired by a new style – for one can truly say today that there is a new architectural style – and which fully satisfy the requirements of worship, of a fresh appreciation of artistic beauty, and of an enlightened economic sense.[22]

The 'Instruction on Sacred Art' was specifically designed to attack the kind of modern art seen at the chapel of Notre Dame de Toute Grâce at Assy in France. Here Marie-Alain Couturier managed the artistic programme and commissioned well-known modern artists including Henri Matisse, Fernand Léger and Georges Rouault to decorate a church by Maurice Novarina of the late 1930s. The project created controversy in France surrounding the elite and abstract nature of the artworks, particularly because many of the artists were not even Christian, let alone Catholic, and it was a controversy in which the Church felt obliged to intervene.[23] Yet Assy, and similar projects such as the church of the Sacré-Coeur at Audincourt and the chapel decorated by Matisse at Vence, were widely published and highly influential despite the Vatican pronouncements. Meanwhile modern Catholic church architecture proliferated throughout Europe, especially in France, Germany and Italy, becoming increasingly well-known as European journals such as *Casabella* became more accessible in Britain.

By 1960, when a Picasso retrospective at the Tate Gallery in London drew enormous audiences, modern art had become so generally accepted that it could no longer be deemed to be shocking even in a church. Moreover, as a theology emerged that wanted the Church to be fully expressed in its local contexts, the Vatican changed its stance. At the Second Vatican Council, the document with the most importance for church-building, the 'Constitution on the Sacred Liturgy' of 1963, was distinctly positive in its encouragement of modern design:

> The art of our own days, coming from every race and region, shall … be given free scope in the Church, provided that it adorns the sacred buildings and holy rites with due honour and reverence. It will thereby be enabled to contribute its own voice to that wonderful chorus of praise in honour of the Catholic faith sung by great men in times gone by.[24]

Its only proscriptions were against art that might be considered irreligious through 'distortion' or 'mediocrity'. Good modern art and architecture were now to be actively sought.[25] Just as the liturgy had to be adapted to the local circumstances of the Church, especially through the greater use of local languages, the liturgy, and the Church itself, were to be made relevant and meaningful to diverse cultures, whether the mission fields of Asia or Africa or the modern industrial West.

Since the Vatican's mid-century statements on art and architecture condemned extremes but failed to advocate anything definite, individual members of the clergy had to interpret this advice as they felt best. Hence, while Cardinal Godfrey in Westminster repeatedly called architects to order and condemned modernism in church design, other bishops promoted the cause of modern church architecture. In the northern edition of the *Catholic Building Review* George Andrew Beck, bishop of Salford, recommended that architects and clergy planning new buildings read *L'Art sacré* for its theologically informed approach to modern church architecture.[26] Beck argued that architects had been too hesitant to adopt modern architecture, erring too much towards tradition:

> Discriminating judges may well say that, on present showing, we have not yet found the ecclesiastical idiom in modern architecture. Some of our best modern churches are still being built in what may be called 'traditional' style. … Are we justified in asking architects for a contemporary style of ecclesiastical building? I think we are; but I do not think that they have yet provided it. Many 'contemporary' buildings are a compromise between what might be called 'Festival of Britain' forms of construction and traditional ecclesiastical style.[27]

For Beck, the favoured middle course had been interpreted too conservatively: church architects and clergy had to be braver in building modern churches.

TURNING POINTS FOR MODERNISM

In 1960, Heenan in his post as archbishop of Liverpool announced that the winner of the competition for Liverpool Metropolitan Cathedral was a well-established non-Catholic modern architect, Frederick Gibberd. On receiving this news, Beck argued that the decision should be viewed by architects and clergy as an encouragement to develop an appropriate language of modern architecture for the Church, one which could represent its relevance to the modern world:

> The Liverpool award will have given a great impetus to church design and planning in the direction which may be described as 'modern' rather than 'traditional'.

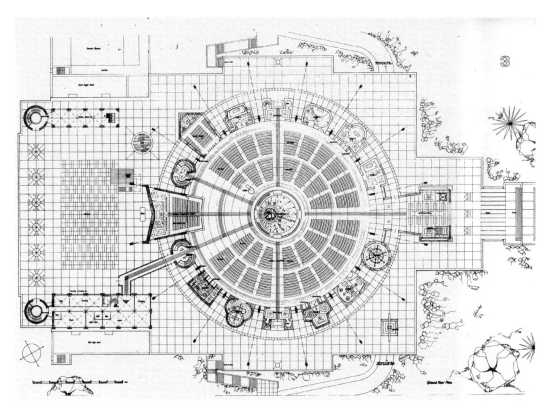

3.4   Frederick Gibberd, competition-winning plan for Liverpool Metropolitan Cathedral, 1960. Source: RIBA Library Photographs Collection. Courtesy of the Gibberd Garden Trust and Frederick Gibberd Partnership

This is bound to be a good thing in the long run, for church art which is not vital, contemporary and, to some extent, controversial must be approaching stagnation and death. … We have still to find a style of architecture, particularly in elevation, which will suggest the 'God-dimension' in human living, which will express dignity, majesty, and the sense of worship, while at the same time showing clearly that these qualities do not belong to a past and dead age but are the expression of an active and energetic spirit in the contemporary world.[28]

While for Beck the designs of modern architecture in elevation were as yet insufficient – too much like 'factories, swimming pools and municipal buildings',[29] he wrote – he enthusiastically approved of the new types of ground plan, like Gibberd's circular nave, developed by modern church architects to gather the congregation around the altar (Figures 3.4, 3.5).

Liverpool Metropolitan Cathedral was therefore seen as a turning point that marked, for many architects and clergy, the Roman Catholic hierarchy's endorsement of modern church architecture in Britain. Heenan had sacked Adrian Gilbert Scott from his post as architect of the cathedral only a year after becoming archbishop in 1957, deciding to interrupt the progress of the building when the crypt, designed by Edwin Lutyens in 1932, reached completion. In place of Scott's reduced version of Lutyens's enormous Byzantine-Renaissance design, Heenan wanted a cathedral built quickly and cheaply – and whose cost limit of £1 million would, it was implied, preclude traditional materials.[30] A modern building

was clearly intended. Heenan had previously been bishop of Leeds, where he had begun a campaign of new church buildings, encouraging modern architects: Peter Hickson described how Heenan had studied his model for the church of Our Lady of the Assumption at Stainforth, near Doncaster, in 1956, explaining that 'it was felt that the church must express the age in which it was built'.[31] After transferring to Liverpool, Heenan continued his interest in architecture, encouraging new building, including significant modern churches by architects such as Weightman & Bullen. In 1963, when he was appointed archbishop of Westminster following the death of Cardinal Godfrey, his arrival in this diocese brought an atmosphere in which modern church architecture could develop more freely in the capital.

Before then, Godfrey had not only insisted on tradition in print but had sometimes exerted his influence in person. Architect Alfred Archard tentatively proposed a church for the parish of Carpender's Park in north-west London in 1958 combining modern features with some traditional elements, arguing that the situation in a new housing area demanded a modern treatment. He wrote to Godfrey:

> We shall be only too ready to submit alternative designs for approval and obviously these would be traditional in character. When building Churches in new areas we often find that the Architects to the [Local] Authority have very decided views about what they will permit. In this case we have tried to adopt a middle course, we realise that middle courses are sometimes fraught with danger, but we

3.5   Metropolitan Cathedral of Christ the King, Liverpool, by Frederick Gibberd, 1960–67. Bell tower sculpture by William Mitchell. Photo: Elsam, Mann & Cooper. Source: Architectural Press Archive / RIBA Library Photographs Collection

> *honestly believe that the Town Planning Authority would not accept a completely*
> *traditional Church, on the other hand we do realise that strongly contemporary*
> *design does not commend itself to Ecclesiastical Authority.*[32]

Their 'middle course', an implicit reference to *Mediator Dei*, was too middling for Godfrey, however, who replied:

> *We examined it briefly yesterday and we do not feel satisfied with it in its present*
> *form. We shall, no doubt, make certain suggestions for an adjustment or possibly*
> *a radical change. I appreciate the point about the housing estate but we hope*
> *that a new church can be built which will satisfy both local requirements and our*
> *own ideas of what a Catholic place of worship should be.*[33]

The church finally built at Carpender's Park was a plain brick building with more than a hint of the Romanesque style, suggested by round-headed lancet windows and a square brick campanile.

When the Church did accept modern architecture at an early date, therefore, it could be due to the personal interest of the bishop, especially in major and exceptional commissions such as that for Liverpool Metropolitan Cathedral. In most cases, however, the bishop might have prompted new building but did not intervene on stylistic grounds. Heenan, for instance, certainly had a personal interest in modern architecture but did not censure traditional designs. In dioceses such as Glasgow and St Andrews and Edinburgh, traditional architects such as Reginald Fairlie and Alexander McAnally received just as many commissions as modernising colleagues such as Gillespie, Kidd & Coia and Peter Whiston. Modern church architecture therefore resulted just as much from the decisions of individual members of the clergy as it did from the tolerance or promotion of bishops.

Several other cases contributed to a changing atmosphere in the Church. Our Lady of Victories in Kensington, London, perhaps first showed that there could be a general parish and lay interest in modern architecture. This was another church whose design was entrusted to Adrian Gilbert Scott, replacing a bombed-out Victorian building on a narrow but prominent site in a wealthy area of central London (Figure 3.6). When the choice of architect became public in 1954, several distinguished parishioners raised complaints, first with the diocese and then in the Catholic press. Amongst them Lord William Forbes-Semphill wrote to Cardinal Griffin, the archbishop of Westminster, deploring the architect's proposals.[34] His despair became a public campaign undertaken by a group of parishioners against the design. The Royal Fine Art Commission became involved, invited to comment by the parish priest, John Bagshawe, in order to settle the controversy.[35] Its members, who included Frederick Gibberd, advised the diocese to commission a completely new design, considering Scott's proposals 'quite unsatisfactory and unworthy'.[36] The grounds of criticism were unclear, however; Scott argued that the commission had found his work 'too modern and not traditional enough, hence the difficulty of satisfying everyone'.[37] In the end, with agreement from members of the commission, Cardinal Griffin asked Goodhart-Rendel to modify Scott's design. He agreed, making the design plainer and modifying Scott's parabolic arches to a more conventional Gothic outline (Figure 3.7).[38]

3.6   Our Lady of Victories, Kensington, London, by Adrian Gilbert Scott,
1952–59. Perspective of first design, drawn by J. D. M. Harvey, 1954. Source: parish
archive. Courtesy of the parish of Our Lady of Victories, Kensington

3.7   Our Lady of
Victories, Kensington,
by Adrian Gilbert
Scott, 1952–59.
The sculpture of
the Risen Christ
by Michael Clark
replaced a crucifix
in the 1980s. By
permission of Joseph
Lindsey-Clark. Photo:
Robert Proctor, 2009

When this decision was announced and construction began in 1955, it might have
seemed that an opportunity for abandoning tradition in favour of modernism in
church architecture had been lost.

Yet the controversy had been partly played out through the Catholic newspaper,
The Tablet, becoming a highly significant debate over modern church architecture.
The debate was especially stimulated by Nairn's condemnation of Scott's church
at Poplar, which suggested that his work was poorly regarded by the architectural
profession.[39] One concerned parishioner at Our Lady of Victories was Nicolete
Gray, an art critic and historian of typography who had written for the *Architectural
Review*.[40] She wrote to *The Tablet* to lament the design and explain the importance
of commissioning a modern building:

> The sort of churches which we build are the most explicit sign which we give to
> the world of the nature of our Faith. … We want our churches to be symbols of the
> Catholic Church alive. There are plenty of people who think that Christianity is dead,
> a relic of the middle ages; what better confirmation could they have than the sight of
> Catholics building new pseudo-Gothic churches in the twentieth century?[41]

Others defended Scott and wrote against modern art and architecture, one
writer citing Pius XII in his favour and arguing that 'nine out of ten of those who
worship in the present temporary church … would find an ultra-modernistic
church completely repugnant'.[42] Simon Elwès, a portrait artist, argued instead
that Pius XII had not condemned modern art at all, but only bad taste. Elwès cited
what soon became a familiar passage of the 'Instruction on Sacred Art': 'Let new

churches be resplendent also for the simple beauty of their lines, abhorring all deceitful ornament'.[43] While this important Vatican statement could apply equally to traditional as to modern architecture, Elwès explicitly used it to promote the latter. The debate in *The Tablet* was concluded by a young Catholic architect, Lance Wright, who later designed several modern Catholic churches. He summarised the case for modern church architecture, arguing that to reject modernism was 'to further a break between the Church and our society in the sphere of culture, which is the same as saying in the sphere of everyday life', confirming Gray's view that the church building should express the relevance of the Church to the world around it, implying that the Church should be seen as an active agent within the world.[44]

    While Our Lady of Victories may therefore have appeared to represent a defeat for those within the Church who favoured modernism, it caused the arguments over church design to be aired amongst Catholics, and the prevailing argument was in favour of modernism. By the time Scott's church opened in 1958, several architects in London had had modern church designs accepted. David Stokes's church of Our Lady of the Visitation at Greenford was designed in 1956 with dramatic broad parabolic arches of reinforced concrete forming the interior and an unornamented brick exterior with a modern tower (Figure 3.8), while John Newton designed his church of St Aidan in East Acton around 1958 as a reinforced concrete and brick basilica containing significant works of modern art.[45] Both of these architects were already well established and had the trust of the diocese. Even as a strongly opinionated archbishop, therefore, Godfrey could not prevent the adoption of modern architecture when it was desired by parish priests and cogently defended by Catholic architects.

3.8   Our Lady of the Visitation, Greenford, London, by David Stokes & Partners, 1956–60. Photo: Colin Westwood, c.1960. Source: RIBA Library Photographs Collection

ECONOMY AND THE IMAGE OF ECONOMY

Even in places where the clergy were ambivalent about modern architecture, one reason for choosing it was cost, or at least a perception that it was cheaper than traditional building. Despite the gradual easing of post-war austerity in the 1950s, the morality of austerity remained an important consideration for architects and churchmen alike. Traditional architecture, especially in the hands of architects such as Adrian Gilbert Scott and Goodhart-Rendel who preferred durable and high-quality materials, was expensive. Modern architecture could also be expensive when a client had a significant budget to spend, but when a building was needed and the budget was small, modern architects could use simple materials, new building technologies and an absence of ornament to meet financial constraints without aesthetic compromise – indeed, the expressive adherence to cost limitations was seen as a virtue by modern architects. In some places cost was hardly an issue. Parishes receiving war-damage compensation had substantial budgets: the cost of Our Lady of Victories was estimated at around £125,000 in 1955, over £100,000 of which was due to be met by compensation; Sts Mary and Joseph in Poplar was projected in 1953 as costing £150,000; Velarde's St Alexander in Bootle was built for £90,000.[46] New churches built for long-established parishes whose congregations had saved substantial sums might also reach such amazing figures: Goodhart-Rendel's church in Marylebone was estimated at £144,250 in 1957 (and, including its presbytery, totalled £190,000 by its completion in 1963).[47]

Yet as costs for labour and materials rose rapidly between 1955 and 1975, economies had to be continually sought: on a single project, costs could escalate alarmingly between the quantity surveyor's estimate and the opening of the church a few years later. Clergy often wanted to build quickly before costs rose out of reach. Throughout the period, general economic conditions deteriorated. In 1956, a brief 'credit squeeze' was imposed by banks, which refused to lend money; an economic boom in the late 1950s and early 1960s fizzled out with a second credit squeeze in 1966, followed by a period of spiralling inflation, the devaluation of the pound and a disastrous depression in the early 1970s.[48] The Roman Catholic Church in Britain was especially vulnerable to economic vagaries because of its reliance on bank loans for funding new buildings: when credit was unavailable, churches could not be built; when interest rates soared, debt repayments became crippling, reducing the capacity for further borrowing. Furthermore, as new parishes were created in new housing areas following post-war population movements, the majority of churches were needed for recently established parishes that had not yet accumulated significant funds. Throughout the two decades considered here, cost was a pressing concern, and modernism in architecture seemed to promise convenient and economical new church buildings.

Liverpool Metropolitan Cathedral was not the only case where a traditional architect lost a commission to a modernist one at least ostensibly on grounds of cost. Adrian Gilbert Scott failed to complete several other projects because a perception of extravagance invited criticism and delay. At St Aloysius, Somers Town, in central London, the parish priest, Arthur Welland, had agreed with Godfrey in 1959 to appoint Scott to design a new church to replace an early nineteenth-century building damaged by bombing. Scott's first design was costed at £150,000; his second at £90,000. After three years, the chairman of the diocese's Parochial Development Commission, auxiliary bishop David Cashman, wrote to Godfrey that 'Scott is either unable or unwilling to produce drawings and plans for a church less ambitious and, consequently, we wonder whether Your Eminence would approve of changing the architect'.[49] In the time taken to reach this decision, the Liverpool Cathedral competition had already pointed Catholic church architecture in a new direction. Godfrey died in 1962, and Scott in 1963. John Newton of Burles, Newton & Partners was then appointed to design a modern church with a concern for liturgical planning, as delays took the project well beyond the Second Vatican Council to the eventual opening of the new church in 1968.[50] During this time the parish had raised new funds, but inflation had taken its toll: including hall and presbytery, the building's final cost was £150,000, the same as Scott's original proposal a decade before.[51]

In Birmingham, Scott's optimism had also caused difficulties. The parish priest of Our Lady Help of Christians at Tile Cross, Timothy Dinan, commissioned drawings from Scott in 1962 and presented them to his parishioners to arouse their enthusiasm and elicit donations for the new building.[52] His plans were quashed by the diocese, which insisted he raise half the capital for the building, projected to cost over £90,000.[53] A meeting between Dinan and an advisor of Francis Grimshaw, archbishop of Birmingham, was recorded for the latter's information: 'Fundamental difference of thinking. Final wish to see fine grandiose church. Does not believe it possible to seat 600 for £60,000', the diocese noted; 'it is possible to seat 600 comfortably for less. So don't wait, start on adequate church', was to be Grimshaw's response.[54] After Scott's death, the diocese wrote to his partner with a reduced cost limit of £50,000. 'The Archbishop must beg architects to be realistic', wrote his secretary, adding that Scott had 'had a generous notion of what parish resources can provide' and urging him to eliminate unnecessary features, including side chapels, from Scott's design.[55] Richard Gilbert Scott then took over the practice, and, in 1965, his new plan for a modernist design with soaring reinforced concrete vaults forming a tower over the centre of a T-shaped plan was submitted and approved (Figure 3.9). During the delay, Dinan had, like Welland at Somers Town, managed to raise substantial further funds, and the diocese eventually approved a sum of £100,000.[56] The diocese's objections were therefore not merely on financial grounds; rather, the desire for 'a fine grandiose church' was regarded as an irresponsible ambition. The delays imposed by the diocese meant that, again, the project was overtaken by the Second Vatican Council, after which Scott's architecture seemed both extravagant and impractical.

By contrast, modern architects could offer the Church a reassuring image of simplicity and even of poverty, and therefore of the wise husbandry of resources. One of the most important and widely published modernist churches of the 1950s was said to have been built for a mere £14,000. Gillespie, Kidd & Coia's church of St Paul in the Scottish New Town of Glenrothes, completed in 1958, was admired by the architectural press because of its striking simplicity, though it used conventional materials, brick walls painted white and cheap timber.[57]

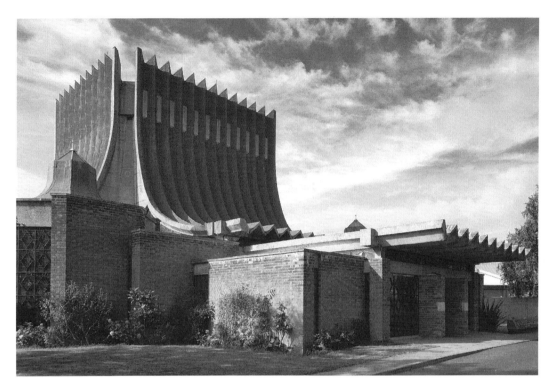

3.9 Our Lady Help of Christians, Tile Cross, Birmingham, by Richard Gilbert Scott, 1965–67. Photo: Robert Proctor, 2009

Though cheap, however, it was not small: it could seat a congregation of 350, about a third of the size of Our Lady of Victories, but at a tenth of the cost.[58] In the discourse of modern church architecture, St Paul's was an example of how good design could result from severe cost restrictions.

Yet the fact that cost was an important constraint in most cases of church-building was only the case because members of the Church – parish priests and their parishioners and often also bishops – wished in the first place to build so many churches and so often on a large scale. Parish priests pressed for permission to build and often had their way because church buildings were seen as a necessity. There was a cultural desire amongst Catholics for the 'grandiose church' that only waned by the end of the 1960s. Modernism could satisfy the clergy's desire, and the desire of the people, to build ambitiously and quickly. But perhaps more importantly, it could give churches the same serious and austere sobriety as the modern buildings of the cities which surrounded them. This, it seems, may be the underlying motive behind the Church's acceptance of modernism: an anxiety to show to the modern world a socially acceptable face, not only to show that the Church belonged in the modern world and was relevant to it, but also to show that the Roman Catholic Church deserved a place as an institution in the British establishment, on a par with other Churches and civic institutions. Economic responsibility was one aspect of this engagement, good taste was another, and both could be supplied by modern architects.

NOTES

1   For example, John Summerson, 'The Case for a Theory of Modern Architecture', *RIBA Journal* (June 1957), 307–10, cited in John R. Gold, *The Practice of Modernism: Modern Architects and Urban Transformation, 1954–1972* (London: Routledge, 2007), 265.

2   Throughout this book I use the terms 'modernism', 'modern movement' and 'modern architecture' fairly broadly to describe aspects of both principle and style, informed to some extent by (though partially also in disagreement with) Sarah Williams Goldhagen ('Something to Talk About: Modernism, Discourse, Style', *Journal of the Society of Architectural Historians*, 64 [2005], 144–67); my use of 'modernity' follows Hilde Heynen (*Architecture and Modernity: A Critique* [Cambridge, MA: MIT Press, 2009], 9–12).

3   On the modernist discourse in the architectural journals, see Andrew Higgott, *Mediating Modernism: Architectural Cultures in Britain* (London: Routledge, 2007).

4   Andrew Saint, *Towards a Social Architecture: The Role of School-Building in Post-War England* (London: Yale University Press, 1987).

5   Austin Winkley, interview with Robert Proctor, London (8 Dec. 2011); Desmond Williams, correspondence with Robert Proctor (7 Aug. 2008); Peter Langtry-Langton, interview with Robert Proctor, Bradford (17 July 2009).

6   'News', *Architects' Journal* (25 June 1969), 1732–40.

7   Robert W. K. C. Rogerson, *Jack Coia: His Life and Work* (Glasgow: n.p., 1986), 2, 12; Gavin Stamp, 'The Myth of Gillespie Kidd & Coia', *Architectural Heritage* 11 (2000), 68–79 (69).

8   Rogerson, *Jack Coia*, 18.

9   Proctor, 'Churches for a Changing Liturgy', 292, 302.

10   For example at Kilsyth ([Gordon Gray] [archbishop of St Andrews and Edinburgh] to Thomas McGarvey [parish priest, St Patrick, Kilsyth] [14 June 1956; 21 Jan. 1958] [Scottish Catholic Archives, Edinburgh (SCA), DE/59/317]).

11   For example, minutes of Sites and Buildings Commission, Archdiocese of Liverpool (24 May 1955; 20 Sept. 1955) (Liverpool Metropolitan Cathedral and Roman Catholic Archdiocesan Archives [LRCAA], Finance Collection, 12/S3/III); Patricia Brown and David Brown, interview with Ambrose Gillick, York (3 Apr. 2012).

12   Eric Mumford, *The CIAM Discourse on Urbanism, 1928–1960* (Cambridge, MA: MIT Press, 2000), 151–2; Bullock, *Building the Post-War World*, 49–50.

13   'Church and Presbytery at Glenrothes New Town', *Architects' Journal* (5 Feb. 1959), 231–8; A. M. Doak, 'Buildings in Prospect', *Architectural Prospect* (Summer 1959), 10–13.

14   James Stirling, 'Ronchamp: Le Corbusier's Chapel and the Crisis of Rationalism', *Architectural Review* (Mar. 1956), 155–61; Colin Rowe, 'Dominican Monastery of La Tourette, Eveux-sur-Arbresle, Lyons', *Architectural Review* (June 1961), 400–410.

15   *CBRN* (1961), 76–7; (1965), 86–7.

16   Little, *Catholic Churches*, 219.

17   Walter Glancy (secretary, Finance Committee, Archdiocese of St Andrews and Edinburgh) to Peter Whiston (24 Feb. 1959) (SCA, DE/71/15).

18   John Carmel Heenan to Albert Stafford (9 Dec. 1968) (WDA, He1/A7).

19   Brian Mooney, telephone interview with Robert Proctor (7 Dec. 2012).

20   Watters, *Cardross Seminary*, 25.

21   Isi Metzstein, interview with Robert Proctor, Glasgow (23 June 2003); Proctor, 'Churches for a Changing Liturgy', 300.

22   Celso Costantini, *Osservatore Romano* (30 July 1952), quoted in O'Connell, *Church Building*, 44, 34–5, 41.

23   William S. Rubin, *Modern Sacred Art and the Church of Assy* (New York: Columbia University Press, 1961); Lai-Kent Chew Orenduff, *The Transformation of Catholic Religious Art in the Twentieth Century: Father Marie-Alain Couturier and the Church at Assy, France* (Lewiston, NY: Edwin Mellen Press, 2008).

24   'Constitution on the Sacred Liturgy', in Walter M. Abbott (ed.), *The Documents of Vatican II* (New York: Geoffrey Chapman, 1966), 175.

25   'Constitution on the Sacred Liturgy', in Abbott, *The Documents of Vatican II*, 175.

26   George Andrew Beck, 'Value for Money', *CBRN* (1958), 196–7.

27   George Andrew Beck, 'Plans and Prices', *CBRN* (1959), 215–16.

28   George Andrew Beck, 'Design, Price and Value', *CBRN* (1960), 171–2; see also Walker, 'Developments in Catholic Churchbuilding', 187–93.

29   Beck, 'Design, Price and Value', 171.

30   *Architectural Competition for the Metropolitan Cathedral of Christ the King, Liverpool: Conditions and Instructions to Competing Architects* (Liverpool: Roman Catholic Archdiocese of Liverpool, 1959), 3; John C. Heenan, *A Crown of Thorns: An Autobiography, 1951–1963* (London: Hodder & Stoughton, 1974), 285, 289.

31   *CBRN* (1956), 98.

32   A. Hodsdon Archard (Archard & Partners), 'Report to Accompany Sketch Plans for Proposed Catholic Church, Carpender's Park, Oxhey' (28 Jan. 1958); Archard to Godfrey (28 Jan. 1958) (WDA, Go/2/132).

33   Godfrey to Archard (30 Jan. 1958) (WDA, Go/2/132).

34   [William Forbes-Semphill to Cardinal Bernard Griffin] (8 July 1954); 'Notes on the Rebuilding of OLV in Kensington' (n.d.); Anthony Sefi to [Derek] Warlock (Archdiocese of Westminster) (7 Dec. 1954) (WDA, Gr/1/36h).

35   [Adrian Gilbert Scott] to [Godfrey] Samuel (secretary, Royal Fine Art Commission) (14 Sept. 1954) (WDA, Gr/1/36h).

36   [Balcarres, Colinsburgh, Fife] to Griffin (21 Sept. 1954); 'Notes on Meeting with the Royal Fine Art Commission' (5 Aug. 1954) (WDA, Gr/1/36h).

37   Adrian Gilbert Scott to *The Tablet* (n.d.) (WDA, Gr/1/36h); edited version of Scott's letter (*The Tablet* [4 Dec. 1954], 558).

38   Goodhart-Rendel to Griffin (2 Dec. 1954); Scott to Griffin (6 Dec. 1954) (WDA, Gr/1/36h).

39   Nairn's article is mentioned in the debate (for example Erica O'Donnell, letter to the editor, *The Tablet* [20 Nov. 1954], 502).

40   Biographical details from Nicolas Barker, 'Obituary: Nicolete Gray', *The Independent* (13 June 1997), http://www.independent.co.uk/news/people/obituary-nicolete-gray-1255651.html (accessed 28 Oct. 2011).

41   Nicolete Gray, letter to the editor, *The Tablet* (6 Nov. 1954), 454.

42   Edward A. de Courcy-Cameron, letter to the editor, *The Tablet* (20 Nov. 1954), 502.

43   Simon Elwès, letter to the editor, *The Tablet* (27 Nov. 1954), 526.

44   Lance Wright, letter to the editor, *The Tablet* (27 Nov. 1954), 526.

45   *CBRS* (1958), 54–7. Our Lady of the Visitation was designed under Griffin but not begun until Godfrey arrived, when its details were personally overseen by him (David Stokes to Canon A. Rivers [finance secretary, Archdiocese of Westminster] [15 May 1956]; Griffin to Stokes [18 May 1956]; Rivers to Stokes [11 Aug. 1959] [WDA, Gr/2/132]).

46   [John] Bagshawe (parish priest, Our Lady of Victories) to [Derek] Warlock (Archdiocese of Westminster) (27 July 1955) (WDA, Gr/1/36h); 'Church and Presbytery of St. Mary and St. Joseph, Canton Street, Poplar', *Architect and Building News* (24 Dec. 1953), 774; 'Archbishop Opens New City Church of St Alexander', *Liverpool Daily Post* (29 July 1957), Liverpool History Projects, http://www.liverpoolhistoryprojects.co.uk/stalexander/news.htm (accessed 4 Nov. 2011).

47   Agenda for vicars general meeting with archbishop (24 May 1957) (WDA, Go/2/132).

48   For credit squeezes associated with changes to church-building programmes, see for example, Canon Rivers to Godfrey (31 May 1957) (WDA, Go/2/132); minutes of meeting of the Council of Administration, Archdiocese of Westminster (12 Oct. 1966) (WDA, He/1/C23(a)).

49   David [Cashman] (Parochial Development Commission, Archdiocese of Westminster) to Godfrey (22 May 1962); Godfrey to Cashman (24 May 1962) (WDA, Go/4/25).

50   Minutes of meeting of the Council of Administration, Archdiocese of Westminster (15 Apr. 1964; 7 Sept. 1964; 30 Sept. 1967); [Canon A. Rivers] (financial secretary) to G. M. Reeves (Durrant, Westmore & Reeves) (7 July 1964); Reeves to Rivers (30 June 1964) (WDA, He/1/C23(a)).

51   Campaign document (*c.*1967) (parish archive, St Aloysius, Somers Town, London).

52   Timothy J. Dinan to [Francis Grimshaw] (archbishop of Birmingham) (5 June 1963) (ARCAB, Parish File, P53/T4).

53   B. Gould (Birmingham diocesan treasurer) to Dinan (13 Oct. 1962) (ARCAB, Parish File, P53/T4).

54   Anonymous memo, 'Tile Cross. Visit 10/9/63' (ARCAB, Parish File, P53/T4).

55   Archbishop's secretary to F. G. Haddon (26 Sept. 1963) (ARCAB, Parish File, P53/T4).

56   Dinan to unnamed recipient (5 Feb. 1965) (ARCAB, Parish File, P53/T4).

57   For example Edward D. Mills and William E. A. Lockett, 'Plans of Churches Here and Abroad', *Church Buildings Today* 1 (Oct. 1960), 9–13.

58   'Church and Presbytery at Glenrothes New Town'.

4

Forms of Modernism

While some consensus had been reached amongst architects by the 1950s on the general principles of the modern movement in architecture, the way those principles were articulated through design remained open to a wide range of variation. In part this was because of changing tastes in architecture: the movement from a Scandinavian-inspired 'soft' modernism, called the 'New Empiricism' in the 1950s, to a 'hard' style amongst the younger generation more influenced by Le Corbusier from the 1950s to the 1960s has been widely documented, and there were further new trends. In the context of church architecture, each interpretation of modernism brought different qualities and meanings to the parish church.

MUNICIPAL MODERNISM

> *It has been said that some of our modern churches might be mistaken for*
> *factories or swimming-pools, and indeed not far from where I live there is a Fire*
> *Station with its adjacent tower which might easily be mistaken for a new church.*
> *The cynics tend to say that churches, schools, factories, swimming-pools and*
> *municipal buildings are all much of a muchness so far as a distinctive style is*
> *concerned.*[1]

So wrote Bishop Beck of Salford in 1960. He was right: many new churches of the 1950s and early 1960s were designed in the same brand of modernism as other civic buildings. Beck wanted a distinctive church style of modernism capable of signifying the sacred, but his thoughts were not shared by all modern architects or clergy. Many deliberately followed the style of the developing post-war city, integrating their churches into new urban and suburban landscapes. Their approach might best be called 'municipal modernism', and stylistically it followed the prevailing New Empiricism.

The New Empiricism maintained many of the principles of the International Style of modern architecture before the war, but, inspired by Swedish architecture of the 1940s particularly celebrated by the *Architectural Review*, architects now used a broader palette of materials, including brick, slate, mosaic and stone, often with simple decorative touches and artworks, sometimes reintroducing traditional elements such as pitched roofs. It became a characteristic style of the 1950s for all kinds of urban buildings, especially those associated with the welfare state – schools, hospitals, early new university buildings and, above all, social housing.[2] The pavilions of the 1951 Festival of Britain and its permanent buildings such as the Royal Festival Hall were especially influential: indeed the latter, designed by Leslie Martin and others at the municipal London County Council architects' office, was clad outside in stone and inside in wood, bringing this form of modernism to a building of national significance.[3]

The New Empiricism was often associated with socialism: its architects claimed to consider the psychological as well as functional needs of their buildings' occupants, and wished to work for public benefit through government rather than for commercial interests.[4] The Royal Festival Hall, and many other major public buildings of the late 1940s and 1950s, such as the Belgrade Theatre in socialist-run Coventry, exemplified an ideal of the modern city endowed by democratic government with communal and egalitarian institutions.[5] By the mid-1950s, the New Empiricism was becoming not only the style of the welfare state but also more generally that of the modern city. Even commercial buildings adopted its language of brick and stone, concrete window frames, slate hangings and chequered slot or lozenge patterns, enlivened by modern sculpture or murals.

This municipal modernism proved attractive to Roman Catholic architects and clergy. Because it balanced pre-war modernism with a recognition of conventional forms and materials, it could be seen as the 'middle way' between modernity and tradition that the Vatican apparently advocated. Moreover municipal modernism in church architecture was often accompanied by claims of new, egalitarian possibilities in worship for the faithful, adapting the rhetoric of the welfare state to the liturgical movement. The association between this architecture and the new communal spaces of the city could assist the Church's claim to be a contemporary and valid part of modern British society.

Beck's complaint about the secular appearance of recent modern churches was especially apt because he had presided over the building of so many in the new housing estates of his own diocese. One of the most prolific local Catholic architects was Geoffrey Williams of Greenhalgh & Williams, based in Bolton, who specialised in a New Empiricist approach to church design. His church of St Columba in Bolton, sited on a hill at the centre of a pre-war housing estate at Tonge Moor, and his adjacent Catholic school were the only public buildings in this small suburban neighbourhood. Completed in 1956, the church was a simple shed-like building with a broad pitched roof and attached tower, built of a similar red brick to the surrounding houses, patterned with blue bricks, concrete tiles and a variety of simple window designs (Figures 4.1, 4.2).[6] The building looked familiarly church-like, with its decorated gable wall and tower, but omitted any historical references in favour of a gentle use of modern motifs, square windows, projecting frames, patterned tiles and brickwork, all widely used elements in modern architecture in the 1950s. Inside, the modern structure of laminated timber portal frames was revealed, becoming a visual feature of the building. An elegant timber ciborium

covered the conventional marble altar, its thin tapering supports and gently undulating canopy suggesting an influence from certain pavilions of the Festival of Britain. At the west end of the church, a small narthex was formed with a curved wall of irregular rough-cut stone supporting a pine-clad choir loft reached by an elegant concrete staircase. This was a modest and unassuming church seating 500, but its architecture was handled with care, drawing intelligently on modern secular design. Williams's design may have been conventional in plan and massing, but its modest modernism suggested that this church's parish wanted to claim an institutional status in the modern nation. As Beck suggested, it could almost have been mistaken for a fire station; like a fire station, the church was altruistically offered to the city for the well-being of its citizens.

Several of Williams's churches related the social democratic ideal in post-war modernism to a liturgical understanding. Williams frequently declared his intention that everyone in the church should see the liturgy: at St Michael, Ancoats, a rebuilding of Manchester's Italian church in 1956, he explained that 'the people have an uninterrupted view of the High Altar' because he had eliminated columns that must have previously obscured the view for many in the original Victorian church.[7] Architects' descriptions throughout the 1950s frequently stressed this quality of the 'uninterrupted view'. Modern structural techniques such as steel trusses allowed wider naves and fewer columns, giving large churches unobstructed interiors. A good view was thought to enable participation in the liturgy by allowing the congregation to follow the actions of the priest at the altar, a concept that had become conventional in British Catholic church architecture in the nineteenth century,

4.1   St Columba, Bolton, by Greenhalgh & Williams, 1956. Photo: Robert Proctor, 2008

4.2   St Columba, Bolton, by Greenhalgh & Williams, 1956. Interior view towards sanctuary;
furnishings reordered since construction. Photo: Robert Proctor, 2008

though it originated in the Counter Reformation. Uninterrupted sightlines also suggested the equality of all those present, as they did in post-war theatre design, where the new civic theatres reduced audience divisions and emphasised the functional requirements of good sightlines and acoustics for all.[8]

At Greenhalgh & Williams's church of Our Lady of Lourdes at Farnworth, an elongated hexagonal plan was suggested by an awkward site, but Williams wrote that he had turned this to his advantage by placing the communion rail across the widest part, enabling the church 'to provide for the largest possible number of communicants'.[9] Frequent communion as an act of participation in the liturgy was a core principle of modern Catholic liturgical thought, promoted in the early twentieth century by Pope Pius X. Yet, if the architect's emphasis on the width of the communion rail suggested this ideal, the dimensions alone had no effect in achieving it; rather, the shape of the church was a symbolic image intended to accentuate this role of ordinary people in the liturgy. Though wide in plan, the church at Farnworth had no pillars thanks to its steel roof, giving clear views for the whole congregation; moreover, since the church became wider towards the front, more people would sit at the front than at the back (Figure 4.3). The interior approached a modern theatre or cinema in atmosphere, a similarity only strengthened by the 126 star-like downlights in the originally blue-painted ceiling.[10] The municipal modern style of the church gave it a civic presence, its simple brick campanile a focal point for several nearby housing estates (Figure 4.4). Inside, its patterned glazing in primary colours and modern pews made a contemporary contrast to the conventional form of the altar. Williams's church architecture associated contemporary taste in design with the ambition of modern designers to cultivate an egalitarian society. The church building, and thus the Roman Catholic Church, positioned itself as the means by which this aim could be achieved in the world.

Greenhalgh & Williams built widely in the Salford diocese in the late 1950s and, besides churches, also built many schools for the diocese, which, though Catholic, were partly funded by the state. Schools were modern in style by necessity, since government guidelines applied strict cost limits and daylight requirements that could only be met through modern techniques: at their junior school of St John Bosco at Blackley, for example, the architects used a standard metal glazing and cladding for rows of classrooms, softening their utilitarian appearance with end walls of stone and brick, and later building a new church to complement the school.[11] The firm was also engaged for housing by the local authority. Though a private practice, therefore, Greenhalgh & Williams's work for the Church was continuous with the developing civic infrastructure of the welfare state that was an important part of the work of most architecture practices in the 1950s.

The approach continued into the 1960s: Harrison & Cox's church of St Patrick in Walsall was opened in 1964, but resembled a 1950s theatre or assembly hall. Its exterior suggested the volumes of a fan-shaped auditorium and raised reception room overlooking the urban scene, and decorative touches in its concrete glazing and brickwork implied a civic status (Figure 4.5). Its exterior did not align with the interior, however: the nave was a single space, and the dominant facade window indicated merely the rear of the choir gallery (Figure 4.6).

4.3   Our Lady of Lourdes, Farnworth, Bolton, by Greenhalgh & Williams, 1957. Photo: Ambrose Gillick, 2012

4.4   Our Lady of Lourdes, Farnworth, Bolton, by Greenhalgh & Williams, 1957. Photo: Robert Proctor, 2008

The external design followed the typology of the theatre to make a statement of responsible civic modernity to its urban audience at the expense of a logical connection to internal functions. Yet its interior did sustain the political implications of the building's external modernism. To promote congregational participation in the liturgy, the largest proportion of seating was close to the altar at the wide end of the fan-shaped plan, and the pews were arranged in curves to focus attention on the sanctuary.[12]

Like much post-war municipal architecture, there was often an emphasis on external artworks in municipal modern churches. For the socially concerned state, this was a way of introducing something of the colour and artistic modernity of the Festival of Britain into the everyday lives of citizens and was often used to reinforce a city's identity through displays of regalia and local history. For the Church, the use of public artworks could demonstrate a civic mentality through similar munificence, helping to anchor the parish in its local context. This intention was present at St Thomas of Canterbury in Rainham, Kent, built by Eduardo Dodds of London (Figure 4.7). In response to the growing number of Catholics in the town, a site was acquired in 1921 in a highly significant location alongside the ancient Roman road and medieval pilgrimage route connecting London to Canterbury.[13] The church was designed in a typical municipal modern idiom: a long brick basilica, vertical concrete windows with a rhythmic pattern, a modern tower dominating the street. Over the entrance a colourful ceramic mural by Catholic artist Adam Kossowski depicted scenes from the life of St Thomas alongside the emblem of Pius XII.

4.5   St Patrick, Walsall, by Harrison & Cox, 1964. Photo: Robert Proctor, 2009

4.6   St Patrick, Walsall, by
Harrison & Cox, 1964. View from
sanctuary towards main entrance.
Photo: Robert Proctor, 2009

While anchoring the church in its local context of the cult of St Thomas in a way
that evoked the typology of civic architecture, this panel stressed its connection
to the Vatican, while celebrating a saint who had asserted the superiority of the
Church over the state. Kossowski had been working since 1950 on artworks for
the nearby Roman Catholic Carmelite priory at Aylesford, also associated with the
Canterbury pilgrimage, so his commission at Rainham cemented this parish's local
allegiance to an emerging Catholic culture in Kent. Kossowski, who also made
ceramic works inside the church, was later commissioned for an external secular
ceramic frieze at the North Peckham Civic Centre, a work he carried out in the same
modern figurative style.[14] The frieze at Rainham had a religious message to convey
about the universal Church in its local context, and it communicated it through a
form of civic art.

4.7   St Thomas of Canterbury, Rainham, Kent, by E. G. Dodds and K. C. White, 1959. Exterior with
ceramic panel of St Thomas of Canterbury by Adam Kossowski. Photo: Robert Proctor, 2010

While Beck complained that Catholic church architecture in the 1950s was too similar to modern secular institutions, his opinion was not shared by all modern architects. As modernism became the accepted architecture of the democratic state in the modern British city, many Catholic architects and clergy co-opted a municipal modern architecture for churches to claim a place for the Church in contemporary society. If the church building appeared to share some of the altruistic values of the beneficent state, it did so in order to claim those values as its own right. Yet Beck's desire for an architecture in elevation that expressed the transcendent qualities of the Church was soon to be embraced by modern architects.

STRUCTURAL EXPRESSION

While municipal modernism emphasised its allegiance to secular architecture, modern architects were also fascinated with the expressive and spatial potentials of new building technologies. New structural techniques had more progressive symbolic and spatial implications. Structural expression in modern architecture could be used to explore new ways in which the Church understood itself, its place in the world and its realisation in space.

In the 1950s, a canon of modern architecture was becoming established in which the development of new building forms from new materials was an important feature, promoted by Reyner Banham and Peter Collins amongst others.[15] The idea that new building technologies should be frankly expressed rather than concealed under historicist cladding or ornament was an important principle of modernism in architecture. One building that was prominent in histories of modernism was Auguste Perret's Catholic church of Notre Dame du Raincy of 1922. In the 1950s, it was well known as a pioneering building in the use of reinforced concrete: the slim columns which lined the nave were gently tapered towards the top, their straight sides determined by the timber formwork that left the imprint of its grain on the concrete; concrete vaults spanned the aisles and nave; the walls were made with pierced concrete blocks filled with coloured glass. It was a modern but economical interpretation of a medieval church, with its emphasis on the slenderness of the supports, the structural daring of its covering and the light-filled colour of its walls. Le Raincy inspired many less well-known successors in church architecture in France and elsewhere, and in Britain in the 1950s became one model for church architects interested in the possibilities of reinforced concrete, most importantly at Basil Spence's Anglican Cathedral at Coventry, designed with engineer Ove Arup.

Of British Roman Catholic examples of such an approach, perhaps the most impressive was St Charles Borromeo in Glasgow by Gillespie, Kidd & Coia, designed by Jack Coia in 1956 and completed by MacMillan and Metzstein (Figure 4.8). St Charles was less overtly Gothic than the modern Gothic churches of Reynolds & Scott, with a more striking modernity of structure thanks to its *in situ* reinforced concrete frame, in which 'the fine detailing of the concrete and the deliberate exploitation of the shuttering board marks', as the architects wrote, made an aesthetic virtue of the material's qualities.[16] Yet the diagonally folded planes of the concrete vaults were clearly a visual reference to medieval vaulting, much like

Spence's coffered ceiling at Coventry. The concrete at St Charles was influenced by Italian engineer Pier Luigi Nervi, awarded the RIBA Gold Medal in the year St Charles was opened, and perhaps especially by Marcel Breuer's Abbey Church of St John at Collegeville, Minnesota, where Nervi was consulted and which was then nearing completion. Breuer explicitly linked his modern folded vaulting to ecclesiastical traditions:

> *Although the church may be a new sensation to the eye, its architectural concepts resemble in some ways those of religious buildings in the Middle Ages and the Classic period. … Church architecture at its best is always identical with the structural logic of the enclosure. … The means of construction by which the large space is framed and roofed-over must be clearly shown as the dominant visual fact of both the interior and exterior and must grow out of contemporary building technology.*[17]

4.8   St Charles Borromeo, Kelvinside, Glasgow, by Gillespie, Kidd & Coia, 1956–60. Photographer unknown , c.1960. Source: Glasgow School of Art

This structurally expressive mode of modernism gave the church interior a powerful visual effect as a statement of advanced contemporary engineering, while retaining aspects of the traditional image.

Yet the use of new structural techniques had great potential for innovation in spatial forms, allowing the plans of churches to be reconsidered, a possibility that became especially relevant in relation to the new thinking on the liturgy. As early as 1955, David Stokes had designed the church of Our Lady of the Visitation at Greenford with similar ideas. Its exterior was municipal in style, resembling a theatre or swimming pool: a curved roof emerged from a brick box next to a square tower that lacked even a cross. Inside, parabolic ribs of reinforced concrete were derived from an important pre-war civic building, Easton & Robertson's Royal Horticultural Hall in Kensington, also a model for several 1930s swimming baths in London and often used for churches in that decade. At Greenford, however, this exciting structure was explicitly intended to eliminate aisles and columns and to allow a broad rather than long nave to bring the congregation close to the altar (Figure 4.9).[18]

Another firm of architects interested in both the expressive and liturgical potential of new structural forms was Lionel Prichard & Son of Liverpool, especially with the arrival of younger staff including Francis Prichard and Ben Naylor.[19] Their church of St Agnes at Huyton marked a novel departure from the modern Gothic approach. Its design was published in 1959, half a hexagon in plan, its sanctuary against the longest wall, while in elevation a reinforced concrete structure, not yet well defined, gave a pointed, bird-like profile.[20] Built from 1963 to 1965, it employed a technique that was still novel in Britain: thin-shelled reinforced concrete on a hyperbolic paraboloid geometry.[21] The roof billowed over the interior in three curved canopies, descending to buttressed piers in the corners, and its sides were fully glazed, heightening the effect of lightness (Figure 4.10, Plan 3c). The flowing roofline, pointed gables and angled spire manipulated the structure for expressive effect (Figure 4.11). It was a bold statement of the potential of this recent technique to transform the appearance and plan of church buildings.

The hyperbolic paraboloid thin-shelled reinforced concrete structure was already becoming popular for churches elsewhere, particularly in America: the technique had been pioneered by Felix Candela in Mexico, who employed it for numerous churches, sometimes to accommodate new types of plan. It was economical with materials, allowed large spans and was simple to build, since all the formwork could be made with straight planks. In 1951, Alison Smithson and Peter Smithson had proposed an inverted hyperbolic paraboloid roof in their entry for the Coventry Cathedral competition, on a square plan whose walls would have been made of glass, and interest in this design resurfaced later, when it was published in *Churchbuilding* in 1963, just as the structure at Huyton was being finalised.[22] In parallel with the advantage of this type of structure in generating new plan types was its unconventional curved form that could lend churches an unmistakeable prominence: as a special, one-off kind of modern architecture, it was perhaps considered to be especially suited to the expression of the sacred. Nevertheless shell concrete was a technique also used for significant civic buildings, including Eliel Saarinen's Kresge Auditorium in Cambridge, Massachusetts, of 1954 and Robert Matthew, Johnson-Marshall & Partners' Commonwealth Institute in London, completed in 1962.[23]

This combination of liturgical innovation and expression of a special character was also the reason for the use of hyperbolic paraboloids in other Roman Catholic churches. At St Mary, Denton in Manchester, designed in 1961 and opened in 1963, the plan was a square, the altar in one corner and the seating arranged on the diagonal. The architects, Walter Stirrup & Son, explained that the hyperbolic paraboloid form made the roof sweep upwards at the corners, giving expressive definition to the sanctuary, 'reminiscent in feeling of soaring Mediaeval structures'.[24] Its exterior, with upturned corners like angels' wings,

4.9   Our Lady of the Visitation, Greenford, London, by David Stokes & Partners, 1956–60. View towards
entrance before completion. Photo: Colin Westwood, *c.*1960. Source: RIBA Library Photographs Collection

4.10   St Agnes, Huyton, Liverpool, by Lionel A. G. Prichard & Son, 1959–65.
Interior view towards choir gallery. Photo: Ambrose Gillick, 2011

4.11   St Agnes, Huyton, Liverpool, by Lionel A. G. Prichard & Son, 1959–65. Photo: Robert Proctor, 2008

made a dramatic gesture of religious purpose in the surrounding grid of Victorian terraced houses (Figure 4.12). This extraordinary form of structure was therefore one way of showing the Church's engagement with the modern world at the same time as emphasising its desire to set itself apart as a communal and religious space, while indulging the modern architect's interest in novel structural techniques. The hyperbolic paraboloid form, often delicate and tent-like in appearance, also had a theological motivation, expressing an idea of the Church as a 'pilgrim people' – a concept that became especially important after the Second Vatican Council and will be considered later.

4.12   St Mary, Denton, Manchester, by Walter Stirrup & Son, 1961–63. Photo: Robert Proctor, 2008

Besides reinforced concrete, other materials were also subject to innovation and used in churches. Laminated timber was cheap and strong and could be used in similar ways to precast concrete portal frames, being prefabricated in standard components for that purpose. Greenhalgh & Williams claimed that their church of St Columba in Bolton was the first such use of this material in north-west England and proudly exposed its portal frames inside.[25] Gillespie, Kidd & Coia's church of St Benedict, Drumchapel, made more dramatic use of curved laminated timber beams to create a soaring roof over a centralised sanctuary. Steel was also frequently explored. While it had frequently been used for roof structures and concealed under imitation vaulting – in many of Reynolds & Scott's churches, for example – modernist architects gave it an architectural language of its own. In the 1960s, the popularisation of the space frame, a triangulated grid structure, gave architects the potential for an expressive, vault-like play of structural elements over interiors, though it was used only on a few occasions, including at St John Stone, Woodvale by Richard O'Mahony and Gillespie, Kidd & Coia's St Margaret, Clydebank, both of the 1970s. In both cases the space frame had a liturgical rationale, suggesting the homogeneity of the interior space and thus the unity of congregation and liturgy. Elsewhere steel was exposed in combination with other materials – steel columns were combined with sheer brick and timber at Liam McCormick's church of the Holy Family in Southampton (Figure 4.13), and with brick and glass, in a frame construction inspired by Mies van der Rohe at the church of the Holy Ghost, St Leonards-on-Sea, by B. Stevens & Partners.[26]

These churches and many others suggest that even when the articulation of new structural forms appeared to be a primary concern of the modern architect, this preoccupation would often have a spatial rationale as well. New structures enabled new forms of plan that transformed the church building to meet new liturgical and symbolic requirements, while being equally concerned with the building's relationship to its urban context. For parishioners and clergy, meanwhile, modern architects' adoption of technical innovations satisfied a need to participate in the transformations taking place in the modern world. Parish photograph albums recorded construction processes: at Huyton, the parish priest was photographed standing on the hyperbolic paraboloid roof, amazed and delighted at his building's technical achievements.[27] Of the church of the Immaculate Conception in Maryhill, Glasgow, designed by Cordiner with a reinforced concrete A-frame, the parish priest wrote: 'The design of our new church, both inside and out, has not been copied from the past. It might be called revolutionary. It is a bold attempt to employ the new materials and the new techniques of the present times, the second half of the twentieth century.'[28] In his sermon at the opening of St Columba, Bolton, Bishop Beck thanked the architect: 'he said it was a lovely contemporary church, an expression of life, a church of modern design, showing all that was best in modern architecture. It was far removed from Gothic architecture and was indeed a church of the twentieth century.'[29] Architects and clergy collaborated in this enterprise, and adopting and expressing new technologies was seen as one way of achieving this vision of the twentieth-century Church.

BRUTALISM: MODERNISM AND THE SACRED

Many of the younger generation of architects, meanwhile, rejected a primarily technological approach to architectural design, becoming interested in the expressive possibilities of conventional and heavy materials such as brick and plain timber and using reinforced concrete not for its possibilities of lightweight span but for its mass and surface effect. Several influences combined in this new approach to materials. Most importantly, Le Corbusier's work of the 1950s showed a marked departure from his pre-war International Style buildings. Ronchamp and La Tourette were both commissioned through Couturier, editor of *L'Art sacré*, and were dramatically published in special issues of the journal especially aimed at

4.13   Holy Family, Southampton, by Liam McCormick, 1966. Photo: Robert Proctor, 2010

church architects and clergy.[30] These buildings showed Le Corbusier's new interest in an architecture of mass, weight, surface texture, sculptural form and dramatic effects of light.[31] Despite a suspicion that Le Corbusier was indulging in 'sheer plastic virtuosity', James Stirling and partner James Gowan soon popularised the use of exposed untreated brick, concrete and timber at their Ham Common flats, designed with 'rich complexities of rough and smooth' and a 'variety of internal lighting effects', influenced also by Le Corbusier's brick and concrete Maisons Jaoul.[32] Alison and Peter Smithson likewise promoted an architecture of mundane materials: their Soho House project, intended to be crudely made in unplastered brick, became a manifesto statement for young architects when published in *Architectural Design* in 1953.[33] American architect Louis Kahn was also influential, having come to prominence by the late 1950s.[34] Early illustrations of his First Unitarian Church in Rochester, New York, showed sheer brick walls articulated with deep buttresses and towers and a single broad rectangle for a nave.[35]

Post-war monumental Brutalism had several strands. The 'New Brutalism' was defined in the mid-1950s by Banham as a riposte to the New Empiricism, beginning with reference to the Soho House.[36] At first this movement was associated with the avant-garde Independent Group of artists and architects, including Banham, the Smithsons and Eduardo Paolozzi, centred on the Institute of Contemporary Arts in London and going much further than an approach to materials: its artists aimed to celebrate ordinary aspects of modern life and to explore the accidental effects of materials and processes. The Smithsons also led Team 10, an international group of young architects that succeeded and displaced the core organisation of modern movement architects, the Congrès Internationaux d'Architecture Moderne. Team 10 argued for an urbanism that rejected technical and social rationalism in favour of greater attention to local contexts, including existing urban forms and social habits. The term 'brutalism', however, was soon applied more loosely to the monumental brick and Corbusian concrete architecture of this period, a new style of modern architecture that retained modernism's broad principles without always adhering to the Smithsons' theories.[37]

The earliest and most enthusiastic adherents of brutalism amongst Roman Catholic church architects were MacMillan and Metzstein of Gillespie, Kidd & Coia. In 1957, when Coia was away on holiday, they made their first designs for the church of St Bride's at East Kilbride. Their balsa-wood model indicated a large, box-like windowless church, with surface texture in the form of striations and a detached tower.[38] Delays in construction led to an opening date in 1964, by which time brutalism was becoming a more mainstream movement amongst architects, and the church was accordingly well received in the architectural press.[39] Its massive walls were made with loadbearing brick. Inside, one wall contained deep top-lit shafts within its depth; the pulpit was a curved brick platform supported on a concrete cantilever that required the priest to pass through the wall (Figure 4.14). The church's entrance was a full-height slot containing a heavy timber door, leading to the underside of a concrete gallery on one side of the nave (Plan 2a). Corbusian roof cowls directed light onto the altar, a detail added late in the design following the publication of La Tourette. Factory glazing roofed the nave, its light filtered by a ceiling of timber slats. The building raised the ordinary materials of brick and timber to the level of the sublime. The architects' statements reinforced this attention to material qualities: 'inside and outside the deep brick walls are pierced, recessed and modelled to provide an expressive enclosing surface', they wrote, adding that the furnishings were 'simply conceived in timber of a rugged quality'.[40] The brickwork was laid in a random bond: the builders were asked to lay the bricks as they came, giving a deliberately coarse appearance to the walls. This unusual feature shows the architects' interest in certain artistic themes of the New Brutalism, the desire to emphasise the processes of production and the love of the 'as found' object or situation, the aestheticisation of the ordinary and awkward. They conceived of modern architecture as a form of avant-garde art, making a radical break with both tradition and the popular modernism of the New Empiricism.

There are indications that St Bride's was controversial amongst Catholics in the diocese of Motherwell. When a new parish priest, James Kilpatrick, took up his post, he wrote to Coia to complain about his assistants' designs:

> I learnt for the first time today, with considerable horror, that it was intended to construct the footpace and steps of the High Altar in brick. I had thought that the extreme of ghastliness had been reached in the monstrous concrete gallery, but I find the idea of a mass of brick in the middle of the Sanctuary even more repelling.[41]

The materials were evidently too ordinary for some to consider suitable for sacred ends, used as they were to sanctuaries covered in marble. In the souvenir booklet accompanying the opening, diocesan administrator John Hughes wrote: 'The fact that it is not in any way a traditional building may disappoint many; but it has architectural distinction – of that there can be no doubt, and it makes a very strong impact on all who enter and worship in it.'[42]

Its 'distinction' was to be a building that associated itself with an elite artistic taste that challenged conventional assumptions of beauty. It showed not only the youth of its architects but also the high-brow aspirations of the clergy who commissioned it, and who felt obliged to defend the design. In his sermon at the opening Mass, Archbishop Gordon Gray of St Andrews and Edinburgh tried to convince the congregation that there were timeless and traditional qualities in the church's architecture. Acknowledging that the modern architect 'may shock traditional taste' with a 'modern, striking concept of a House of God', he interpreted the church as a 'great massive building whose fortress-like strength seems to symbolise the Church built upon a rock, impregnable against the assaults of her enemies'. It was 'simple in lines, beautiful in its proportions' and a 'monumental building'.[43] Several churches in Gray's diocese were also built by Gillespie, Kidd & Coia: St Patrick, Kilsyth, was designed in 1962 to replace a burned-down Victorian building.[44] 'You have seen the official opening of a splendid church', wrote Gray to its parish, 'which will stand as a monument to the faith and generosity of the Catholics of Kilsyth, and as an example of the finest modern ecclesiastical architecture in Britain'.[45] MacMillan and Metzstein's version of brutalism therefore satisfied the conflicting needs of the local Roman Catholic hierarchy to commission an elite form of modern design while also maintaining an ultimately conventional view of the church building.

4.14   St Bride, East Kilbride, by Gillespie, Kidd & Coia, 1957–64. Interior viewed from side gallery, c.1964.
Photo: Sam Lambert. Source: Architectural Press Archive / RIBA Library Photographs Collection

4.15   St Patrick, Rochdale, by Desmond Williams, 1964–69. Perspective drawing of early design, c.1964: the design was subsequently much reduced and simplified, and a circular drum added over the centre. Courtesy of Desmond Williams. Source: parish archive

With its monumental tendency, brutalism could be seen as the answer to Beck's desire for a church architecture that was 'dignified and impressive' and expressive of the sacred purpose of the building. Desmond Williams of Manchester designed the church of St Patrick in Rochdale in 1964 with sheer red brick walls articulated as buttresses alternating with slot windows, clearly influenced by Stirling and Gowan and Louis Kahn (Figure 4.15).[46] In north-west England, particularly around Manchester, brick had long been the local building material and vast brick Victorian factories and warehouses were a familiar sight. Such factories were celebrated by J. M. Richards and photographer Eric de Maré in the *Architectural Review* in the mid-1950s for their sublime aesthetic and for a presumed absence of self-conscious design, their supposedly unmediated response to functional demands a template for modern architecture. This invention of a 'functional tradition' was a formative influence on many architects who designed in a brutalist style.[47] Williams's church at Rochdale, however, also evoked the tradition of Catholic church architecture in the region: its circular drum formed a distinctive feature over the nave, a clerestory around its edge lighting the broad interior and suggesting the Byzantine style, like a brutalist reinterpretation of Norris's nearby pre-war church of St John the Baptist (Figure 4.16). Williams's use of exposed brickwork continued the Byzantine revival's fascination with this material in Catholic churches, and also derived from his enduring memories of childhood visits to Quarr Abbey on the Isle of Wight, a Gothic-inspired brick building of 1912 by Paul Bellot.[48] St Patrick in Rochdale may have positioned itself in the mainstream of modern architecture of the 1960s, but it also suggested associations with local and Roman Catholic traditions.

4.16   St Patrick, Rochdale, by Desmond Williams, 1964–69. Photo: Robert Proctor, 2013

Williams's church of St Augustine in Manchester was designed in a similar vein but without any such hints of tradition: the church was a brick box, square in plan, with slot windows in *dalle de verre* and rising clerestories bathing the interior in yellow light (Plate 4). The role of art in this church illustrates another aspect of brutalism that could make it palatable to the Church. Sculptor Robert Brumby was commissioned for a scheme of artworks to complete the interior, including a reredos of Christ in Glory in ceramics and *ciment fondu*. This work was conceived as an extension of the architecture: Williams considered the piece early in the design process, wanting it to be 'as one' with the brick, and Brumby obtained samples of the bricks to give his stoneware a similar earthy hue.[49] The reredos combined two different styles of art: the figure recalled Jacob Epstein's modern figurative sculpture, suitable because of the textural properties and method of assembling of component pieces of the ceramic; meanwhile, the background was made of cement panels and swathes of ceramic pieces in swirling circular patterns. This was an unusual and experimental technique. Its effect was similar to the many large-scale abstract murals that were then being commissioned as public art for building exteriors, architecturally integrated into schools, housing and university buildings, sometimes in ceramic and also often in sculptural concrete.[50] The liturgical elements at St Augustine's, the tabernacle, sanctuary lamp and casket of holy oils, were embedded in the reredos, treated as collaged objects in a sculptural composition. The effects of randomness and collage and the interest in material experimentation in Brumby's mural were allied to the Independent Group's fascination with process and material, and, like that group's members, Williams and Brumby viewed their work as a total collaboration. Nevertheless the reredos retained some more conventional notions of ecclesiastical art, especially the dominating figure, almost Byzantine in character, and the desire for an altar backdrop.

In contrast, Gillespie, Kidd & Coia's version of brutalism dispensed almost entirely with artworks: at St Bride's, a few niches allowed the parish to place its own statues in the sculptural nave wall, so that the inevitably kitsch images that would enter the church would be framed in the manner of 'as-found' objects. This arrangement recalls Le Corbusier's framing of the painted wooden statue of the Virgin Mary in the sanctuary wall at Ronchamp. Like the Smithsons and Team 10, Metzstein and MacMillan accepted the everyday practices of the building's users. Yet in framing such objects the architecture bracketed them outside itself, to be viewed as primitive ritualistic elements, much as *L'Art sacré* celebrated the apparently primitive human urge to create figurative icons with its photographs of religious folk art.[51] Meanwhile the architecture of St Bride's restricted the possible places for statues, limiting their use in line with the Church's increasing emphasis on the liturgy. Metzstein and MacMillan's approach was brutalist in more than simply style.

The brutalist ideas of accepting the ordinary and responding to local context could have an ethical dimension, suggested by Richard O'Mahony's church of St Patrick at Clinkham Wood, St Helens, first designed around 1962.[52] O'Mahony had visited Sweden, including Sigurd Lewerentz's modernist churches, and St Patrick's also shows the influence of English architects, notably Stirling and Gowan and Colin St John Wilson, with plain, exposed brickwork alongside concrete columns and pine boarding (Figure 4.17).[53] The floor was laid with quarry tiles,

4.17   St Patrick,
St Helens, by F. X.
Velarde Partnership,
1962–65. Photo:
Elsam, Mann &
Cooper, c.1965.
Source: RIBA Library
Photographs
Collection

a utilitarian, domestic material much liked by brutalist architects; in the baptistery the quarry tiles turned to black, rising from the floor to clad the rectangular font, which became an integral architectural feature rather than a piece of furnishing (Figure 4.18). The lid of the font and an overhanging canopy were made of copper, a standard building material treated here like industrial equipment rather than the more ornamental approach that was conventionally used for such sacred items. O'Mahony's church gave expression to an idea of the sacred through space and light, achieved with the simplest and cheapest of materials. The location of the church might have suggested such an approach: Clinkham Wood was a new local authority housing estate at the edge of this industrial town, and many in its congregation were factory workers in the local glass industry.[54]

Common materials had recently been promoted elsewhere as an appropriate form of modernism for churches in industrial, working-class areas and as an architecture that would express the sacred in the visual language of the people. The Anglican church of St Paul, Bow Common, by Robert Maguire, a Roman Catholic architect, and Keith Murray was especially influential (Figure 4.19). Writing about the building for *Churchbuilding*, Maguire emphasised the 'industrial' and ordinary materials and their local relevance: the walls were of exposed brick; the internal floors used common concrete paving slabs; steel was used for the ciborium over

4.18   St Patrick, St Helens, by F. X. Velarde Partnership, 1962–65. Baptistery. Photo: Robert Proctor, 2008

the altar and for an external frame supporting the bell; the font cover, made of slate, was raised with a mechanism made by 'a local dockside firm'. The design, they argued, was centred on 'the *actual* life of the real local Christian community', an attempt to give the architecture 'particularity'.[55] This argument about materials related to the principles of the New Brutalism: the Smithsons and other members of Team 10 argued that architecture and urbanism had to relate to and express the needs and existing identities of local communities, eschewing the totalising rationalism of earlier modernism. At St Helens, O'Mahony endorsed this new thinking: its stylistic similarities were also similarities of principle.

4.19   St Paul, Bow
Common, by Robert
Maguire and Keith
Murray, 1958–60.
Photo: Reginald
Hugo de Burgh
Galwey. Source:
Architectural Press
Archive / RIBA
Library Photographs
Collection

German church architect Rudolf Schwarz, much admired by Maguire and
O'Mahony, had already argued that church architecture in the modern world
should embrace increasing limitations of cost and accept a modern impossibility of
material richness. In *The Church Incarnate*, translated into English in 1958, he set out
a modern approach to church architecture where the building's 'sacred function'
would be analysed and accommodated in the techniques of the present time. 'For
the master builder', he thought, 'what proves true is true, real what realizes. In his
bare workshop the things are worth only as much as they can perform. When he
perseveres in the genuine he does what God wants of him, even if this genuine
thing be poor.' Schwarz echoed Maritain's notion of the artist pursuing technique
with an attitude of faith, but for Schwarz modernity was irreparably separated from
the past, and even past ideas of the sacred might no longer be available. 'This, then
is our task', he urged, 'to build churches out of that reality which we experience and
verify every day; to take this our own reality so seriously and to recognize it to be
so holy that it may be able to enter in before God.'[56]

In the issue of *Churchbuilding* in which Maguire discussed Bow Common, a
translation of an article appeared from *L'Art sacré* by one of its editors, Dominican
Marie-Robert Capellades, who argued that poverty should be welcomed in church
architecture partly for pragmatic reasons but also as an ethical stance. Capellades
echoed and reinterpreted St Bernard of Clairvaux's famous objection to material
richness in the church, espousing the virtues of asceticism:

The Christian Temple is the House of God but it is also the house of men.
Should it not be a welcoming sort of house to us pilgrims? Shouldn't the poor
also feel at home in this dwelling? And shouldn't it in return speak to us of the
blessedness of the poor?[57]

Brutalism in church architecture was not merely a design trend, therefore, but could have important religious and social justifications. O'Mahony's church of Our Lady of the Rosary at Donnington perhaps expressed this most clearly: it was closely modelled on Schwarz's church of St Christophorus at Cologne-Niehl (Figure 6.1), both small, simple and plain, brick and concrete cubic buildings, the concrete frame defining the location of the sanctuary.[58] With a modest budget, O'Mahony accepted that 'simplicity, dignity and even austerity will play their part' in a church that visually emphasised these qualities (Figure 4.20).[59]

While the expressive economy of brutalism could have theological justifications, as brutalism became an increasingly mainstream form of modernism in the 1960s it also began to take on the same municipal associations as the New Empiricism in the previous decade. Like the New Empiricism, it became fashionable for public works such as civic centres, libraries and universities. Le Corbusier's government buildings for Chandigarh showed the possibilities for a modern monumental and institutional use of sculptural concrete; Paul Rudolph in America popularised brutalism as a distinctive style more associated with exposed and textured concrete than with brick in government and university buildings. In several cases of churches designed in this mode there were obvious references to a municipal brutalism. Sts Peter and Paul, Lichfield, for example, designed by Timothy Armstrong and completed in 1967, had brick planes and slot windows, concrete vaults forming a distinctive motif echoing Basil Spence's monumental Falmer House for the University of Sussex.[60] The church had a weighty presence in its context: facing a road junction in a leafy suburban estate, a neighbourhood centre nearby, its scale dominated its surroundings, and the absence of religious symbols (neither cross nor tower) gave it the appearance of a civic building (Figure 4.21).

In Dumbarton, meanwhile, the church of St Peter was designed in a brick brutalist style with timber beams, copious board-marked concrete and quarry tiles (Figure 4.22).[61] The architects Garner, Preston & Strebel admitted that the congregation expressed 'alarm' at their design, only warming to it when they found the church conducive to worship.[62] In 1960, the architects had won a competition for the redevelopment of the central area of Dumbarton and built a shopping centre, council offices and even a Masonic temple.[63] They designed the Catholic church in the new style of civic architecture that they were bringing to the town in contrast to the church's surrounding municipal houses and tower blocks. In commissioning these architects the Roman Catholic parish sought to integrate itself into the town's emerging expression of civic identity.

Brutalism, whether in Corbusian concrete or following more nuanced influences from Schwarz to Kahn and stretching over two decades, therefore, had a variety of motivations: a modern asceticism, contextual relevance, civic aspiration, avant-garde artistic taste and, throughout, a reassuringly traditional sense of permanence and monumentality. Yet brutalism was much more than a style.

4.20   Our Lady of the Rosary, Donnington, by Richard O'Mahony & Partners, 1965–67. Photo:
Elsam, Mann & Cooper, c.1967. Source: archive of OMF Derek Cox Architects, Liverpool

4.21   Sts Peter and Paul, Lichfield, by Gwilliam & Armstrong, 1967. Photo: Ambrose Gillick, 2012

4.22 St Peter, Dumbarton, by Garner, Preston & Strebel, 1971. Photo: Robert Proctor, 2010

Many of its architects thought that the New Empiricism had abandoned the rigorous functionalism of pre-war modernism and wanted to restore the pre-eminence of functional analysis to the modern movement. In the case of church architecture, this would lead to a radical approach to the ways in which architecture could accommodate liturgy.

RATIONAL SYSTEMS: MODERNISM AND BUILDING

One further strand of modern architecture would have a very different effect on church architecture: the development of rationalised and industrialised approaches to building. In accepting industrialisation as an aspect of modernity, many modern architects were keen to explore its implications for building construction and design; yet, it was a route that threatened to undermine and even eliminate the position of the architect. For many clergy in the 1960s, the concept of the institutional Church as a bastion of sacred values was fading in favour of a less monumental idea, of a more responsive and flexible Church for congregations in perpetual movement – an approach that made industrialised systems seem attractive. In that later period's worsening economic climate, the promises of cheapness and efficiency offered by building systems would make the theology of the small, cheap church both appealing and pragmatic.

This approach in British modernism originated in the development of new building techniques for schools in the 1940s and 1950s.[64] For a welfare state that proposed universal education for burgeoning populations of children, architects at the Ministry of Education invented new methods for the design and construction of schools for economy in space and materials. These methods included the use of prefabricated building systems, increasingly methodically employed from the 1940s and eventually becoming the norm. The most important such system was CLASP, using steel frames with various cladding materials, commissioned by a consortium of local authorities from 1957 to gain economies of scale. This system was also adapted to other building types, notably at the University of York, whose campus was designed by Robert Matthew Johnson-Marshall architects from 1961, and, with the encouragement of the government, to housing.[65] Roman Catholic church architects were involved in these developments, almost all being commissioned for schools. Catholic school building in England and Wales was substantially funded by government, and the Ministry of Education's funding was increasingly determined by assuming the savings that would be obtained through building systems.[66] Architects studied new methods carefully: Greenhalgh & Williams, for example, established a London office in the 1950s led by Charles Wilfrid Childs, who had previously worked in the Ministry of Education helping to develop rationalised techniques for schools. Geoffrey Williams took plans of the firm's schools from Bolton to London to receive his advice.[67] In Scotland, full state funding had been agreed for denominational Catholic education in 1918 in return for cessation of Church control over schools, and clergy had little influence over sites, buildings or architects, but Catholic architects received many school commissions directly through local authorities.

In England and Wales, the clergy were deeply involved in school building. George Beck, bishop of Brentwood from 1951, Salford from 1955 and archbishop of Liverpool from 1964, had been headmaster of a Catholic grammar school in Nottingham before joining the hierarchy, when he accepted the job of representing the bishops of England and Wales in negotiations with the government over education policy.[68] In Salford, Beck created a department called the Building Office in 1959, whose remit was to monitor the progress of all new diocesan buildings and to check plans and estimates and any cost increases on projects, potentially intervening in cases of dispute.[69] A full-time surveyor, Bernard Flood, vetted architects' plans to curtail excesses, established standardised briefs and monitored construction costs and building contracts.[70] Guidelines were issued to reform the design and construction process: architects were told to complete their designs for buildings before work began to reduce delays and cost increases.[71] The Building Office also styled itself as a National Catholic Building Office offering advice to other dioceses, particularly on school building.[72] It is probably no coincidence, then, that Beck favoured modern church architecture, arguing that churches should adopt similar methods of standardising costs as schools and working out a yardstick based on cost-per-seat figures for average churches. Even so, he acknowledged that an expression of the building's sacred status might mean that such desirable factors as increasing height with scale would make such rationalisation difficult.[73]

Archbishop Heenan of Liverpool followed Salford's developments closely, also appointing a surveyor, Richard Edge, in the late 1950s to advise that diocese's Sites and Buildings Committee.[74] Weightman & Bullen's church of St Margaret Mary in Liverpool became something of a test case for the diocese when Edge insisted in 1959 that its estimated cost was excessive. The committee then demanded 'a more imposing and aesthetic building' for the money.[75] Instead, the parish priest asked the architects to revise the design to a lower cost.[76] Two years later the design was still being discussed, and the diocese asked Bullen to compare his plan with another modern church that had just been completed.[77] Bullen argued that the other church's lower cost was due to its traditional plan: the wider nave at St Margaret Mary came at a higher cost than a basilica with simple portal frames. Yet when Bullen analysed the two churches in terms of cost-per-place, his emerged the winner. He concluded that the diocese should consider the costs of churches in a more rigorous way – by deciding the sizes of new buildings for parishes and setting a cost-per-place limit that might be lifted for wealthier areas. The effect, he argued, would be 'a more rational Church building programme' and clearer briefs for architects.[78] Such a programme was never strictly implemented, partly because parish priests maintained their autonomy in defiance of diocesan attempts at centralisation, but the debate over rationalising the building process increasingly affected the design of churches.

The possibilities of new rationalised building techniques for church architecture were much discussed in the 1960s. Catholic architect John Wells-Thorpe argued in *Churchbuilding* that dioceses and denominations needed to collaborate to obtain a prefabrication system that was suitable for the building type.[79] Later the Anglican diocese of Chichester commissioned him to design a prototype lightweight 'movable church' and to study the potential of building systems.[80]

4.23   St Michael &
All Angels,
Wombwell,
Barnsley, by
Weightman &
Bullen, 1967–68.
Photo: Robert
Proctor, 2009

At a Catholic conference, the 'Visual Arts Week', he had already proposed an
inter-denominational 'building consortium' alongside Catholic architect Patrick
Nuttgens, who had recently become director of the Institute for Advanced
Architectural Studies at the University of York and was involved with the building
of the campus with his former tutor at Edinburgh University, Robert Matthew.[81]
Several Catholic and Anglican dioceses declared themselves interested in such a
plan to coordinate a church-building system, though nothing came of it.[82]

One architectural result of this preoccupation of both clergy and architects
with rationalised methods was the church of St Michael and All Angels at
Wombwell near Barnsley, completed in 1968 (Figure 4.23). Its architects
were David Brown and Patricia Brown of Weightman & Bullen's office in York.
They may have been aware of a contemporary Anglican experiment, the
church of St Francis in Duston, Northamptonshire, by Hamish McLachlan,
built with the 'A75 Metric System'.[83] Wombwell used the CLASP Mark IV
system of prefabrication, having the same modular dimensions and concrete
cladding panels as those of the University of York's new campus, a system
Weightman & Bullen had already used in several schools. They adapted the
system for their church: the elongated hexagonal plan required several
specially designed elements, and local artist Reg Williams was commissioned
to create vividly coloured translucent window panels in polyester resin.
At Wombwell, however, the reason for using CLASP was that the church was on
a site of mining subsidence that had damaged the previous church of 1952, and
CLASP's lightweight, flexible form of construction had been devised especially

for such difficult conditions in the mining areas of the Midlands.[84] While this building proved that construction systems could successfully be used for a church, it remained an isolated experiment in the application of this line of thought to Catholic church architecture in Britain.

Despite architects' willingness in the 1960s to consider this rationalising modernist approach, those clergy who needed new churches quickly and cheaply and without pretension were increasingly likely to reject architects altogether. The problem with architects was that their disorganisation could lead to costly delays on the building site. The diocese of St Andrews and Edinburgh, for example, became exasperated with problems in Gillespie, Kidd & Coia's church buildings, complaining of frequent design changes, a cost over-run and poor construction at St Patrick, Kilsyth.[85] This experience led the diocese to recommend that parish priests force architects to work with contractors at an early stage and that only large building firms should be employed because their drawing staff could detail buildings themselves and because they would be able to use 'semi-industrialised building' techniques.[86] Many clergy turned instead directly to building companies. The most prolific of these was Lanner Limited, a company in Wakefield that offered to design and build churches to a set budget. In the 1950s, they worked with a consultant architect, Kimball Pollitt, to create their own 'Preform' system of laminated timber and reinforced concrete A-frames and portal frames.[87] Occasionally Lanner's system was also adopted by architecture firms: Weightman & Bullen, for example, adopted it for a small chapel of 1958, Our Lady and the Welsh Martyrs at Overton in Wales, with a budget of only £6,000.[88] More often, however, Lanner would supply a complete design-and-build service including wiring, plumbing and furnishing for a fixed cost. At first Catholic parishes employed them for church halls that would be temporarily used for worship until a proper church could be afforded, but even then Lanner built several permanent churches: Holy Family, Thurnscoe, of 1959, with reinforced concrete portal frames and pointed windows, and Our Lady, Thurcroft, of 1961, both in small rural towns and both chapels-of-ease rather than parish churches in their own right.[89] Throughout the 1960s, Lanner churches were built in Sussex, at Rotherfield, Henley Road in Brighton, Bosham and Burwash.[90]

By the late 1960s, even city parishes considered Lanner seriously. Cardinal Heenan looked afresh at the company when prompted by the need for a new church at Neasden on an overstretched budget. He had known the firm when he was bishop of Leeds and wrote to a colleague there to find out how Lanner's churches had fared, complaining of the excessive cost of architects' designs.[91] Joseph McShane replied with a detailed and favourable assessment of the firm's productions, noting that dispensing with architects' fees saved a considerable sum and that the buildings had lasted well. He also reminded Heenan of the notorious case of architect Derek Walker's 'avant-garde' church of St Benedict, Garforth, which collapsed in a ruin within days of opening in 1964. 'If their products are not monuments of architectural beauty', wrote McShane, 'they are not ugly, but they are serviceable, they are economical for those anxious of costs.'[92] Westminster's Council of Administration considered Lanner churches under the headings of

4.24   Our Lady
of Walsingham,
Bootle, by Lanner
Ltd, 1973. Interior;
view towards main
entrance. Carved
frieze of the Last
Judgement by Eric
Carr, c.1976. Photo:
Robert Proctor, 2008

'system-built churches' and 'prefabs', but Lanner's publicity was keen to downplay these terms: 'our buildings are constructed of traditional building materials and are not prefabricated', insisted its brochure, explaining that every church was specially designed and showing perspectives by its architect, Brian Godward.[93] Lanner offered a perfect combination of modernity of design and method without the risks of high-profile architecture and with a reassuring combination of permanence and economy in construction.

Both Westminster and Liverpool employed Lanner by the early 1970s for large-scale churches, many even with plans influenced by the liturgical movement. Our Lady of Walsingham in Bootle, Liverpool, was a broad, low octagon designed to seat 500. Undemonstratively modern from without, its interior revealed laminated timber beams rising to a point over the expansive nave, while coloured-glass windows and imitation stonework gave a reassuring religious atmosphere (Figure 4.24).[94] When a member of the clergy at Westminster, F. A. Smyth, was dispatched to Liverpool and Manchester to visit Lanner churches there, he returned with a favourable impression, even praising their 'prayerfulness'.[95] The effects of modesty, simplicity and self-effacement of Lanner churches could by this time be viewed by clergy as more relevant to their concept of the Church as an institution that served rather than dominated its community in contrast to more experimental, iconic modes of modern church architecture that had often prevailed until then.

The irony that many modern architects advocated industrialised systems of construction only to find that building companies could take over and make them redundant was a constant preoccupation of this period. Architects defended themselves as uniquely able to investigate and solve the complex functional needs of their clients.[96] Wells-Thorpe argued that building companies were not interested in a serious study of the liturgy or the needs of a church and that industrialised systems could not give a church building a distinctive identity without modification by architects.[97] There was also continual suspicion about the lifespan of new techniques. While architects only rarely accepted industrialised systems for churches, however, they eagerly employed the standardised products of the building industry: prefabricated elements that were common in post-war church architecture included laminated timber and reinforced concrete portal frames, standard windows, factory glazing, common stock brick, engineering brick or concrete blockwork and pine planks, a post-war palette of ready-made materials that modernist architects of all persuasions adopted as a matter of course. Some architects thought these materials had to be used with artistry and inventiveness to create modern sacred space; others, such as Weightman & Bullen and Greenhalgh & Williams, particularly in their more modest churches, aimed at something like a modern vernacular. Their pragmatism was also endorsed in theoretical writing. In his article 'Transparent Poverty', Capellades called for a more modest modern church architecture: 'let us at last get away from the mania of trying to make each of our parish churches a cathedral', he wrote, arguing that contemporary church architects should instead take inspiration from medieval village churches, built to standardised patterns and techniques in great numbers, varied according to context: a concept of a vernacular approach that could serve as a model for an industrialised and anonymous modern church architecture.[98] Such an approach always remained, however, one amongst many strands of church design, and the high artistic taste, theological awareness and inventiveness of architects remained attractive to clergy even in times of greater financial pressure.

NOTES

1   Beck, 'Design, Price and Value', 171.

2   This movement has been summarised but rarely examined in depth (see for example Mumford, *The CIAM Discourse*, 163–7).

3   See Miles Glendinning, 'Teamwork or Masterwork? The Design and Reception of the Royal Festival Hall', *Architectural History* 46 (2003), 277–319.

4   Bullock, *Building the Post-War World*, 102–5; Gold, *Practice of Modernism*, 24–8; Stephen Kite, 'Softs and Hards: Colin St. John Wilson and the Contested Visions of 1950s London', in Mark Crinson and Claire Zimmerman (eds), *Neo-Avant-Garde and Postmodern: Postwar Architecture in Britain and Beyond* (New Haven: Yale University Press, 2010), 55–77.

5   Alistair Fair, ' "A New Image of the Living Theatre": The Genesis and Design of the Belgrade Theatre, Coventry, 1948–58', *Architectural History* 54 (2011), 347–82.

6   *CBRN* (1957), 100–103.

7   *CBRN* (1956), 61–3.

8   Fair, '"A New Image of the Living Theatre"', 367–72.

9   *CBRN* (1957), 104–7; 'Church is Built on "Raft"', *Catholic Guardian* (18 Oct. 1957), 7 (parish archive, Our Lady of Lourdes, Farnworth); Walker, 'Developments in Catholic Churchbuilding', 372–5; id., 'Liturgy and Architecture', 48.

10 'Farnworth's New Church Opened', *Catholic Guardian* (18 Oct. 1957), 6 (parish archive).

11 *St John Bosco's, Blackley: The Diamond Years: 1940–2000 AD* (Manchester: n.p., [c.2000]), 11 (Salford Diocesan Archives, Manchester [SDA], Parish Files).

12 *CBRS* (1964), 120–23.

13 Dorothy Morris, *The Catholic Church in Rainham, 1921–2000* (Rainham: n.p., 2000), 1–10 (parish archive, St Thomas of Canterbury, Rainham, Kent).

14 Benedict Read, 'Introduction' to Benedict Read et al., *Adam Kossowski: Murals and Paintings* (London: Armelle Press, 1990), 17.

15 For example Collins, *Concrete*.

16 Architects' description of the church [typescript] (*c.*1960) (GSAA, GKC/CHK/1).

17 Marcel Breuer and Hamilton Smith, 'The Buildings at St John's Abbey, Collegeville, Minnesota', *Design Quarterly* 53 (1961), 1–31 (5, 13).

18 *CBRS* (1956), 36–7; (1958), 77–8; (1959), 56–7; (1960), 44–5; (1961), 38–41; Walker, 'Developments in Catholic Churchbuilding', 361; on similar pre-war buildings, see Andrew Saint, 'Some Thoughts About the Architectural Use of Concrete', *AA Files* 22 (Autumn 1991), 3–16.

19 Jonathan Prichard, telephone interview with Robert Proctor (1 Oct. 2008).

20 *CBRN* (1959), 64–5.

21 *CBRN* (1965), 62–3.

22 John Catt et al., 'Design for Coventry Cathedral 1951', *Churchbuilding* 8 (Jan. 1963), 5–17.

23 Saint, 'Some Thoughts About the Architectural Use of Concrete', 12–14.

24 *CBRN* (1961), 94.

25 *CBRN* (1957), 100.

26 *CBRS* (1964), 60–63.

27 Parish archive, St Agnes, Huyton, Liverpool.

28 *Solemn Opening of the New Church of the Immaculate Conception, Maryhill, Glasgow, Sunday, 8th December, 1957: Souvenir Brochure* (Glasgow: n.p. 1957) (GRCAA, Y/14).

29 *Souvenir to Commemorate the Consecration, 12th December, 1956 and Solemn Opening, 16th December, 1956, of St Columba's Church, Bolton* (Bolton: n.p., 1956) (parish archive).

30 *Ronchamp*, special issue of *L'Art sacré* (Sept.–Oct. 1955); *La Tourette* special issue of *L'Art sacré* (Mar.–April 1960).

31 For example Rowe, 'Dominican Monastery of La Tourette'.

32 James Stirling, 'Garches to Jaoul: Le Corbusier as Domestic Architect in 1927 and 1953', *Architectural Review* (Sept. 1955), 145–51; 'Flats at Ham Common', *Architectural Review* (Oct. 1958), 218–25.

33 'House in Soho, London: Alison and Peter Smithson', *Architectural Design* (Dec. 1953), 342.

34 Vincent Scully, *Louis I. Kahn* (London: Prentice-Hall, 1962). On Kahn's influence in Britain, see Murray Fraser and Joe Kerr, *Architecture and the 'Special Relationship': The American Influence on Post-War British Architecture* (London: Routledge, 2007), 353–8.

35   Scully, *Louis I. Kahn*, 34.

36   'The New Brutalism', *Architectural Review* (Apr. 1954), 274–5; Reyner Banham, 'The New Brutalism', *Architectural Review* (Dec. 1955), 355–61; 'The New Brutalism', *Architectural Design* (Jan. 1955), 1.

37   Reyner Banham, *The New Brutalism: Ethic or Aesthetic?* (London: Architectural Press, 1966), 89.

38   J. A. Coia (Gillespie, Kidd & Coia) to Gerard M. Rogers (diocese of Motherwell) (16 Sept. 1957) (GSAA, GKC/CEK/1/1); photograph of model for St Bride's Church, East Kilbride (GSAA, GKC/CEK/2/2).

39   See David Buri, bibliography to Rodger, *Gillespie, Kidd & Coia*, 245.

40   'St. Bride's Church, East Kilbride' (n.d.) (GSAA, GKC/CEK/1/4); edited version in 'Public Buildings', *Architectural Review* (Jan. 1961), 40–41.

41   James Kilpatrick to J. A. Coia (Gillespie, Kidd & Coia) (1 May 1963) (GSAA, GKC/CEK/1/5).

42   *Solemn Opening: St Bride's Church, East Kilbride* (GRCAA, Y/15).

43   'Church Building: A Great Challenge', *The Universe*, Scottish edn (4 Sept. 1964), 4.

44   Design date based on drawings in GSAA (see Proctor, 'Churches for a Changing Liturgy', 302).

45   *Centenary, Parish of St. Patrick's, Kilsyth, 1865–1965: Souvenir Brochure* (1965) (SCA, HC/51).

46   *CBRN* (1964), 100–101.

47   Higgott, *Mediating Modernism*, 92, 101–3; J. M. Richards and Eric de Maré, *The Functional Tradition in Early Industrial Buildings* (London: Architectural Press, 1958).

48   Desmond Williams, email to Robert Proctor (13 June 2009).

49   Desmond Williams, email to Robert Proctor (6 Aug. 2008).

50   See Lynn Pearson, 'Broad Visions: Ceramics in the Twentieth Century Church', paper presented at Tiles and Architectural Ceramics Society Conference, 'Church Ceramics: Decorative Tiles, Mosaic and Terracotta During and After the Gothic Revival', Coalbrookdale, 2006, http://www.lynnpearson.co.uk/Broad%20Visions.pdf (accessed 4 May 2012); see also Lynn Pearson, 'To Brighten the Environment: Ceramic Tile Murals in Britain, 1950–70', *Journal of the Tiles and Architectural Ceramics Society* 10 (2004), 12–17; Robert Brumby, telephone interview with Robert Proctor (11 June 2013).

51   For example *Le Douleureux problème des arts missionaires*, special issue of *L'Art sacré* (Mar.–Apr. 1951).

52   Richard O'Mahony (F. X. Velarde Partnership) to T. Barry (17 Aug. 1962) (LRCAA, Parish Files, 211).

53   Richard O'Mahony, interview with Robert Proctor, Liverpool (6 Nov. 2008).

54   Visitation report for St Patrick, Clinkham Wood (1971) (LRCAA, Parish Files, 211).

55   'Anglican Church in Stepney', *Churchbuilding* 7 (Oct. 1962), 14–23 (14, 18).

56   Rudolf Schwarz, *The Church Incarnate: The Sacred Function of Christian Architecture*, trans. Cynthia Harris (Chicago: Henry Regnery, 1958), 10–11.

57   M.-R. Capellades, 'Transparent Poverty', trans. Keith Harrison, *Churchbuilding* 7 (Oct. 1962), 4–8; originally published in *L'Art sacré* (1958).

58   Walker, 'Developments in Catholic Churchbuilding', 489; Rudolf Schwarz, *Kirchenbau: Welt vor der Schwelle* (Heidelberg: F. H. Kerle, 1960).

59   *CBRN* (1965), 84; (1967), 82–5; Kenneth Nugent, 'Review of New Church: Our Lady of the Rosary, Donnington, Shropshire', *Clergy Review* 52 (1952), 1001–8.

60   Timothy Armstrong, correspondence with Robert Proctor (20 Feb. 2012).

61   Peter Ansdell Evans, 'Six Churches: Part 1', *Architects' Journal* (12 Dec. 1973), 1459–73 (1460).

62   Stephen Garner, 'St Peter's Church and Presbytery, Dumbarton', *Clergy Review* 59 (1974), 237–43 (238, 243).

63   John Gifford and Frank Arneil Walker, *Stirling and Central Scotland*, Buildings of Scotland (London: Yale University Press, 2002), 402, 409, 414–15.

64   Saint, *Towards a Social Architecture*; Ministry of Education, *The Story of Post-War School Building* (London: HMSO, 1957).

65   Gold, *Practice of Modernism*, 63–7, 189–99.

66   Mary J. Hickman, *Religion, Class and Identity: The State, the Catholic Church and the Education of the Irish in Britain* (Avebury: Ashgate, 1995), 240–42; George Scott, *The R.C.s: A Report on Roman Catholics in Britain Today* (London: Hutchinson, 1967), 149–50.

67   Austin Winkley, interview with Robert Proctor, London (8 Dec. 2011).

68   Stewart M. Foster, *A History of the Diocese of Brentwood, 1917–1992* (Brentwood: Diocese of Brentwood, 1994), 101; Michael Gaine, 'Beck, George Andrew (1904–1978)', in *Oxford Dictionary of National Biography* (Oxford: Oxford University Press, 2004), http://www.oxforddnb.com/view/article/65084 (accessed 5 June 2013).

69   Beck, circular letter 'To All Architects Employed on Building Contracts for the Salford Diocese' (18 June 1959) (SDA, Building Office papers, 094).

70   For example Bernard Flood to Bishop Beck (30 Jan. 1961); see also Bernard Flood and Salford Roman Catholic Diocesan Trustees, 'Procedure for Diocesan Building Projects' (June 1959) (SDA, Building Office papers, 094).

71   'Report for Father Slevin' (13 Nov. 1958) and attached memo, George Andrew Beck, 'General Note to Architects and Quantity Surveyors' (21 Mar. 1960) (SDA, Building Office papers, 094).

72   For example draft 'Building Procedure for Catholic Voluntary School Building Projects' and letter, Flood to Beck (8 Apr. 1960) (SDA, Building Office papers, 094); see also George Andrew Beck, 'Buildings and Costs', *CBRN* (1964), 162.

73   Beck, 'Value for Money', 197–8.

74   'Report on a Visit to Salford Building Office' (*c.*1958) (LRCAA, Finance Collection, 12/S3/III).

75   Minutes of the Sites and Buildings Commission (21 July 1959) (LRCAA, Finance Collection, 12/S3/III).

76   Minutes of the Sites and Buildings Commission (17 Nov. 1959); Francis C. Harvey (parish priest, St Margaret Mary, Liverpool) to [Taylor] (secretary, Sites and Buildings Committee, Archdiocese of Liverpool) (4 Nov. 1959) (LRCAA, Finance Collection, 12/S3/III).

77   On St Margaret Mary, see *CBRN* (1962), 46–7; (1963), 42–3; (1964), 46–7; see also minutes of meeting of the Liverpool Archdiocesan Sites and Buildings Commission (23 Apr. 1961) (LRCAA, Finance Collection, 12/S3/III), which suggests that the design was substantially changed at this point. The reference church used as a comparison was St Stephen, Orford, Warrington; see *CBRN* (1958), 64–7; (1961), 60–63.

78   A. G. Bullen (Weightman & Bullen) to Heenan (14 Apr. 1961) (LRCAA, Parish Files, 154).

79   J. A. Wells-Thorpe, 'Church Building and New Construction Techniques', *Churchbuilding* 14 (Jan. 1965), 11–13.

80   'Editorial: Chichester Report', *Churchbuilding* 20 (Jan. 1967), 2.

81   *Bulletin of the Society of Catholic Artists* (Apr. 1964) (Archive of the Society of Catholic Artists, London [ASCA]); Fiona MacCarthy, 'Obituary: Patrick Nuttgens', *The Guardian* (17 Mar. 2004), http://www.guardian.co.uk/news/2004/mar/17/guardianobituaries. highereducation (accessed 18 June 2012); for York University, see Saint, *Towards a Social Architecture*, 214–21.

82   Walker, 'Developments in Catholic Churchbuilding', 267–73.

83   'Church of St. Francis, Duston', *Churchbuilding* 20 (Jan. 1967), 8–10; 'From Our Notebook', *The Tablet* (11 Feb. 1967), 151.

84   'Wombwell: St. Michael and All Angels', *Churchbuilding* 23 (Jan. 1968), 21; *CBRN* (1967), 98–101; (1968), 71–3; 'The Sinking Church is Now "Refloated"', *The Universe*, Scottish edn (30 Jan. 1970), 14; Walker, 'Developments in Catholic Churchbuilding', 512; Patricia Brown and David John Brown, interview with Ambrose Gillick, York (3 Apr. 2012); Saint, *Towards a Social Architecture*, 164–70.

85   Walter Glancy (finance secretary, Archdiocese of St Andrews and Edinburgh), summary of correspondence with Gillespie, Kidd & Coia over St Patrick, Kilsyth (Sept. 1962–Dec. 1967) (SCA, DE/39/30).

86   [Walter Glancy], 'Memo for Finance Committee. Method of Contracting' (7 July 1964) (SCA, DE/39/25).

87   'Leeds Diocese', CBRN (1957), 146–7.

88   *CBRN* (1958), 167–9.

89   *CBRN* (1959), 152–3; (1962), 142–3.

90   *CBRS* (1964), 128; (1965), 88–9; (1969), 50–53.

91   John C. Heenan (archbishop of Westminster) to Joseph McShane (diocese of Leeds) (15 Mar. 1969) (WDA, He1/C23(b)).

92   McShane to Heenan ([1969]) (WDA, He1/C23(b)). On the collapse of St Benedict, Garforth, see ' "It Was to Have Been Church of Our Times"', *The Universe*, Scottish edn (27 Nov. 1964), 11.

93   Minutes of meeting of the Council of Administration and Finance Committee of the Archdiocese of Westminster (10 Sept. 1969); Lanner Ltd, publicity brochure (1969) (WDA, He1/C23(b)).

94   'Some Interesting Liverpool Development Information Supplied by Lanner Ltd of Wakefield', CBRN (1971), 176–80; *CBRN* (1973), 81–3; (1974), 176–9.

95   F. A. Smyth to Heenan (11 Dec. 1970) (WDA, He1/C23(b)).

96   Gold, *Practice of Modernism*, 63–7.

97   Wells-Thorpe, 'Church-Building and New Construction Techniques', 12; id., 'Relevance in Church Building', *Clergy Review* 55 (Jan. 1970), 81–8 (85).

98   Cappellades, 'Transparent Poverty', 6–7.

5

Modern Church Art

Just as the Roman Catholic Church saw the adoption of a modern municipal architecture as a way to claim an accepted position within British society, the commissioning of modern art for churches could also contribute to achieving a higher social and political status. Art and architecture that adhered to mainstream British culture represented cultural capital, an investment that could repay the Church through an increasing recognition in society of its importance and legitimacy.[1] Acquiring cultural capital for conversion into social capital could be particularly urgent for a Church that historically had a marginal status in Britain and a high proportion of whose members were of Irish descent. Modern architects, too, wished to incorporate art in their churches. Yet the Church would only adopt modern art on its own terms, not least because church art had to be functional, satisfying the needs of devotion and liturgical use. Artists therefore also contributed to the production of the church in partnership with architects and clergy.

The patronage of modern artists was an important aspect of modernist architectural culture in this period, even in the service of the post-war welfare state. The use of fine art, and particularly high modernist art, in a public context for such buildings as schools, theatres and civic centres was espoused by architects such as J. M. Richards of the *Architectural Review* and much debated. It was a persistent theme at the CIAM meeting of 1951 in Hoddesdon entitled 'The Heart of the City', whose delegates visited the Festival of Britain, its South Bank site the subject of a comprehensive programme of artistic installations.[2] There had already been discussion of the need for the 'emotions' of the people to be considered in modern architecture and the role that artists could play in fulfilling this spiritual need.[3] It was an argument that was especially allied to the New Empiricism and was sometimes contentious within modern movement discourse. Modern architects in Britain, however, often coming from a background in Arts and Crafts design, frequently took an unproblematic approach to working with modern artists, who welcomed opportunities for collaboration. A pioneering venture in involving artists with architectural projects was established by the London County Council, which, in 1954, decided it had a social duty to provide modern art to the masses and allocated an annual budget for artworks to be provided for new schools and housing estates. Two young artists, Antony Holloway and William Mitchell, were employed to produce art for new public buildings, working with architect Oliver Cox at the Council's Architects' Department. It was an important model for the integration of art and architecture, and Mitchell would later undertake significant Catholic commissions in a similar vein at Liverpool and Clifton cathedrals.[4] The Arts Council, established on a permanent basis in 1946 to dispense funding to arts organisations and local authorities, was likewise a product of the post-war welfare state's desire to make high culture accessible to the masses.[5] The provision of modern public art was seen as an intrinsic duty of the new socially concerned state: modern architects willingly concurred, and the Church shared in this climate of cultural benevolence.

ART AND THE CHURCH

In church architecture, of course, art had well-established historical precedents. The churches at Assy and Audincourt in France were influential models for a modern approach to integrating church art and architecture. Both were simple basilican buildings designed by Maurice Novarina. At Assy, Couturier invited the best modern artists regardless of their faith to create works of varying degrees of abstraction: Henri Matisse produced an image of St Dominic that was a faceless linear design on ceramic tiles; André Lurçat designed a tapestry depicting the Apocalypse to hang within the apse; Jewish artists Jacques Lipchitz and Marc Chagall were commissioned for further pieces in the 1950s.[6] Couturier and his colleagues at L'Art sacré followed Maritain in believing that the artist had to take a spiritual stance in devotional art, but thought that the artist's creative intelligence and willingness to adopt a Christian attitude were more important than their adherence to religious duties.[7] Furthermore, Couturier argued that it was the artist's accomplished ability to convey a spiritual message through formal composition that made religious art devotional rather than its literal content, opening the way to non-realistic and non-figurative approaches.[8] Good modern art was therefore to be preferred to the conventional realism of most pious imagery.

The arguments were controversial and evoked a response from the Vatican. Pius XII's encyclical *Musicae sacrae disciplina*, on sacred music, of 1955 criticised the employment of non-Catholic artists in the Church and insisted that artists had to meet the Church's own expectations, not just the hermetic methods of art.[9] The Church's position on abstraction was more ambivalent: it could be accepted when it might be considered decorative, especially for stained glass, which contributed to a religious atmosphere rather than being an object of prayer; but it was less acceptable for images purporting to represent Christ or the saints, when the Church's prohibition of distortion applied.[10] Abstraction was especially condemned for the sanctuary crucifix, an object of devotion within the liturgy that represented the Incarnation – Christ in the form of a man.[11]

On the other hand, mass-produced art had long been forbidden from churches by canon law, though the rule was widely ignored. Even the most stereotyped images were frequently therefore hand-made, parishes often purchasing them from craft producers such as Stüflesser in the Italian Tyrol, a firm that specialised in a rococo style of painted wooden statuary and that was endorsed by the Vatican.[12] The 1952 'Instruction on Sacred Art' went further than canon law, however, also forbidding 'second rate and stereotyped statues' from public veneration, balancing its condemnation of excessively modern art with an equal rejection of kitsch.[13] The arguments against kitsch were widely repeated. In the *Clergy Review*, a British magazine aimed at parish priests and edited by O'Connell, Charles Blakeman, a Catholic artist, condemned the 'inferior, standardized article', urging priests to trust artists and to allow them freedom.[14] A decade later, when the Second Vatican Council's 'Constitution on the Sacred Liturgy' of 1963 explicitly endorsed modern art for churches, J. D. Crichton, an English parish priest and liturgical writer, emphasised the sacredness of individual work in the creation of art for the Church:

> *A picture that is no more than a painted photograph, a statue that is poured out of a mould, made of inferior material by people who have no care for its quality or for its purpose, is incapable of arousing a response from the user, unless it be one of disgust. The Constitution … uses the expression humanis operibus which we may translate as 'the works of man's hands' and we may add that it is because they are the works of man's hands that they can give glory to God and reflect his beauty. Anything less cannot.[15]*

Popular devotional art was criticised as being sentimental and overly feminine, a view Blakeman extended to other aspects of churches such as typical lace-adorned altars.[16] Modern art, by contrast, needed to be virile, and so the 'hieratic' figure was advocated: recognisably human, yet sufficiently abstracted and reinterpreted as to possess symbolic qualities, severe enough to inspire devotion without arousing undue emotion.[17] Emotional restraint was seen as a quality of liturgical prayer in contrast to popular devotions and was therefore advocated for liturgical art by Romano Guardini in his widely published book, *The Spirit of the Liturgy*.[18] The 'Constitution on the Sacred Liturgy' continued this theme by emphasising the liturgical role of church art, as 'signs and symbols of heavenly realities'.[19] Throughout this period, therefore, the Church demanded a good quality of original art and permitted some aspects of modern styles depending on context, a desire that coincided with the interests of many modern architects who wanted to work with artists.

Undeterred by controversy and spurred by sympathetic patrons, Couturier and his colleagues in the Art Sacré movement in France were a major force in popularising modern sacred art and making it acceptable within the Church. Audincourt employed a more unified scheme than Assy: Fernand Léger designed a series of clerestory windows with recognisable but non-figurative emblems of the Passion, while Jean Bazaine created entirely abstract *dalle de verre* windows for the cylindrical baptistery, dark nervous lines crossing swathes of orange and grey (Figure 5.1).

5.1   Église du Sacré-Coeur, Audincourt, by Maurice Novarina, 1951. View of baptistery with glass by Jean Bazaine. © ADAGP, Paris, and DACS, London, 2013. Photo: Denis Mathieu, 2013

The use of *dalle de verre* as an element of the church's modern architecture was an important aspect of this widely published building: in Anton Henze and Theodor Filthaut's book, *Contemporary Church Art*, published by Catholic publishers Sheed & Ward, Audincourt's glazing was said to be unified with the substance of the architecture, 'technically part of the wall', a statement of great significance for any modern architects who doubted the desirability of ornament.[20] The French model of sacred artistic commissions would become highly influential in Britain in the 1950s.

MODERN CHURCH ART IN BRITAIN: COVENTRY CATHEDRAL

Uniting the New Empiricism of post-war British architecture with the concept of the basilica of sacred art inspired by these French models was Coventry Cathedral. Basil Spence won the competition for this Anglican cathedral in 1951 with a design that aroused much controversy in the press for its modernism, despite his insistence on its historical basis, its conservative basilican plan and his intention to build it substantially in stone. Behind the altar Spence planned a magnificent tapestry by Graham Sutherland, while modern stained glass would line the nave and form a dramatic backdrop to the baptistery. Spence visited Sutherland in France to invite him to take on the commission, and the two visited the chapel at Vence decorated by Matisse. Significantly, the subject of Sutherland's tapestry, Christ in Glory, was interpreted through the book of Revelation, also the source for Lurçat's apocalyptic tapestry at Assy. Spence had thought of Sutherland because he had seen a crucifixion painting the artist had made for the Anglican church of St Matthew in Northampton, a striking commission from a patron who also emulated the Art Sacré movement, its vicar Walter Hussey.[21]

For Coventry's baptistery window, Spence approached John Piper and Patrick Reyntiens around 1955. Part of the attraction of Piper for Spence was that he was a well-established modern painter, and his move into working with stained glass, sympathetically executed by Reyntiens, resembled the trajectory of Fernand Léger when the latter designed the windows for Audincourt.[22] Piper and Reyntiens were also keen to emulate modern French stained glass.[23] At Coventry, their baptistery window consisted of small panels of leaded glass in an abstract design of a blaze of coloured light: a similar approach to Bazaine's at Audincourt, though more traditional in technique. Spence modelled Coventry closely on the pioneering French churches, and the cathedral aroused widespread public interest in Britain in modern church architecture and sacred art. Though Coventry was not always well received by architectural critics, it had a great impact on the architectural profession in Britain that was sustained throughout the lengthy process of its building, which only began in 1955 and was not complete until 1962.[24] Spence's concept of a basilica of modern art was adopted and imitated by many Roman Catholic architects and clergy.

5.2   St Aidan, East
Acton, London, by
Burles & Newton,
1959–61. View of
nave: frieze of the
Stations of the
Cross by Arthur
Fleischmann;
painting of the
Crucifixion by
Graham Sutherland,
c.1964. Courtesy of
the Estate of Graham
Sutherland. Photo:
Robert Proctor, 2009

FROM COVENTRY TO CATHOLICISM

Coventry's connections to subsequent Roman Catholic church art were often literal, as two case studies will show. In Lancaster, the church of St Bernadette, designed by Tom Mellor, was opened in 1958, a New Empiricist building of brick, stone and steel. Shortly after the church was opened, the timber panels of its reredos were daringly painted with an outline figure of Christ in Majesty, flanked by angels and overlaid with bold patches of primary colours, commissioned from John Piper. The church also included artworks by well-known Catholic sculptors Peter Watts and Michael Clark. At St Aidan at East Acton in London, meanwhile, a basilican reinforced-concrete church designed by Burles & Newton was opened in 1961 and subsequently filled with works of art, most of which were planned from the beginning. Behind its high altar was a bright red canvas of the Crucifixion by Graham Sutherland with an emaciated, tortured figure of Christ, while more conventional works adorned the church throughout (Figure 5.2, Plate 5).

Sutherland's Crucifixion at East Acton was similar to his canvas at Northampton: red, instead of blue, but the same gaunt figure; and it was in fact his third, since another similar scene was woven into the base of the Coventry tapestry. St Aidan's Crucifixion was the most overtly modern of the three: over the cross was an electric light and at its base a chain-link fence, references to the prison camp that had been only implicit in his previous images, a frequent theme of post-war Crucifixions, including that of Germaine Richier at Assy. Significantly, Sutherland was a Roman Catholic convert, and his work for St Aidan was his first for a Catholic church, answering a complaint that architectural critic Joseph Rykwert had made in France that Sutherland had so far been overlooked by Catholics.[25]

Sutherland's appointment at East Acton was eagerly endorsed by the parish priest, James Ethrington, who evidently wished to assume the role of enlightened patron of modern art in emulation of Hussey at Northampton and, later, Chichester Cathedral. Around 1964, when his church's artistic commissions were complete, Ethrington published a booklet on St Aidan's artworks, inviting an art critic for a national newspaper, Terence Mullaly, to contribute an endorsement. Ethrington noted that the booklet was intended to reach beyond Catholics, 'to draw attention to features of St. Aidan's Church likely to be of interest to the general public'.[26] Its purpose, and therefore also one purpose of the artworks, was to bring this church to a certain level of elite appreciation and to raise awareness of a Catholic artistic culture. Sutherland was here claimed for Catholicism, lending his credentials to the other more conventional artists whose work was placed alongside his: Kossowski, already well known and requested by churches across Britain; Arthur Fleischmann, a Hungarian artist who had made work for the Vatican at its 1958 Brussels Exposition pavilion; Roy de Maistre, an Australian painter who had earlier completed a series of Stations of the Cross at Westminster Cathedral; Philip Lindsey Clark, an eminent sculptor; and several others.[27] Mullaly emphasised the importance of this original sacred art in transforming the reputation for kitsch that adhered to Christian and especially Roman Catholic churches: 'during rather more than the last 150 years religious art has plumbed the depths of sentimentality and triviality', he wrote; 'St Aidan's has broken with this bad old tradition'.[28]

This was exactly what the Vatican's 'Instruction on Sacred Art' demanded. Had Sutherland's Crucifixion painting at East Acton been made in the 1950s, it might have tested the limits of acceptability, but by the time of its unveiling in 1963 modern religious art was tolerated by Church and public alike, and the painting was well received. Catholic weekly *The Tablet* explained its purpose in relation to the new modern architecture and atmosphere of Catholic churches: 'Clean lines, unpainted wood, and beauty unadorned are the order of the day. Gone are the wedding-cake altars, the sugar-plum statues and sad-eyed madonnas, and many heaved a gusty sigh of relief at their departure'.[29] Another writer, however, questioned Sutherland's emphasis on suffering at the expense of other interpretations of the Crucifixion and, interviewing teenage parishioners, thought its devotional purpose not wholly satisfied.[30] Yet the fact that such a work could be commissioned without substantial controversy was no doubt largely thanks to Coventry Cathedral. Coventry made modern sacred art acceptable and desirable, motivating Catholics to participate in modern high culture and to welcome it into their churches.

The collaboration of Piper and Reyntiens at Coventry was equally significant to Roman Catholic church architecture. At St Bernadette, Lancaster, the choice of Piper was exceptional, since he was not Catholic (Plate 6, Figure 5.3). The impact of his work in suburban Lancaster must have been potent, though, significantly, it was a young parish. A reporter for the *Daily Express*, attempting to whip up a scandal, found only praise for Piper: 'We should feel honoured that an artist of Piper's quality has been able to paint it for us', said a 'church committee man';

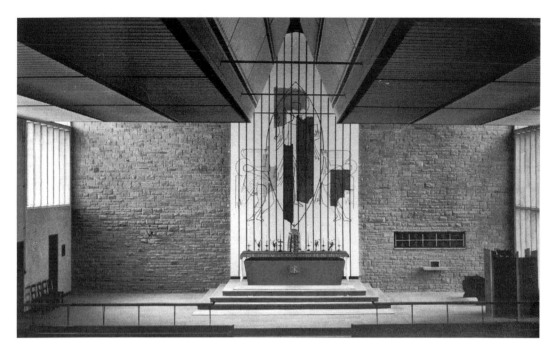

the parish priest who commissioned it, Christopher Aspinall, was said to have 'loved the painting'; and a 29-year-old 'churchgoer' added: 'Some people around here are too old-fashioned. They seem to think no one could pray properly with such a "loud" painting above the altar. But times are changing.'[31] Like Sutherland at East Acton, Piper's mainstream renown lent cultural credibility to the Church. His painting, dominating Mellor's building though integrated with it, was an act of faith by the parish in the capacity of the artist to speak to modern people about Christian themes in a new way that also inspired devotion.

Reyntiens, meanwhile, was a Catholic, a graduate of Edinburgh College of Art who had trained in the stained-glass workshop of Joseph Nuttgens. Following the Coventry commission, Piper and Reyntiens were invited by Frederick Gibberd to provide stained glass in *dalle de verre* for the Metropolitan Cathedral in Liverpool. Gibberd had investigated another prolific stained-glass designer of this period, Charles Norris, a Benedictine monk at Buckfast Abbey in Devon. Norris had made an enormous scheme of *dalle de verre* windows for Our Lady of Fatima in Harlow New Town – a church Gibberd knew well, since he was the architect planner for Harlow. Eventually Gibberd admitted he disliked Norris's work and recommended Geoffrey Clarke, one of the designers of Coventry's nave windows.[32] Gibberd sent Heenan to visit Coventry, and the decision to commission Piper and Reyntiens followed.[33] A Dominican, Illtud Evans, advised Heenan that Reyntiens was 'an excellent Catholic, with an informed knowledge of his faith which is of such importance in the iconography and design of glass for a sacred building' and 'the best stained glass artist working in England today'.[34] Reyntiens had already been at work in the Archdiocese of Liverpool for the church of St Mary, Leyland by Weightman & Bullen, where early discussions about commissioning artists also began with reference to Coventry.[35] The national prestige that Piper and Reyntiens's partnership had attained through Coventry Cathedral was a significant factor in the decision to employ them, and Reyntiens's Catholicism reassured the clergy. Gibberd was impressed by the broad architectonic scale of their work at Coventry, in contrast to Norris's crowded figurative windows at Harlow, a taste that Piper and Reyntiens amply satisfied with their trinity of sunbursts in the Liverpool lantern (Plate 7).

In one point, however, Basil Spence had himself been influenced by a British Catholic precedent for modern religious art. Coventry's external bronze sculpture by Jacob Epstein of the cathedral's patron St Michael defeating the devil seemed to hover weightlessly against the sandstone wall, a form that suited Spence's modernist intentions since it did not appear to be an ornament but an autonomous object. Spence had already seen a similar work at the Catholic convent of the Holy Child Jesus at Cavendish Square in London (Figure 5.4).[36] Here Epstein had been commissioned in 1951 to create an external sculpture of the Madonna and Child, a work made of lead salvaged from the rooftops during their repair and suspended on the wall of a bridge linking two convent buildings. The commission came from the architect of the rebuilding of the bomb-damaged convent, Louis Osman, who claimed to have invented the idea of the levitating sculpture. Osman invited Epstein, a Jew, to work on the project without telling the convent's nuns, who were eventually persuaded to accept the piece through encouragement from art historian Kenneth Clark, alongside a substantial donation from the Arts Council and Epstein's willingness to be instructed on the subject of the Virgin Mary.[37]

Epstein had long been interested in Christian iconography, and though many of his pre-war religious figures had been condemned as blasphemous, they had all been speculatively made for sale rather than commissioned. Though they were titled with Christian themes, their intention was to evoke universal principles. His image for Cavendish Square was more theologically specific: the Virgin presented the Christ child to the secular world (literally, since it overlooked Oxford Street, the commercial heart of London); the child's outstretched arms recalled the Crucifixion, and his horizontal draperies reprised the shroud in Epstein's earlier figure of the Resurrection. When this sculpture was inaugurated in 1953 by Rab Butler, Chancellor of the Exchequer, it had an electrifying effect: architecture critic Robert Furneaux Jordan thought it the most important public artwork in London for centuries, and Epstein found himself suddenly a celebrity, in demand for monumental and religious sculpture.[38] It caused a debate in the Catholic press equivalent to that over Our Lady of Victories: Catholic sculptor Peter Watts, who made the Stations of the Cross at St Bernadette, Lancaster, thought it essentially un-Christian and non-devotional, while Lance Wright countered that the modern artist's personal interpretation of a religious theme made Christianity accessible to the world in a comprehensible language.[39] It was not a work of church art, but it catalysed the acceptance of modern art by the Catholic Church in Britain.

Gillespie, Kidd & Coia's church of St Charles Borromeo in Glasgow drew on this appreciation of Epstein. Sculptor Benno Schotz, a Jewish immigrant often compared to Epstein, was commissioned for major work, his modern figurative sculpture crowding Coia's Coventry-like church: near-life-size terracotta figures depicted the Stations of the Cross; a bronze angel clapping cymbals held the sanctuary lamp;

5.4   Madonna and Child by Jacob Epstein at Convent of the Holy Child Jesus,
Cavendish Square, London, 1951–53. Photo: Steve Cadman, 2011

IPPED
IENTS

IX
JESUS FALLS
THE THIRD TIME

VIII
THE WOMEN OF JERUSALEM
MOURN OUR LORD

and a crucifix with bronze figures of Christ, the Virgin Mary and St John stood behind the marble altar surrounded by a halo of golden shards (Figure 5.5). Coia invited Schotz, a colleague at the Glasgow School of Art, to carry out the commissions, which were completed by around 1961. If Coventry was a reference point, however, Coia's intentions were different: Schotz's sculpture was to be integrated with the wall rather than detached from it, giving a 'horizontal wavy movement', so Schotz used the reinforced concrete beams as a base and chose terracotta to match the brickwork.[40] In contrast to Coventry's mainly symbolic and abstract internal artworks, this commission filled the church with figures intended for devotional use. Schotz's work was accordingly less challenging to Catholic taste than Epstein's more radical reinterpretations, yet the fact that these artworks were commissioned from a well-established non-Catholic modern artist was a substantial advance in the spirit of the Art Sacré movement. Schotz worked concurrently for Gillespie, Kidd & Coia's church of St Paul, Glenrothes, whose parish priest, Pierce Grace, had seen and appreciated Schotz's work for St Charles. MacMillan, approving his appointment, gave the sculptor a sketch for the crucifix based on photographs of Catalan crosses that he had seen in *L'Art sacré*. To the arms of the cross Schotz attached symbols of the Passion, like those in Léger's windows at Audincourt (Figure 5.6). Grace, though he was impressed by the restrained devotional feeling of Schotz's crucifix, felt unable to inform Archbishop Gray of its authorship in advance, but the sculpture was widely admired on the opening of the church in 1958, and, when he discovered that Schotz was its artist, Gray declared that he thought it was 'fit for the Vatican'.[41]

5.5   St Charles Borromeo, Kelvinside, Glasgow, by Gillespie, Kidd & Coia, 1956–60. Stations of the Cross by Benno Schotz, RSA. Courtesy of the Trustees of the late Benno Schotz, RSA. Photo: Robert Proctor, 2010

PATRONAGE AND DEBATE: LIVERPOOL AND LEYLAND

On at least one occasion the Church's desire for figurative art conflicted with an architect's preferences. At Liverpool Metropolitan Cathedral, Robert Brumby was commissioned to make a sculpture of the Virgin and Child for the lady chapel (Figure 5.7). This commission was made by the clergy without consulting Gibberd, who angrily complained when he discovered it. Augustine Harris, auxiliary bishop of Liverpool, defended their action, arguing that Gibberd's emphasis on abstract art was inappropriate for a figure of popular devotion.[42] The clergy on the cathedral committee had already been concerned about Gibberd's appointment of established abstract painter Ceri Richards for a canvas and designs for the tabernacle and stained glass in the Blessed Sacrament chapel. His yellow and white painting and blue and yellow glass design for Liverpool were entirely abstract, some more overt symbolism entering the tabernacle panels (Figure 5.8). Richards's work received a mixed reception from the cathedral committee, some of whom could not conceal their disliked of it from Gibberd.[43] The choice of artist had been tentatively accepted by Beck, however, who took over from Heenan in 1964, and Beck had personally approved the designs at various stages. Beck had debated the desirability of abstraction with Gibberd, accepting abstract art in certain contexts, but advocating a more conventional treatment for devotional images.

5.7 Metropolitan Cathedral of Christ the King, Liverpool, by Frederick Gibberd, 1960–67. Lady chapel:
sculpture of Madonna and Child by Robert Brumby; stained glass by Margaret Traherne. By permission of
Robert Brumby and the Dean of the Metropolitan Cathedral of Christ the King. Photo: Robert Proctor, 2012

5.8   Metropolitan Cathedral of Christ the King, Liverpool, by Frederick Gibberd, 1960–67. Blessed Sacrament chapel: painting, tabernacle and stained-glass design by Ceri Richards © Estate of Ceri Richards, all rights reserved, DACS, London, 2013; stained glass executed by Patrick Reyntiens, © Patrick Reyntiens, all rights reserved, DACS, London, 2013. By permission of the Dean of the Metropolitan Cathedral of Christ the King. Photo: Henk Snoek. Source: Architectural Press Archive / RIBA Library Photographs Collection

Reassured by advice from Reyntiens supporting Richards's appointment and having inspected some of the artist's earlier work, Beck approved the commission because it required 'something which will give a visitor to the Chapel, particularly the ordinary visitor who comes to pray there, a sense of peace, tranquillity and majesty, with some awareness, I hope, of the presence of God'.[44] In other words it was specifically the theocentric nature of the Blessed Sacrament chapel that made abstraction possible, and seemingly also a desire to engage non-Catholic visitors.

In contrast, Beck refused Gibberd's request to appoint Leslie Thornton for the crucifix after viewing samples of this modernist sculptor's earlier renditions of the subject. Beck wrote to Gibberd:

> I do not think it is possible to regard the crucifixes and statues which are placed in our churches simply and solely as works of art, in the sense in which a work of art can be presented in secular surroundings. The purpose of these objects is also to foster devotion, and I would maintain that they are more truly works of art in the measure in which they achieve this purpose. I do not believe that this necessarily restricts the artist to a realistic and representational design, but I think it does exclude the abstract and impressionist presentation.[45]

After several prominent artists refused the commission for a crucifix suspended from the baldachino, Elisabeth Frink was asked for a smaller work to place behind the altar, with Gibberd's approval (Figure 5.9).[46] Frink made a thin, barely distinguishable figure whose arms alone formed the cross beam, but despite its novelty the clergy were favourable: 'We are not sure about the liturgical correctness of the absence of the cross-beam', wrote Beck, 'but I, personally, and others of the committee think the symbolism of this is very striking since it portrays a gesture of love for all men, and not merely the suffering of a victim'.[47] Frink's work balanced the requirement for a recognisable crucifixion figure with a novel form and complexity of meaning.

At St Mary's church in Leyland, a similar and earlier unified programme of modern artworks completed this church in the Archdiocese of Liverpool. The church was run by Benedictines from Ampleforth, who appointed one of their number, Edmund Fitzsimons, as the parish priest. Fitzsimons undertook unusually extensive preparatory studies. Not only did he read about modern church architecture, subscribing to *Churchbuilding*, but in 1959 he went on a tour organised by the Birmingham University Institute for the Study of Worship and Religious Architecture titled 'Modern Glass in France and Switzerland', including visits to Le Raincy, Audincourt and Ronchamp.[48] Fitzsimons also took advice on church art from Crichton, who warned him against resorting to ecclesiastical suppliers.[49]

Crichton attended a meeting in 1961 between Fitzsimons and architect Jerzy Faczynski of Weightman & Bullen, where commissions and schemes for the church's artworks were decided. Geoffrey Clarke, Charles Norris and Reyntiens were proposed for the stained glass, the latter eventually appointed. The Stations of the Cross were to be 'based on [a] linear conception such as "wired sculpture" or on "statuette types"', Faczynski proposing Henry Moore as the sculptor. David John was to be asked for a statue of the Virgin Mary, and, for the external tympanum, Crichton suggested Kossowski.[50] Most of this ambitious scheme went to plan (Plate 8, Figure 5.10):

5.9   Metropolitan Cathedral
of Christ the King, Liverpool,
by Frederick Gibberd,
1960–67. Crucifix by Elisabeth
Frink © Estate of Elisabeth
Frink, all rights reserved,
DACS, London, 2013; stained
glass behind by John Piper
and Patrick Reyntiens, ©
Patrick Reyntiens, all rights
reserved, DACS, London,
2013. By permission of the
Dean of the Metropolitan
Cathedral of Christ the King.
Photo: Robert Proctor, 2010

Reyntiens made an abstract composition in *dalle de verre* whose blue and green
colours symbolised the Creation and the Immaculate Conception of the Virgin
Mary; Kossowski produced one of his most dramatic works, an external ceramic
frieze of the Last Judgement and also made a ceramic cross depicting Christ as High
Priest to hang over the altar. Faczynski himself designed a tapestry to hang behind
the Blessed Sacrament chapel altar, visible from the nave of the church, directly
inspired by Sutherland at Coventry, but here with an image of the Crucifixion
more orthodox than those of Sutherland. The diocese made little objection to
the scheme of artworks. Its one complaint was that Kossowski's cross was not
adequately liturgical and an additional crucifix had to be added for the altar.[51]

A Liverpool sculptor, Arthur Dooley, accepted the commission for the Stations of the Cross, producing a striking series in bronze placed in the V-shaped pillars surrounding the nave. Dooley was by then a local celebrity, a Catholic convert and a communist. He used his sculptures at Leyland as an opportunity to explore modern political themes allied to the narrative subjects. 'St. Veronica of the Stations', he wrote, 'embodies the idea of the natural goodness and humanity in the very nature of women (and men)'; and he explained how the figure of Simon of Cyrene not only helped Christ carry the cross but was also the soldier nailing Christ to it: 'I hope to show by this that in a society where the ruling classes have the power to govern and dictate to the workers, then the ordinary man loses his right to make personal decisions'.[52] Christ's death was announced by a newspaper seller's billboard; the Roman soldiers were faceless and machine-like, some with swastikas, others with Franco-era Spanish coins embedded in them; the imprint of Christ's face on Veronica's veil became graffiti on a brick wall (Figure 5.11); an emaciated child symbolised global poverty.[53] This radical commission brought Leyland widespread publicity after it was installed in 1965, a television documentary bringing it to a national audience while the Catholic press delighted in the sensational story.[54] Fitzsimons evidently wanted to position Leyland at the summit of Roman Catholic avant-garde art at a time when Liverpool Metropolitan Cathedral was still under construction, demonstrating the Church's modernity and culture to the nation.

5.10   St Mary, Leyland, by Weightman & Bullen, 1960–64. Suspended crucifix in ceramic by Adam Kossowski; Virgin and Child by Ian Stuart; Blessed Sacrament chapel tapestry of the Crucifixion by Jerzy Faczynski, made by the Edinburgh Tapestry Company; stained glass by Patrick Reyntiens, © Patrick Reyntiens, all rights reserved, DACS, London, 2013. Photo: Elsam, Mann & Cooper, c.1964. Source: parish archive

CATHOLIC ARTISTIC CULTURE

While the use of such notable artists as Schotz, Sutherland, Piper and Dooley made headlines and attracted non-Catholic interest, most church art remained relatively conventional. At St Aidan, Sutherland's Crucifixion painting contrasted with the more familiar forms of works by Philip Lindsey Clark and Adam Kossowski, and at St Bernadette, Lancaster, the Stations of the Cross were representational, carved in stone by Peter Watts, while other sculptures there were made by Clark's son, Michael. These artists contributed a wealth of sculpture to new churches across Britain. The inspiration for their approach was Eric Gill. Gill's most important church work had been the series of Stations of the Cross he produced for Westminster Cathedral from 1915, which, though controversial at the time for their unfamiliar hieratic style, were soon accepted and long remained influential.[55] Watts's Stations of the Cross at Lancaster, for example, used a tough formal style of figure, conveying emotions associated with their subject matter through angular and calculatedly uncomfortable compositions (Figure 5.12). In a similar mode, artist David John produced a great many pieces for churches of all kinds. For F. X. Velarde, he created integrated architectural sculpture at the shrine of Our Lady of Lourdes in Blackpool and sculptural reliefs for the entrance front of St Luke, Pinner. In wood, he carved modern figurative statues, many in churches by Weightman & Bullen, including that at Leyland. One of his most interesting and expressive works was a long frieze of the Stations of the Cross in wood for the church of St Mary Magdalene, Cudworth, in 1961, one of several of his works there for architect John Rochford (Figure 5.13). These artists and others sustained and developed a distinctive culture – even a 'tradition' – of twentieth-century Roman Catholic church art owing more to Gill's version of the Arts and Crafts movement than to avant-garde modernism.

One important means of cultivating the sense of a unified Catholic artistic culture was the Guild of Catholic Artists and Craftsmen, founded in 1929, its name suggestive of a medieval corporation as interpreted by William Morris and Gill, though it was renamed the Society of Catholic Artists in 1964.[56] Architects were just as prominent within it as artists. The older generation included Philip Lindsey Clark and Goodhart-Rendel; Alfred Bullen of Weightman & Bullen was its secretary in the 1950s.[57] Younger members later took over, including Paul Quail, a stained-glass artist, Lance Wright, Gerard Goalen, David John and Adam Kossowski. Through the organisation of exhibitions and meetings it brought together all generations and disciplines of artists and designers, often with a special focus on liturgical art. In 1960, for example, the guild staged an exhibition, 'Church Building and Art', at the Building Centre in London, including Stations of the Cross made for the church of the Holy Apostles, Pimlico, by Philip Lindsey Clark; Graham Sutherland's Crucifixion painting at Chichester; competition designs for Liverpool Metropolitan Cathedral by Frederick Gibberd, Denys Lasdun and Lance Wright; and works by Robert Maguire, Francis Pollen, Patrick Reyntiens and others.[58] It is tempting to see this exhibition as another catalyst for the acceptance of modern art in Catholic churches in the 1960s.

Perhaps this group's most important activity for developing an intellectual approach to art as well as for attracting patronage was its annual 'Visual Arts Week' at Spode House in Staffordshire. Spode House was a wing of a Dominican priory, and this event took place with the encouragement and organisation of Conrad Pepler, a Dominican priest who had been raised by his father Hilary in Gill's artistic community at Ditchling. The 'Visual Arts Weeks' were well attended by artists, architects, clergy and Catholic intellectuals and involved a brief but often transformative ferment of creative energy. In 1956, for example, delegates engaged in team design projects for a convent chapel and a parish church: an architect led each team, and members designed artworks and liturgical furnishings together.[59] The title of the 1962 event was 'Sacred Art in a Geometric Environment', and its programme included a demonstration of sculpture by David John and lectures from Joseph Rykwert, architectural critic Colin Rowe and Christopher Cornford, newly appointed at the Royal College of Art.[60] Speakers were sometimes invited from France, including theologian Louis Bouyer, who wrote on liturgy and architecture, and Maurice Cocagnac, a Dominican, editor of L'Art sacré and an architect and painter.[61] These conferences were evidently vital events both in the development of a Catholic culture of the arts and in its engagement with wider modern culture.

There was an extremely broad range of art and of architects' collaborations with artists in post-war British Roman Catholic church architecture, from the conventional statuary that many still liked to the thoughtful and comprehensive integration of contemporary art and architecture at Leyland and Liverpool. Modern artists and architects aimed to explore the limits of acceptability in church art by presenting familiar devotional elements in unexpected new forms, forcing the faithful to think more deeply about how their devotions might be interpreted in ways that were relevant in the modern world. At the same time, modern art was commissioned for a wider public audience, intended to demonstrate Catholic participation in modern culture to the world beyond the Church.

5.12   St Bernadette, Lancaster, by Tom Mellor, 1958. Stations of the Cross by Peter Watts (Nailing of Christ to the Cross). By permission of Richard Watts. Photo: Robert Proctor, 2011

5.13   St Mary Magdalene, Cudworth, by John Rochford, 1960–61. Stations of the Cross by David John. By permission of David John. Photo: Robert Proctor, 2009

NOTES

1   The idea comes from Pierre Bourdieu, *Outline of a Theory of Practice*, 187–97.

2   Mumford, *The CIAM Discourse*, 203–13; Jacqueline Tyrwhitt, Josep Luis Sert and Ernesto Rogers (eds), *The Heart of the City: Towards the Humanisation of Urban Life* (London: Lund Humphries, 1952).

3   Seemingly this is a subject which has not yet been well researched (see for example Robert Melville, 'Personnages [*sic*] in Iron', *Architectural Review* [Sept. 1950], 147–51).

4   Dolores Mitchell, 'Art Patronage by the London County Council (L.C.C.), 1948–1965', *Leonardo* 10 (1977), 207–12.

5   Nigel J. Abercrombie, 'The Approach to English Local Authorities, 1963–1978', in John Pick (ed.), *The State and the Arts* (Eastbourne: John Offord, 1980), 66–7; John Pick, 'Introduction: The Best for the Most', ibid. 9–14.

6   Rubin, *Modern Sacred Art and the Church of Assy*, 35–7.

7   Ibid. 37–8; Joseph Pichard, *L'Art sacré moderne* (Paris: B. Arthaud, 1953), 97, 113–14; Régamey was less open to non-Christian artists, but did not exclude them (P.-R. Régamey, *Art sacré au XXe siècle?* [Paris: Éditions du Cerf, 1952], 75–7).

8   Orenduff, *Transformation of Catholic Religious Art*, 62.

9   Rubin, *Modern Sacred Art and the Church of Assy*, 70–71.

10 For a substantial and detailed discussion of abstract art in post-war Catholic thought and practice, see George Mercier, *L'Art abstrait dans l'art sacré: La Tendance non-figurative dans l'art sacré chrétien contemporain* (Paris: Éditions E. De Boccard, 1964).

11 Adrian Fortescue, *The Ceremonies of the Roman Rite Described*, revd J. B. O'Connell (London: Burns Oates & Washbourne, 1948), 7; J. B. O'Connell, 'Questions and Answers', *Clergy Review* 43 (1958), 41; but see id., 'Questions and Answers', *Clergy Review* 46 (1961), 49–50; Orenduff, *Transformation of Catholic Religious Art*, 135–55.

12 For Stüflesser statuary (though some may have been by Tyrolean competitor firms), see for example St Joseph, Ramsbottom, *CBRN* (1963), 90–91; Brian Moorhouse, *St Augustine's, Lowerhouse: Centenary, 1896–1996* (1996), 28 (SDA, Parish Files); St Thomas More, Sheldon, in Bryan Little, 'Four New Birmingham Churches', *Clergy Review* 55 (1970), 1009–14 (1014). In many more cases a reference to statuary 'carved in Italy' seems to be Stüflesser.

13 Colleen McDannell, *Material Christianity: Religion and Popular Culture in America* (New Haven: Yale University Press, 1995), 171, ch. 6.

14 Charles Blakeman, 'The Problem of Church Art', *Clergy Review* 40 (1955), 22–33.

15 J. D. Crichton, 'Art at the Service of the Liturgy', in id. (ed.), *The Liturgy and the Future* (Tenbury Wells: Fowler Wright Books, 1966), 164–73 (164–5).

16 Blakeman, 'The Problem of Church Art', 27; McDannell, *Material Christianity*, 180–85; for another view, see Susan O'Brien, 'Making Catholic Spaces: Women, Décor, and Devotion in the English Catholic Church, 1840–1900', in Diana Wood (ed.), *The Church and the Arts: Papers Read at the 1990 Summer Meeting and the 1991 Winter Meeting of the Ecclesiastical History Society*, Studies in Church History 28 (Oxford: Blackwell, 1992). Walker notes that anti-kitsch rhetoric had a longer history ('Developments in Catholic Churchbuilding', 138–9).

17 McDannell, *Material Christianity*, 177–8; see also for example Roulin, *Modern Church Architecture*, 805.

18   Romano Guardini, *The Spirit of the Liturgy*, trans. Ada Lane (London: Sheed & Ward, 1930), 12–19 (esp. n. on p. 12).

19   'Constitution on the Sacred Liturgy', in Abbott, *The Documents of Vatican II*, 174.

20   Anton Henze, 'The Potentialities of Modern Church Art and Its Position in History', in Anton Henze and Theodor Filthaut (eds), *Contemporary Church Art*, trans. Cecily Hastings (New York: Sheed & Ward, 1956), 15–48 (31).

21   Basil Spence, *Phoenix at Coventry: The Building of a Cathedral* (London: Geoffrey Bles, 1962), 36–8; Garth Turner, ' "Aesthete, Impresario, and Indomitable Persuader": Walter Hussey at St Matthew's, Northampton, and Chichester Cathedral', in Wood (ed.), *Church and the Arts*, 524–5.

22   Spence, *Phoenix at Coventry*, 52–3.

23   June Osborne, *John Piper and Stained Glass* (Stroud: Sutton Publishing, 1997), 41–8, 27–33.

24   Spence, *Phoenix at Coventry*, 88, 105.

25   Joseph Rykwert, 'Passé récent et problèmes actuels de l'art sacré', in D. Mathew et al., *Catholicisme Anglais* (Paris: Éditions du Cerf, 1958), 291–8 (297–8).

26   James Ethrington, 'The Church of St Aidan, East Acton, London, W3', in James Ethrington and Terence Mullaly (eds), *St Aidan's, East Acton: The Church and its Art* (London: n.p., *c.*1964), unpaginated.

27   'Biographical Notes', in Ethrington and Mullaly (eds), *St Aidan's, East Acton*.

28   Terence Mullaly, 'Art at St Aidan's', in Ethrington and Mullaly (eds), *St Aidan's, East Acton*. Mullaly later wrote an article on the church for *The Telegraph*, reprinted as 'Challenge in the Church', *Bulletin of the Society of Catholic Artists* (May 1968), 2–4 (ASCA).

29   'From Our Notebook', *The Tablet* (23 Feb. 1963), 200.

30   Anthony P. Kirwin, 'A Way Through the Weeds: Graham Sutherland's "Crucifixion" in East Acton', *The Tablet* (11 Jan. 1964), 181–2.

31   'Should This Painting be Rubbed Out?', [*Daily*] *Express* (n.d.) [newspaper clipping] (LRCDA, parish file for St Bernadette).

32   Minutes of meeting of the Cathedral Executive Committee (12 Oct. 1961); Frederick Gibberd, 'Report on Progress and Points for Discussion with his Grace the Archbishop and the Cathedral Committee' (11 Jan. 1961) (LRCAA, Cathedral Collection, S2/XI/A/2).

33   Frederick Gibberd, *Metropolitan Cathedral of Christ the King, Liverpool* (London: Architectural Press, 1968), 69.

34   Illtud Evans to Archbishop Heenan (9 Dec. 1961) (LRCAA, Cathedral Collection, S2/IX/A/93).

35   'Notes on a Meeting with Dr. J. D. Crichton, Fr. B. E. Fitzsimons and J. Faczynski at Manchester, 10th August, 1961, concerning the art works for the new Church' (parish archive, St Mary, Leyland, 'New Church: Art Works'); Libby Horner, 'Patrick Reyntiens' Autonomous Panels: Myth, Music and Theatre', *Decorative Arts Society Journal* 35 (2011), 63–80 (64–7).

36   Spence, *Phoenix at Coventry*, 68.

37   Jonathan Cronshaw, ' "This Work Has Never Been Commissioned At All": Jacob Epstein's Madonna and Child', *Art and Christianity* 66 (Summer 2011), 5–7; Evelyn Silber, *The Sculpture of Epstein* (Oxford: Phaidon, 1986), 55, 209; Jacob Epstein, *Epstein: An Autobiography* (London: Hulton Press, 1955), 235–6.

38   Spence, *Phoenix at Coventry*, 68; Epstein, *Epstein*, 236; Silber, *The Sculpture of Epstein*, 55.

39   For example Peter Watts, letter to the editor, *The Tablet* (31 Apr. 1952), 442; Iris Conlay, letter to the editor, *The Tablet* (7 June 1952), 465; Peter Watts, letter to the editor, *The Tablet* (14 June 1952), 482; W. E. Pattin, letter to the editor, *The Tablet* (14 June 1952), 482; Lance Wright, letter to the editor, *The Tablet* (21 June 1952), 502; Peter Watts, letter to the editor, *The Tablet* (21 June 1952), 502; Lance Wright, letter to the editor, *The Tablet* (28 June 1952), 524.

40   Benno Schotz to Jack Coia (24 Mar. 1961) (GSAA, GKC/CHK/1/7); Benno Schotz, *Bronze in My Blood: The Memoirs of Benno Schotz* (Edinburgh: Gordon Wright, 1981), 208–9.

41   Schotz, *Bronze in My Blood*, 210–12.

42   Augustine Harris to Gibberd (29 Oct. 1966) (LRCAA, Cathedral Collection, S2/X/A/114).

43   Gibberd to Monsignor Thomas G. McKenna (Aug. 1966) (LRCAA, Cathedral Collection, S2/X/A/108).

44   Beck to Gibberd (29 June 1965) (LRCAA, Cathedral Collection, S2/X/A/75).

45   Beck to Gibberd (4 Mar. 1965) (LRCAA, Cathedral Collection, S2/X/A/82).

46   Gibberd to Beck (20 Jan. 1967) (LRCAA, Cathedral Collection, S2/X/A/123).

47   Beck to Gibberd (27 Feb. 1967) (LRCAA, Cathedral Collection, S2/X/A/125).

48   Frank Harrison, *St Mary's, Leyland: The History of a Catholic Community* (Preston: n.p., 1995), 92–3; Edward Corbould, 'St Mary's Priory Church, Leyland', *Churchbuilding*, 13 (Oct. 1964), 3–9 (3); see also George G. Pace, 'Review of New Church: St Mary's Priory, Leyland', *Clergy Review* 50 (1965), 81–8. At the time of research, the parish archive of St Mary's 'New Church: Art Works' box contained, amongst other things: a postcard and leaflet of Audincourt; a programme and papers from a conference on 'New Church Architecture' at Liverpool University of 1960, including papers by for example Robert Maguire and William Lockett on 'New Church Buildings in France and Germany', with Fitzsimons listed as a delegate; a leaflet on Gabriel Loire's *dalle de verre* glass in France; and the itinerary for the Birmingham tour, dated 1959, including visits to Le Raincy, Audincourt and Ronchamp; an article on Pierre Fourmaintraux (Marian Curd, 'Playing With Light', *Catholic Herald* [12 May 1962]); an unreferenced newspaper cutting on modern churches in Mexico, including work by Felix Candela; copies of *Churchbuilding*; newsletters from the University of Birmingham Institute for the Study of Worship and Religious Architecture; correspondence with artists.

49   J. D. Crichton to Edmund Fitzsimons (9 July 1959) (parish archive, St Mary, Leyland, 'New Church: Art Works').

50   'Notes on a Meeting with Dr. J. D. Crichton, Fr. B. E. Fitzsimons and J. Faczynski at Manchester, 10th August, 1961, concerning the art works for the new Church'; Jonah Jones to Fitzsimons (26 Jan. 1962) (parish archive, St Mary, Leyland, 'New Church: Art Works') .

51   Sites and Buildings Commission (19 July 1960) (LRCAA, Finance Collection, 12/S3/III).

52   Arthur Dooley, 'Stations of the Cross' (n.d.) (parish archive, St Mary, Leyland, 'New Church, Art Works').

53   Simon Caldwell, 'One Man's Passion', *The Universe* English edn (26 Nov. 1995), 7.

54   A transcript of the BBC film, *A Modern Passion* (broadcast 7 Apr. 1966), is present in the 'New Church, Art Works' box of the parish archive of St Mary, Leyland.

55   Roulin, *Modern Church Architecture*, 34–5; Rykwert, 'Passé recent et problèmes actuels', 295–6.

56   *Bulletin of the Society of Catholic Artists* (Dec. 1964) (ASCA).

57   For example A. Bullen (Weightman & Bullen) to David John (5 Nov. 1956) (ASCA).

58   Guild of Catholic Artists and Craftsmen, 'Church Building & Art' [exhibition notice] (Nov.–Dec. 1960) (ASCA); Iris Conlay, 'Patronage the Only Answer', *Catholic Herald* (9 Dec. 1960), 5.

59   Paul Quail, newsletter (June 1956) (ASCA). The following year the idea was extended to a design project for a 'Catholic City Centre': Conrad Pepler (Spode House) to Paul [Quail] (honorary secretary, Guild of Catholic Artists and Craftsmen), 13 July [1956]; Paul Quail, typed news sheet (June 1957) (ASCA).

60   Programme for 'Visual Arts Week' (1962) (ASCA).

61   David John, telephone interview with Ambrose Gillick (12 June 2013); Louis Bouyer, *Liturgy and Architecture* (Notre Dame, IN: University of Notre Dame Press, 1967).

6

Modernism and the Liturgical Movement

The year 1960 was a watershed in the creation of a modern Catholic church architecture, not least because it was then that one of the most important books for church design of the twentieth century was published. Peter Hammond's *Liturgy and Architecture* set out for architects and clergy the case for a modern church architecture based primarily on the function of liturgy. Hammond argued that the basilican form of church had developed in the Middle Ages to enshrine an excessively clerical liturgy remote from the congregation. Instead, he urged a church architecture that promoted congregational involvement, a 'corporate worship', which, he thought, would recapture the spirit of early Christian liturgy.[1] The Anglican church of St Paul at Bow Common in London by Robert Maguire and Keith Murray opened the same year and was widely published in connection with Hammond's arguments. The book and the building contributed to an architectural discourse that outlined a new approach to church design, drawing from the liturgical movement in the Roman Catholic Church, already then gaining ground in Britain, and substantially influencing architects and clergy in the design of Catholic churches. This chapter examines some pioneering examples of architectural and clerical collaboration in producing this new liturgical architecture.

Hammond's book was polemical in tone and arose in the context of an organisation he helped to found in 1957, the New Churches Research Group (NCRG). Most of this group's members were young architects, and they met regularly in the basement bar of the Architectural Press offices in London. Catholic architect Maguire and his colleague Murray, an ecclesiastical designer, were founding members. Also involved was Catholic architect Lance Wright, frequent contributor to *The Tablet* and technical editor for the *Architects' Journal*, giving the group access to professional publications. As the NCRG publicised its ideas in the 1960s, its membership expanded, including John Newton of Burles, Newton & Partners, designer of a large number of Catholic churches in London, and Austin Winkley, a Catholic church architect and lay activist. Patrick Nuttgens, Patrick Reyntiens and Liverpool architect Peter Gilbey were also involved. The group was interdenominational, later also including Anglican church architect George Pace among its members. Clergy were also present. Hammond himself was an Anglican priest and theological writer.[2] Charles Davis, a Catholic priest and theologian teaching at St Edmund's Seminary at Ware was an early participant. Most founding members of the NCRG were young and sympathetic to the emerging avant-garde architectural discourse of the New Brutalism, and indeed Peter Smithson was invited to speak at an early meeting. The NCRG and New Brutalism had much in common: theoretically, in their rejections of prevailing conventions in architecture, and socially, as groups of 'angry young men'.[3]

The NCRG organised lectures and conferences and undertook a campaign of publication.[4] Following the publication of *Liturgy and Architecture*, Hammond edited a book of talks given by early group members including Wright and Davis, entitled *Towards a Church Architecture* in evocation of Le Corbusier's manifesto of modern architecture.[5] Meanwhile the quarterly magazine *Church Buildings Today*, started in 1960 by publisher John Catt, began its first issue with a polemical article by Maguire and Murray summarising Hammond's demand that architects understand the functions of a church from first principles.[6] For a few years Maguire and Murray edited the magazine, changing its name to *Churchbuilding*. It acted as a forum for debate amongst members of the NCRG and others, including critical accounts of new buildings in Britain and abroad. Another group had an equally important and related role: the NCRG's aims were shared by the Institute for the Study of Worship and Religious Architecture at Birmingham University, founded around the same time and led by Anglican theologians Gilbert Cope and John Gordon Davies. This academic organisation also contributed to *Churchbuilding* and organised tours and lecture series that complemented the NCRG's activities.

Meanwhile Lance Wright also wrote reviews of churches, sometimes anonymously, for the *Architects' Journal*, further propagating the group's thinking. Under his chairmanship from 1964, NCRG members published a series of functional studies of each denomination's requirements in the *Architects' Journal*, issued in book form as a 'briefing guide' in 1967, a publication that fulfilled Hammond's original call for a 'liturgical brief'.[7] Wright also organised a conference on Roman Catholic church architecture attended by 60 architects that, at Cardinal Heenan's suggestion, produced a guide for clergy and architects involved in reordering existing churches.[8] Wright's practice, in which Peter Ansdell Evans and Nigel Melhuish were also partners, went on to design three small Catholic churches in the late 1960s, St Cecilia, Trimley; St Gregory, Alresford; and Christ Our Hope, Beare Green, all incorporating NCRG principles: indeed Trimley was really a collaborative and experimental design by the Catholic group in the NCRG.[9] The group's work was not only confined to architectural discourse, however. When Charles Davis became editor of the Catholic *Clergy Review* in 1963, he substantially changed its tone, commissioning critical reviews of new churches, many written by fellow group members including Wright, Nuttgens and Winkley. Beginning as a relatively informal avant-garde organisation, therefore, the NCRG embarked on a successful campaign of publication which soon made modern church architecture synonymous with the liturgical movement.

The group had two core ideas: an emphasis on functional analysis as the primary determinant of architecture and a concept of the liturgy as a communal act undertaken by the whole congregation. Church architects, they insisted, had to analyse liturgy as the church's primary function. Yet rather than enshrine existing rites, architects were to employ an ideal concept of liturgy. Modern church architecture therefore had an agenda of religious and social reform.[10] Congregational involvement in the liturgy was the primary aim, since the original, authentic purpose of liturgy in early Christianity was thought to have been the collective, participatory worship of God by everyone present. The new concept of liturgy would be socially liberating: 'We still have to face the fundamental problem of restoring to the Christian layman his true priestly liturgy – both in and out of church', wrote Hammond, 'and of overcoming the psychological proletarianism that is part of the legacy of the Middle Ages'.[11] Thus modern church architecture would bring dignity to the laity with their involvement in worship. New spatial forms could change the congregation's perception of itself and its role in liturgy, affecting people's behaviour. The altar had to be close to the congregation; divisions between congregation and sanctuary had to be reduced, though a hierarchy of spaces was still preferred; distractions from the Eucharistic liturgy had to be removed; and the faithful were to be brought into relation with each other as an 'organic unity'.[12]

If liturgical function was the most important aspect of a church, symbolism therefore took second place. Hammond discouraged overt symbolism or expressive design in a pointed reference to Liverpool Metropolitan Cathedral and certain recent American churches:

> Churches are built to 'express' this and to 'symbolize' that. We have churches which look like hands folded in prayer; churches which symbolize aspiration or the anchor of the industrial pilgrim's life; churches which express the kingship of Christ; churches shaped like fishes, flames, and passion-flowers. There are still very few churches which show signs of anything comparable to the radical functional analysis that informs the best secular architecture of our time.[13]

Artworks were also considered with caution as potential distractions from the liturgy. Coventry Cathedral, for Basil Minchin writing in *Churchbuilding*, employed modern art for mere 'religious sentiment', becoming a 'museum of religious art', while the domination of the church by Sutherland's tapestry detracted from the altar.[14] Even church towers were suspect, ecclesiastical clichés now that they no longer served their original functions.[15]

The principles of architectural modernism resonated with those of liturgical reform and scholarship. Hammond wanted to restore a supposedly primitive and pure idea of liturgy, recovering its fundamental principles. Likewise the architecture of the church could be analysed for its principles: 'Reduced to its bare essentials, it is a building to house a congregation gathered round an altar', he argued, and his simple but potent diagrams claimed to show how a congregation would arrange itself if unconstrained by architecture or convention.[16] Liturgical historians such as Jesuit Josef Jungmann and Anglican Gregory Dix had sought the underlying stable principles of the liturgy beneath its historically shifting surface appearances: the 'primitive picture' of worship, as Jungmann put it; Dix's 'shape of the liturgy'.[17]

Modernist architects also proposed to discard the inessential. Siegfried Giedion, for example, had divided architecture into 'constituent' and 'transitory facts': the latter were ephemeral characteristics and motifs across history, and the former were the stable underpinnings of architectural form that architects had to identify in developing a 'new tradition'.[18] To divest themselves of acquired but unnecessary habits in design, architects increasingly studied social activities, often through diagrams like Hammond's, to design buildings as sheltering envelopes for essential functions. The aesthetics of modern architecture continued this essentialism by rejecting ornament in favour of plain materials and volumes, revealing the human activities they contained.

Hammond's ideas therefore resonated with those of young brutalist architects, who maintained an idealistic social agenda and felt that modern architecture itself needed to return to its principles. The Smithsons and other members of Team 10 published polemical articles arguing that architects had to consider human social groups and communities as the primary motivations in design:

> Architecture is concerned with finding the pattern of buildings and communications which make the community function and, at the same time, give it meaning. To make the community comprehensible to itself, to give it identity, is also the work of the politician and the poet, but it is the work of the architect to make it visible.[19]

Similarly, for the founders of the NCRG, the church architect's task was to effect and reveal the community of the faithful brought together in worship.

The NCRG's ideas led to an interest in alternative European precedents in church architecture, shifting attention from France to Germany. While Le Corbusier's handling of materials remained influential, his religious architecture was seen as liturgically conventional. 'Ronchamp', wrote Maguire and Murray, 'has provided a justification for architects to ignore any discipline, to pursue private whimsy without concern for function .... In the development of church building, it is a blind alley.'[20] Instead, Hammond and his colleagues looked to Rudolf Schwarz, who had been designing churches since the 1920s for the Diocese of Cologne based on theological and liturgical study, using modern construction techniques and an austere approach. Hammond illustrated Schwarz's pre-war churches of Corpus Christi at Aachen, completed in 1930, praising the essentialism of its white walls and prominent altar, and St Albert, Leversbach, of 1932, a 'liturgical shed of the utmost simplicity for a small rural community'.[21] Similarly, highlighting buildings from a trip to Europe organised by the Birmingham Institute in 1961, Gilbert Cope and Giles Blomfield praised Schwarz's new church of St Christophoros at Niehl, an industrial suburb of Cologne (Figure 6.1):

> The church at first seems as harsh as its surroundings; in fact it is a salutary reminder of the essentials of the Christian faith. Here is a severely simple eucharistic room; the crude expression of the plain brick box derives from the singleness of purpose, clearly understood and fulfilled. ... The great value of the building is to remind us what a church is really for; the place where the community meets to offer worship.[22]

6.1   St Christophorus, Niehl, Cologne, by Rudolf Schwarz, 1958–60. Stained glass and painting of the Risen Christ by Georg Meistermann © DACS, London, 2013. Photographer unknown. Source: © Rheinisches Bildarchiv Köln

For post-war British church architects, Schwarz was a model for the integration of architectural modernism and liturgical thinking.

Schwarz had been associated early in his career with the Catholic liturgical movement through contact with Romano Guardini, theologian and author of *The Spirit of the Liturgy*, for whom Schwarz had designed a small chapel at a Catholic youth centre in a castle at Rothenfels. Schwarz's first book, *Vom Bau der Kirche*, translated for an American publisher as *The Church Incarnate: The Sacred Function of Christian Architecture*, was especially powerful for modern architects because of its abstracted diagrams of relationships between congregation, celebrant and God.[23] Like Hammond later, Schwarz wanted to consider the church's fundamental needs:

> *Table, space and walls make up the simplest church. The little congregation sits or stands about the table. ... We cannot continue on from where the last cathedrals left off. Instead we must enter into the simple things at the source of the Christian life. We must begin anew and our new beginning must be genuine.*[24]

For Schwarz, however, the purpose of this analysis of liturgical space was more symbolic and mystical than British architects' often more strictly functionalist approaches.[25] Though sometimes creatively misread by British writers and architects, Schwarz's architecture indicated a path for reform.

Other German architects, especially Emil Steffan and Dominikus Böhm, were also influential. These architects and their clerical clients engaged with a political discourse in Germany of community cohesion: worship, and therefore church architecture, it was argued, should bring people together to counteract the tendency to anonymity in modern urban life.[26] Their approach made them especially attractive to British church architects inspired by the New Brutalism and liturgical thought. Italy could provide further inspiration: Joseph Rykwert, for example, argued as early as 1956 for a church architecture based on programmatic analysis, praising the circular-naved church of S. Maria Nascente in the experimental housing district of QT8 in Milan.[27]

Maguire and Murray's Anglican church at Bow Common explored these emerging concepts, working them out through practice. Maguire and Murray benefited from collaboration with their client, Gresham Kirkby, an Anglo-Catholic and socialist with knowledge of the European liturgical movement.[28] In the temporary hall used before the church was built, Kirkby had developed liturgical forms that attempted to embody an idea of communal worship: at communion the congregation gathered, standing, around the altar, each member receiving the Eucharist before the whole congregation returned to their seats, and congregational processions were also encouraged.[29] Maguire and Murray incorporated these practices with a broad plan, slightly longer than it was wide, a processional route around its edge marked with paving slabs and defined by reinforced-concrete columns and a vaulted ceiling; the altar was placed off-centre under the lantern, on a low platform in an open sanctuary, and the seating was set back from it around three sides allowing room for communion (Figure 6.2). A metal ciborium added shortly after the opening in 1960 enhanced the altar's presence. Maguire and Murray described their church using similar spatial and mystical terms to Schwarz:

The liturgy may be seen as a movement towards the place of the altar; in other words the incorporation of the individual person into the sacrificial life of Christ, or movement towards the transfiguring light. ... A church is the place of the assembly of the people of God. It is a holy place, consecrated, set apart, for this purpose.[30]

6.2   St Paul, Bow Common, London, by Robert Maguire & Keith Murray, 1958–60. Photograph taken on completion *c.*1960 but before installation of the ciborium. Photo: Eric de Maré. Source: Architectural Press Archive / RIBA Library Photographs Collection

Bow Common went some way beyond Hammond's more severely functionalist intentions, retaining High-Church notions of sacred space and sacrifice. Yet it provided a convincing and widely published model of a liturgical modern church architecture, and did so with a brutalist material expression that emphasised fundamental characteristics.[31]

Hammond's *Liturgy and Architecture* had received some criticism, even from sympathisers, for its almost exclusive emphasis on the Eucharistic rite. Cope wrote that the church was 'a liturgically dual purpose volume', its other most important function being to accommodate baptism.[32] His colleague at the Birmingham Institute, Davies, was just then working on a book about the architecture of baptism for Hammond's publisher.[33] At Bow Common, Maguire and Murray made baptism a significant element in their design, with a prominent font placed near the entrance in one corner of the church's processional circuit, symbolising the sacrament as the entrance into the kingdom of God, as Davies later urged in his book. Yet Bow

Common was also criticised for reductivism, since it did not include any permanent place for readings, contradicting many Anglicans' emphasis on scripture.[34]

Bishop Beck of Salford warned Catholics against taking Hammond too literally: Catholics, he wrote, differed from Protestants in viewing the liturgy as a 'sacrifice of propitiation' rather than solely a commemoration of the Last Supper, a distinction that he thought 'is bound to affect not only the liturgy of worship but the character of the building in which that worship takes place'. He supported Hammond's arguments, but gave them a Catholic inflection: 'We must seek to build churches which will be adapted to the needs of a more consciously corporate worshipping community, performing in its own locality through the power of its own priest the sacrificial action of the Mystical Body of Christ'.[35] This complexity was also present in the liturgical movement itself as it developed in the Roman Catholic Church in the twentieth century until its eventual acceptance at the Second Vatican Council. Liturgical reformers received qualified approbation from Church authorities, and were already influencing Catholic church architecture in Britain when the NCRG was established.

THE LITURGICAL MOVEMENT IN THE CHURCH

The liturgical movement originated in the nineteenth century when new scholarship on the history and theology of liturgy resulted in a desire to change liturgical practice.[36] In the early twentieth century, the Benedictine abbey of Maria Laach in Germany pursued liturgical theology and innovation, becoming a centre for conferences and publications. Influenced by early Christian writers, Abbot Ildefons Herwegen and fellow monk Odo Casel insisted on the liturgy's central place in the Church, which they described as the 'Mystical Body of Christ' composed of all its members. Liturgy, it was argued, brought the Church together to constitute this body, and Christ became present in the congregation through their gathering to effect redemption. An influential moment in the liturgical movement was a Mass said by Herwegen at Maria Laach during a conference in 1914: a wooden altar was placed in the church's crypt, the celebrant faced the people, and the congregation recited parts of the Mass together.[37] The 'dialogue Mass', as it was known, became widespread in Germany after its approval in 1929.[38] Meanwhile historical studies such as Jungmann's *Mass of the Roman Rite* argued that the liturgy's history was characterised by gradual formalisation and ceremonial enrichment, trends that made it increasingly clerical and detached from the congregation, who were reduced to 'spectators looking on at a mystery-filled drama'. The early Christian Mass, in contrast, had been fluid and extemporised, characterised by a 'community spirit', a 'feeling of oneness', now lacking.[39] The historical study of liturgy and its architectural settings showed its variety and contingency, opening the way for reform.

A further development in the liturgical movement took place in France, where parish clergy developed the idea of a 'pastoral liturgy' that could educate the laity in its meanings as it was performed. The Centre de Pastorale Liturgique was founded in Paris in 1943, promoting this concept through conferences and its journal, *La Maison Dieu*.[40] In France the worker-priest movement saw priests assuming working-class occupations as a missionary technique, and 'Catholic Action' was especially strong, a movement to involve the laity in all aspects of parish organisation and evangelisation. Missionary approaches were applied to ordinary city parishes. Henri Godin, a priest in a Paris suburb, argued that the majority in his parish were not effectively Christian and needed conversion. For that to work, Christian worship had to be adapted to the culture of the urban poor. 'Our religion must be religion pure and simple', argued Godin, 'stripped bare of all the human adjuncts, rich though these may be, which involve a different civilisation'.[41] The Mission de Paris followed, a programme of missionary activity, including plain-clothes priests who declared a spirit of poverty, a communal social view of the parish and adaptations of the liturgy and its setting, including Mass in parishioners' houses.[42] Dominican theologian Yves Congar followed these developments closely, and his book *Lay People in the Church* consequently argued for a central role in the Church for the laity, including in the liturgy.[43] The Mission de Paris became well known and influential in Britain, directly influencing Kirkby at Bow Common, for example. The missionary and pastoral approach had important implications for church architecture, which had to provide for an engaging and communal liturgy, but to do so in a spirit of poverty and an awareness of context.

All these movements were independent of the Vatican. The Vatican generally endorsed and encouraged the liturgical movement, allowing moderate developments and adopting many of its proposals through incremental reforms of Church regulations and liturgy while condemning extreme views and experiments. Pius X, on acceding to the papacy in 1903, affirmed the primacy of Gregorian chant for liturgical music, encouraging the laity to form church choirs to restore this ancient liturgical function, and he urged the faithful to receive frequent communion as the highest form of participation in the Eucharist.[44] Pius XII, in office from 1939 to 1958, took great interest in the liturgical movement and confirmed its most important principles. His encyclical of 1943, *Mystici corporis Christi*, endorsed the concept of the Church as the Mystical Body of Christ, and in *Mediator Dei* he encouraged the 'active participation' of the faithful in liturgy, with 'earnestness and concentration'.[45] The Vatican made significant liturgical changes during his office, including the formalisation and dissemination of the dialogue Mass.[46]

The Second Vatican Council, begun by John XXIII and continued by Paul VI, brought the liturgical movement to maturity within the Church. The 'Constitution on the Sacred Liturgy' of 1963 enshrined its principles and announced the reform of the liturgy that took place over the following years, culminating in the new rite of Mass in 1969. The constitution asserted the importance of lay participation and the pastoral nature of liturgy. The liturgy and sacraments had to be 'restored', becoming simpler and more accessible: 'texts and rites should … express more clearly the holy things which they signify. Christian people, as far as possible, should be able to understand them with ease and to take part in them fully, actively, and as befits a community'. Taking its cue from missionary concerns, the constitution encouraged regional diversity, permitting bishops to make alterations relevant to their contexts and encouraging the incorporation of local cultural forms in sacred rites and liturgical objects and furnishings.[47] Behind the making of the constitution were theologians and liturgy scholars at the centre of the liturgical movement, including Congar; voting to implement it at the council in the nave of the basilica of St Peter's in Rome were all the Catholic bishops of the world.

In Britain, knowledge of the liturgical movement before the 1950s was limited and arrived mainly through papal pronouncements: Pius X's statements led to widespread galleries in churches for lay choirs, the elimination of aisle seating so that congregations had unobstructed views of the altar and broad sanctuaries so that large numbers could kneel at the communion rail, all still important in the 1950s.[48] Before the Second World War, the few British Catholics who noticed the liturgical movement tended to be regarded as eccentric. Amongst them was Eric Gill, who wrote an essay on the subject, 'Mass for the Masses', published for a Catholic socialist magazine in 1938. Gill argued that the altar should be in the centre of the church, as a symbol of sacrifice: 'not only does Christ offer Himself in the Holy Sacrifice, but the people also offer themselves. It is a corporate offering', he wrote. Bringing the laity into such a relationship with the altar required new spatial forms, eliminating hierarchies, so that Christianity could 'become again the religion of the people, the common people, the masses'. Architecture could help to achieve this: 'the altar must be brought back again into the middle of our churches, in the middle of the congregation, surrounded by the people', and the church should be plain and humble.[49]

Gill implemented these ideas in the church he designed with parish priest Thomas Walker, St Peter at Gorleston-on-Sea, a simple brick barn-like building opened in 1939, a cross in plan with transepts filled with seating so that the congregation was arranged on three sides of the altar. Another parish priest who was friendly with Gill was John O'Connor, whose chapel-of-ease of Our Lady and the First Martyrs in Bradford, built in 1935 by local architect J. H. Langtry-Langton, sited the altar at the centre of an octagon, the congregation arranged around it (Figure 6.3). Despite their innovations, neither church attracted much attention until the 1950s, when they could be viewed as precursors by Hammond and the NCRG and, perhaps, by certain former bishops of Leeds who knew the church at Bradford: John Heenan as archbishop of Liverpool and later of Westminster and George Dwyer, who became archbishop of Birmingham.

By the 1950s, British awareness of the liturgical movement was growing and the Vatican was reported to be favourable to reform.[50] Clergy with international connections played an important role in disseminating the movement.[51] Clifford Howell, for example, a Jesuit and former missionary, wrote on the liturgical reforms for Catholic newspapers, and published *The Work of Our Redemption* in 1953, a colloquial guide to the Mass for the laity. This work arose from his involvement with the American Benedictine journal, *Worship*, published by the monks of St John in Collegeville, who were at the forefront of liturgical thought in that continent thanks to their connections with German monasteries.[52]

Another important figure was James Crichton, parish priest at Pershore in Worcestershire, where he undertook a small but significant architectural experiment. Crichton was an early member of the Society of Saint Gregory, founded in 1929 to promote the revival of Gregorian chant, its interests soon expanding to the liturgy itself, and he edited its journal, *Liturgy*, from 1952, becoming an important writer on the subject.[53] Crichton followed developments in Europe closely, travelling to

the continent for conferences. In 1953, he went to Lugano for the International Congress on Liturgy, which proposed liturgical reforms around the theme of 'active participation' and where Cardinal Alfredo Ottaviani of the Vatican celebrated Mass facing the people.[54] In 1956, Crichton went to Assisi to attend perhaps the most important post-war conference of the liturgical movement, the International Congress on the Pastoral Liturgy, whose keynote speaker was Pius XII. Crichton attended with his superior, Archbishop Francis Grimshaw of Birmingham and the expert on canon law and liturgy, O'Connell, who summarised the conference for the *Clergy Review*.[55] On returning to Pershore, Crichton began to implement liturgical movement ideas in the design of his new church.

6.3   Our Lady and the First Martyrs, Bradford, by J. H. Langtry-Langton, 1935. The interior has been reordered twice, most recently in 1971 by Peter Langtry-Langton to restore aspects of its original arrangement. Photo: Robert Proctor, 2009

A decade before, he had already written a description of his 'dream church' for the Society of St Gregory. Beginning with a complaint that architects did not adequately consider the liturgy in their designs, he set out the primary functions of the church building, summarising liturgical movement theology in relation to architecture:

> *A church is a miniature of the Mystical Body, a concrete realisation of the heavenly Jerusalem. … It is a cell of the Catholic Body, it is the ecclesia, the meeting place of the people of the parish. … The church exists to make possible the due performance of the principal acts of the Christ-Body. The chief of these is the Eucharist, the Action par excellence of the Church. The altar, then, which is the place of sacrifice, becomes the centre of the church, not merely in the sense that all can see it but, because the sacrifice is also the people's sacrifice … in the sense that the people can gather round it.*[56]

The remainder of the article proposed a church building, including a plan (Figure 6.4). The church would be a domed circle, the altar off-centre in the central part, the seating arranged in a crescent in front of it and to the sides; the altar, he thought, should not be in the centre because the congregation had to be addressed directly by the priest in the liturgy. The sanctuary was to be lower than the nave, but the altar elevated so that it appeared to be at floor level while retaining a modest separation. The altar would be intended for Mass facing the people and the tabernacle placed in a chapel behind the nave. A choir, leading the congregation in liturgical chant, would be located behind the altar. Instead of a pulpit there would be two ambos, a feature taken from early Christian basilicas, for reading the Epistle and the Gospel directly to the congregation instead of facing the altar as the liturgy then required. A broad circuit around the edge of the nave was marked off by columns and devoted to 'solemn processions'. The baptistery would be given a prominent place at the entrance, the holy-water stoups placed alongside it so that when people entered the church they would be reminded of this sacrament of initiation. Side chapels would allow private devotions to be pursued away from the nave so that they did not detract from its liturgical functions. All these innovations became commonplace after Vatican II, though Catholic rules on liturgical furnishings prevented many from being implemented earlier.[57]

At his church of the Holy Redeemer at Pershore, Crichton partially achieved this model in 1959 with the help of architect Hugh Bankart (Figure 6.5, Plan 4d). The church was simply built with red brick and stone trim, necessarily cheap in this rural parish. A steel roof structure gave a broad span over a single interior space. The sanctuary was placed within the main body of the church halfway into the two blocks of seating. 'The whole purpose of the square plan is to gather all the people around the Altar and as close as possible to it', wrote Bankart, adding that the altar was designed so that Mass could be said facing the people if it were ever to be permitted.[58] A communion rail surrounded the sanctuary, but it was removable and often only in place during services. Broad aisles between the seats allowed congregational processions. The font was placed on the central axis of the church in the vestibule, flanked by timber holy-water stoups. The tabernacle was placed away from the altar in a recess beside it to form a Blessed Sacrament chapel. The importance of this move, much discussed at Assisi, was both pragmatic, as it made it easier for the priest to say Mass facing the people across the altar, and theological, since it separated the reservation of the previously consecrated sacrament from the liturgy of consecration at the altar, clarifying the altar's liturgical purpose. On the front of the simple, almost primitive stone altar, was carved the text, *Congregavit nos in unum Christi amor*, 'Christ's love has gathered us into one', taken from the liturgy of the washing of the feet on Maundy Thursday, and therefore a complex statement here of the purpose of liturgy, the desire to create a parish community through the Mass, and of the humility of Christ amongst his followers.

Simple though it was, the church at Pershore attracted attention because of its distinguished patron. Even before it was built it was discussed in *The Tablet*, which noted its proposed liturgical arrangements with interest.[59] Pershore's consecration Mass was also reported:

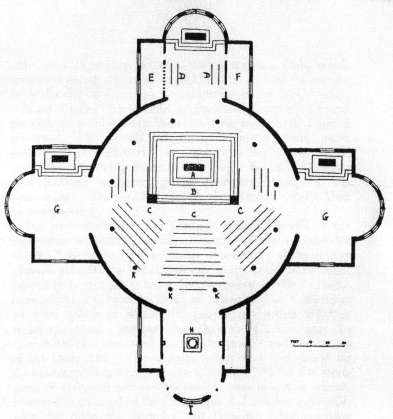

NOTES ON THE PLAN.[1]

A. If the High Altar may not face the people, it will have to be moved a little further back to allow floor space for the ceremonies. The seating could be adapted accordingly.

B. Sanctuary, lines marking the steps down.

CCC. Seating. It might be argued that there is a deal of waste space in this church. That objection will not be urged if the liturgical function of the church is the criterion. (This church would accommodate about 400 people).

DD. Choir Stalls.

E. Organ space.

F. Sacristies.

GG. Side Chapels with room for confessionals.

H. Font and baptistery.

I. Main Entrance.

KKK. Columns. The Stations of the Cross might be painted on the wall. There would be room enough for the people to follow the priest in the *Via Dolorosa*.

[1] I have to thank Mr Leighton Bishop who drew the plan for me and gave it quite a professional appearance.

6.4   J. D. Crichton, 'A Dream-Church', *Music and Liturgy* (June 1943), 73. Plan drawn by 'Mr Leighton Bishop'. Courtesy of the Trustees of the Society of St Gregory

6.5   Holy Redeemer, Pershore, by Hugh Bankart, 1957–59. Photographer unknown, c.1960. Source: parish archive

At once [we] saw, as we had not been able to see with the church empty, just how successful Fr Crichton had been in his aim to bring the altar and consequently the Mass right down into the body of the congregation. He reckons that no one need sit more than twenty-five feet away from the sanctuary, which cuts a deep semi-circle into the wide, shallow church; even with the altar rails in position … there was a strong impression of being embraced in the sweep of the sanctuary. This impression was reinforced by the unanimity and enthusiasm with which the congregation played its part in the dialogue Mass.[60]

Significantly, the church was appreciated by Catholic architects in the NCRG. Winkley wrote to *The Tablet* praising it as a 'landmark' in church architecture that gave 'fresh and clear expression to the relationship between priest, people and their church'.[61] He also took a group of fellow architects, including Maguire, to visit.[62] Pershore signalled that the Roman Catholic Church in Britain was open to the possibility of a modern liturgical church architecture.

NETWORKS OF REFORM

Though Hammond, Maguire and the NCRG were the most important force in promoting the new approach to church design, there were other routes within the Catholic Church in Britain through which reform was cultivated, until in the 1960s

the liturgical movement in church architecture became the dominant mode of
design. Reform was transmitted through networks of clergy and architects, often
formed around church-building projects.

Even before Bankart designed Crichton's church at Pershore, another architect
received similar advice from a parish priest to produce another influential early
example of modern liturgical church architecture. Gerard Goalen, a Catholic
architect, was commissioned by the parish priest of Harlow New Town, Francis
Burgess, to design the church of Our Lady of Fatima in 1953. Goalen had been
trained at the Liverpool School of Architecture, one of the first schools to adopt a
modernist, sociological and functional approach to design.[63] In Burgess he found
a client sympathetic to his approach and interested in liturgical reform. Goalen's
outline design for the church of Our Lady of Fatima in Harlow was shown on a
site plan for the new church in 1953, and his design was largely complete the
following year, though not built until 1960.[64] The church was T-shaped in plan,
the nave divided into three sections, the sanctuary located at the crossing with
the high altar in its centre (Figure 6.6, Plan 4a). Goalen explained his intentions in
the opening booklet: 'The Parish Priest asked me to design a church which would
give to the altar its proper importance and dignity, and which would enable the
congregation to gather very closely round it at Mass.'[65] Burgess, meanwhile, cited
Pius XII's encyclical, *Mediator Dei*, expanding Goalen's statement:

> One of the outstanding features of our new church is the fact of its being built
> specifically for worship which is, by its nature corporate and communal. As the

6.6   Our Lady of
Fatima, Harlow,
by Gerard
Goalen, 1954–60.
View showing
original liturgical
arrangements:
stained glass by
Charles Norris.
Photo: John McCann,
c.1960. Source: John
McCann / RIBA
Library Photographs
Collection

*magnet draws the iron filings to itself, so the priest at the Altar has his people
all around him. Everyone will be near the Altar, surrounding it on three sides.
Everyone will see, everyone will hear, everyone will be able to take part.*[66]

Priest and architect shared the same desire for an architecture that would promote
new conceptions of the liturgy.

The liturgical furnishings at Harlow also incorporated liturgical movement ideas,
but were subject to much negotiation. Goalen was appointed under Beck, then
bishop of Brentwood before his move to Salford, but Beck's successor, Bernard
Patrick Wall, was less sympathetic to Goalen's and Burgess's intentions. Burgess
wanted to say Mass facing the people across the altar, placing the tabernacle on
a second altar at the back of the sanctuary and drawing a curtain across it during
Mass. The purpose of this arrangement was to separate the Blessed Sacrament
in the tabernacle from the liturgical Eucharist, so that during the Mass the
congregation would give all their attention to the consecration of the sacrament at
the altar. Wall objected to these proposals, quoting at length from Pius XII's speech
at Assisi the year before in which the pope had urged priests to maintain devotion
to the Blessed Sacrament and opposed the reformers' desire to separate the high
altar and tabernacle.[67] Goalen and his client at Harlow were clearly aware of this
liturgical movement debate, attempting to position their church at the forefront
of reform in Britain.

Though the bishop blocked their plans, several innovations were achieved
at Harlow. The altar was placed in the centre of its platform in the middle of the
sanctuary; the tabernacle, though fixed to the altar as the bishop required, was low
in shape so that the altar could be used in future to say Mass facing the people.
Furthermore the candlesticks were not placed on the altar as in other churches,
but were designed to stand on the floor alongside it. This arrangement drew on
ancient precedent: Jungmann described how the candlesticks in Roman basilicas
were originally carried in procession as the liturgy began and placed on the floor
around the altar.[68] This arrangement left the altar clear of furnishings so that it
stood out as the most important element of the sanctuary, its Eucharistic function
and symbolism taking precedence and sightlines unhindered to allow for Mass
facing the people. Another important feature at Harlow was the pair of permanent
stone ambos in the sanctuary, substituting for the more conventional pulpit. They
were intended for liturgical readings, the Epistle and the Gospel, and, following
the bishop's instructions, were slightly different in design to indicate their separate
functions.[69] The design for the church at Harlow resulted from a considered
engagement with liturgical movement theology on the part of both the parish
priest and a modern architect committed to putting this theology into practice.

A few years after it opened, the church of Our Lady of Fatima was discussed
in the *Clergy Review*. Though praised as 'one of the best new Catholic churches in
this country', it was also criticised for having divided the congregation into three
separate parts, undermining the desired expression of the unity of the laity and
thus the sense of corporate worship. The significance of the baptistery was, it was
thought, inadequately shown in the design, since the font had been placed in a
corner of the vestibule (at the bishop's insistence).[70] By the time this article was

written, however, the NCRG had been promoting debate about the relationship between liturgy and church architecture for several years. Goalen himself, benefiting from these discussions, was already working on churches that showed a more complex and mature awareness of the liturgical movement.[71] In 1959, Goalen attended the Birmingham Institute's tour of modern churches and stained glass in France, Switzerland and Belgium, an event that became a turning point in his thinking about church architecture.[72] Whilst Our Lady of Fatima drew primarily from Perret's church at Le Raincy for its architectural expression – a reinforced concrete frame with *dalle de verre* walls – Goalen's later churches drew on a wider knowledge of European church architecture and an admiration for Schwarz.

On this trip to Europe Goalen would have met another parish priest who was also in the process of building an influential new church. Edmund Fitzsimons, parish priest of St Mary at Leyland, undoubtedly knew about the liturgical movement through his membership of the Benedictine community of Ampleforth. Fitzsimons had a broader frame of reference than most parish priests, subscribing to the Birmingham Institute and the NCRG and attending a conference in Liverpool, 'New Church Architecture', that included a talk by Hammond.[73] For advice on the design of the church at Leyland, he corresponded with other Benedictine congregations in America. The priory of St Louis in Missouri, a daughter community of Ampleforth, sent him a plan of their chapel, just then being designed by Hellmuth, Obata & Kassabaum and Pier Luigi Nervi: it was circular with a central altar, the choir sited behind it, under tiers of thin-shell reinforced concrete vaults (Figure 6.7).[74] The Benedictines at Portsmouth Priory in Rhode Island later sent an article about their newly opened chapel of St Gregory the Great, designed by Pietro Belluschi with an octagonal nave and separate sanctuary.[75] Fitzsimons also consulted Crichton, who sent him a plan of his church in Pershore: 'We started with the altar and the font – all else has come from that', wrote Crichton, advising him to consider the liturgy and to consult Maguire.[76] Even before approaching an architect, Fitzsimons made a model for an octagonal church and circulated it widely for advice.[77]

In his choice of architect Fitzsimons found a sympathetic partner in Weightman & Bullen, whose architects Jerzy Faczynski and Stanislaus Pater produced numerous sketch designs for centrally planned churches.[78] The design that Fitzsimons finally accepted in 1960, and which was completed in 1964, had a circular platform at the centre of the circular plan with a central marble block altar, evidently intended for Mass facing the people (Plan 3a). The congregation occupied a ring around it, its seating rising gently towards the outer edge, the choir directly behind the altar; a circular processional aisle ran around the edge of the building, separated from the nave by V-shaped concrete supports containing the Stations of the Cross; side chapels for private devotions projected from the perimeter. The baptistery occupied a significant space on the central axis near the door, and a Blessed Sacrament chapel containing the tabernacle was placed at the far end of the church beyond the high altar, open to the nave.

Its liturgical form was not only due to Fitzsimons's insight: Weightman & Bullen had also previously employed a knowledge of the liturgical movement. Pater and Patricia Brown designed St Ambrose in Speke, near Liverpool, in 1958, with a broad,

6.7   Chapel of the Priory of St Louis and St Mary, Missouri, by Hellmuth, Obata & Kassabaum, c.1959–62. Photo: G. E. Kidder Smith, mid-1960s. Source: © Massachusetts Institute of Technology. Courtesy of MIT Libraries, Rotch Visual Collections

almost square nave and unusually wide aisles, 'designed to enable the laity to actually participate in the liturgy by walking in processions', as the architects wrote; a large baptistery was located on axis under the reinforced concrete campanile, and the choir gallery was omitted, as 'it is intended that the people themselves will sing the Mass led by a small *schola* and organ placed near the Sanctuary' (Figure 6.8, Plan 3b).[79] The original designs submitted to the diocese placed a Blessed Sacrament chapel behind the altar, but the diocese insisted the tabernacle had to be placed on the high altar.[80] These innovations at Speke were inspired by Pius XII's desire for 'active participation' and the liturgical reforms already under way. Shortly before, Brown had designed the more modest church of St Catherine of Siena, Lowton, a hexagon in plan with pews canted at the sides to create a 'gathered' congregation, the sanctuary projecting from its apse into the nave (Figure 6.9).

6.8   St Ambrose, Speke, Liverpool, by Weightman & Bullen, 1958–61. Photo: Ambrose Gillick, 2012

6.9   St Catherine, Lowton, by Weightman & Bullen, 1957–59. Photo: Robert Proctor, 2008

The aim was 'a closer sense of unity between the Sanctuary and the Nave', even if other aspects – the position and form of the altar and pulpit, for example – remained conventional.[81] For Weightman & Bullen, Leyland represented the culmination of several years of development of a liturgical modern church architecture, catalysed by an especially progressive client.

In August 1960, Gibberd's proposal for Liverpool Metropolitan Cathedral was announced as winner of the design competition. It is no coincidence that Gibberd's plan for a circular nave, originally intended to slope gently towards the central altar, projecting side chapels and axial Blessed Sacrament chapel was similar in layout to St Mary, Leyland. One of the three assessors of the competition was John Heenan, archbishop of Liverpool. A month before, Heenan had been present on the Sites and Buildings Commission of the diocese when the plans for Leyland had been presented, discussed in detail with their parish priest, and provisionally approved.[82] It is therefore easy to see how Heenan would have been drawn to such a similar plan amongst the nearly 300 entries displayed for judging. Though Gibberd would not have known of the plans for Leyland, he was certainly influenced by Goalen's church of Our Lady of Fatima at Harlow. In his role as architect-planner for Harlow New Town, and as colleague and friend of Goalen, Gibberd attended the opening ceremony of the church in March that year. A Nonconformist with no previous knowledge of Catholic liturgy, he was immediately impressed by the ceremony and its setting at Harlow and, as he told Heenan, rushed home to draw plans for Liverpool that day in a frenzy of inspiration.[83]

CIRCULAR ARGUMENTS

For a short period in the early 1960s, the circular plan became fashionable, but it was always criticised by members of the NCRG as showing insufficiently serious liturgical understanding. It was often used for symbolic associations as much as for any liturgical advantages. Peter Whiston's St Columba at Cupar, for instance, opened in 1964, was circular with a central altar, a central axis defined by font and pulpit at opposite ends (Figure 6.10), yet its approach to the participation of the laity was symbolic as well as functional: 'The church was originally conceived as a circular unit expressing the idea of unity', said an article probably written by the architect, the conical roof and tower 'symbolising the ascent of prayer'.[84] The church of the Blessed Sacrament at Gorseinon near Swansea had similar contradictions. It was designed by a parishioner, Robert Robinson, in 1965 and completed in 1967, the same year as Liverpool Metropolitan Cathedral. It was a polygonal church with a lantern over a central sanctuary, the seating arranged in a square on all sides of the altar. Its parish priest Gerald Hiscoe described the plans in terms that echoed Heenan's brief at Liverpool: the altar would be 'the focal point of the Church around which the Church is designed, flooded with light from the circle of windows above – concentrating attention on the Table of the Sacrifice of the Mass', and the congregation would be 'all around

the Table of the Lord's Supper (just like a family)'. Yet the symbolism of the central design was more prominently advertised than its liturgical motivations: 'The theme of the New Church – the Church of the Blessed Sacrament – is that of a Monstrance', wrote the priest, explaining that the nave formed the base, the lantern the stem and the finial (a circle at the centre of a cross) represented the pyx.[85]

6.10   St Columba, Cupar, by Peter Whiston, 1964. Photo: Robert Proctor, 2012

Liverpool Metropolitan Cathedral was much criticised by NCRG members, becoming a foil against which they defined their position (Figure 6.11). In his book about the cathedral, Gibberd acknowledged the liturgical movement's importance in modernist architectural discourse, asserting the primacy of function, but he also asserted that symbolism was necessary, and explained the cathedral's crown-like lantern as a reference to its dedication to Christ the King.[86]

6.11 Metropolitan
Cathedral of Christ
the King, Liverpool,
by Frederick
Gibberd, 1960–67.
View from side
gallery: entrance
on the left; Blessed
Sacrament chapel
on the right; stained
glass by John
Piper and
Patrick Reyntiens,
© Patrick Reyntiens,
all rights reserved,
DACS, London,
2013. By permission
of the Dean of
the Metropolitan
Cathedral of Christ
the King. Photo:
Robert Proctor, 2012

His design process did not follow the rigid programmatic approach and
theological agenda advocated by the NCRG. Charles Davis considered Gibberd's
use of symbolism essentially irrelevant.[87] Maguire argued that the competition
design lacked consideration for the programme and showed 'theological
unsoundness' in its relationship of congregation to altar. The raked floor, he
thought, suggested congregational spectatorship rather than participation
and inverted the proper hierarchy of priest and people, while the off-centre
altar of the original design precluded Mass facing the people.[88] Gibberd and
the archdiocese changed both elements, but the criticisms were aimed more
seriously at the overall process of design. The function of a church was so
complex that more serious study and thorough engagement with the client was
needed, as Richard O'Mahony and William Lockett advised in writing about the
cathedral for the *Clergy Review*: 'To think about the natural shape of a gathered
community, its general orientation and the shape of its activity is a better
beginning than thinking up a good shape first and then discovering how best
to adapt it for use.'[89]

Because Liverpool Metropolitan Cathedral had been designed in competition,
no negotiation with the client was possible before designs were made, and the
process of selection inevitably resulted in a strong image over more sophisticated
and thoughtful designs. This was indeed the intended effect of the competition. The
competition conditions, written by Heenan with David Stokes and the cathedral
committee, gave a general liturgical movement aspiration but were deliberately
imprecise. The high altar, they said, 'must be the focus of the new building.

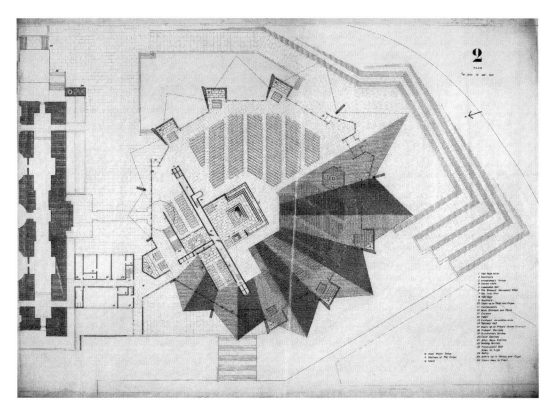

The trend of the liturgy is to associate the congregation ever more closely with the celebrant of the Mass. The ministers at the altar … must be in sight of the people with whom they offer the sacrifice.'[90] When dozens of competitors wrote seeking clarification, Heenan reassured them: 'for your consolation you should know that the Assessors will look first for a splendid conception'.[91] Gibberd's striking drawings provided just such a conception.

6.12   Metropolitan Cathedral of Christ the King, Liverpool. Unexecuted competition design by Denys Lasdun, 1960. Source: RIBA Library, Drawings & Archives Collections

Heenan and the other assessors, David Stokes and Basil Spence, passed over several liturgically complex proposals. Denys Lasdun, who was closely involved with younger brutalist architects, based his design on a more studied approach to liturgy (Figure 6.12). An open sanctuary was sited off-centre in a circle, surrounded by a horseshoe of seating; behind it was a bar of liturgical elements sandwiched between walls, and, unlike those in Gibberd's design, side chapels were concealed from sightlines to the altar. The low roofline eschewed the monumentality and symbolism of Gibberd's elevations, a fact the assessors counted against it.[92] Many other architects interested in the liturgical movement entered, including Gerard Goalen, with a complex design partly based on his church at Harlow, but without the striking diagrammatic simplicity of Gibberd's design (Figure 6.13). Criticisms of Gibberd's plan were therefore not only of the architect but also of the clergy, whose conception of architecture was deemed inadequate. Liverpool became as influential through its surrounding discourse of criticism as it was through the striking modernism of its elevations.

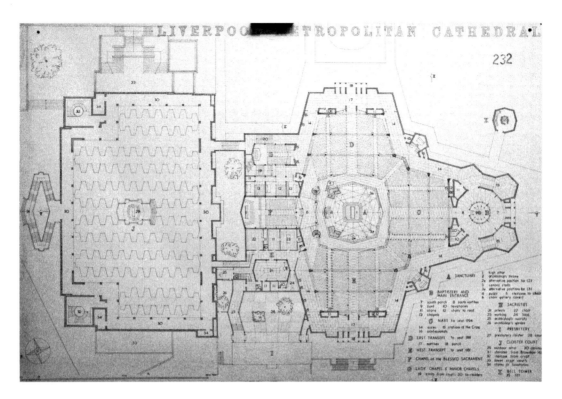

6.13   Metropolitan
Cathedral of Christ
the King, Liverpool.
Unexecuted
competition design
by Gerard Goalen,
1960. Courtesy of
Martin Goalen

LITURGICAL PLANNING

Two final case studies show how the architectural and theological discourses of
the liturgical movement combined in more mature projects of the 1960s, finally
attaining the level of liturgical analysis that the NCRG had called for. The first,
St Margaret of Scotland at Twickenham in London, was designed by an architect
involved with the NCRG, Austin Winkley. Winkley had been a student at the
Architectural Association School of Architecture in the late 1950s, where his tutor
was Peter Smithson, and attended a talk by Maguire when the latter was working at
Bow Common, approaching him for advice on his student project for a pilgrimage
chapel. Winkley began his career at Greenhalgh & Williams's office in London, a
firm already interested in liturgical ideas, before setting up in partnership with
John Williams, a fellow graduate of the Architectural Association, in the early
1960s. Winkley was also involved in several lay organisations, including the Young
Christian Workers and the National Council for the Lay Apostolate.[93] Winkley's
background combined a progressive, reforming Catholicism with modernist
architectural training.

Meanwhile the parish priest at Twickenham, Sydney Dommerson, was also
enthusiastic about reform. Winkley and Dommerson worked closely together and,
unusually for a Catholic church in Britain, they involved a lay parish committee in the
project. In reports to the parish, this committee described their discussions about
liturgical actions in relation to the church's design. The committee established
their brief for the church in 1964, six months before Winkley was appointed.

They closely studied the Vatican instruction 'On Implementing the Constitution on the Sacred Liturgy', which had been issued that year following the constitution's approval at the Second Vatican Council. Using this document they discussed the sanctuary layout and the position of the choir, which had to form 'part of the united community'.[94] They decided that the congregation would be close to the altar but not surrounding it. The Blessed Sacrament was to be reserved in a separate chapel, and the celebrant's 'Presidential function' had to be evident.[95] The purpose of the nave, they wrote, was to be 'the space of the Christian people', and it was not to contain devotional imagery.[96] Twickenham was an unusually well-prepared parish with firm views on their new church.

Winkley's first design for the 'Mass room' of the church was a square with a sanctuary on one side, the entrance doors either side of it leading past the font and altar (together on the sanctuary) to the front of the U-shaped seating. The celebrant would occupy a 'Presidential seat' behind the altar; there would be a 'place for the Word' where the readings and the Gospel would be given, and then the priest would 'step into the middle of the assembly for the Sacrifice-Meal part of Mass'. A separate 'Sacrament chapel' would be enclosed behind the sanctuary.[97] In response, the parishioners asked for a central aisle and a 'main door' so that events such as the Holy Week liturgy, weddings and funerals could include a processional relationship between entrance and sanctuary.[98] Winkley duly provided this in further variations on the plan.[99]

A different design was finally approved by the diocese in 1967, shortly after Winkley had been briefly joined by Chilean architect Jaime Bellalta, who had completed a postgraduate degree in London and had become involved in the NCRG.[100] The new plan was a square with the sanctuary in one corner, two blocks of seating at right angles and another small block further back on the diagonal axis (Figures 6.14, 6.15, Plan 5b). According to Winkley, the position of the central seating permitted a central aisle but also prevented the congregation from being visibly split into two parts, uniting it into a single community. The font was placed at the rear corner on an axis with the altar, although at the expense of associating it with the entrance, which was placed to the side. The floor was very lightly sloped, intended to convey a feeling of being projected forwards to focus worshippers' minds on the liturgy. Devotions to the Blessed Sacrament and the Virgin were given a separate chapel. The congregation had wanted the tabernacle to be concealed from the nave, but at the insistence of Heenan, now archbishop of Westminster, and his diocesan committee, it was placed within a wall between nave and chapel, making it prominent in both spaces (Figure 6.16).[101] An important feature of the church was that the social hall opened directly onto the nave so that the parish could gather after Sunday Mass, welcoming newcomers and forging a parish community as an extension of liturgy.

St Margaret was therefore a fully fledged expression of the liturgical movement in its maturity after the Second Vatican Council. It owed its complex and thoughtful design on the one hand to an architect who was actively involved in reform both within the Church and in church architecture and to a parish priest and indeed a parish with a heightened interest in Vatican II and its espousal of liturgical movement theology.[102] The relationship between architect and clergy here was

6.14 St Margaret of Scotland, Twickenham, London, by Williams & Winkley, 1964–69. View from sanctuary to font: stained glass behind by Patrick Reyntiens, © Patrick Reyntiens, all rights reserved, DACS, London, 2013. Photo: © Richard Einzig, *c.*1969 / arcaidimages.com. Source: archive of Austin Winkley & Associates, London, www.austinwinkley.co.uk

6.15 St Margaret of Scotland, Twickenham, London, by Williams & Winkley, 1964–69. Exterior. Photo: © Richard Einzig, *c.*1969 / arcaidimages.com. Source: archive of Austin Winkley & Associates, London, www.austinwinkley.co.uk

6.16   St Margaret of Scotland, Twickenham, London, by Williams & Winkley, 1964–69. Sanctuary in use, c.1969: stained glass by Patrick Reyntiens, © Patrick Reyntiens, all rights reserved, DACS, London, 2013. Photo: Norbert Galea. Source: archive of Austin Winkley & Associates, London, www.austinwinkley.co.uk

exactly what the NCRG had urged: a client who could formulate an intelligent brief working with an architect prepared to look at the purposes of the church from first principles.

The Cathedral Church of Sts Peter and Paul in Clifton, Bristol employed a liturgical movement approach with perhaps the most rigour of any Catholic church project in Britain. Clifton Cathedral was designed to replace a Victorian church, thought to be structurally unstable. The bishop, Joseph Rudderham, considered running a competition like that at Liverpool, but was advised against it, instead appointing Sir Percy Thomas & Son as architects after consulting the RIBA.[103] It was a decision that led to conversations between the clergy and the architects at Clifton of a kind that had not been possible between Gibberd and the clergy at Liverpool. The project architects, Ronald Weeks, Frederick Jennett and Anthony Poremba had little experience of church architecture, though when appointed in 1965, the firm's office in Shrewsbury had just completed a remarkable small Roman Catholic church at Machynlleth with affinities to those of Schwarz.[104] The architects took a rigorous sociological approach to planning spaces around activities, their design process beginning with an analysis of functions and ending with a plan for a building. Accepting the commission, the architects wrote: 'We are sure that only such a close working relationship between Architect and Client can achieve the level of "Architectural Seriousness" advanced by the New Liturgical Movement.'[105] This was a reference to an essay by Lance Wright for the NCRG urging a church architecture based on genuinely modernist architectural principles, and the conviction expressed in this letter remained throughout their design's development.[106]

Many of those on the cathedral committee who oversaw the new building were connected to the liturgical reforms. One was Gregory Murray, a Benedictine at Downside Abbey and parish priest in the diocese. Since the 1930s, he had helped to make Gregorian chant widespread and understood, writing several books on liturgical music, including simplified versions of chant for use in parishes, most famously *A People's Mass* of around 1950. He was an advocate of lay participation and the use of the vernacular in the liturgy.[107] Another member of the committee was Lancelot Sheppard, a lay Catholic writer who specialised in liturgical scholarship, recently appointed to the Liturgical Committee of the Roman Catholic hierarchy of England and Wales alongside Crichton, O'Connell and others.[108] Joseph Buckley also attended the committee, a canon of the cathedral and parish priest at the Sacred Heart at Westbury-on-Trym in Bristol, where he had established reputedly the first lay parish committee in Britain following the Second Vatican Council and instilled a missionary spirit in his parishioners through weekday house Masses.[109] Rudderham was a self-confessed traditionalist, but with his cathedral committee dominated by well-informed proponents of liturgical reform, the liturgical movement modernism that resulted at Clifton was perhaps inevitable.

The committee began by educating their architects about the liturgy. At their second meeting, the architects asked introductory questions. 'The first question was one of the most difficult to ask in front of such a powerful gathering of clergy', wrote Weeks: ' "What is the purpose of the Altar?" The answer was not simple and straightforward much to everyone's astonishment, and the dialogue had begun.'[110] Weeks and his colleagues sat with the cathedral administrator, Thomas Hughes, as he described each part of a high Mass and a pontifical high Mass (where a bishop is present) in turn. The architects drew analytical diagrams of the positions and movements of liturgical participants, leaving their spaces undefined: the sanctuary was given a notional circular form with central altar, and the nave was an open field. Symbols and lines showed the movements of liturgical celebrants and congregation through space in relation to the altar and other elements (Figure 6.17).

In the next stage of the design process the architects drew up a document they called a 'liturgical brief'. Each page explored a predetermined aspect of the church – sanctuary, nave, baptistery and so on – incorporating their understanding of liturgy to suggest spatial arrangements. This document abstracted liturgical elements and studied them in relation to the movements, positions and meanings of the liturgy and sacraments. The sanctuary, for example, was shown in several possible configurations for different events and its furnishings were studied for the movements that took place around them and their relationships with other elements. Sanctuary and Blessed Sacrament chapel were explored in section to examine arrangements for the bishop's throne, altar, ambo and tabernacle in relation to sightlines between celebrants and congregation. Symbolic meanings were also important: the ambo was shown both in use and in a schematic diagram of liturgical foci, 'Word', 'Sacrament' and 'Celebrant'. Baptism was considered as 'the "Illumination" (white light)', symbolism given physical form with the baptistery near a dark entrance, the font lit from a skylight, leading to the bright, high space of the sanctuary.

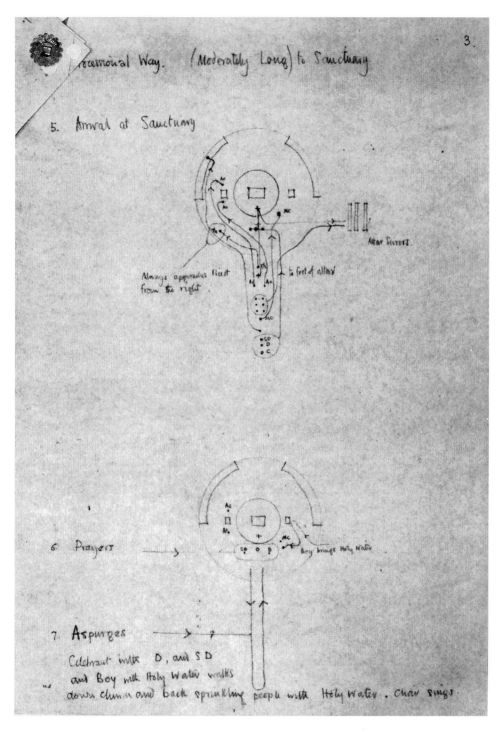

3.

Processional Way. (Moderately Long) to Sanctuary

5. Arrival at Sanctuary

Always approaches Priest from the right.

to feet of altar

Altar Servers

6. Prayers →

Boy brings Holy Water

7. Asperges → ✝

Celebrant with D, and S D
and Boy with Holy Water walks
down church and back sprinkling people with Holy Water. Choir sings.

6.17   Cathedral of Sts Peter and Paul, Clifton, Bristol, by Percy Thomas Partnership, 1965–
73. Architects' sketch of the liturgical entrance procession, 1965. Source: Clifton Diocesan
Archives. Courtesy of Ronald Weeks and the Trustees of the Diocese of Clifton

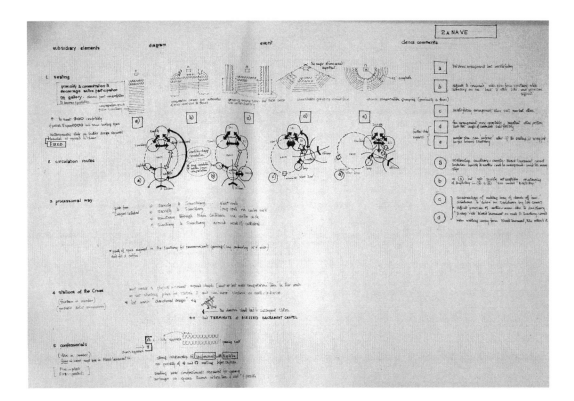

6.18   Clifton Cathedral, Bristol, by Percy Thomas Partnership, 1965–73. Architects' studies for the nave, 1966. Source: Clifton Diocesan Archives. Courtesy of Ronald Weeks and the Trustees of the Diocese of Clifton

Five different nave seating layouts were sketched, studying the 'grouping' of the congregation around the 'focus' of the sanctuary (Figure 6.18). The cathedral design was summarised with a single bubble diagram showing the 'relationships of basic elements', combining lines of physical movement and axes of vision (Figure 6.19).[111]

It could be argued that in paying so much attention to liturgical functions the architects reinforced conventional patterns of highly ritualised liturgical performance. Indeed the liturgies they studied in 1965 were those of a Church in transition, and in the following decade even the assumption of formal ceremonial was questioned: clergy were increasingly likely, as Winkley anticipated, to adopt a more domestic and informal approach to the Mass. Nevertheless Clifton represented one of the most serious attempts amongst architects in that decade to understand how the church could be designed for liturgy.[112]

The design process relied on dialogue with the clergy on the cathedral committee, many features of Clifton Cathedral resulting from their decisions. The fan-shaped plan was chosen by the clergy: the option of a U-shaped seating plan was dismissed as an 'unsatisfactory arrangement where seats overlook others', while it was 'difficult to "command" [a] wide plan from [the] sanctuary while addressing one side', and a semi-circular plan might 'unfocus' the altar. The fan-shaped nave was considered 'very acceptable' if the altar could be placed 'such that [the] angle of command [be] satisfactory'.[113] Similarly the Blessed Sacrament chapel was debated by the committee, who concluded that it need not be open to the nave.[114] It was therefore closed off with a side wall from the nave, while the tabernacle was accessible through a slot from the main sanctuary (Figure 6.20).

When completed after much delay in 1973, Clifton Cathedral tangibly embodied liturgical ritual, confronting visitors with spaces that made movement and meaning inescapable. The exterior was almost blank, precast panels revealing interior volumes and the tower indicating the sanctuary (Plate 9). The principal entrance, approached by a processional bridge, was a solid door with a sculptural surface by William Mitchell, making the entrance area dark, enlivened by Henry Haig's abstract stained glass. The plan's hexagonal geometry encouraged a freedom of spatial juxtapositions in the building's design (Plan 5a).[115] As the worshipper moved around the edge of the hexagonal plan, the tabernacle would be glimpsed in the Blessed Sacrament chapel. The top-lit font followed, surrounded by a low wall containing the stoups. Then the view opened up to the sanctuary, seen across the baptistery as a tall light space, and the single ambo and high altar lined up on an axis from the font. The visitor moved through a processional sequence in spaces also used by the clergy: processions filed around the edge of the interior, taking time that would be filled with liturgical music or congregational singing, imbuing the liturgy with a ceremonial atmosphere. The fan-shaped nave brought the congregation close to the liturgy, the absence of separation from the sanctuary allowing physical participation. Nevertheless the sanctuary was emphasised as the highest place in a hierarchy of spaces, marked across the top with the reinforced-concrete ring beam supporting the lantern and flooded with light (Figure 6.21).

6.19   Clifton Cathedral, Bristol, by Percy Thomas Partnership, 1965–73. Architects' summary of design studies, 'Relationships of Basic Elements', 1966. Source: Clifton Diocesan Archives. Courtesy of Ronald Weeks and the Trustees of the Diocese of Clifton

6.20   Clifton Cathedral, Bristol, by Percy Thomas Partnership, 1965–73. View of consecration ceremony, 1973, showing Blessed Sacrament chapel with sanctuary and nave visible behind through openings. Photo: Brian Middlehurst, 1973

Throughout, an absence of decoration made the building's occupants the focus of attention, nowhere more so than within the sanctuary, where celebrants' actions unfolded against the backdrop of a sheer white concrete wall.

Architect and NCRG member Peter Evans compared Clifton favourably with Liverpool Metropolitan Cathedral:

> The primitive arrangement of bishop presiding in the apse with his college of presbyters about him, facing the people across the altar, with the congregation around three sides of the projecting sanctuary, has generated the basic form of the building, rather than the building forcing the form of the assembly.[116]

6.21   Clifton Cathedral, Bristol, by Percy Thomas Partnership, 1965–73. Stained glass by Henry Haig. Photo: Brian Middlehurst, c.1973

The design process and the building were exactly as the NCRG advocated: a functionalist approach, modelling space around the primary purpose of the liturgy with a focus on congregational participation, balanced with an understanding of the meanings of liturgical elements. It was a serious attempt to analyse the needs of a church as if churches had never been built before – a fundamental modernist principle. If Clifton's exterior, 'gaunt and forbidding', as a Catholic newspaper described it, 'will not satisfy everyone's picture of what a church should look like', this was exactly as Hammond had argued: the interior and its spatial organisation of function took precedence, while the exterior showed that the building was merely an envelope around the real human and divine Church that manifested itself in liturgical action.[117]

NOTES

1   For example Peter Hammond, *Liturgy and Architecture* (London: Barrie and Rockliff, 1960), 138.

2   Keith Murray and Esther de Waal, 'Obituary: Canon Peter Hammond', *The Independent* (24 Mar. 1999), http://www.independent.co.uk/arts-entertainment/obituary-canon-peter-hammond-1082634.html (accessed 27 June 2012).

3   See Thomas Schreggenburger and Claude Lichtenstein (eds), *As Found: The Discovery of the Ordinary* (Zurich: Lars Muller, 2001).

4   Beginning with Peter Hammond, 'A Liturgical Brief', *Architectural Review* (Apr. 1958), 240–55.

5   Peter Hammond (ed.), *Towards a Church Architecture* (London: Architectural Press, 1962).

6   Robert Maguire and Keith Murray, 'The Architect Must Ask Questions', *Church Buildings Today* 1 (Oct. 1960), 3–4.

7   New Churches Research Group, *Church Buildings: A Guide to Planning and Design* (London: Architects' Journal, 1967).

8   Lance Wright to John C. Heenan (archbishop of Westminster) (6 Nov. 1964); conference notice, 'The Reordering of Existing Roman Catholic Churches', RIBA (18 Mar. 1965), list of attendees; New Churches Research Group, report to His Eminence Cardinal John Heenan Archbishop of Westminster, 'The Reorganisation of Existing Churches to Meet the Needs of Liturgical Renewal' (c.1967) (WDA, He1/A7); Catholic Architects Study Group, memo. (2 Apr. 1964) (ASCA).

9   'Low Cost Church the Shape of a House', *Catholic Herald* (3 June 1966), 3.

10 Hammond, *Liturgy and Architecture*, 9; Maguire and Murray, 'Architect Must Ask Questions', 3.

11 Hammond, *Liturgy and Architecture*, 23.

12 Ibid. 41, quoting 'Diocesan Building Directives' of the Roman Catholic Diocese of Superior, WI, 1957.

13 Hammond, 'A Radical Approach', 23.

14 Basil Minchin, 'Review of *Phoenix at Coventry* by Basil Spence', *Churchbuilding* 8 (Jan. 1963), 26–7.

15 Hammond, *Liturgy and Architecture*, 48.

16 Ibid. 28, 84.

17 Joseph A. Jungmann, *The Mass of the Roman Rite: Its Origins and Development*, trans. Francis A. Brunner, ed. Charles K. Riepe (Westminster, Md.: Christian Classics, 1980; first Eng. trans. 1951), 168; Gregory Dix, *The Shape of the Liturgy* (London: Dacre Press, 1945).

18 Siegfried Giedion, *Space, Time and Architecture: The Growth of a New Tradition* (Cambridge, MA: Harvard University Press, 1982; originally published 1941), 18–19.

19   Alison Smithson and Peter Smithson, 'The Function of Architecture in Cultures-in-
     Change', *Architectural Design* (Apr. 1960), 149; see also Mumford, *The CIAM Discourse*,
     225–65; Max Risselada and Dirk van den Heuvel (eds), *Team 10, 1953–1981: In Search
     of a Utopia of the Present* (Rotterdam: NAi, 2005); Alison Smithson (ed.), *Team 10 Primer*
     (London: n.p., c.1963); id. (ed.), *Team 10 Meetings, 1953–1984* (Delft: Publikatieburo
     Bouwkunde, 1991).

20   Maguire and Murray, *Modern Churches*, 51.

21   Hammond, *Liturgy and Architecture*, 131–2.

22   Gilbert Cope and Giles Blomfield, 'A Survey of Six Continental Churches', *Church
     Buildings Today* 4 (Oct. 1961), 3–11 (5).

23   Schwarz, *Church Incarnate*; see also Schnell, *Twentieth-Century Church Architecture in
     Germany*, 48.

24   Schwarz, *Church Incarnate*, 34–5.

25   Richard Kieckhefer, *Theology in Stone: Church Architecture From Byzantium to Berkeley*
     (Oxford: Oxford University Press, 2004), 232–70.

26   Kathleen James-Chakraborty, *German Architecture for a Mass Audience* (London:
     Routledge, 2000), 10, 57–67.

27   Joseph Rykwert, 'The Churches We Deserve?', *New Blackfriars* 37 (Apr. 1956), 171–5.

28   Kenneth Leach, 'Obituary: Father Gresham Kirkby', *The Guardian* (22 Aug. 2006),
     http://www.guardian.co.uk/news/2006/aug/22/guardianobituaries.religion (accessed
     13 July 2012); Gerald Adler, *Robert Maguire and Keith Murray* (London: RIBA Publishing,
     2012), 16–29.

29   Robert Maguire, 'Church Design Since 1950', *Ecclesiology Today* 27 (Jan. 2002), 13.

30   'Anglican Church in Stepney', 15–16.

31   See also, 'Church at Bow Common, London', *Architectural Review* (Dec. 1960), 400–405.

32   Cope and Blomfield, 'Survey of Six Continental Churches'.

33   J. G. Davies, *The Architectural Setting of Baptism* (London: Barrie and Rockliff, 1962).

34   'Anglican Church in Stepney', 23.

35   George Andrew Beck, 'Liturgy and Church Building', *CBRN* (1962), 159–64 (161).

36   My principal guides are John Fenwick and Bryan Spinks (*Worship in Transition: The
     Twentieth Century Liturgical Movement* [Edinburgh: T. & T. Clark, 1995]).

37   Ernst B. Koenker, 'Objectives and Achievements of the Liturgical Movement in the
     Roman Catholic Church since World War II', *Church History* 20 (June 1951), 14–27;
     Fenwick and Spinks, *Worship in Transition*, 26–8; Ernst B. Koenker, *The Liturgical
     Renaissance in the Roman Catholic Church* (Chicago: Chicago University Press, 1954);
     Kieckhefer, *Theology in Stone*, 232–3; Odo Casel, *The Mystery of Christian Worship and
     Other Writings*, ed. Burkehard Neunheusen (London: Darton, Longman & Todd, 1962).

38   Jungmann, *The Mass of the Roman Rite*, 122–4.

39   Ibid. 14–15, 88, see also 20, 63–4 for characteristic arguments.

40   Fenwick and Spinks, *Worship in Transition*, 28.

41   Henri Godin and Yvan Daniel, 'France A Missionary Land?', in Maisie Ward, *France
     Pagan? The Mission of Abbé Godin* (London: Sheed & Ward, 1949), 65–191 (128).

42   G. Michonneau, *Revolution in a City Parish* (London: Blackfriars, 1949).

43   Congar, *Lay People in the Church*; Jürgen Mettepenningen, *Nouvelle Théologie – New Theology: Inheritor of Modernism, Precursor of Vatican II* (London: T. & T. Clark International, 2010), 41–2.

44   Pius X, *Tra le sollecitudini: sulla musica sacra* (1903), The Holy See, http://www.vatican.va/holy_father/pius_x/motu_proprio/documents/hf_p-x_motu-proprio_19031122_sollecitudini_it.html (accessed 18 July 2012); Lancelot Sheppard, 'L'Assemblée liturgique', in Mathew et al., *Catholicisme Anglais*, 226–35 (228–9); Jungmann, *The Mass of the Roman Rite*, 120–21.

45   Pius XII, '*Mediator Dei*: On the Sacred Liturgy' (1947), http://www.vatican.va/holy_father/pius_xii/encyclicals/documents/hf_p-xii_enc_20111947_mediator-dei_en.html (accessed 19 July 2012).

46   J. B. O'Connell, 'The New Instruction of the Congregation of Rites', *Clergy Review* 44 (1959), 90–99; Michael J. Walsh, 'Pius XII', in Adrian Hastings (ed.), *Modern Catholicism: Vatican II and After* (London: SPCK, 1991), 20–26 (24–5).

47   'Constitution on the Sacred Liturgy', in Abbott (ed.), *The Documents of Vatican II*, 146; Pierre Marie Gy, 'The Constitution in the Making', in Austin Flannery (ed.), *Liturgy: Renewal and Adaptation* (Dublin: Scepter, 1968), 9–18; Colman O'Neill, 'General Principles', ibid. 19–32.

48   Little, *Catholic Churches*, 160.

49   Eric Gill, 'Mass for the Masses', in *Sacred and Secular &c.* (London: J. M. Dent & Sons, 1940), 143–55, originally published in *The Cross and the Plough: The Organ of the Catholic Land Associations of England and Wales* 4 (June 1938); see also id., 'The Problem of Parish Church Architecture', in *Art Nonsense and Other Essays* (London: Cassell, 1929), 124–30; id., 'Westminster Cathedral', *New Blackfriars* 1 (June 1920), 148–53.

50   Clifford Howell, letter to the editor, *The Tablet* (21 Nov. 1953), 502; 'Liturgical Reform: An International Conference at Mont Sainte-Odile', *The Tablet* (1 Nov. 1952), 365.

51   J. D. Crichton, 'The Liturgical Movement from 1940 to Vatican II', in J. D. Crichton, H. E. Winstone and J. R. Ainslie (eds), *English Catholic Worship: Liturgical Renewal in England Since 1900* (London: Geoffrey Chapman, 1979), 60–61.

52   Clifford Howell, *The Work of Our Redemption* (Oxford: Catholic Social Guild, 1953).

53   Crichton, 'The Liturgical Movement', 64–6.

54   Walker, 'Developments in Catholic Churchbuilding', 75; Crichton, 'The Liturgical Movement', 72–3.

55   J. B. O'Connell, 'The International Liturgical Congress at Assisi', *Clergy Review* 41 (1956), 641–9; 'Pastoral Liturgy: British Delegates to Assisi Congress', *Catholic Herald* (11 May 1956), 1.

56   Crichton, 'A Dream-Church', 71–2.

57   Ibid.

58   *CBRS* (1957), 88.

59   'From Our Notebook', *The Tablet* (31 May 1958), 512.

60   'From Our Notebook', *The Tablet* (4 July 1959), 383–4.

61   Austin S. Winkley, letter to the editor, *The Tablet* (7 June 1958), 536–7.

62   Austin Winkley, telephone interview with Robert Proctor (21 Nov. 2011).

63   Gerard Goalen to George Andrew Beck (bishop of Brentwood) (7 Nov. 1953); Gerard Goalen to Francis Burgess (parish priest, Our Lady of Fatima, Harlow New Town) (14 Nov. 1953); Frederick Gibberd to Burgess (19 Nov. 1953); letters (Brentwood Diocesan Archives [BDA], I3).

64   (Office of) Frederick Gibberd, site plan (29 Dec. 1953) (BDA, I3).

65   Gerard Goalen, 'A Place for the Celebration of Mass', in *Our Lady of Fatima, Harlow: Opening Souvenir Booklet* (Harlow New Town: n.p., 1960), 38 (BDA, I3).

66   Francis Burgess, ' "Think on These Things" ', in *Our Lady of Fatima, Harlow*, 33 (BDA, I3).

67   Wall to Burgess (18 Oct. 1957) (BDA, I3).

68   Jungmann, *The Mass of the Roman Rite*, 52.

69   On the bishop's comments, Eric H. Goldingay (diocese of Brentwood) to Burgess (8 Sept. 1958) (BDA, I3).

70   'Review of New Church: Our Lady of Fatima, Harlow New Town: Architect: Gerard Goalen', *Clergy Review* 48 (1963), 69–72.

71   For good summaries of Goalen's church architecture, see Harwood, 'Liturgy and Architecture', 66–8; Zeidler, 'Die Einheit des Raumes'.

72   Harwood, 'Liturgy and Architecture', 65; the itinerary included Paris, Audincourt, Besançon, Basel, Zurich and Brussels (parish archive of St Mary, Leyland, 'New Church: Art Works').

73   Undated programme (parish archive of St Mary, Leyland, 'New Church: Art Works').

74   Timothy Horner (St Louis Priory, Missouri) to Edmund Fitzsimons (16 Apr. 1959); 'Abbey Arches in Concrete', *Daily Telegraph* (6 Apr. 1960) (parish archive of St Mary, Leyland, 'New Church: Art Works').

75   Peter Sidler (Portsmouth Priory School, Portsmouth, Rhode Island) to Fitzsimons (28 July 1961) (parish archive of St Mary, Leyland, 'New Church: Art Works'); Meredith L. Clausen, *Spiritual Space: The Religious Architecture of Pietro Belluschi* (Seattle: University of Washington Press, 1992), 81–5.

76   J. D. Crichton to Edmund Fitzsimons (9 July 1959); Crichton to Fitzsimons (21 Aug. 1959); Fitzsimons to Crichton (16 Sept. 1959); Fitzsimons to Crichton ([1959]) (parish archive of St Mary, Leyland, 'New Church: Art Works').

77   Pace, 'Review of New Church', 84; postcards and other ephemera (parish archive of St Mary, Leyland, 'New Church: Art Works'); see also Corbould, 'St Mary's Priory Church', 3–4.

78   Pater and Faczynski are both represented in correspondence about the building: for example Patrick Reyntiens to Fitzsimons (n.d.); Reyntiens to Fitzsimons (8 June 1962) (parish archive of St Mary, Leyland, 'New Church: Art Works'); Patricia Brown and David John Brown, interview with Ambrose Gillick, York (3 Apr. 2012); G. Pace attributes the design to Pater ('Review of New Church', 85); Corbould attributes it to Faczynski ('St Mary's Priory Church').

79   *CBRN* (1958), 64.

80   Drawings (n.d.) (Archive of Weightman & Bullen, Liverpool); minutes of meeting of the Liverpool Archdiocesan Sites and Buildings Commission (20 May 1958) (LRCAA, Finance Collection, 12/S3/III).

81   *CBRN* (1957), 42; the plan was approved by the diocese at the Liverpool Archdiocesan Sites and Buildings Commission meeting of 21 May 1957 (LRCAA, Finance Collection, 12/S3/III); Brown and Brown, interview with Gillick; photograph of opening ceremony (n.d.) (parish archive of St Catherine, Lowton).

82   Meeting of Liverpool Archdiocesan Sites and Buildings Commission (19 July 1960) (LRCAA, Finance Collection, 12/S3/III).

83   Heenan, *A Crown of Thorns*, 301.

84   'Opening of St Columba's Church, Cupar, Fife', *St Andrew Annual: The Catholic Church in Scotland* (1964–65), 43.

85   Gerald Hiscoe, fundraising leaflet (22 Dec. 1965) (Menevia Diocesan Archives, Swansea [MDA], parish file for Blessed Sacrament, Gorseinon); see also Paul Robinson and Robert Robinson, *Fanfare for a Church: The Story of the Church of the Blessed Sacrament, Gorseinon* (Talybont, Gwynedd: Y Lolfa, 2010), 38, where the authors cite what appears to be the same document but seem to misinterpret it as an architectural brief.

86   Gibberd, *Metropolitan Cathedral*, 12, 17, 22, 32, 35, 46; though earlier Gibberd had admitted a lack of knowledge of liturgy (Frederick Gibberd, 'The Liverpool Metropolitan Cathedral', in William Lockett [ed.], *The Modern Architectural Setting of the Liturgy* [London: SPCK, 1964], 55–69 [55]).

87   Charles Davis, 'Church Architecture and the Liturgy', in Hammond (ed.), *Towards a Church Architecture*, 107–27 (108).

88   'R. C. Cathedral Design Criticised by Architect', *Liverpool Daily Post* (20 Sept. 1960) (parish archive of St Mary, Leyland, 'New Church: Art Works'); 'Comment on the Liverpool Catholic Cathedral Competition', *Architectural Design* (Oct. 1960), 425–6.

89   Richard O'Mahony and William E. A. Lockett, 'The Metropolitan Cathedral of Christ the King', *Clergy Review* 52 (1967), 753–60 (756–7).

90   *Architectural Competition for the Metropolitan Cathedral of Christ the King*, 3.

91   'Comment on the Liverpool Catholic Cathedral Competition', 425; letter from Heenan for preface to answers to competitors' questions (LRCAA, Cathedral Collection, S2/VIII/A/17).

92   Denys Lasdun, drawings for competition entry for Liverpool Metropolitan Cathedral (1960) (RIBA Library, Drawings Collection, PA2100/5, 1–8); 'Competition: Metropolitan Cathedral of Christ the King, Liverpool', *Architects' Journal* (1 Sept. 1960), 313–33 (333).

93   Austin Winkley, interview with Robert Proctor, London (8 Dec. 2011).

94   'St Margaret's Parish: Planning for the New Church', report of meeting (12 Nov. 1964) (parish archive); 'Inter Oecumenici: On Implementing the Constitution on Liturgy. Instruction of the Congregation of Rites', trans. Austin Flannery, in Flannery (ed.), *Liturgy*, 37*–59*.

95   'The Parish of St Margaret's: Planning for the New Church', report of meeting (29 Oct. 1964) (parish archive).

96   'St Margaret's Parish: Planning for the New Church', *St Margaret's Page* [parish newsletter] (11 Dec. 1964) (parish archive).

97   'Report of the Parish Meeting Held on 24 June 1965', *St Margaret's Page* (16 July 1965) (parish archive).

98   'Report on the Parish Meeting Held on Thursday 22nd July', *St Margaret's Page* (30 July 1965) (parish archive).

99   Williams and Winkley, plan drawings (1965, n.d.) (parish archive of St Margaret, Twickenham).

100   See for example 'Low Cost Church the Shape of a House'; Bellalta named as partner of Williams & Winkley (*CBRS* [1966], 48).

101   J. Anthony McCall (assistant financial secretary, Archdiocese of Westminster) to Sidney Dommerson (28 Sept. 1966) (parish archive, St Margaret, Twickenham); Archdiocese of Westminster Council of Administration (22 Nov. 1967) (WDA, He1/C23(a)); also, Gemma Dommerson, letter to the editor, *Clergy Review* 55 (1970), 734–5.

102   For further discussion of St Margaret, see also Lance Wright, 'Evolution of the Multi-Cell Church: Appraisal of St Margaret's, Twickenham', *Clergy Review* 55 (1970), 497–504.

103   Rudderham to Anthony Rossi (23 July 1965) (Clifton Diocesan Archive, Bristol [CDA], Cathedral File).

104   *CBRN* (1965), 159–61; according to Ronald Weeks, this church was designed by Bill Marsden, and links between the bishop of Shrewsbury and Rudderham may have been influential in gaining the Clifton commission (Ronald Weeks, telephone interview with Robert Proctor [24 Sept. 2008]). It is equally possible that the architects were recommended by the cathedral's benefactor, since he had also funded Machynlleth (see *CBRN* [1965], 159–61).

105   Frederick S. Jennett (Sir Percy Thomas & Son) to Rudderham (19 July 1965) (CDA, Cathedral File).

106   Lance Wright, 'Architectural Seriousness', in Hammond, *Towards a Church Architecture*, 220–44.

107   'Out on a High Note', *Catholic Herald* (24 Jan. 1992), 1; Harold Butcher, 'Dom Vernacular Tours the United States', *Catholic Herald* (28 Aug. 1959), 5; Gregory Murray, *A People's Mass* (London: Cary & Co., n.d.); Rosemary Hughes, 'La Musique sacrée', in Mathew et al., *Catholicisme Anglais*, 283–90 (284, 289).

108   For example see Sheppard, 'L'Assemblée liturgique'; id. (ed.), *The New Liturgy* (London: Darton, Longman & Todd, 1970); 'E-Day is Nov. 29', *The Universe*, Scottish edn (31 July 1964), 1. He also wrote articles on liturgical reforms for the Catholic press: for example 'Reforming the Liturgy', *The Tablet* (15 Jan. 1955), 57–8; (22 Jan. 1955), 81–2; (29 Jan. 1955), 104–5; 'The Changing Liturgy II: The People's Role in Public Worship', *The Tablet* (4 July 1964), 742–4; see also T. F. B., 'Obituary: Lancelot Sheppard', *The Tablet* (3 Apr. 1971), 343.

109   Joseph C. Buckley, 'The Parish and the Future', *Clergy Review* 50 (1965), 931–40; Kevin Donovan, 'Influences on the English Liturgical Scene', in Crichton, Winstone and Ainslie (eds), *English Catholic Worship*, 111; 'Obituaries', *Catholic Herald* (1 Nov. 2002), 6.

110   Ronald Weeks, 'The Design and Construction of the Cathedral Church of SS. Peter and Paul, Clifton', *Pax* 63 (Autumn–Winter 1973), 60–69 (61).

111   Percy Thomas & Son, 'Liturgical Brief' (Dec. 1965) (CDA, Cathedral File); see also Kate Wharton, 'Genesis of a Cathedral', *Architect and Building News* (1, 15 Jan. 1969), 22–9.

112   For a more critical analysis, see Robert Proctor, 'Modern Church Architect as Ritual Anthropologist: Architecture and Liturgy at Clifton Cathedral', *Architectural Research Quarterly* 15 (2011), 359–72; see also Robert Llewellyn, 'The Congregation Shares in the Prayer of the President', in Sheppard (ed.), *New Liturgy*, 103–12 (109).

113   'Clerics' Comments' column on Percy Thomas & Son, 'Liturgical Brief' (Dec. 1965) (CDA, Cathedral File).

114 Cathedral Working Committee (26 Apr. 1966) (CDA, Cathedral File, 'Miscellaneous Correspondence').

115 Perhaps inspired by Robert Maguire's Anglican church of St Matthew, Birmingham (Peter Ansdell Evans, 'Clifton's Catholic Cathedral', *Architects' Journal* [11 July 1973], 70–72 [71]; Walker, 'Developments in Catholic Churchbuilding', 418).

116 Evans, 'Clifton's Catholic Cathedral', 70. Other contemporary accounts of the building include Kenneth Nugent, 'Clifton Cathedral Church of SS Peter and Paul', *Clergy Review* 58 (1973), 737–44; Kate Wharton and Ronald Weeks, 'Architectural Heritage Year 2075…? Clifton Cathedral', *Architect* (May 1975), 24–5.

117 'The Tablet Notebook', *The Tablet* (23 June 1973), 590.

7

Liturgical Change

CHURCH ARCHITECTURE BEFORE LITURGICAL REFORM

The previous chapter aimed to give a brief narrative of the liturgical movement in British Roman Catholic church architecture through a small number of protagonists, examining people and buildings that were unusually advanced in their thinking and influential on later developments. This chapter considers the more typical experiences of church architects and clergy in Britain during this time of change, looking at the transformations that took place in the liturgy from the 1950s until the 1970s, the influence of NCRG debates on architects, and their effects on parish church architecture.

I begin by looking at the architectural aspects of liturgy before reform. Liturgical movement writing viewed contemporary liturgy as the culmination of a long deterioration characterised by clericalisation, the liturgy becoming distant from the people, performed in splendidly decorated chancels divided from the laity and viewed from afar, with the congregation reduced to mere spectators. Such accounts, however, were motivated by a reforming agenda. While there is evidence for passive congregations, the basilican form itself did not preclude participation and could be designed with participation in mind: practices were more complex than the theory suggests.

Most large churches of the 1950s and early 1960s had long rectangular naves, but it had been an important principle since the Counter Reformation, accepted with renewed interest in Britain in the late-nineteenth century, that everybody should see the sanctuary and follow the Mass. Seeing was the key, yet visibility was a principle that the liturgical movement questioned, since vision implied spectatorship whereas 'active participation' demanded action. The NCRG and others therefore criticised churches that appeared to limit lay involvement in liturgy. The separation of sanctuary and nave with solid altar rails, high contrasts of light between nave and sanctuary, and a monumental distant altar implied a supposedly faulty conception of liturgy as a spectacle.

Britain was relatively late in adopting European styles of liturgical innovation and participation. While the dialogue Mass was common across France and Germany by the 1940s, as late as 1958 at least six British dioceses still prohibited it.[1] In 1958, the Vatican allowed parishes to say the dialogue Mass without diocesan permission, and only then did it become common in Britain.[2] Yet even in the 1960s, the dialogue Mass was often rare enough to be remarkable.[3] Dioceses varied widely: 'In Edinburgh, dialogue Mass is widespread and congregational participation is often excellent', wrote one observer in 1962. 'To go to Glasgow to Mass is to pass into a different world, mute and frustrating.'[4] The Latin Mass without congregational participation remained normal in many places until relatively late. Mass facing the people was rarer still. Even when a priest followed the liturgical movement, he would not necessarily face the congregation. At Desmond Williams's circular church of St Mary in Dunstable, certainly influenced by liturgical movement notions when it was designed around 1960, the altar was placed against a reredos at one side of the seating (Figure 7.1). Early designs for the circular church of St Catherine of Siena at Birmingham similarly placed the altar against a reredos at the rear of its platform, and though it was built with a central altar, the opening Mass of 1964 was said facing away from the congregation (Figure 7.2).[5]

The faithful did not always apparently want to participate in the liturgy. The liturgical movement aimed to direct the congregation's attention to the liturgy because many worshippers indulged in unrelated devotions during the Mass. These included public recitation of the rosary, advocated during Mass throughout October by Leo XIII in 1884 and sometimes maintained in Britain until the Vatican discouraged 'pious exercises' during the liturgy when promoting the dialogue Mass in 1958.[6] A common objection to the dialogue Mass, meanwhile, was that it disturbed the worshipper's meditation and the church's feeling of sanctity.[7] There were further ways in which congregation and liturgy could be divided, as sociologists John Rex and Robert Moore studying Irish immigrants at a temporary church in Birmingham found:

> The … Mass Centre is filled at each Mass with men, women, children, and babies; these latter two groups maintain continuous diversions and a level of noise that makes it difficult to follow the service. Sermons are short and the setting of the liturgy on a stage under stage lights with the congregation below and occasionally engulfed by noise and disturbances, separates the people from the ritual and heightens the observer's sense of 'us down here' watching something going on 'up there'.[8]

Before Vatican II, the normal experience of liturgy for most Catholics was of a Latin rite performed by the priest, often with psychological or social barriers to participation.

Architects could therefore endorse modern architecture without engaging with the liturgical movement. Long, narrow churches with splendid sanctuaries were built for clergy without a culture of liturgical innovation. Sanctuaries were often framed as separate spaces, as seen at Reynolds & Scott's Sacred Heart, Gorton, Manchester (Figure 7.3); or more subtly with wider structural supports and a richer ceiling decoration, as at the same architects' church at Hackenthorpe in Sheffield.

7.1 St Mary, Dunstable, by Desmond Williams, 1961–64. The altar position has
not changed since completion, but it was originally furnished with the tabernacle
and six candlesticks along its rear edge. Photo: Robert Proctor, 2013

St Stephen, Droylsden, in Manchester by Greenhalgh & Williams, though it was modern in style and its architects were aware of the liturgical movement, employed a conventional basilican plan: prominent brick walls flanked the sanctuary and splayed out towards the nave, the altar rail extending across them, while the altar was typically monumental in form and set against a reredos (Figure 7.4). Greenhalgh & Williams conceived of congregational participation primarily as a visual emphasis on the sanctuary achieved by making it the dominating feature of the building, visible to all and attracting attention through scale, richness, light and framing devices.

Liturgical movement writers criticised churches with proscenium arches, where the sanctuary seemed like a stage and the liturgy appeared theatrical. By 1950s churches were only occasionally built with such a feature: the Immaculate Conception in Leeds by R. A. Ronchetti, for example, was a simple brick church with passage aisles, where deep brick chancel arches framed the altar and yellow glass transmitted an otherworldly glow to the sanctuary. The most theatrical new churches were, however, those that were intended for temporary use. Early church buildings in the life of a parish were often dual-purpose halls, serving as churches on Sundays and ceremonial occasions and otherwise as social halls, intended for purely secular use once a church was built. Their secular uses often included theatre or music, so a stage would occupy one end opposite the sanctuary or double as a sanctuary on Sundays, as Rex and Moore described.

7.3　Sacred Heart, Gorton, Manchester, by Reynolds & Scott, 1958–62. Photo: Robert Proctor, 2013

7.4   St Stephen, Droylsdon, Manchester, by Greenhalgh & Williams, 1958–59. Photo: Robert Proctor, 2012

7.5   St Paul, Glenrothes, by Gillespie, Kidd & Coia, 1956–58. Photo: William Toomey, c.1958. Courtesy of Architectural Press Archive / RIBA Library Photographs Collection. Source: Glasgow School of Art

Separate sanctuaries would be closed off by folding partitions. When opened and folded up at the sides, these partitions visually defined the sanctuary like curtains, while screens above closed off the openings in these portal-framed interiors. Such theatrical elements could be interpreted as liturgically desirable. When the parish of St Mary at Levenshulme in Manchester bought a cinema for conversion to a temporary church, their architects Mather & Nutter explained its liturgical advantages. The sanctuary occupied the raised stage and the congregation the auditorium, whose raked floor gave worshippers 'an excellent view of the Altar from all parts of the Church'. Concealed lighting illuminated the proscenium strip, painted red, 'which gives richness to the decoration and focuses attention on the Sanctuary'.[9]

Despite receiving much praise from NCRG members, Gillespie, Kidd & Coia's church of St Paul, Glenrothes was criticised for a theatrical sanctuary.[10] Its altar was placed in a taller space than the nave, illuminated from a concealed lantern (Figure 7.5, Plan 2b). 'The recess in which the altar is placed tends to form a proscenium arch, and to produce a slightly stagey effect', wrote Edward Mills, an effect he thought was increased by the use of natural light. William Lockett added that this aspect of the design would detract 'from the congregation/priest relationship'.[11]

Though they were building for the relatively progressive diocese of St Andrews and Edinburgh, Gillespie, Kidd & Coia were based in liturgically conservative Glasgow without the benefit of a clerical culture of interest in the liturgical movement. Their church of St Bride at East Kilbride, for example, may have been avant-garde in style but was liturgically conventional, with a large altar and tabernacle in a raised sanctuary at one end of a long nave. It was opened in 1964 by the bishop of Glasgow, James Scanlan, with a pontifical high Mass in Latin making no concessions to the Second Vatican Council's 'Constitution on the Sacred Liturgy' of the year before.[12]

Patrick Nuttgens gave a talk about St Bride the following year in London, followed by a discussion attended by Coia, Metzstein and MacMillan. Nuttgens praised the church's architecture, but admitted that the reinforced concrete gallery along one side of the nave created an awkward space underneath it: 'during Mass', he noted, 'the whole area of the church under the side gallery was crowded with people not paying attention'. Its design was also considered too inflexible for the liturgical changes that were now expected. Winkley, then beginning work on St Margaret, Twickenham, 'suspected that the building was more obsolete than people seemed to realize'. The acoustics were also criticised: electrical amplification was thought to create a distancing effect between clergy and congregation and should have been unnecessary. The architects admitted that their client's brief had been incomplete and that they had been concerned less with liturgical function than with the creation of a numinous space. Coia concluded that 'at the end of the day, the church was a place for religious worship and had to feel right for that purpose'.[13]

By then, however, Metzstein and MacMillan had begun to embrace the liturgical functionalism of the NCRG with more centralised church designs. St Bride had been designed in 1958, before the liturgical movement discourse in architecture had become widespread. When the *Architectural Review* asked the architects for material for an article on St Bride after its opening, the architects requested publication of another church instead, St Joseph at Faifley in Glasgow, since it was 'of a more advanced liturgical form'.[14] St Joseph, designed in 1960 and opened in 1963, was the firm's first church to depart from a linear plan, with seating on three sides of the sanctuary, all contained in a single pitched-roofed volume (Plan 2c). Even this building was designed for the old liturgy, however; its altar platform at the far side of the sanctuary platform, and the altar on the far side of its platform, designed for a priest to stand in front of it facing away from the people, gave the church a directional quality (Figure 7.6). The tabernacle was originally on the altar and a conventional heavy pulpit was constructed outside the sanctuary.[15] Faifley drew on an awareness of liturgical movement principles, yet without anticipating the new liturgical practices that were soon to become the norm.

At Glenrothes, Gillespie, Kidd & Coia incorporated a liturgical arrangement common in many other churches across Britain of this period and before, but which would soon be regarded as a solecism: a devotional side altar behind the altar rails and within the space of the sanctuary. Liturgical movement writers, evoking the convention of the altar as a symbol of Christ, advocated only one altar in the sanctuary. Secondary shrines were thought to distract the congregation from the

liturgy, and so, as the Second Vatican Council confirmed, they were to be few in number and visually discrete. Yet before the council many new churches were built with side altars inside the sanctuary, even by architects who knew of the liturgical movement in the 1950s, including Greenhalgh & Williams at St Columba and Our Lady of Lourdes in Bolton. Side altars had a necessary function in busy parishes and wherever there were several priests. Until the mid-1960s, priests had to say Mass every day. The result was a great many 'private Masses', as they were called, invariably said at side altars with little ceremony. Sandy & Norris's chapel at Ratcliffe College in Leicester, for example, was dotted with side chapels in niches around the nave to cater for its ordained teaching staff. Even as late as 1967, the chapel by Greenhalgh & Williams at the Salesian school at Thornleigh in Bolton had only one side altar in the body of the chapel in response to the Second Vatican Council, yet a separate priests' chapel was built behind it with ten small altars where staff could say their private Masses.[16] Gillespie, Kidd & Coia, similarly, incorporated rows of silo-like side chapels at their seminary, St Peter's College at Cardross (Figure 7.7).[17]

In 1964, the first Vatican-approved experiments with concelebration took place, and the rite was soon approved for gatherings of clergy, replacing individual Masses with a liturgy celebrated by several priests around a single altar. Cardross was therefore outdated when it opened. So, too, was Liverpool Metropolitan Cathedral, its ring of side chapels largely redundant by 1967: the cathedral was opened with a concelebrated Mass, to which its sanctuary was considered perfectly suited.

7.6   St Joseph, Faifley, Glasgow, by Gillespie, Kidd & Coia, 1960–63. View after early reordering, c.1965, when the tabernacle was moved to an altar behind the sanctuary. Photographer unknown. Source: Glasgow School of Art

Ample sanctuaries with broad altars were now desired, such as that at Clifton Cathedral, where only one secondary altar was included.

While centralised plan types were being explored in the late 1950s and early 1960s, the prevailing type remained the big basilica with passage aisles or the single-volume rectangular box. Many such churches were built in the Archdiocese of Westminster, where Archbishop Godfrey espoused traditional forms in church architecture even while acknowledging the need for lay participation.[18] John Newton of Burles, Newton & Partners built several such churches for Westminster with plain and open sanctuaries for liturgical visibility. Newton's basilican church of St Aidan at East Acton opened the same year as his church of the Immaculate Heart of Mary in Hayes, an even larger and more impressive modern basilica seating up to a thousand (Figure 7.8). Constructed in steel, it had a wide nave with sail-like vaults, its aisles filled with seating to maximise capacity. Even as he began exploring liturgically innovative plans, joining the NCRG, Newton continued to design longitudinal churches. Our Lady, Queen of Apostles at Heston, opened in 1964 but designed in 1961, retained seated aisles and framed the sanctuary with paired columns, though its broad interior was stark to focus attention on the liturgy (Figure 7.9).

St Francis de Sales at Hampton Hill was designed before the 'Constitution on the Sacred Liturgy' had been promulgated, but despite its longitudinal plan it could still be interpreted according to the constitution's principles (Figure 7.10). It had a single nave and wide sanctuary, and only one side chapel, set back and partly screened from the pews. Newton wrote about his design using liturgical movement ideas,

7.8   Immaculate Heart of Mary, Hayes, London, by Burles, Newton & Partners, 1958–62. View towards choir gallery over entrance: Stations of the Cross by Arthur Fleischmann. Photo: Robert Proctor, 2010

7.9   Our Lady, Queen of the Apostles, Heston, London, by Burles, Newton & Partners, 1961–64. Photo: Robert Proctor, 2010

7.10   St Francis de Sales, Hampton Hill, London, by Burles, Newton & Partners, 1964–67. Nave windows by Jerzy Faczynski and J. O'Neill & Sons; chapel on the right with stained glass by Gilbert Sheedy. Photo: Robert Proctor, 2010

saying that he had excluded stylistic mannerisms so that 'the fabric of the church as an enclosing envelope does not exert itself but only contributes to the worship of the faithful'. One important function was that 'the Priest is to be seen in the central position in the place of Christ with the people around him and united with him in what is being done by him'. Sanctuary and nave had to remain distinct but yet unified enough to express the unity of priest and people in the Mass.[19] A group of parishioners wrote a further interpretation of the church's architecture in terms close to those of Hammond and Maguire: 'the important consideration is that the Liturgy can function in dignified surroundings where the people of God form one worshipping community', they wrote. However, 'one of the more recent problems of modern church architecture is that the round and D-shaped churches, which were regarded by many people to be the answer to the present demands of the Liturgy, are not fulfilling that function'. Noting that the church had been planned several years before, they nevertheless thought it

> admirably suited to the new Liturgy. The people of God are gathered in one group and speak with one voice; the free-standing Altar at low level, with the priest on one side and the people on the other … lends itself to the familiar pattern of the Last Supper. Together, very much together, we offer the Holy Sacrifice of worship.

More allegorically still, they thought that the 'frieze' – simple timber panels containing the Stations of the Cross – could be considered 'an extension of the priest's arms … [seeming] to enfold the whole congregation in the arms of Christ'.[20]

Though the longitudinal church often did result from liturgical conservatism, therefore, it did not necessarily equate to a passive or devotionally minded laity but could be rich in its meanings and open to liturgical emphasis.[21]

CANON LAW AND LITURGICAL FURNISHINGS

A perennial obstacle to reform in the Roman Catholic Church in Britain was a legalistic mentality. Every aspect of the liturgy and many aspects of church design were governed by canon law and the rubrics of the Roman Missal. These constraining texts made it hard for those who wished to introduce change to do so; yet the rules themselves could also stimulate creativity, and reading them with liturgical movement principles in mind was one method of reform. The Second Vatican Council cut across this approach by interrupting the continuity of canon law, leaving creativity suddenly unconfined. Before that moment of interruption, architects exercised their ingenuity within and through these strictly held parameters.

The rule-bound attitude in British Catholicism differed from the more contingent approach to canon law that was often seen on the continent. Joseph Rykwert, writing for a French audience, saw the British approach as a barrier to the development of a modern church art and architecture: 'In England more than elsewhere … Catholics are obsessed by a meticulous liturgical observance', he wrote. He explained that at an exhibition in London of modern French church architecture 'even the most receptive critics fixated on one thing: that the candles on the altar are rather low, and that there are too often only two instead of six'.[22] Rykwert believed the development of modern church architecture in France had been possible because of a freedom from rigidly applied rules. Such restrictions as the number, style and position of the candlesticks were viewed as formal conventions that architects who took a traditional approach accepted; modern architecture, in contrast, was defined by its desire to transgress past conventions to envision new forms. Architects, however, generally prohibited from making such transgressions, probed the interstices of the text-bound rubrics to exploit their ambiguities and, in the process, revealed their contingency.

O'Connell's *Church Building and Furnishing* and articles in the *Clergy Review* explained and clarified the rules on liturgy and church architecture. His book could be read in different ways. Because it explained the laws in detail, with diagrams and photographs to show the correct forms of liturgical furnishings, it could lead architects and clergy to an especially rule-based attitude, and indeed the book was widely consulted for this purpose. On the other hand it also explained the historical development of liturgical furnishings and the origins of the rules, suggesting their contingent status and arming architects with knowledge that could unlock possibilities for new forms, especially through an understanding of historical precedents that might seem more 'authentic' expressions of purpose than the current forms of furnishings. O'Connell accepted the liturgical movement and in setting out the forms and histories of liturgical elements wanted to make them better understood. Canon law did not stipulate general forms for churches other than a vague condition of adherence to tradition, giving wide potential for innovation in church design, but when it came to smaller liturgical components the Church gave detailed prescriptions, mostly derived from liturgical texts. In diagrams and photographs O'Connell showed the acceptable forms for the altar: a stone table top (the *mensa*) with stone supports that could have an infill to give a solid form and a recess (the sepulchre) to contain relics, all aspects implied by the consecration rite, which required the anointing of the joints between altar and supports and the insertion of relics. Six candlesticks had to be set on the altar and a tabernacle fixed to it in the centre; a stepped platform raised it up and a ciborium or baldachino sheltered it. The altar also had to be covered with prescribed cloths including a frontal and the tabernacle had to be veiled. Finally, there had to be a crucifix, 'not an accessory, but the principal thing on the altar'.[23]

The element that would become most passionately debated after the Second Vatican Council was the tabernacle. O'Connell explained how the Blessed Sacrament had originally not been the subject of private devotions and that at first it had been reserved away from the high altar, only becoming associated with the altar in the Middle Ages and fixed upon it from the seventeenth century (except in cathedrals and monasteries where the high altar was used for choral services). Twentieth-century canon law prescribed this arrangement and the Assisi Congress temporarily reinforced it: after delegates had discussed the desirability of alternative locations for the tabernacle, Pius XII's speech denounced attempts to separate tabernacle and high altar, and the Vatican's Sacred Congregation of Rites issued a ruling in 1957 restating the existing law and rejecting innovation.[24] In Britain such regulations were accepted literally, as the argument between priest and bishop at Our Lady of Fatima in Harlow shows.

Dioceses would often take an interest in liturgical furnishings, censoring anything that seemed incorrect or unprecedented. Archbishop Gray of St Andrews and Edinburgh, for example, visited Gillespie, Kidd & Coia's church of St Mary and the Angels at Camelon in Falkirk on its completion in 1960 and gave a list of alterations to the parish priest Anthony Flynn. The candlesticks, he insisted, had to be separate, suggesting that the architects had designed a combined version that did not comply with the rules. The side altars also had to be repositioned to be centred within their spaces and the baptistery was to be provided with railings according to canon law.[25] At St Paul, Glenrothes, a few years earlier the architects had proposed an altar in the form of a single large block, to be told by Gray that, according to O'Connell, the supports and table top had to be distinguished and their joints visible.[26] As a result they designed an altar more table-like in form, though usually invisible beneath its frontal. Similarly Archbishop Godfrey of Westminster demanded that architects submit detailed drawings of liturgical furnishings, especially if the design was likely to be unusual. David Stokes, for example, was quizzed over Greenford, asked for a detailed drawing of the altar and baldachino and told to show the parish priest a similar built example.[27] In Liverpool, the Sites and Buildings Commission checked liturgical furnishings and scrutinised plans. Not only did the diocese prevent Weightman & Bullen from placing the tabernacle in a separate chapel at St Ambrose, Speke, they also made small modifications to their other designs. At St Catherine, Lowton, the altar platform had to be raised from one step to three in line with convention; at St Ambrose, an initial proposal for a tabernacle raised on legs was swiftly rejected; and at Leyland, the ceramic suspended crucifix by Adam Kossowski was approved but was interpreted as 'an ornament or decoration' and a liturgical altar cross was also required.[28] In all these cases the architects were attempting to change the normal formulae for liturgical elements, even if only in subtle ways. When architects repeated designs from one church to another, they often did not need to submit drawings for special approval but could simply indicate a precedent that had already been approved. Diocesan scrutiny was therefore a powerful incentive against innovation.

Sanctuaries generally had a familiar appearance, a recognisable Catholic form that varied little from one church to another. Nevertheless there was room for creativity within the rules and a variety of treatments of liturgical objects in modern churches. For example some form of canopy over the altar was a canonical requirement. In traditional guise it might follow the early Christian or Romanesque ciborium. One striking example was that of Hector Corfiato's St William of York at Stanmore, where art deco style columns in black and gold supported a hat-like confection over the high altar, in a church that the parish priest had asked to be 'in the style of the Romanesque' (Figure 7.11).[29] The more usual treatment of this feature was an ornamented suspended baldachino such as those at St Stephen, Droylsden, and St Boniface, Salford, elegantly designed to complement the modern architecture of their churches. In the late 1950s and early 1960s, it was often reinterpreted as a corona. At Massey & Massey's St Raphael, Stalybridge, for example, a square rig of lights hung from the centre of the dome over the freestanding altar; and at St Teresa of Avila in St Helens by William & J. B. Ellis, opened in 1965 but designed before the Second Vatican Council, a cylindrical crown of timber slats was suspended over the imposing marble altar (Figure 7.12). Gillespie, Kidd & Coia experimented with different approaches: at St Charles in Glasgow and St Bride at East Kilbride, concrete cantilevered projections constituted baldachinos; at their church of the Sacred Heart, Cumbernauld, open coffers in the timber ceiling suggested this form (Figure 7.13). The canonically required feature became a pretext for expressive architectural experiment, in some cases integrated into the structure of the building.

The design of the altar was especially carefully considered. The rule that the front should be covered was often ignored, however, in favour of a permanent decorative treatment of the altar face. Altars were generally made to resemble single heavy blocks, concealing their internal structures with facings of stone, and designed to complement other furnishings. At St Nicholas at Gipton in Leeds by Patricia Brown and David Brown of Weightman & Bullen, for example, liturgical movement aims were clearly stated by the architects, yet the treatment of the altar remained conventional, if stylistically modern: it was broad and deep and placed close to the rear wall of the sanctuary, which was described as a 'reredos' and ornamented with pieces of gold mosaic (Figure 7.14).[30] The altar had a heavy overhanging *mensa*, and its base was clad in white marble, its front decorated with slate panels containing gilded crosses. Its scale and richness made the altar a strong visual feature complementing the dramatic modern interior.

7.11   St William of York, Stanmore, London, by Hector O. Corfiato &
Partners, 1960–61. Photo: Robert Proctor, 2010

7.12   St Teresa, Newtown, St Helens, by William & J. B. Ellis, 1964–65. Photo: Robert Proctor, 2008

7.13 Sacred Heart, Cumbernauld, by Gillespie, Kidd & Coia, 1961–64. Stations of the Cross in *dalle de verre* by Sadie McLellan. Photo: Robert Proctor, 2011

7.14   St Nicholas, Gipton, Leeds, by Weightman & Bullen, 1960. Altar and communion rails: the sanctuary has been partly reordered since completion. Photo: Robert Proctor, 2009

7.15   St Theresa of Lisieux, Borehamwood, London, by F. X. Velarde Partnership, 1961–62. Photo: Elsam, Mann & Cooper, c.1962. Source: archive of OMF Derek Cox Architects, Liverpool

At the Holy Apostles, Pimlico, London, a modern basilican church by Hadfield, Cawkwell & Davidson, the altar was set against the rear wall. A sandstone *mensa* rested on a rectangular base with slate panels engraved with gilded symbols, the alpha and omega and a central image of the lamb symbolising the sacrifice of Christ. At both Gipton and Pimlico the treatment of the altar extended to the communion rails: brass and white marble in Leeds, slate with gilded figures of the Apostles in London.

The symbol of the lamb was frequently used: at St Charles, Kelvinside, for example, where Gillespie, Kidd & Coia's sanctuary was richly decorated in Mexican onyx and other valuable stones, its high altar incorporated a bronze sculpture of the lamb by Benno Schotz. Occasionally the pelican also appeared, a symbol of the self-sacrifice of Christ: engraved onto marble at Weightman & Bullen's St Catherine of Siena, Lowton, for example, where photographs of the opening ceremony showed the altar in use without a frontal.[31] For every case of an altar that received the liturgically correct coverings there was another whose decoration was meant to take the place of such covering. Some rules could therefore be broken, provided the general appearance of the furnishings remained familiar.

In most cases of such a decorative treatment of liturgical elements, the intention was to harmonise each feature with the architecture of the building, and architects often designed minor furnishings such as candlesticks for the same reason. By 1960, the heavy decorative altars typical of this period were questioned. Hammond argued that altars had become little more than shelves for objects and artworks; instead, he approved of the European trend for putting furnishings, including candlesticks, on the floor, leaving altars free to express their functions of sacrifice and of the 'holy table of the eucharistic banquet'.[32] NCRG members thought liturgical elements should be designed to show their functions as objects for human use and particular purposes, made evident in their outline forms rather than through applied ornament. Charles Davis elaborated on the origins of the altar in the table, the meal being the principal aspect of the Christian sacrifice in distinction to pagan sacrificial altars.[33] These ideas later led to a preference for smaller altars, often explicitly referencing the table form.

For some architects, a careful study of O'Connell's historical analysis of liturgical elements led to new forms that obeyed the letter of the rules but also attempted to recover their ancient meanings and purposes. Velarde noted that the earliest altars consisted of 'a tomb and a mensa' and thought that these two elements, with a minimum of decoration, were still most suitable.[34] Continuing his interest in early Christian church architecture, his practice experimented with the altar form at St Theresa at Borehamwood in London. Here a pillar-style of altar had a thin table top: made only of two relatively small pieces of plain stone, lightly decorated with the symbol of the lamb, it evoked early Christian pillar altars known from Ravenna, adding the *mensa* to reaffirm the symbolism of the Eucharistic meal (Figure 7.15).

Gerard Goalen also used liturgical rules to create meaningful forms. At his church of the Good Shepherd in Nottingham, opened in 1964, the altar was integrated with the architecture, its unusual vaulted form following the geometry of the ceiling vaults (Figure 7.16, Plate 10). It was given a low, veiled tabernacle and six candlesticks as required, and a baldachino was suspended high above it. The communion rails were given the same distinctively vaulted form as the altar. At Harlow, Goalen had written about the relationship of these two elements: 'The communion rail is similar in design and construction because it is, in a sense, an extension of the altar'.[35] O'Connell, too, had pointed out this relationship: 'the communion rail is really regarded as a continuation of the altar "of which we partake" ... when we receive Communion as the completion of the sacrifice', he wrote, and insisted that, like the altar, it should be covered with a linen cloth, theoretically required by the liturgy's rubrics though rarely used in practice.[36] For Goalen the communion rail became a feature that did not so much divide the congregation from the sanctuary, as was commonly thought, but could actually serve to unite them with the liturgy.

It is clear therefore that the rules of canon law were broadly upheld by parish priests, architects and dioceses in modern church architecture, generally strictly and sometimes with more licence. Altar arrangements differed little between churches, yet there was still scope for architects' creativity. Enhancing the altar's visual dominance aimed to concentrate attention on the liturgy, while in some cases careful thought about the rules could prompt new insights into the meanings and purposes of liturgical furnishings.

7.16 Good Shepherd, Nottingham, by Gerard Goalen, 1961–64. Stained glass by Patrick Reyntiens, © Patrick Reyntiens, all rights reserved, DACS, London, 2013. Photo: Henk Snoek, c.1964. Source: RIBA Library Photographs Collection

All this would suddenly change when the Second Vatican Council revised the very concept of a rule-based church architecture. Liturgical movement writers questioned rule-bound approaches not just in church architecture but in liturgy itself. Liturgy was governed by minute rules about ritual actions whose transgression might threaten the sacred effects of the ceremony.[37] The architecture of the sanctuary was governed by a similar fear of failure to adhere correctly to ritual stipulations. Increasingly, however, the liturgy was desired to be a genuine communication between priest, people and God rather than a ritual. In the past, wrote one commentator, the priest 'had "mechanised" words and gestures to be certain of not breaking the rubrics'; in the revised liturgy, he had to 'invent authentic gestures'.[38] 'The priest has to keep constantly in mind the style of celebration that is suitable for the community over which he presides', wrote Lancelot Sheppard. 'There can be no rule of thumb following of the rubrics, no routine celebration.'[39] The same was true of architecture: having followed and explored liturgical conventions, architects and clergy were soon to be confronted with a state of unprecedented uncertainty over liturgical design.

LITURGICAL REFORM

Throughout the period covered by this book, liturgy was reformed in a long process of which the Second Vatican Council was only one crucial stage, with continuing effects on parish church architecture. Pius XII's reforms of the liturgy did not affect its texts so much as the way it was conducted and understood. His revisions to the Holy Week liturgies from 1951 to 1955 had an especially significant impact and some specific effects on church architecture. On Palm Sunday the congregation was urged to join in the clergy's procession outside and into the church building. Other Easter services were simplified and their timings changed, aiming to restore them to their supposedly original times.[40] With the reforms came a revival of lay interest in the Holy Week ceremonies and a surge in attendance.[41]

Greater attention to these ceremonies followed in church design. Weightman & Bullen were especially interested in providing processional circuits wide enough for the congregation to participate, as they did at St Ambrose in Speke. They also emphasised baptisteries in a way that was then unusual. At Speke, like several of their other churches of the period (St Mary, Leyland; St Margaret Mary, Liverpool) the baptistery was centred in a space immediately beyond the vestibule, where the Easter Vigil ceremony might be carried out in especially dignified surroundings: the fire would be lit in the porch, the paschal candle brought in procession down the nave and returned to the baptistery for the blessing of the water, when the candle was dipped into the font. The liturgy required this ceremony to be conducted in sight of the congregation whenever possible. The visual prominence of the baptistery in these churches therefore suggests they were designed with the Easter Vigil in mind, the congregation turning to witness the blessing in a space that lent it symbolic significance. Another architectural feature of Holy Week was the need for an altar of repose for temporary reservation of the Blessed Sacrament, which generally took place in a side chapel: in many churches a chapel was designated for this annual use and given a second tabernacle.

A revival of interest in the sacramental ritual of baptism was another reason for prominent baptisteries. The liturgical rubrics stipulated that the font had to be railed off, and the rite itself implied its location: it was a three-part ritual, beginning in the narthex, entering the nave of the church and proceeding to the baptistery to culminate in the pouring of water. O'Connell and many other writers thought that it was important that the baptistery floor was lower than the nave so that movement into it became an enactment of Christ's baptism and evoked the analogy with death and resurrection made by St Paul.[42] In many churches before the council, however, the baptistery was treated like another side chapel, baptism being attended only by close relatives with little ceremony: at St Joseph, Wembley, by Reynolds & Scott, for example, it originally occupied one of the side chapel spaces, stepped down and given a mosaic floor with watery symbolism; even that at Liverpool Metropolitan Cathedral occupied a chapel, railed off from the nave.[43] Similarly, even though architect Richard O'Mahony was keenly aware of the liturgical movement, his early baptisteries were relatively insignificant: that at St Patrick in St Helens was architecturally innovative in material and detailing, but too small for use by any more than a small gathering and barely visible from the nave.

Weightman & Bullen's churches were thus comparatively significant in their treatment of this feature. So, too, were those of Gillespie, Kidd & Coia: in their churches, the position of the font often became an anchoring point for an orchestrated entrance sequence. At St Bride, East Kilbride, worshippers entering the main door walked under the gallery, turning left to walk to the rear of the building, where the font was visible beyond the gallery, then turning right at the font and up a step before entering the nave (Figure 7.17). At Our Lady of Good Counsel in Glasgow, the door opened to a stepped ramp with the font at its summit; once reached, the nave opened up on turning to the right (7.18).[44] These exceptionally well-studied entrance sequences linked the ordinary arrival of worshippers to the ritual of baptism. In the newly prominent liturgy of the Easter Vigil, they would have made the solemn entrance ritual especially dramatic, extended in time and framed within hinged strips of space.

Until the Second Vatican Council, liturgical reform proceeded with caution. In December 1963, however, the 'Constitution on the Sacred Liturgy' was approved by the council, giving official endorsement to the liturgical movement and prompting major reforms. The principle of 'active participation' was amplified into an urgent imperative: 'In the restoration and promotion of the sacred liturgy the full and active participation by all the people is the aim to be considered before all else, for it is the primary and indispensable source from which the faithful are to derive the true Christian spirit.'[45] To achieve this it announced that the liturgy was going to be reformed. New church architecture, it said, had to be 'suitable for the celebration of liturgical services and for the active participation of the faithful'. Not only would liturgy be revised, but so would the rules on church architecture and furnishing: 'Laws which seem less suited to the reformed liturgy should be amended or abolished. Those which are helpful are to be retained, or introduced if lacking.'[46] Far-reaching change was anticipated in both liturgy and the requirements of church architecture.

The following year the Vatican issued the document 'On Implementing the Constitution on Liturgy'. Its chapter 'On Building Churches and Altars for Active Participation' insisted that this principle be used to plan new churches. This document now permitted Mass to be celebrated facing the people, and altars had to be made suitable for it if necessary. The tabernacle therefore had to be small, but, with the approval of the bishop, the Blessed Sacrament could now be reserved in another part of the church 'provided it is really dignified and properly ornamented'.[47] Crucifix and candles could, if the local bishop approved, be placed alongside the altar. The celebrant now had to have a seat that indicated his role of 'presiding over the assembly'.[48] Side altars were to be few in number and set away from the sanctuary. The choir had to be positioned so that it was part of the congregation, suggesting that galleries were no longer desirable.[49] The document implied that a new form of church architecture was now required. A few years later the Vatican's 'Instruction on the Worship of the Eucharistic Mystery' added a new emphasis on the unity of the faithful at the Mass: 'In the celebration of the eucharist', it said, 'a sense of community should be fostered so that all will feel united with their brothers and sisters in the communion of the local and universal Church and even in a certain way with all humanity.'[50] It was a passage that would be imaginatively heeded by architects and clergy, and applied not just to furnishings but to churches as a whole.

7.17   St Bride, East Kilbride, by Gillespie, Kidd & Coia, 1957–64. View of rear of nave showing font. Photo: Sam Lambert, *c.*1964. Source: Architectural Press Archive / RIBA Library Photographs Collection

Meanwhile, canon law relating to church buildings was effectively suspended, causing great uncertainty. Many churches were designed before the 'Constitution on the Liturgy' and completed after it, and many more were still being designed during this crucial period. Liturgical reform followed only slowly: English was permitted incrementally in the Mass, the Eucharistic canon remaining in Latin, until the new rite was eventually approved and made compulsory in 1969. In the meantime, further documents were issued by the Vatican and by national hierarchies of bishops concerning church architecture and furnishing, while the rubrics of the Missal underwent continual adjustment. The uncertainty of this period gave increasing freedom of experimentation to architects and clergy until the new rite was adopted.

The location of the tabernacle was one of the most contested problems of the liturgical reforms, touching a central point of Roman Catholic belief and practice, the doctrine of the real presence of Christ in the consecrated host that was maintained by Catholics as a defining feature of their faith, enacted through devotional practices. In 1967, the 'Instruction on the Worship of the Eucharistic Mystery' advised clergy to place the tabernacle in a chapel away from the main altar.[51] If retained in the sanctuary, the tabernacle now required a special arrangement apart from the altar.[52] Instead of clarifying the Vatican's position, however, this document created further uncertainty and unease over the apparent demotion of the Blessed Sacrament from its position of prominence. Architects and clergy often remained cautious. Archbishop Gray, for example, wrote to his finance secretary, 'I do feel that even if we have a Blessed Sacrament Chapel it should be in such a position that the Tabernacle can be seen from the main Church. … The presence of the Blessed Sacrament largely accounts for the wonderful reverence with which people treat our Churches.'[53]

These concerns were negotiated in the sanctuaries of churches. Before Mass facing the people was permitted in 1964, architects and clergy sought altar designs that would allow Mass facing in either direction, uncertain of the future. As early as 1958, O'Connell had recommended a double altar, stepped down at the front: a celebrant behind it would stand at a higher level and celebrate across the altar, while the tabernacle was fixed at the lower level, where Mass could be said facing away from the people if required. It would prevent the tabernacle from obstructing the celebrant when it was retained on the altar as the Vatican at first insisted.[54] One such altar was built for the church of St Andrew in Dumfries in 1964 by local architects Sutherland, Dickie & Partners, to great interest from the Catholic press.[55] Sometimes a new altar was added close to the nave, effected at Westminster Cathedral in 1965, where the original high altar remained intact, and in the new church of St Teresa of Avila at St Helens, where the tabernacle was placed on a shallow gradine at the back of the sanctuary, as if the altar had been split into two parts, the archdiocese having ruled out a second altar.[56] This arrangement was considered unsatisfactory by many writers, as it suggested there were two high altars in the church. O'Connell also thought it 'unbecoming' for the priest to stand with his back to the Blessed Sacrament.[57] One solution was to raise the tabernacle over the head height of the celebrant; or, as at John Newton's church of St Aloysius at Somers Town in London, to place the tabernacle on one side of the sanctuary in a specially decorated shrine.

Negotiations over church design could often be lengthy. At Our Lady Help of Christians at Tile Cross in Birmingham, Richard Gilbert Scott tried out different arrangements, submitting sketches to the Archdiocese of Birmingham. His first designs for the church in 1964 showed a T-shaped plan like that of Our Lady of Fatima in Harlow with the tabernacle on the altar. In 1965 he submitted a proposal for a double altar like that at Dumfries (Figure 7.19). To this the diocese responded that it was 'undignified'. Scott's proposal for a celebrant's seat on a platform behind the altar was also questioned, as it was thought to be too much like a bishop's throne. Scott drew a new sanctuary layout the following month, the tabernacle high on the wall so that it was over the celebrant's head, reached by cantilevered steps, and a chair in a niche to the left (Figure 7.20). Two ambos were now added at the front of the sanctuary.[58] The seat was still thought too prominent: a temporary and movable one was requested instead; and Scott was asked to move the ambos back to address the transepts.[59] As completed in 1967, the sanctuary was a single composition in white marble under the soaring concrete tower, the tabernacle placed on axis on a pedestal at the rear, the ambos built in beside it, and the chair made of wood (Figure 7.21). Like many other architects building churches in the mid-1960s, Scott had to counter the clergy's uncertainty with coherent ideas of his own.

Richard O'Mahony, meanwhile, solved the Vatican's preference for separating Eucharistic reservation from the Mass with a unique idea: a sliding screen across a Blessed Sacrament chapel located behind the sanctuary. At St Patrick in St Helens, the Archdiocese of Liverpool permitted this arrangement in 1964.[60] The tabernacle was contained in its own chapel, its seating concealed behind the sanctuary wall; a large opening on one side made the tabernacle visible to the nave. During the Mass, the screen was drawn across. On it was a fibreglass sculpture of the Resurrection by artist Norman Dilworth, intended as a complement to the Stations of the Cross and to the same artist's altar crucifix. O'Mahony wrote that this arrangement was especially significant for the Easter liturgy: the screen would be drawn across at midnight when the Easter Vigil Mass began, revealing the image of the Resurrection.[61] O'Mahony obtained permission for the same layout at a church in the diocese of Shrewsbury: St Michael and All Angels at Woodchurch was already under construction when it was revised to adopt this layout, the screen being installed some time after its opening in 1965 (Plan 4c).[62] Reviewing the church, a writer in the *Clergy Review* approved the arrangement and recommended it to others, though it never caught on.[63]

Many of Gillespie, Kidd & Coia's Catholic churches were built during this period of transition, before the new liturgy was published. Our Lady of Good Counsel at Dennistoun in Glasgow was designed in 1962 and completed in 1965, its liturgical arrangements modified during construction (Figure 7.22). The position of the altar and the shape of the *predella* were changed late in 1964 for Mass facing the people.[64] The side chapel became a Blessed Sacrament chapel, and the candlesticks were redesigned to be placed on the steps beside the altar.[65] The celebrant's chair was placed under a tall free-standing crucifix, and an ambo was built within the sanctuary, giving different locations for each part of the Mass.[66] At St Benedict in Drumchapel, Glasgow, with a C-shaped seating plan on a diagonally oriented square, several proposals were made for the tabernacle: one placed it against a supporting pillar at one side of the sanctuary, and the final layout incorporated it into a low brick screen at the rear, where it could also be seen from a chapel behind.[67] Slow progress on the building site allowed time to adjust the interior before the church was opened in 1970, when the new liturgy was fully in use. By now, Gillespie, Kidd & Coia's response to the liturgical movement made their churches increasingly adaptable to new liturgical practices with relatively small modifications.

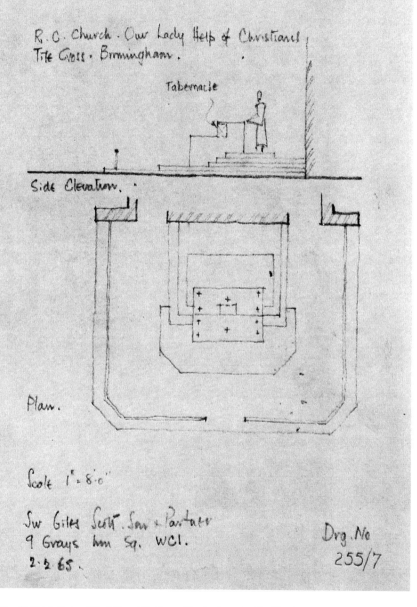

R. C. Church. Our Lady Help of Christians,
Tile Cross. Birmingham.

Tabernacle

Side Elevation.

Plan.

Scale 1" = 8'-0"

Sir Giles Scott. Son + Partner
9 Grays Inn Sq. WC1.
2.2.65.

Drg. No
255/7

7.19   Our Lady Help of Christians, Tile Cross, Birmingham, by Sir Giles Scott, Son & Partner, 1962–67. Sketch proposals by Richard Gilbert Scott for a double altar, 1965. Source: Archives of the Roman Catholic Archdiocese of Birmingham. Courtesy of Richard Gilbert Scott

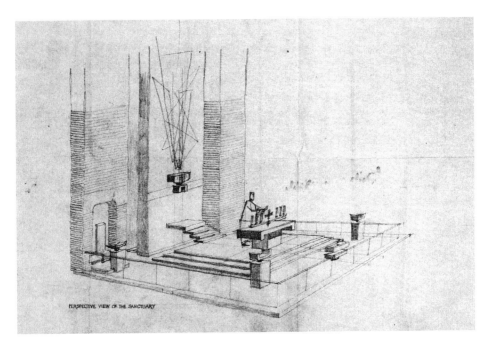

7.20 Our Lady Help of Christians, Tile Cross, Birmingham, by Sir Giles Scott, Son & Partner, 1962–67. Sketch proposals by Richard Gilbert Scott for sanctuary arrangement, 1965. Source: Archives of the Roman Catholic Archdiocese of Birmingham. Courtesy of Richard Gilbert Scott

7.21 Our Lady Help of Christians, Tile Cross, Birmingham, by Sir Giles Scott, Son & Partner, 1962–67. View from transept: stained glass by John Chrestien. Photo: Robert Proctor, 2009

7.22   Our Lady of Good Counsel, Dennistoun, Glasgow, by Gillespie, Kidd & Coia, 1962–65.
Photo: Studio Brett, *c.*1965. Source: RIBA Library Photographs Collection

At Liverpool Metropolitan Cathedral, indecision over liturgical arrangements during the Second Vatican Council resulted in Gibberd's iconic structure housing relatively informal furnishings. When Gibberd and his assistant Jack Forrest asked about the design of the high altar, proposing a single large block of marble, the cathedral committee deliberated and disagreed over the form the altar should take, acknowledging that the matter was currently in a 'state of flux'. They passed on to Gibberd the rules of canon law: 'the Altar should consist of one piece of solid stone table or mensa with a support or supports', they wrote, noting that the altar would in any case be covered with frontals.[68] Gibberd retained his solid block, which he had already ordered, but raised it on a platform. In 1964, after the 'Constitution on the Sacred Liturgy' had announced the suspension of canon law but before any further documents had been published on the subject, the detailed design of the side chapels became urgent. The Blessed Sacrament chapel, it was decided, would be designed for Mass facing away from the people, and the Lady chapel for Mass facing towards them.[69] A year later, however, it was clear that the Blessed Sacrament chapel would have to be redesigned to allow Mass facing the people, and hasty revisions were made.[70] Gibberd had pressed hard for a decision to avoid temporary furnishings being used in this chapel, something he thought would be 'visually disastrous'.[71] As Paul Walker argues, the indecision of Liverpool Metropolitan Cathedral's clergy at a time of suddenly shifting liturgical practices led to a building with a contradictory interior. Some elements were fixed and monumental; others were temporary and movable: the archbishop's throne and canons' stalls were of timber; most of the side chapels had temporary altars; and there was no permanent lectern or ambo.[72] On a lesser scale, such problems resulting from the Second Vatican Council were felt by Catholic church architects and clergy engaged in church projects all over Britain.

Separate Blessed Sacrament chapels, always a feature of cathedrals, began to become common for parish churches. John Newton's church of the Immaculate Heart of Mary at Hayes had included one as early as 1962, probably adapting a chapel during construction, placed prominently at the head of an aisle and decorated with stained glass containing Eucharistic symbols. In 1964, Newton included such a chapel in his design for St Anselm in Southall, London, a large fan-shaped church clearly inspired by the 'Constitution on the Sacred Liturgy', opened in 1968, the tabernacle placed on a pedestal behind an altar at the head of an aisle.[73] At St Aidan, Coulsdon in south London, Newton rebuilt an incomplete pre-war church by Adrian Gilbert Scott when a new parish priest, Kenneth Allan, requested a church that addressed 'the Liturgical thinking of our times', and while keeping some of Scott's shell, he created an entirely new plan, roughly a square with seating on three sides of the altar and a separate Blessed Sacrament chapel on one side (Figure 7.23).[74] The Blessed Sacrament chapel was this church's only separate space for devotion.

Looking at this period of transition, it is, perhaps unfairly, easier to locate and examine the sites of progress and reform than it is to acknowledge the sites of resistance to change. In reality reform occurred slowly and unevenly. When Archbishop Beck established a Liturgy Commission at Liverpool in 1968, its members realised that the diocese did not know what liturgical practices were

actually in place in its parishes and undertook a survey. Of 102 parishes, only 64 had Mass facing the people; only 39 had any music at Mass on Sunday and, of those, few had congregational singing; only 41 had lay readers, seen as an index of congregational participation.[75] The 1960s was a decade of increasing diversity in religious practice: just as new churches were being built that embodied liturgical movement concepts of worship, older churches continued to be used in much the same way as before.[76] This situation began to change in 1970, when the new rite of Mass was made compulsory.

7.23   St Aidan, Coulsdon, London, by Burles, Newton & Partners, 1966. Photo: Robert Proctor, 2010

THE NEW LITURGY: ACTION AND INTIMACY

The new rite of Mass not only used the local language throughout, it included many new actions, drastically simplified the liturgy and changed its emphasis and meanings. Lay readers, encouraged in earlier reforms, were now expected to read the two scripture readings. An offertory procession, derived from early Christian liturgy, further required the physical participation of the faithful: members of the congregation brought the bread and wine from the back of the church to the celebrant. The laity also now read 'bidding prayers' before the canon. The Mass took place in full dialogue between priest and people, and the canon was said aloud. The new rite took many of its forms from the former high Mass, which had only rarely been celebrated before, including ceremonial movement around the sanctuary between chair, ambo and altar, in contrast to the more customary low Mass largely conducted at the altar.

Only one ambo was now required, from where the readings and sermon (now called the 'homily') were to be given as part of the liturgy. Several elements were left to local hierarchies to define: so, for example, the British hierarchies decided that communion would normally be received standing rather than kneeling, and the 'kiss of peace' that in a high Mass had been a ritualised gesture between the clergy in the sanctuary became an exchange of handshakes amongst the laity.

The intentions of the new rite were declared in its preface and rubrics, the 'General Instruction on the Roman Missal'. The instruction began by defining the centrality of the liturgy, incorporating the role of the faithful into its first statement about liturgical worship: 'The celebration of the Mass, as an action of Christ and the people of God hierarchically ordered, is the centre of the whole Christian life.'[77] This was already a spatial statement – celebrant and congregation formed one 'people' in a hierarchical distribution; and more followed. The instruction required an expressive zoning of the interior by function: 'the shape of the church ought in some way to suggest the form of the assembly and the different functions of its members', it advised, while at the same time 'they should also bring everyone together in a way which shows that the Church is one'.[78] Audibility was emphasised. The ambo and the liturgy of the word were given considerable significance: 'the table of God's word and the table of Christ's Body' formed the two main foci of the Mass, as Christ became present through scripture in a manner related to his sacramental presence in the Eucharist.[79] Whereas the rubrics on liturgical furnishings had previously been prescriptive laws about form, the new rubrics were more informal and encouraged diversity: conventional materials for furnishings could be substituted with others relevant to the local context. The capacity of church buildings and liturgical objects to convey meaning was now viewed as contingent on culture and on their reception by the laity.

This was a different conception of liturgy to that prevailing before the council. Commentators felt that the Mass would no longer be as fixed as it had been: 'The whole spirit abroad in the Church … is quite opposed to the mentality that would seek to impose a rigid uniformity of eucharistic celebration on all for a long time to come', wrote Sheppard.[80] Experimentation and change were seen as inevitable after a decade of transformation. The participation of the faithful was seen as crucial for the effectiveness of liturgy. The prayerful silence of the pre-conciliar liturgy would give way to a liturgy of acclamation and action, as, it was claimed, had been its original mode of performance.[81] The church architecture that would make possible this new kind of liturgy had been set out by the Catholic hierarchy of England and Wales the previous year in a booklet of 1968, the *Pastoral Directory for Church Building*. It endorsed recent developments in church architecture, virtually insisting on new plan types: the 'assembly of the faithful should embrace the sanctuary', it said; and it even instructed architects on a design method for liturgical architecture: 'It is of first importance to locate in the sanctuary the centres of action in their ordering of priority and to consider the movements of all in the sanctuary'; the congregational seating plan would follow logically, and furnishings 'should be integrated with the architectural concept of the whole building'. The congregation had to be able to see, hear and join in worship with the celebrant.[82]

Ideas about the rite of baptism also changed: while the liturgical movement led to a renewed emphasis on baptisteries, later reforms made baptism more liturgical by assuming a witnessing congregation, symbolising the incorporation of the individual into the Church represented by the gathered parish. The 'Constitution on the Sacred Liturgy' had already hinted that baptism would be integrated into the Mass. By the mid-1960s, even churches by O'Mahony, Goalen and Winkley were criticised for having separate baptisteries ill-suited to congregational celebration.[83] A new, simplified rite of baptism was published in 1969, making it a more public event. The baptistery now had to be capable of holding a congregation or to be 'in clear view of the faithful', and if that was not possible baptism was to be performed outside it in a more suitable location.[84] Fonts were therefore increasingly placed near the sanctuary. At St Michael in Wolverhampton, Desmond Williams placed the font here as early as 1968 to emphasise ' "reception" rather than entry into the church and … for occasional public baptisms' (Figure 7.24).[85] Nevertheless the desire for a symbolic place near the entrance remained. Winkley resolved this tension at St Elphege at Wallington by siting the entrance near the sanctuary at the front of the church in view of the congregation, the font placed beside the entrance on an extended sanctuary platform (Figure 7.25).[86]

As the new decade approached, modern church architecture settled into established forms. Square and oval plans with curved seating around an open sanctuary with the altar placed well forward became the norm. Side chapels were few and often contained the tabernacle. Churches also became smaller, not only because of dwindling congregations and decreasing funds but also because it was felt that large churches were unable to provide the level of intimacy that the new liturgy demanded. Altars also became lower, smaller and simpler. Candlesticks became small and unobtrusive, and decorative cloth hangings were often dispensed with in favour of a single white cloth. The ambo and celebrant's chair had to be specially designed and related to everything else. Amongst typical churches of this period was St Thérèse of Lisieux at Sandfields, Port Talbot, by F. R. Bates, Son & Price, designed around 1969 (Figure 7.26).[87] The plan was a semicircle, and the sanctuary was a lobe-shaped platform of green marble, its material distinguishing it as a separate space as required by the 'General Instruction on the Roman Missal'. Ambo and altar were of the same material, linking them as the primary liturgical centres, while the celebrant's chair was of wood so its position could be changed. The tabernacle was originally placed in a chapel to the left of the sanctuary. Other side chapels were placed behind the congregation so that they were not visible during the Mass. Overhead, reinforced concrete folded vaults splayed out from the sanctuary to express the unity of the congregation.

Circular churches continued to be built but became more carefully considered in terms of liturgical function after the criticisms of Liverpool Metropolitan Cathedral. The church of Corpus Christi at Stechford in Birmingham by Ivor Day & O'Brien had a central altar, but it occupied a sanctuary that extended to the rear like a thrust stage, backed by a plain brick reredos with the tabernacle on a pillar.[88] The congregation was arranged in a horseshoe shape; the altar was small,

7.24   St Michael, Wolverhampton, by Desmond Williams, 1965–67. The liturgical furnishings, including font, are mostly original: reredos, tabernacle, candlesticks, altar and font inserts by Robert Brumby. By permission of Robert Brumby. Photo: Robert Proctor, 2009

and there were no communion rails. A pine-boarded ceiling and corona emphasised the unity of the interior. The square plan on a diagonal axis was more commonly used for new churches in the late 1960s and early 1970s, with many possibilities for detailing and liturgical arrangement. At Cantley in Doncaster, John Black designed a small square church on this plan, castle-like on the outside, intimate inside, its simple table altar at the front of the sanctuary and the tabernacle a decorated aumbry in a side wall.[89] The Bradford father-and-son firm of Langtry-Langton favoured this plan type, building it at large and small scales. St Peter-in-Chains, Doncaster, was a big town-centre church designed by J. H. Langtry-Langton, planned around a geometry of two overlapping angled squares: 'An ideal grouping was … drawn at the sketch plan stage, and when this had been achieved, a geometric structure was transposed over it', claimed the architect.[90] St Joseph at Hunslet in Leeds by Langtry-Langton's son Peter was a variant on the diagonal square plan whose motivating factor, he argued, was the centrality and closeness of the altar amidst the congregation (Figure 7.27). The celebrant's chair occupied a special platform linked to the sanctuary. The tabernacle was set in a niche at one side in an arrangement that the bishop of Leeds, William Wheeler, thought was an 'ideal placing … giving it a position of the highest dignity and availability'.[91] The altar was made of plain Yorkshire stone in a departure from conventional decorative materials to relate this church to its locality. Even smaller was Langtry-Langton's rural church of St Margaret Clitherow at Threshfield, a pyramidal tent-like building with two small groups of curved pews close to a small, rubble-stone altar.

7.25   St Elphege, Wallington, London, by Williams & Winkley, 1969–72. The font is visible beyond the altar, next to the main entrance door. Photo: Robert Proctor, 2010

7.26   St Thérèse, Port Talbot, by F. R. Bates, Son & Price, c.1969. The tabernacle was originally housed in a chapel to the left of the sanctuary. Photo: Robert Proctor, 2012

In London, the churches of Our Lady and St Peter in Wimbledon and St Paul, Wood Green, made similar uses of the angled square plan with a monumental employment of brick and reinforced concrete. In Wimbledon, Tomei, Mackley & Pound's design was capped with a pyramidal roof and bright lantern over a high central space and lower secondary seating areas (Figure 7.28). At Wood Green, much the same plan was given brutalist expression by John Rochford & Partners with a reinforced concrete grid in-filled with brick inspired by Schwarz's churches of the 1950s (Plate 11). A deep concrete beam over the sanctuary concealed a lantern that washed light over it, defining the sanctuary without dividing it from the nave, the altar and ambo projecting out beyond it. In both these churches the tabernacle was placed in a chapel to one side of the sanctuary where it could be accessed by the celebrant while giving a place for devotion outside the liturgy. In Glasgow around the same time, Gillespie, Kidd & Coia used the diagonal square plan that they had previously employed at Cumbernauld for their only Catholic church designed specifically for the new liturgy, St Margaret in Clydebank (Plan 2d). Here, raked seating descended to a broad sanctuary with the liturgical elements arrayed in a sculptural composition around the altar. Rippling walls of brick and a red-painted steel space-frame roof embraced sanctuary and nave in an expression of unity. By the end of the decade, architects and clergy had reached a consensus on the forms and principles of church design and on the theological ideas they wished to convey.

These churches could nevertheless be seen as ultimately conventional in their concept of the liturgy. Their liturgical arrangements were generally fixed

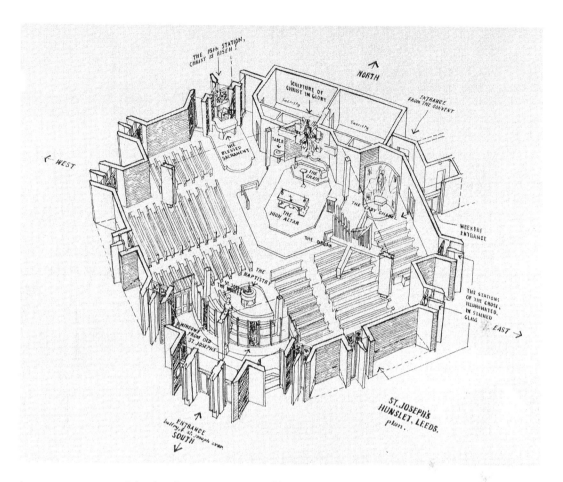

in permanent materials, despite expectations of further changes to come. Their architects and clergy retained a pre-conciliar idea of the church as a monumental and devotional sacred space for ritual, even if the ritual of the Mass was now no longer the performance of a single celebrant but the action of a community. An alternative approach already becoming significant in the 1960s was to accept instability and intimacy in worship as new conditions of the Church, embedding these qualities into church design. Flexible churches, with moving partitions and furnishings, previously only considered temporary, started to become theologically and architecturally appealing in their own right, offering spaces that could be adapted for future changes and for different congregations. In the 1970s, Winkley argued that churches should be small and that the fixed arrangements of the previous decade were a hindrance: 'Our intention now should be to develop freer plan arrangements where people can move, see and be seen', he wrote, adding that the use of chairs rather than pews would assist such movement.[92] A new and further reform of church architecture was now being suggested that addressed the fundamental principles of what a church was, not just its liturgical layout – a reform that will be considered in more detail in the final chapter.

7.27   St Joseph, Hunslet, by J. H. Langtry-Langton & Partners, 1968–71. Diagram of plan by Peter Langtry-Langton, c.1971. By permission of Peter Langtry-Langton. Source: souvenir booklet accompanying church opening, 1971, Leeds Diocesan Archives

7.28   Our Lady and St Peter, Wimbledon, London, by Tomei, Mackley & Pound, 1970–73. The tabernacle was originally placed in the chapel to the right of the sanctuary. Photo: Robert Proctor, 2010

One such experimental church had a particular significance in relation to liturgical development in Britain. The church and pastoral centre of St Thomas More at Manor House in London was always much more than a parish church: its parish priest, Harold Winstone, established a Centre for Pastoral Liturgy for the Archdiocese of Westminster there in 1969. Winstone wrote widely about liturgy, becoming involved in the Liturgy Commission for England and Wales under Archbishop Grimshaw of Birmingham from 1963. The centre at Manor House was intended as an educational and experimental facility for the liturgy, including the creation of national publications and demonstrating liturgical forms, particularly new music, to others. It was the first church in the Archdiocese of Westminster to implement new rites as they were published and tested new translations, rites and music.[93] John Newton, its architect, became a member of the Liturgical Commission of the archdiocese which oversaw the centre's activities.[94]

Built around 1974, St Thomas More occupied a small site in a street of Victorian terraced housing and was domestic in appearance. On the ground floor was a social hall and offices for the liturgical centre; above was the church (reminiscent of the 'upper room' of the Last Supper), its sanctuary in a cantilever; on top were flats for Winstone and his assistant. The presence of Catholic West Indians in the parish was a pretext for Winstone to experiment with adapting the liturgy to their needs through 'spontaneous forms of worship'.[95] Accordingly the space of the church was flexible, with sliding partitions that could be drawn across secondary spaces to unify the nave or divide it into more intimate areas (Figure 7.29). The liturgical furnishings were made of timber, including the altar and tabernacle

stand, so that the space could be reconfigured whenever desired.[96] The building was designed to accommodate experiment and continual change in liturgy, as well as to minimise effects of ritual by reducing any appearance of formality or artificiality, hoping thereby to engage the congregation more effectively in the liturgical celebration.

7.29   St Thomas More, Manor House, London, by Burles, Newton & Partners, c.1974. View of the chapel. Photo: Robert Proctor, 2010

The process of reform in liturgy and church architecture from the 1950s to the 1970s was complex and often fragmented. While the shape of the church building changed dramatically across this relatively brief period, ideas about its liturgical function and actual liturgical practices shifted at different rates: architecture and religion had parallel trajectories, but different speeds and changes of gear. Yet Roman Catholicism in this period was even more complex than this focus on liturgy would suggest. The NCRG and the liturgical movement before it argued for a primary focus on the Eucharist, and were also concerned with the sacraments, especially baptism; but this emphasis shifted attention from an area of religious practice that remained of great importance in Roman Catholic culture, namely non-liturgical devotions. Popular devotions of all kinds were significant in Roman Catholic religious practice in Britain throughout this period, and, as I will show in the next chapter, were often given special prominence in new church buildings, despite and alongside liturgical reform. However important in both architectural and religious narratives of this period, therefore, liturgical reform must be seen as one amongst many other factors behind the Church's making of itself through architecture.

NOTES

1   Crichton, 'The Liturgical Movement from 1940 to Vatican II', 68; Walker, 'Developments in Catholic Churchbuilding', 61 n. 47; Lancelot C. Sheppard, letter to the editor, *The Tablet* (16 Mar. 1957), 258.

2   J. B. O'Connell, 'The New Instruction of the Congregation of Rites', 97–8; press reports suggest its novelty (for example Mary Crozier, 'A Dialogue Mass', *The Tablet* [14 Mar. 1958], 249).

3   'Dunbar Church Re-Opened', *St Andrew Annual: The Catholic Church in Scotland* (1960–61), 56.

4   P. G. Walsh, letter to the editor, *The Tablet* (10 Nov. 1962), 1084.

5   Photograph (parish archive).

6   Leo XIII, 'On the Recitation of the Rosary' (1884), art. 4, http://www.vatican.va/
holy_father/leo_xiii/encyclicals/documents/hf_l-xiii_enc_30081884_superiore-anno_
en.html (accessed 10 Aug. 2012); James R. Reynolds, letter to the editor, *The Tablet* (15 Oct. 1955), 379; H. E. Calman, letter to the editor, *The Tablet* (22 Oct. 1955), 410; Terence J. Howes, letter to the editor, *The Tablet* (29 Oct. 1955), 438;
R. G. Webb, letter to the editor, *The Tablet* (12 Nov. 1955), 486; see also J. B. O'Connell, 'Questions and Answers', *Clergy Review* 45 (1960), 300–301. A further article by O'Connell suggests it was current in Liverpool in 1962 (J. B. O'Connell and L. L. McReavy, 'Questions and Answers', *Clergy Review* 47 [1962], 497–8).

7   A. M. Wood, letter to the editor, *The Tablet* (29 Sept. 1962), 915.

8   John Rex and Robert Moore, *Race, Community, and Conflict: A Study of Sparkbrook* (London: Oxford University Press, 1967), 175.

9   *CBRN* (1957), 98–100.

10   It was praised, for example, in Hammond, *Liturgy and Architecture*, 105.

11   Mills and Lockett, 'Plans of Churches Here and Abroad', 13.

12   *Solemn Opening: St Bride's Church, East Kilbride* [souvenir brochure] (East Kilbride: n.p., 1964) (GRCAA, Y/15).

13   'St Bride's: An Appraisal', *RIBA Journal* (Apr. 1966), 170–79 (172, 179).

14   Isi Metzstein (Gillespie, Kidd & Coia) to J. M. Richards (editor, *Architectural Review*) (23 June 1965) (GSAA, GKC/CEK/1/7); see also Proctor, 'Churches for a Changing Liturgy', 305–6.

15   Proctor, 'Churches for a Changing Liturgy', 311–12.

16   *CBRN* (1967), 48.

17   Watters, *Cardross*.

18   William Godfrey, foreword to *CBRS* (1960), 33.

19   John Newton, 'The Catholic Church, Hampton Hill', in *St Francis de Sales, Hampton Hill, Middlesex: Souvenir Brochure* (London: n. p., 1964), 7 (parish archive).

20   Parishioners [*sic*], 'Our Church', in *St Francis de Sales*, 7 (parish archive).

21   See esp. Kieckhefer, *Theology in Stone*, 18.

22   Rykwert, 'Passé recent et problèmes actuels', 297.

23   O'Connell, *Church Building*, 129–203 (202).

24   J. B. O'Connell, 'The Care of the Blessed Sacrament', *Clergy Review* 43 (1958), 11–18 (17).

25   Anthony Flynn (parish priest, St Mary and the Angels, Camelon) to Jack Coia (Gillespie, Kidd & Coia) (4 Dec. 1960) (GSAA, GKC/CCF/1/7).

26   Pierce Grace (parish priest, St Paul, Glenrothes) to Gordon Gray (archbishop of St Andrews and Edinburgh) (24 Jan. 1958); Gray to Grace (4 Feb. 1958) (SCA, DE/59/202).

27   A. Rivers (financial secretary, Archdiocese of Westminster) to David Stokes (11 Aug. 1959) (WDA, Go/2/132).

28   Minutes of meetings of the Sites and Buildings Commission, Archdiocese of Liverpool (16 Dec. 1958; 19 July 1960) (LRCAA, Finance Collection, 12/S3/III).

29   *CBRS* (1960), 54; (1961), 63–5.

30   *CBRN* (1961), 120.

31   Parish archive.

32   Hammond, *Liturgy and Architecture*, 38–9.

33   Charles Davis, 'The Christian Altar', in Lockett (ed.), *Modern Architectural Setting*, 13–31.

34   Velarde and Velarde, 'Modern Church Architecture', 519.

35   Gerard Goalen, 'A Place for the Celebration of Mass', in *Our Lady of Fatima, Harlow: Opening Souvenir Booklet* (Harlow: n.p., 1960), 38 (BDA, I3).

36   J. B. O'Connell, 'Questions and Answers', *Clergy Review* 41 (1956), 304.

37   Kieran Flanagan, *Sociology and Liturgy: Re-Presentations of the Holy* (Basingstoke: Macmillan, 1991), 150–85.

38   Llewellyn, 'The Congregation Shares in the Prayer of the President', 104–5.

39   Lancelot Sheppard, 'The New "Ordo Missae"', in id. (ed.), *New Liturgy*, 37.

40   For pre-1955 Holy Week rites, see Fortescue, *Ceremonies*, 262–323. On the liturgical changes, see for example Gaspar Lefebvre, *The New Liturgy of Holy Week: Supplement to the Saint Andrew Daily Missal* (Bruges: Liturgical Apostolate, Abbey of Saint André, 1956).

41   J. G. McGarry, 'Holy Week 1956', *Furrow* 7 (1956), 323–32 (325).

42   O'Connell, *Church Building*, 117–20.

43   Paul D. Walker, 'Prophetic or Premature? The Metropolitan Cathedral of Christ the King, Liverpool', *Theology*, 105 (2002), 185–93 (188).

44   Proctor, 'Churches for a Changing Liturgy', 316–17.

45   'Constitution on the Sacred Liturgy', trans. Joseph Rogers, in Flannery (ed.), *Liturgy*, 7*.

46   Ibid. 28*.

47   '*Inter Oecumenici*: On Implementing the Constitution on Liturgy. Instruction of the Congregation of Rites', trans. Austin Flannery, in Flannery (ed.), *Liturgy*, 58*.

48   Ibid. 58*.

49   Ibid. 59*.

50   Sacred Congregation of Rites, 'Instruction on Worship of the Eucharistic Mystery' (1967), art. 18, Catholic Liturgical Library, http://www.catholicliturgy.com/index.cfm/FuseAction/DocumentContents/Index/2/SubIndex/11/DocumentIndex/338 (accessed 12 Sept. 2012).

51   Ibid., art. 53.

52   Ibid., art. 55.

53   Gordon Gray to William Glancy (finance secretary, Archdiocese of St Andrews and Edinburgh) (22 Feb. 1965) (SCA, DE/39/27).

54   J. B. O'Connell, 'Questions and Answers', *Clergy Review* 43 (1958), 41; id., 'Questions and Answers', *Clergy Review* 44 (1959), 435–6.

55   'New Church a Challenge', *The Universe*, Scottish edn (4 Dec. 1964), 5; ' "A Centre of Spiritual Life": Pope Paul', *The Universe*, Scottish edn (4 Dec. 1964), 5; 'St Andrew's Day, 1964, in Dumfries', *St Andrew Annual: The Catholic Church in Scotland* (1964–65), 10.

56   Austin Winkley, 'Some Changes in Existing Churches: Westminster Cathedral and Waxwell Farm Chapel', *Clergy Review* 50 (1965), 817–24 (818–21); *CBRN* (1965), 59; minutes of meeting of the Council of Administration, Archdiocese of Liverpool (8 Mar. 1965) (LRCAA, Beck Collection, 5/S3/1).

57   J. B. O'Connell, 'Questions and Answers', *Clergy Review* 44 (1959), 435–6; George Beck to O'Mahony (parish priest, Our Lady of Sorrows, Liverpool) (16 Aug. 1965) (LRCAA, Parish Files, 212).

58   Richard Gilbert Scott, drawings (1964, 1965); archbishop's secretary to Dinan (parish priest, Our Lady Help of Christians, Tile Cross) (15 Feb. 1965); Dinan to [archbishop's secretary] (8 Mar. 1965) (ARCAB, Parish Files, P53/T4).

59   Archbishop's secretary to Dinan (10 Mar. 1965) (ARCAB, Parish Files, P53/T4).

60   Minutes of meetings of Council of Administration, Archdiocese of Liverpool (5 Oct. 1964; 16 Nov. 1964) (LRCAA, Beck Collection, 5/S3/l).

61   *CBRN* (1965), 48.

62   Gerald Corcoran (parish priest, St Michael and All Angels, Woodchurch) to William Grasar (bishop of Shrewsbury) (1 Dec. 1964); Grasar to Corcoran (9 Dec. 1964) (Shrewsbury Diocesan Archives, Birkenhead, Parish File).

63   C. Fleetwood-Walker, 'Review of New Church: St Michael and All Angels, Woodchurch, Birkenhead', *Clergy Review* 51 (1966), 825–32 (829). Dating from *CBRN* (1962), 94–5; (1963), 62–3; (1964), 120–21; (1965), 74–9.

64   Gerald Barrett (Gillespie, Kidd & Coia) to Calidec Ltd (27 Nov. 1964) (GSAA, GKC/CDE/1/2).

65   Barrett to J. & C. McGloughlin Ltd, Dublin, Kingston Brass Co. Ltd and M. H. Gill & Son Ltd, Dublin (14 Dec. 1964) (GSAA, GKC/CDE/1/2).

66   'New Church of Our Lady of Good Counsel, Dennistoun', *St Andrew Annual: The Catholic Church in Scotland* (1964–65), 41.

67   Gillespie, Kidd & Coia, drawings for St Benedict, Drumchapel (1964–69) (GSAA, GKC/CHDU/3).

68   Minutes of meeting of the Liverpool Metropolitan Cathedral Executive Committee (8 Oct. 1964) (LRCAA, Cathedral Collection, S2/XI/A/5).

69   Minutes of meeting of the Liverpool Metropolitan Cathedral Executive Committee, Liturgical Sub-Committee (21 Apr. 1964) (LRCAA, Cathedral Collection, S2/XI/A/5).

70   Minutes of meeting of the Liverpool Metropolitan Cathedral Executive Committee (9 July 1965) (LRCAA, Cathedral Collection, S2/XI/A/6).

71   Frederick Gibberd to T. G. McKenna (Cathedral Executive Committee) (5 Feb. 1964) (LRCAA, Cathedral Collection, S2/X/A/37).

72   Walker, 'Prophetic or Premature?', 187–8.

73   *CBRS* (1964), 36–9.

74   *CBRS* (1966), 63–5; see also 'Architecture and the Artist', *The Tablet* (28 June 1969), 648–9.

75   Survey report (1968) (LRCAA, Beck Collection, 5/S3/IV).

76   See for example Hornsby-Smith, *The Changing Parish*, 67.

77   Paul VI, *Apostolic Constitution (Missale Romanum) and General Instruction on the Roman Missal*, trans. Clifford Howell (London: Catholic Truth Society, 1973), 14; see also Schloeder, *Architecture in Communion*, 50.

78   Paul VI, *Apostolic Constitution (Missale Romanum) and General Instruction on the Roman Missal*, 65.

79   Ibid. 16, 23.

80   Sheppard, 'The New "Ordo Missae"', 19.

81   See for example Lucien Deiss, 'The Gradual Psalm', in Sheppard (ed.), *New Liturgy*, 80–81.

82   National Liturgical Commission of England and Wales, *Pastoral Directory for Church Building* (London: Burnes & Oates, 1968), 10, 13.

83   Fleetwood-Walker, 'Review of New Church', 830–31; Austin S. Winkley, 'Review of New Church: St Gabriel's, Holloway, London', *Clergy Review* 53 (1968), 997–1004 (998–9); Wright, 'Evolution of the Multi-Cell Church', 502; Lance Wright, 'Liverpool Cathedral: An Architectural Appraisal', *The Tablet* (13 May 1967), 520–22 (521).

84   'Infant Baptism: The New Rite', *The Tablet* (28 June 1969), 655; J. D. Crichton, 'The New Rite and Baptism', *The Tablet* (18 July 1970), 702–3; Christopher J. Walsh, 'Initiation', in Harold Winstone (ed.), *Pastoral Liturgy: A Symposium* (London: Collins, 1975), 159–88 (esp. 177); also see Sacred Congregation for Divine Worship, 'General Introduction to Christian Initiation, 1973', in Austin Flannery (ed.), *Vatican Council II: More Postconciliar Documents* (Leominster: Fowler Wright Books, 1982), 22–8.

85   Francis Woodward, souvenir booklet to accompany opening of St Michael, Wolverhampton (1968) (ARCAB, Parish Files, P318/T5).

86   *CBRS* (1972), 98–101.

87   *CBRS* (1969), 130–31.

88   *CBRS* (1973), 158–9.

89   *CBRN* (1972), 22; (1973), 222–3.

90   *CBRN* (1973), 16.

91   *CBRN* (1971), 238.

92   Austin Winkley, 'The Place of Celebration', in Winstone, *Pastoral Liturgy*, 46–9.

93   See Michael Walsh, 'Michael Shaw Obituary', *The Guardian* (13 Sept. 2012), http://www.guardian.co.uk/music/2012/sep/13/michael-shaw-obituary (accessed 4 Oct. 2012).

94   Circular letter (*c.*1971) (WDA, He7/23); see also 'Westminster Centre's Task is Liturgical Renewal', *Catholic Herald* (19 Dec. 1969), 2.

95   'New Liturgy in Centre', *The Tablet* (20 Dec. 1969), 1278–9.

96   *CBRS* (1974), 232–3.

8

Devotion

The devotional functions of churches were frequently important in their design and remained significant throughout the period studied here. The emphasis on the liturgical movement in writing on church architecture at the time and since has tended to obscure this feature of post-war church architecture, a highly distinctive aspect of Roman Catholic culture in post-war Britain. The liturgical movement contrasted the liturgy with popular devotions, which were viewed as motivated by individual piety and sentiment more than reason or doctrine. For Guardini, the liturgy's 'sense of restraint' and rich symbolic world made it a higher form of worship than pious devotions.[1] Yet Guardini argued that devotions were still important, even necessary, and could be improved through the influence of liturgy. Later, the emphasis on liturgy in church architecture marginalised devotional features in churches, as the 'Constitution on the Sacred Liturgy' implied:

> The practice of placing sacred images in churches so that they may be venerated by the faithful is to be firmly maintained. Nevertheless, their number should be moderate and their relative location should reflect right order. Otherwise they may create confusion among the Christian people and promote a faulty sense of devotion.[2]

Liturgical movement writers could be scathing about the proliferation of statues in churches, doubting their efficacy in inspiring devotion.[3] Decades later, however, a perceived loss of devotional imagery and ritual began to be felt with nostalgia, becoming a frequent criticism of the Second Vatican Council. There had been, it was thought, a 'widespread collapse of the older devotional system', as distinctive Catholic iconography had been replaced by banal and generic images.[4]

By the 1970s, many clergy were cautious with statuary. St Aidan in Coulsdon, south London, by Burles, Newton & Partners, for example, was spartan and lacked conventional imagery or indeed any special place for it. A small figurative crucifix by Dunstan Pruden was suspended in the Blessed Sacrament chapel, and a processional cross was placed behind the altar, the only image canonically required in a Catholic church. On a side wall towards the rear of the nave was the only other figure besides the discreet Stations of the Cross, a sculpture of the Virgin and Child.

Beneath it was the stand for placing candles to accompany prayer; but the statue was attached high up on the wall, precluding the pious intimacy of private prayer in a conventional side chapel. Moreover the figure itself was unfamiliar, primitive in feeling and made of black bronze by a Swiss Benedictine artist, Xaver Ruckstuhl, in the style of the altar and other furnishings he designed for the church and its reform-minded parish priest, Kenneth Allan (Figure 8.1).[5] Coulsdon was unusually ascetic for a parish church, however; most had at least a separate Lady chapel.

Before the Second Vatican Council, churches normally had chapels or niches along the sides of the nave containing statue shrines; side altars were placed at the heads of each aisle dedicated to the Virgin Mary, St Joseph or the Sacred Heart, while statues of lesser saints were placed elsewhere. At Weightman & Bullen's St Clare in Blackley, for example, the Lady altar was placed at the front to the left of the sanctuary, the Sacred Heart to the right, and three side chapels along one side contained statues of St Francis and associated saints, since this church was run by Franciscans (Figure 8.2). Architects would often design spaces in anticipation of an accumulation of statues: at St Paschal Baylon in Liverpool, architect Sydney Bolland incorporated shelved niches for statues framed from the nave with plain columns, and designed bare panels above each column to receive the Stations of the Cross, all acquired later rather than designed for the church. Church buildings were populated with familiar figures that supplemented worshippers' experience of divine transcendence with more accessible intercessors with God.

The Church often intervened to approve, moderate or condemn popular devotional practices.[6] The arrangement of images in the church was also a method of constraining the laity's enthusiastic devotions within an authorised and co-ordinated space. Nevertheless clergy and dioceses in Britain were often active in promoting non-liturgical devotions. Many devotional events took place in and around church buildings built by clergy specifically to accommodate them and formed an important part of the architect's brief.

8.2   St Clare, Blackley, Manchester, by Weightman & Bullen, 1956–58. Mosaic of St Clare by George Mayer Martin; Stations of the Cross by David John. By permission of David John. Photo: Ambrose Gillick, 2012

EUCHARISTIC DEVOTIONS

Despite the liturgical movement's emphasis on the sacramental action of the Eucharist, the Vatican also affirmed the importance of non-liturgical devotion to the Blessed Sacrament in the tabernacle, maintaining its significance even after the Second Vatican Council. The 'Instruction on the Worship of the Eucharistic Mystery' advised that 'devotion, both private and public, toward the sacrament of the altar even outside Mass … is strongly advocated by the Church, since the eucharistic sacrifice is the source and summit of the whole Christian life'.[7] Exposition of the Blessed Sacrament, its display outside the tabernacle in a monstrance for public veneration, was encouraged, provided it was separate from the Mass, which now could not take place with the sacrament exposed.[8] For Catholics in Britain, devotion to the reserved sacrament was one of the most important activities outside the Mass and required specific architectural forms. It was also a characteristic aspect of Catholicism in relation to other denominations, contributing to a Catholic sense of identity. Bishop Beck warned that liturgical developments should not weaken devotion to the sacrament: 'The frequent reception of Holy Communion, as well as public and private visits to the Blessed Sacrament, form part of the Catholic way of life', he wrote, cautioning architects against excluding this important custom.[9]

One form of this devotion was private prayer in view of the tabernacle. The view was important: as David Morgan observes, devotional images are used for their effects of concentrating the mind and stimulating profound internal engagement with their object.[10] The tabernacle with its veil and lamp was such a focal point for meditation, a recognisable sign of the 'real presence' of God within the church. Prayers could be said anywhere, but in front of the tabernacle they had a focused character, and the sense of divine presence was more keenly felt. Catholics who passed a church would doff a hat or make the sign of the cross, but would also feel an urge to enter, to 'visit' the Blessed Sacrament.

Devotion to the Blessed Sacrament could be an argument for having a church in the first place. The liturgy did not require a church – it could take place in a room in a house or a rented hall; reservation of the Blessed Sacrament, however, did require a dedicated space. At the new parish of the Holy Family at Pontefract in Leeds, parish priest John Hudson began by saying Mass in a school, but urged Bishop Dwyer to allow him to build a church, hoping not to have to begin with a temporary church hall:

> A Church-Hall never seems to be regarded as more than a glorified Mass-Centre, and it seems almost impossible to prevail upon parishioners to pay visits to the Blessed Sacrament etc. For the sake of all the Catholics in the Parish, but especially the children, I feel that a Church is a necessity.[11]

Hudson's wish was soon granted, and one of the most striking modern churches of the diocese opened in 1964, designed by Derek Walker with liturgical movement principles in mind. On the opening of the church, Dwyer was keen to emphasise its primary function of accommodating the liturgy, but he also acknowledged its devotional use:

The Parish of the Holy Family is rightly delighted that a permanent home for Our Lord in the Blessed Sacrament is now in its midst. … We have the great privilege of His abiding presence in the tabernacle. Make it your practice to visit the Blessed Sacrament as often as you can.[12]

With the altar set forward for Mass facing the people, the tabernacle was set into the reredos, but it remained a strong visual feature of the interior, set at the foot of Robert Brumby's ceramic mosaic figure of Christ in Majesty (Figure 8.3).[13]

Dual-purpose church halls were often designed to allow visits to the Blessed Sacrament while the building was otherwise closed or in use: in some, folding partitions across the sanctuary enclosed a permanent worship space with separate access to one side. When architect Lionel Prichard & Son presented plans for such a building in Widnes, the Archdiocese of Liverpool requested more room between altar and screen 'to enable people to make private visits whilst the hall was in use'.[14] Even when separate Blessed Sacrament chapels were planned in churches after Vatican II, devotional visits were used as justification, perhaps pre-empting criticism of any weakening of this devotion, an explanation given at St Mary, Leyland, for example.[15] If it was expected that a church would be locked, the visual aspect of devotion to the sacrament could be satisfied by a glazed screen or window in an unlocked vestibule, an arrangement built into many small churches, such as that of St Pius X at New Malden by Francis Broadbent.[16] Visibility could also be problematic. The parish priest of St Alexander in Bootle, a church by Velarde, removed its glazed narthex screen in 1964 and replaced it with a wall to block the view from the street when the doors were open. When questioned by the diocese, he argued that the wall 'ensured protection and reverence for the Blessed Sacrament', presumably from being ignored or mocked by passers-by during Mass. The diocese, however, insisted that he insert a window.[17] Looking into a church and seeing the tabernacle when passing was an important custom for Catholics and one that clergy aimed to sustain.

Public forms of devotion to the Blessed Sacrament also had architectural requirements. The most common was Benediction, a service of prayers and hymns to accompany the display of the host in a monstrance. The monstrance was often placed on a temporary 'throne' or pedestal on or behind the altar, sometimes sheltered with a canopy. A pedestal could be built into the reredos behind the altar, a common arrangement in pre-war churches, also employed by Adrian Gilbert Scott at Sts Mary and Joseph, Poplar, where the crucifix would be removed and replaced by the monstrance, steps behind the altar giving access. Bishop Dwyer of Leeds complained that modern altars, lacking suitable structures behind them, had unworthy arrangements for exposition, and asked all parishes to ensure they at least used temporary thrones.[18] Even in the late 1960s, the use of a high throne was still expected, though the hierarchy preferred it only for 'solemn annual occasions'.[19] Of these occasions the most important was *Quarant'Ore*, consisting of exposition for a continuous period of 40 hours with processions of the monstrance through the church, often co-ordinated across parishes so that there was continual, or at least frequent, exposition throughout each diocese.[20] During this period parishes would compete in the lavishness of their ephemeral church decorations, loading altars with flowers and candles.[21]

8.3   Holy Family, Pontefract, Leeds, by Derek Walker, 1964. Reredos of Christ in Majesty, candlesticks, altar sculpture and tabernacle by Robert Brumby. By permission of Robert Brumby. Photo: J. Roberts & Co., 1964. Source: Leeds Diocesan Archives

In some churches, exposition was not just regular but permanent, the building accommodating this distinctive requirement. Two religious orders made permanent exposition a feature of their rule. The Blessed Sacrament Fathers arrived from branches of the order in America, settling in Liverpool, where Lionel Prichard converted a cinema into a chapel of the Blessed Sacrament, and in Leicester, where they ran the parish of the Blessed Sacrament at Braunstone and commissioned a new church from Bower Norris.[22] The exterior of Norris's Byzantine-Romanesque brick building had a 'monastic simplicity' suited to the order but a 'grand scale in keeping with the noble purpose of perpetual adoration', in the architect's words; symbols of the monstrance on its gateposts were the only decoration. Inside there was a substantial reredos with the monstrance throne high up at the rear of the sanctuary under a framing arch.[23] In London, the convent chapel of the Sisters of the Adoration Réparatrice in Chelsea served a similar function. The order came from France in 1898, and, following war damage, its new chapel of 1959 was designed in a modern, Perret-influenced style by Corfiato. The nuns occupied a screened section of the nave near the sanctuary, while the laity occupied the area behind them. An unusually tall reredos had a high platform to which the monstrance was permanently fixed so that it was visible beyond the screen and dominated the interior.[24]

Meanwhile every parish church celebrated one liturgical event that included formal devotion to the Blessed Sacrament: the feast of Corpus Christi, on a variable date in spring. The monstrance was carried in procession by the celebrant, attended by clergy and servers and followed by the congregation. In many parishes, such processions took place around the grounds of the church or in the streets immediately outside, and so sufficient outdoor space around the building was needed. By the 1950s, public processions reached a peak of enthusiasm and parishes would combine for processions of the Blessed Sacrament through their towns. An article in the *Catholic Herald* in 1951 contrasted the processions of 20,000 people in Middlesbrough, the streets lined with onlookers, with the equally zealous procession of a hundred faithful through the streets of the rural town of Machynlleth.[25] Processions would pause at makeshift altars decorated to receive the monstrance; hymns were sung and Benediction given, often at civic landmarks and private houses.[26] The feast of Corpus Christi was not just a popular devotion but a liturgical one following Sunday Mass, instituted by the Vatican and especially promoted at the Counter Reformation, cultivated by the clergy in Britain and fervently celebrated by the faithful.

Despite the perception of a decline in devotion to the Blessed Sacrament after the Second Vatican Council, it continued to thrive throughout the 1960s with the support of the hierarchy: Cardinal Heenan, writing in 1966, urged Catholics not to abandon devotions as a consequence of the liturgical revival, though the urgency of his appeal suggests they were already beginning to wane.[27]

MARIAN DEVOTIONS

The next most important and frequent devotion was to the Virgin Mary. If a Catholic church had only one shrine or statue outside the sanctuary, it would invariably be dedicated to the Virgin. Separate Lady chapels continued to be common into the 1960s and could be used to celebrate Mass on weekdays. They would often be used for private prayer to the Virgin, such as the recitation of the rosary, accompanied by the lighting of candles. There were many more public forms of devotion, however, with implications for architecture.

Many churches were dedicated to the Virgin Mary, using different titles – Our Lady of Lourdes and of Fatima celebrated her apparitions; Our Lady Help of Christians, Queen of Peace, Queen of Heaven, Star of the Sea, and the Immaculate Heart of Mary were associated with set devotions or prayers. Parishes often acknowledged their dedication in decorating churches. One of the most extravagant was St Mary at Failsworth in Manchester, designed by Tadeusz Lesisz of Greenhalgh & Williams and opened in 1964. Lesisz moved his firm's church architecture away from its earlier modernism towards a Romanesque basilican style, and though designed around 1961 this church ignored the NCRG's ideas about liturgy and architecture and the growing demand to limit the devotional aspects of churches. The artworks at Failsworth were conventional in style (though nothing was mass-produced) and depicted a cycle of Catholic beliefs about the Virgin. Dominating the interior was the mosaic reredos, designed by a young parishioner, B. Nolan, and made by an Italian mosaicist (Figure 8.4). Its image of the Virgin was based on the 'Miraculous Medal', worn by many Catholics as part of a Vatican-approved devotion following the visions of a nineteenth-century French nun, St Catherine Labouré. Over the church's mosaic figure, angels holding a crown indicated the Coronation of the Virgin as Queen of Heaven, recently accepted into Catholic doctrine by Pius XII. This figure dwarfed every other element of the sanctuary, even dominating a frieze of Eucharistic symbols: liturgy was effectively made secondary to the presentation of Marian devotion.

Similar images were scattered throughout the church. Hanging in the entrance arch was a figure of the Virgin in aluminium by E. & J. Blackwell to Lesisz's design depicting the Immaculate Conception – the doctrine of the Virgin's freedom from original sin declared by Pius IX in 1854, a subject of St Catherine's visions and, it was believed, further confirmed by the apparitions at Lourdes. The figure at Failsworth evoked the Lourdes apparitions, the church's surrounding arch recalling the famous grotto (Figure 8.5). In a stone frieze above the windows, also by Blackwell, were depictions of the rosary meditations, suggesting that parishioners might have gathered to recite its prayers in procession around the church. Inside, the Lady chapel contained a statue described as a vision of St Catherine of Mary as Queen of the Universe, while stained-glass windows depicted further Marian attributes. The west window, finally, had been rescued and adapted from the demolished Victorian church and showed the Assumption, the ascension of Mary into heaven, also established as doctrine by Pius XII. Other devotional images were also present: a side chapel to the Sacred Heart containing a reredos from the Victorian church; a chapel to Saint Anthony; the Stations of the Cross.[28] The parish of Failsworth conceived of its church as a devotional shrine, its architecture organising and framing a coherent iconography.[29]

Even when the liturgical movement was accepted, Marian devotions could still be cultivated as one aspect of a participatory parish culture. Gerard Goalen's plan for Our Lady of Fatima at Harlow, for example, may have aimed at a congregational

focus on the central altar, but his elevations were intended as a field for devotional imagery. Charles Norris's *dalle de verre* windows illustrated the apparitions at Fatima in the nave and progressed to the rosary scenes in the transepts (Plate 12).[30] The parish priest, Francis Burgess, was a member of the order of the Canons Regular of Mary Immaculate and encouraged Marian devotions at Harlow. These revolved around two statues of Our Lady of Fatima, circulated between parishioners' houses where they would become the focus for family prayers including the recitation of the rosary, strongly advocated by Pius XII.[31] The church building was undoubtedly also used for such devotional activities, and its stained glass embodied this parish community's cultivation of devotion, especially through the prayers of the rosary. Liturgy and devotion were not so much in tension as complementary to each other in the religious practices of the faithful.

Many parishes in Britain held annual May processions at least until the end of the 1960s, usually in the grounds of the church and sometimes in the streets around it. The May devotions were a Catholic variant of a custom in many British towns of crowning a local girl as the May Queen and holding a procession: Catholics instead channelled this form into a devotional event. The May Queen, chosen from a parish's schoolchildren, led a procession to place a crown of flowers on the statue of the Virgin brought out from the Lady chapel for the occasion. A temporary shrine decorated with flowers would be made, sometimes outdoors, sometimes inside the church: at St Stephen, Droylsden, for example, the statue was taken from its chapel and placed in front of the opening (Figure 8.6). In some places these events even took place in the sanctuary: 'There is not much edification nor

8.4   St Mary, Failsworth, Manchester, by Greenhalgh & Williams, 1961–64. Reredos mosaic of Our Lady of All Graces designed by B. Nolan. Photo: Robert Proctor, 2012

8.5   St Mary, Failsworth, Manchester, by Greenhalgh & Williams, 1961–64. External sculpture of the Immaculate Conception and Mysteries of the Rosary by E. & J. Blackwell. Photo: Robert Proctor, 2012

8.6 St Stephen, Droylsden, Manchester, by Greenhalgh & Williams, 1958–59. May devotions, 1960s. Photographer unknown. Source: parish archive. Courtesy of the Diocese of Salford

encouragement to piety and reverence, to see May Queens and retinue strutting about the High Altar to the accompaniment of clicking cameras and craning necks', wrote one correspondent to a Catholic newspaper; yet it remained a popular practice, approved by parish priests (Figure 8.7).[32] With such events in mind, Catholic churches were designed with prominent chapels for the statue of the Virgin and ample external space.

An important feature of Marian devotion was the pilgrimage to a shrine associated with her apparitions. Pilgrimages to Lourdes featured strongly in post-war Catholic life in Britain thanks to an ever-increasing ease of travel. Devotion to St Bernadette and the Lourdes apparitions also entered British churches. Many were dedicated to Our Lady of Lourdes, St Bernadette or the Immaculate Conception, the doctrine that resulted from the apparitions, and many more churches had images and shrines associated with this devotion. Sometimes such shrines were built outside the church, and some were extravagant facsimiles of the famous grotto. This practice had persisted since the nineteenth century:

8.7   St Catherine of Siena,
Birmingham, by Harrison &
Cox, 1961–65. May devotions,
1960s. Photographer unknown.
Source: parish archive. Courtesy
of the Birmingham Roman
Catholic Diocesan Trustees

the imitation grotto imaginatively transported its viewers to the original shrine,
arousing the devotional fervour of pilgrimage in the more limited confines of the
parish.[33] Occasionally replica grottoes became pilgrimage sites in their own right:
at Carfin in Lanarkshire, parish priest Thomas Taylor had founded such a shrine
in the 1920s that, with inventive plumbing, even possessed the original's sacred
spring, becoming a national centre of pilgrimage in Scotland. A new circular church
was built for it by Charles Gray, opened in 1973, though crowded ceremonies were
normally conducted in the open air.[34] The church of St Bernadette in Lancaster by
Tom Mellor contained plentiful open ground intended from the start to be used
for devotions. A Lourdes grotto was created under Mellor's concrete campanile by
Preston architect Wilfrid Mangan in 1965, several years after the church's opening,
though it had been intended originally: the architect's perspective showed an
arched opening in the tower's basement and a pool of water in front of it; above
the grotto was an open section in the campanile intended as a pulpit (Figure 8.8).[35]
Mangan's plans included a paved 'amphitheatre' intended to accommodate crowds
of visitors for ceremonies under the tower.[36]

8.8   St Bernadette, Lancaster, by Tom Mellor, 1958. Perspective by the architect dated 1955. Courtesy of David Mellor. Source: parish archive

The diocese of Lancaster was in fact dedicated to Our Lady of Lourdes, and, in thanksgiving for having escaped serious bomb damage in the Second World War, its bishop, Thomas Flynn, commissioned a shrine, the votive chapel of Our Lady of Lourdes in Blackpool, designed by Velarde and completed in 1957 (Plate 13, Figure 8.9). The cost was raised from the contributions of parishes across the diocese. It had little real function, not serving as a parish church: it was located near a hospital, where it might have catered for nurses or visitors, and may have been intended as a gathering point for pilgrims to Lourdes, including hospital patients, departing from Blackpool airport.[37] It soon became associated with a convent of the Adoration Réparatrice. Enriched with integral carving by David John, it was a small, elaborate building, a dazzling display of gold mosaic and deep colours framing John's understated figure of the Lourdes apparition over the reredos. Its main purpose seems to have been simply to exist as a continuous act of devotion in its own right by all the Catholics of the diocese.

STATIONS OF THE CROSS

The Stations of the Cross were another important devotion with a prominent place in nearly every Catholic church in Britain. Like Marian devotions, the Stations hinged around visual cues provided by images, and architects often considered them an important function in church design. The Stations, formalised by the Church in the eighteenth century, consisted of a series of prayers and meditations with ritual actions including genuflection at 14 episodes in the Passion of Christ, beginning with the condemnation of Christ by Pilate and culminating in the entombment.

8.9 Votive Shrine of Our Lady of Lourdes, Blackpool, by F. X. Velarde, 1955–57. Integral sculpture by David John. Photo: Robert Proctor, 2011

Some episodes were drawn from the Bible and others were traditional, such as the miraculous imprint of Christ's face on Veronica's veil. Regulations attached to the devotion established rules for its minimum form, prescribing a series of prayers made in procession past wooden crosses attached to the church's walls. Images were not formally required, but were normally hung alongside the crosses, and often included the crosses in their frames. A physical procession was theoretically required, but if necessary the congregation could remain in the pews, turning to watch the priest and servers as they moved.[38] The devotion was practised regularly as a public ceremony and also privately, especially in Lent. The rules set by the Church for this ritual were established in connection with the indulgence it granted and were carefully followed, the *Clergy Review* often advising priests on the correct forms of the devotion.[39]

Though never required in a church, the Stations were nearly always present. The competition brief for Liverpool Metropolitan Cathedral stated that the 14 positions for the Stations had to be marked on competition plans, and when competitor Clive Entwistle asked whether these were obligatory the answer was affirmative and that they must be placed in the nave.[40] Gibberd's design had 16 slim structural supports surrounding the nave, and when in 1964 the cathedral committee came to consider the Stations there was some debate. One member thought they were 'not a necessary part of the furnishing of a church or cathedral, but concerned rather with private devotions', and that as there was already a set in the crypt the cathedral did not need another. Gibberd suggested that plain crosses might be placed in the nave, but, the committee agreed, 'it was felt that this would not be popular with the people'. The faithful expected images, and, though the clergy were sympathetic, they deferred a decision indefinitely.[41] This was an unusual situation, however, and even those writers who followed the liturgical movement generally thought this devotion should have a significant place in the church. Crichton's 'Dream Church', for example, envisaged the Stations as a painted frieze in a circular aisle wide enough for a full procession.[42]

As a popular, non-liturgical devotion, it was important to clergy that the Stations of the Cross should contain images that ordinary parishioners could use as devotional aids, and so the events of the Passion had to take a recognisable form, inspiring meditation on the sufferings of Christ. In Edinburgh, for example, Archbishop Gray assiduously solicited opinions from clergy and laity on abstract designs by Fred Carson for Stations at the new church of St Gabriel at Prestonpans, concluding that the artist's work 'may indeed be the artistic pattern for the future, but if so we are not yet prepared for it' and refusing to endorse the commission, and though what must have been a revised design did eventually proceed, an abstract treatment remained unusual.[43] Eric Gill's Stations at Westminster Cathedral were the most important precedent for artists commissioned by modern architects for stone panels: hieratic figures were thought capable of expressing strong emotions without sentimentality to assist the viewer in meditation.[44] At Our Lady of Fatima, Harlow, for example, Irene Foord-Kelcey's Stations of the Cross were, like Gill's, in Hopton Wood stone and boldy primitive in style, described in emotional terms: her interpretation of the narrative was an unfolding of 'the entire tragedy, Love, Agony, and Death'; the women of Jerusalem demonstrated their 'utter desolation', as 'each figure seems obsessed by grief' (Figure 8.10).[45] Even as late as 1970, a modern church could receive Stations loosely inspired by those of Gill: at John Rochford's church of St Paul at Wood Green in London, the commission was given to Michael Clark, who had stayed at Gill's community at Ditchling. His stone reliefs were less stylised than Gill's but hardly more realist: their figures were taut with unreleased emotive energy, drenched in white raking light from above the processional strip of space that Rochford had designed for them (Figure 8.11).

Such an approach – the stone plaque embedded in or attached to the wall – was only loosely integrated with architecture, and many modern architects tried to incorporate this devotional function more rigorously into their designs. At their church of St Martin at Castlemilk in Glasgow, MacMillan and Metzstein of Gillespie, Kidd & Coia made the Stations an articulating element (Figure 8.12). Windows in the side walls of this church were combined with the Stations. Plaster casts of typical church furnishers' images were cut down and inserted into the 14 splayed embrasures. The pious images therefore satisfied conventional devotional desires, but, in their almost ghost-like presence, must have been intended by the architects as more like quotations of the kitsch, an 'as-found' element brought into the architecture in the manner of the Independent Group. Though integrated, however, these panels revealed themselves to be superfluous, since the wooden crosses that constituted the canonical form were separate, attached to the window sills and silhouetted against the coloured glass.

8.10   Our Lady of Fatima, Harlow New Town, by Gerard Goalen, 1954–60. Stations of the Cross by Irene Foord-Kelcey. By permission of Christopher Foord-Kelcey. Photo: Robert Proctor, 2010

8.11   St Paul, Wood Green, London, by John Rochford, 1967–72. Stations of the Cross by Michael Clark. By permission of Joseph Lindsey-Clark. Photo: Robert Proctor, 2010

These unconventional Stations gave ritual meaning to the architecture of the nave walls as a strong visual feature of the church's interior while creatively exploring the implications of the ritual's rules.

Other architects incorporated Stations more literally into the windows. At Weightman & Bullen's Holy Ghost at Bootle in Liverpool, opened in 1958, Joseph Nuttgens made the Stations in stained glass, lit from outside when used after dark.[46] Stained glass was normally associated with a decorative rather than devotional purpose; here, however, architect and craftsman gave the stained-glass window a new functional role in the church building. Reynolds & Scott later did the same at Christ Church, Heald Green; Peter Langtry-Langton incorporated more modern stained glass Stations at St Joseph, Hunslet, and Gillespie, Kidd & Coia employed Sadie McLellan for this purpose at the Sacred Heart in Cumbernauld (Figure 7.13). At the English Martyrs, Horley, architect Justin Alleyn commissioned stained-glass Stations that were especially clearly related to the church's plan. Fourteen slot-shaped windows articulated a processional circuit around the octagonal nave, with expressive modern versions of the scenes in *dalle de verre* by Fourmaintraux, also lit from outside (Plate 14).[47]

Linear friezes of Stations were perhaps easiest to integrate into the church's design: at St Aidan at Acton, two horizontal slots in the side aisles were filled with blue and gold mosaic, a background for figures by Arthur Fleischmann.[48] More dramatic was F. R. Bates, Son & Price's church of St Francis of Assisi in Cardiff. Adam Kossowski made several sets of Stations for churches across England and Wales

8.12   St Martin, Castlemilk, Glasgow, by Gillespie, Kidd & Coia, 1957–61. Photo: Robert Proctor, 2010

in glazed ceramics, but at St Francis he went much further. Instead of hanging work on walls, he was given a curved balcony frontage in an arc around the church and used it to give the scenes a setting and an effect of movement (Plate 15). A backdrop of green sgraffito depicted buildings and hills and his ceramic pieces were placed over the top, the pink cross making a rhythmic motif across the frieze. A passageway between pews gave a processional route sufficient for priest and servers to pass under the Stations in sequence, the images visible to the worshippers from their seats. It was an innovative work that dominated this small modern church, articulating its space.

The Second Vatican Council prompted a significant shift in ideas about devotions, centring on the practice of indulgences. Devotions before the Second Vatican Council were highly motivated by indulgences, attached by the Church to set prayers and actions: the indulgence would be phrased as an equivalent number of days or months of fasting, or would be 'plenary', fully preparing the subject for heaven. A ritual stance towards devotions was encouraged because indulgences only applied when the actions or prayers to which they were attached were performed correctly, and so indulgences also helped to regulate popular devotion.[49] Reformers, however, worried that the faithful treated such devotions as magical acts rather than genuine prayer capable of bringing the individual closer to God.[50] Consequently Paul VI announced in 1967 that indulgences were to be reduced and simplified and loosened from their connections to specific objects or places.[51] This reform aimed to change the emphasis in devotions from public ritual actions towards personal, thoughtful piety.

The Stations of the Cross were revised the following year. The devotion still attracted a plenary indulgence, but its rules were relaxed: 14 Stations were required, but their visual forms were undefined; a processional movement was still required, but the prayers did not have to relate to the conventional episodes and could instead be a general meditation on the Passion. These changes increased the latitude for creativity in the design of the Stations, a freedom made use of at Clifton Cathedral. Here, the architects wanted the Stations to be integral to the architecture and commissioned William Mitchell, a well-established architectural sculptor who had recently made the doors and bell tower at Liverpool Metropolitan Cathedral. Mitchell had previously refused a commission for Stations for the seminary chapel at Kirkby Lonsdale in Lancashire, doubtful of their contemporary relevance. When he presented his ideas and sketches to the clergy at Clifton in 1972, they constituted such a departure from the norm that they were sent for approval to Annibale Bugnini, Secretary of the Sacred Congregation for Divine Worship at the Vatican.[52] Mitchell's new series omitted all but one non-scriptural event, added the Last Supper to the beginning of the sequence and the Resurrection to the end, and included Christ's forgiving of the repentant sinner on the cross.[53] This revised sequence made significant changes to the focus of this devotion, away from the suffering of Christ and towards the more general significance of the Passion and Resurrection. Mitchell conceived of his new series as more relevant for the

modern world: the agony in the garden, for example, represented contemporary conditions of stress and anxiety.[54]

The architects made the Stations an important feature of the interior of the new Cathedral with large panels along the processional circuit around the rear of the nave (Figure 8.13). Mitchell's technique incorporated them literally into the fabric of the architecture: the building's walls were of a fine board-marked concrete, and the Stations were made with a fast-setting cement called 'Faircrete' into which the designs were rapidly drawn. The immediacy of the technique, Mitchell thought, would prevent conventional forms from creeping into his work.[55] The figures were bold and primitive, heads, hands and clear symbols in low relief. Their placement in the cathedral gave them a distinct relationship with the liturgy, reflecting the primary concern of clergy and architects at Clifton and the liturgical movement aim of making devotions more liturgical. Since the revised sequence began with the Last Supper it already contained a liturgical allusion; the Resurrection scene, moreover, depicted Christ's hands breaking bread in reference to his appearance at Emmaus. Clifton's Stations of the Cross therefore began and ended with Eucharistic motifs, suggesting an understanding of the Passion in relation to liturgy and making this devotion more relevant to the principal purpose of the church building. With newly written prayers and images that were unfamiliar to the faithful, Clifton's Stations were designed to rouse worshippers out of ritual habits to force them to think in a new way about this devotion, even as its customary prominence in the church was maintained.

8.13   Clifton Cathedral, Bristol, by Percy Thomas Partnership, 1965–73. Stations of the Cross by William Mitchell. By permission of William Mitchell. Photo: Robert Proctor, 2013

PILGRIMAGE

In comparison with the sobriety and ubiquity of the Stations of the Cross, the custom of pilgrimage was entirely different, attended with festivity and focused on unique, special places. Though pilgrimages have often been attributed to the laity as spontaneous responses to miraculous events, post-war British pilgrimages were organised by the clergy and deliberately invented – or reinvented – to stimulate the devotion of the faithful. Architects and artists participated in this invention, providing spaces with a heightened sense of the sacred as frames for pilgrimage activity. Victor Turner's anthropological theory of pilgrimage describes it as a rite of passage, occupying a liminal place imbued with qualities associated with sacredness where pilgrims can briefly subvert authorised rules of conduct in an atmosphere of fellowship, or *communitas*: though he also notes that religious authorities often intervene to regulate it and subdue any excesses.[56] Pilgrimage shrines offered the promise of special contact with the sacred and personal transformation, prompted by a surfeit of symbolic objects, images and activities.[57] Moreover, Turner sees a resurgence in pilgrimage in the twentieth century as a popular reaction against modernising and iconoclastic tendencies in the Church.[58] More recently Robert Maniura has noted the highly variable and flexible nature of pilgrimage devotions: 'pilgrimage has no rubric', he writes, and many kinds of actions and experiences may be available at a shrine.[59] As with other devotions, the central principle of pilgrimage is vision: 'the people come "to see the image"' – a principle certainly maintained in the revived pilgrimages of post-war Britain.[60]

A significant concern of British Catholics was that the dissolution of the monasteries under Henry VIII and the subsequent Protestant Reformation had obliterated all historical pilgrimage shrines. Even when the buildings and sites of shrines remained in the care of other denominations, nearly all devotional features, including the bodies of saints, were lost. Throughout the nineteenth and twentieth centuries the absence of the relics and shrines of the saints was keenly felt and nostalgically evoked in new churches. For Catholics the landscapes of England, Scotland and Wales were marked by sites of loss, inspiring efforts to revive and restore the ancient shrines and their pilgrimages. Among them, two post-war examples stand out as particularly important: the shrine of St Simon Stock at Aylesford Priory in Kent, and that of Our Lady of the Taper at Cardigan in Wales.

Aylesford Priory, near the pilgrim route to Canterbury, was a Carmelite foundation established in the thirteenth century and handed over to secular use with the dissolution of the monasteries, its fifteenth-century church subsequently demolished.[61] One of its earliest abbots had been St Simon Stock, reputedly witness to a vision of the Virgin Mary that inspired a devotion known as the 'scapular'. This was a brown cloth, later reduced to a small piece of cloth bearing an image of the Virgin, whose wearers were assured an indulgence, a devotion that became almost as popular as the rosary.[62] The Carmelite order re-established itself in Britain in 1949 when a group of Irish friars purchased the remaining cloistered cottages at Aylesford, arriving with a dignified procession.[63]

Two years later they were given a relic of the skull of St Simon Stock by the cathedral of Bordeaux. The transfer of the relics, hailed as a 'homecoming' of the saint by the Catholic press, was accompanied by ceremonies that attracted over 20,000 visitors.[64] The priory soon became a major pilgrimage site through the enthusiastic publicity of the prior, Malachy Lynch, and a few years later Adrian Gilbert Scott was appointed as architect to build a new chapel and accompanying shrines to transform it into a worthy pilgrimage centre. Lynch also set about creating a hub of Catholic artistic and craft activity along the lines of Gill's colony at Ditchling, and attracted Kossowski to contribute his most important body of work to extend and complete the buildings.[65]

The romantic liminal setting of the priory was an attraction to pilgrims: though the town of Aylesford was easy to reach from London, visitors had to cross a bridge over the Medway river and climb a hill to its concealed site, a journey evoked in spiritual terms in journalistic reports.[66] The site's qualities of loss, ruination and recovery were also powerful, as the ruins of the medieval church were discovered on the site and many of its stones used for new buildings when work began in 1954.[67] Adrian Gilbert Scott's design for a new church did not, however, attempt to replicate the old: instead it preserved the sense of loss by placing a sanctuary under a broad tower and leaving the nave open to the sky (Figure 8.14). The open-air gathering had become a feature of pilgrimage experience in Britain since medieval churches were not available for Catholic use, and it was consciously retained at Aylesford. The building consisted of a complex series of chapels distributed along cloistered walkways framing the open-air nave. It was a network of interconnected shrines, its elevations forming a self-effacing backdrop for a profusion of devotional imagery. The chapels were decorated with vivid ceramics and sgraffito by Kossowski, who also made many of the liturgical furnishings, and Charles Norris contributed *dalle de verre* windows (Figure 8.15). One chapel was dedicated to Carmelite saints, another to the English Reformation martyrs; there was a chapel to St Anne, the mother of Mary; and behind the sanctuary was the shrine to Simon Stock containing Kossowski's towering reliquary, installed in 1964 (Figure 8.16). Michael Clark was commissioned for a figure of the Virgin of the Assumption, ceremonially installed over the high altar against a glittering ceramic backdrop by Kossowski.[68] There was a 'rosary way', Kossowski's earliest work at Aylesford, a series of majolica plaques around a garden behind the shrine. Pilgrims visiting Aylesford would undertake the primary ceremonies of Mass and Benediction in the open nave, but multiple dispersed and secondary devotional activities were available too: visits and prayers at the reliquary and other chapels; the Stations of the Cross; and recitation of the rosary in an imaginative and romantic setting. It was an encapsulation and intensification in one evocative site of all the main devotional activities of Roman Catholicism.

The site became a pilgrimage centre, 'the foremost shrine of Our Lady in England', with the co-operation of the hierarchy.[69] Bishop Cowderoy of Southwark led frequent ceremonies attended by thousands. When the relic was installed, he celebrated Mass in the presence of the bishop of Bordeaux and a representative of the Vatican.[70] Cowderoy declared in a sermon that he 'could never be tired …

8.14   Aylesford Priory, Kent, by Adrian Gilbert Scott, 1954–64. Central sculpture of the Virgin Mary by Michael Clark. Photo: Robert Proctor, 2010

8.15   Aylesford Priory, Kent, by Adrian Gilbert Scott, 1954–64. Chapel of the Forty Martyrs of England and Wales: ceramics by Adam Kossowski; *dalle de verre* windows by Charles Norris. Photo: Robert Proctor, 2010

FLOS CARMELI VITIS FLORIGERA

ST·SIMON OF ENGLAND PRAY FOR US

8.16   Aylesford Priory, Kent, by Adrian Gilbert Scott, 1954–64. Reliquary of St Simon Stock by
Adam Kossowski; *dalle de verre* windows by Charles Norris. Photo: Robert Proctor, 2010

of encouraging by every means in his power this great work destined to play a great part in the bringing of this land back to be Our Lady's Dowry', and the Vatican granted a plenary indulgence for pilgrims at his request.[71] Lynch, meanwhile, was adept at publicity and fundraising, attracting volunteer donors and builders through 'Our Lady's Building Company', whose 25,000 members received a newsletter and reports of miraculous events.[72] It was an orchestrated plan to capture the imaginations and harness the devotional desires of British Catholics.

Pilgrimages in Britain continued to grow after the Second Vatican Council. At Our Lady of the Taper in Cardigan a church was built after the council that reconciled devotional practices to liturgical ceremonies in a manner informed by the liturgical movement. This shrine was also newly 'restored' after the Second World War. In December 1953, on the eve of a 'Marian year' announced by Pius XII, Cardigan appeared on a pictorial map in the *Catholic Herald* showing the modern and medieval Marian shrines of England, Wales and the south of Scotland made by Catholic historian Martin Gillett and illustrator Tim Madden, later also issued as a poster (Figure 8.17).[73] This striking image interpreted Britain as a lost landscape of Marian devotion, complete with iconic statues and miraculous apparitions. The former medieval shrine of Our Lady of Cardigan, the subject of a recent booklet by a local historian, was prominently marked. Gillett and the parish priest of Cardigan, George Anwyll, persuaded the bishop of Menevia, John Petit, to revive the shrine.[74]

Gillett became involved in its establishment at the bishop's request: he had named it 'Our Lady of the Taper', as its medieval statue was thought to have held a candle, and he oversaw the creation of a statue by Benedictine sculptor Vincent Dapré. The new statue was blessed by Cardinal Griffin in Westminster Cathedral in 1956 and toured the diocese of Menevia before arriving in procession at Cardigan, where it was solemnly installed by Petit in the tiny parish church (Figure 8.18).[75] Seamus Cunnane succeeded Anwyll as parish priest in 1962 and assiduously promoted the shrine as a pilgrimage centre, campaigning for a new church capable of accommodating pilgrims and ceremonies. Nevertheless Cunnane thought that the small size of the existing parish church was not a hindrance to the pilgrimage: rather than bringing the statue into an open space, he wanted pilgrims to overflow from the church and to enter later for private devotion, considering the experience of visiting a shrine an important feature of pilgrimage.[76] When a new church eventually became possible, he retained this idea in its design.

The old church was not only too small but was also threatened with demolition to make way for a road, so a new site and building were necessary.[77] Petit wanted to acquire Cardigan's medieval castle, perhaps to recreate a medieval pilgrimage atmosphere and lend historical authority to the restoration of this devotion, but Cunnane instead found a site with room to expand and open grounds for gatherings of the faithful in a more suburban location.[78] Cunnane closely directed the architect, Merrick Sloan of Weightman & Bullen, in the new church's design, considering how pilgrimage activities would take place in and around the building. The statue shrine, a glazed tower with room for only a few people, was separate from the church, linked to it by a wall surrounding a courtyard from where it could be viewed by the assembled crowds (Figure 8.19).

8.17   'Shrines of Our Lady', from *Catholic Herald* (4 Dec. 1953), 7. Drawn by
Tim Madden. Courtesy of the *Catholic Herald*, catholicherald.co.uk

8.18   Pilgrimage of Our Lady of the Taper, Cardigan. Undated photograph, appearing to show installation of new statue in 1956. Photographer unknown. Source: Menevia Diocesan Archives. Courtesy of the Diocese of Menevia and Canon Seamus Cunnane

8.19   Our Lady of the Taper, Cardigan, by Weightman & Bullen, 1970. View from courtyard: statue-shrine to the left; church in the centre; presbytery forming wall to the right. Photo: Robert Proctor, 2010

The shrine kept this devotional activity apart from liturgical events so that congregations attending Mass would not be distracted by devotions. The timber-framed church was relatively small for parish use, but for large gatherings of pilgrims the faithful could stand in the open courtyard, glazing at the rear of the nave allowing them to see inside. Cunnane and his architects embraced the Catholic pilgrimage culture of outdoor settings and the sense of fellowship given by a dense crowd, combining this occasional devotional function with the building's more regular liturgical use. The opening and consecration ceremony for the church in 1970 demonstrated its pilgrimage functions. A procession through the town brought the statue from the old church to the new shrine, and its taper was lit by Gillett in front of the crowds in the courtyard.[79] The church of Our Lady of the Taper demonstrates the enormous and continuing popularity of Marian pilgrimage devotion in post-war Britain even after the Second Vatican Council: modern in style and architectural approach and purpose-built to contain popular devotions in carefully considered relationship to the liturgy, the church sustained the popular religious enthusiasm of Catholics in post-war Britain in accordance with the tenets of the council.

NOTES

1   Guardini, *Spirit of the Liturgy*, 18, 56, 60–61.

2   'Constitution on the Sacred Liturgy', in Abbott (ed.), *The Documents of Vatican II*, 175.

3   Crichton, 'Art at the Service of the Liturgy', 170.

4   Margaret Hebblethwaite, 'Devotion', in Hastings (ed.), *Modern Catholicism*, 240–41.

5   Kenneth Allan, 'Obviously Post-Vatican II', *Catholic Herald* (3 Mar. 1967), 6; 'The Good Church Guide: St Aidan's, Coulsdon', *Clergy Review* 58 (1974), 552–4.

6   See Robert Anthony Orsi, *The Madonna of 115th Street: Faith and Community in Italian Harlem, 1880–1950* (New Haven: Yale University Press, 1985).

7   Sacred Congregation of Rites, 'Instruction on Worship of the Eucharistic Mystery' (1967), art. 58. *The Catholic Liturgical Library*, http://www.catholicliturgy.com/index. cfm/FuseAction/DocumentContents/Index/2/SubIndex/11/DocumentIndex/338 (accessed 12 Sept. 2012).

8   Ibid., arts 60–66; cf. pre-conciliar instructions in Fortescue, *The Ceremonies of the Roman Rite*, 351.

9   George Andrew Beck, 'Liturgy and Church Building', 163.

10   David Morgan, *The Sacred Gaze: Religious Visual Culture in Theory and Practice* (Berkeley: University of California Press, 2005), 50.

11   John E. Hudson (parish priest, Holy Family, Pontefract), visitation paper (12 Oct. 1958) (Leeds Diocese Archives [LDA], Parish File for Holy Family, Pontefract).

12   George Patrick Dwyer, foreword to souvenir booklet, Holy Family, Pontefract (1964) (LDA, Parish File for Holy Family).

13   See also *CBRN* (1964), 131–5; '7 New Churches', *Architectural Review* (Oct. 1965), 256–8.

14 Sites and Buildings Commission (19 Nov. 1957) (LRCAA, Finance Collection, 12/S3/III).

15 *CBRN* (1959), 172.

16 *CBRS* (1956), 48–51.

17 Minutes of meetings of the Council of Administration, Archdiocese of Liverpool (13 Apr.; 6 July 1964) (LRCAA, Beck Collection, 5/S3/I).

18 George Patrick Dwyer, letter to clergy (*ad clerum*) (3 Apr. 1962), *Acta ecclesiae Loidensis* 31 (LDA).

19 'Statement and Directives on Devotion to the Blessed Sacrament drawn up by the Archdiocesan Liturgical Commission and Circulated to the Clergy with the Approval of the Archbishop' (*c.*1968) (LRCAA, Beck Collection, 5/S3/IV); see also National Liturgical Commission of England and Wales, *Pastoral Directory*, 19.

20 Diocese of Salford, *Almanac for 1965*, 25–7 (SDA); Fortescue, *The Ceremonies of the Roman Rite*, 349–58.

21 For example *CBRN* (1956), 93.

22 *CBRN* (1972), 160–61; 'U.S. Priests Coming to Leicester', *Catholic Herald* (24 Aug. 1951), 5.

23 *CBRS* (1956), 98–9.

24 *CBRS* (1959), 39–42; see also 'New Chapel on Site of Saint's Home', *The Universe*, Scottish edn (14 Nov. 1958), 9; Patricia E. C. Croot (ed.), *A History of the County of Middlesex*, vol. 12: *Chelsea* (London: Institute for Historical Research, 2004), British History Online, http://www.british-history.ac.uk/report.aspx?compid=28726 (accessed 18 Oct. 2012).

25 'Parish of 50 Has Its Procession', *Catholic Herald* (1 June 1951), 5.

26 'Benediction in the Market Place', *Catholic Herald* (12 June 1953), 7; 'A Moment of Reverence', *The Universe*, Scottish edn (13 June 1958), 16.

27 John C. Heenan, *Council and Clergy* (London: Geoffrey Chapman, 1966), 90.

28 *St Mary's, Failsworth: 1845–1964* (Manchester: n.p., 1964) (parish archive); see also *CBRN* (1964), 77–81.

29 For a more critical view, see Walker, 'Developments in Catholic Churchbuilding', 382.

30 Charles Norris, 'The Stained Glass Windows', in *Our Lady of Fatima, Harlow: Opening Souvenir Booklet* (Harlow New Town: n.p., 1960), 44 (BDA, I3).

31 Elinor Moreton Smith, 'Recent Catholic Development in Harlow', in *Our Lady of Fatima, Harlow: Opening Souvenir Booklet* (Harlow New Town: n.p., 1960), 21, 27; Francis Burgess (parish priest, Our Lady of Fatima, Harlow) to Bernard Patrick Wall (bishop of Brentwood) (20 Feb. 1956); Burgess to George Andrew Beck (bishop of Brentwood) (14 July 1954) (BDA, I3).

32 Sacerdos, 'May Queen Unsuitable Customs', *Catholic Herald* (31 May 1957), 2.

33 See for example McDannell, *Material Christianity*, 155–62; see also Ruth Harris, *Lourdes: Body and Spirit in the Secular Age* (London: Allen Lane, 1999), 72–84.

34 *Solemn Opening of the New Church of St Francis Xavier, Carfin* (Carfin: n.p., 1973) (SCA, HC/57).

35 Tom Mellor, watercolour painting (1955) (parish archive of St Bernadette, Lancaster); *CBRN* (1958), 135; also *Aedificatio: A History of St Bernadette's Church, Bowerham, Lancaster* (n.d.), 12–14 (Lancaster Roman Catholic Diocesan Archives [LRCDA], Parish File).

36 Wilfrid C. Mangan, plan drawing (9 Aug. 1962) (parish archive, St Bernadette, Lancaster).

37 For example 'A Prayer Fashioned in Stone' [newspaper cutting], *Blackpool Evening Gazette* (13 May 1982), 12 (church archive, Our Lady of Lourdes, Blackpool); see also English Heritage, 'Thanksgiving Shrine of Our Lady of Lourdes' (30 June 1999), http://list.english-heritage.org.uk/resultsingle.aspx?uid=1387319 (accessed 23 Oct. 2012).

38 Fortescue, *The Ceremonies of the Roman Rite*, 242–3.

39 J. O'Connell, 'Questions and Answers', *Clergy Review* 40 (1955), 537–40; L. L. McReavy, 'Questions and Answers', *Clergy Review* 42 (1957), 554–6; Urban Judge, 'Erection of the Stations of the Cross', *Clergy Review* 44 (1959), 682–5.

40 *Architectural Competition for the Metropolitan Cathedral of Christ the King*, 19; Clive Entwistle to Mgr Turner (cathedral competition secretary, Archdiocese of Liverpool) (25 Nov. 1959) (LRCAA, Cathedral Collection, S2/VIII/A/12); competitors' questions and answers (LRCAA, Cathedral Collection, S2/VIII/A/17).

41 Cathedral Executive Committee (12 Nov. 1964) (LRCAA, Cathedral Collection, S2/XI/A/5).

42 Crichton, 'A Dream-Church', 73.

43 Gordon Gray (archbishop of Edinburgh and St Andrews) to Walter Glancy (14 May 1965) (SCA, DE/39/29).

44 Roulin, *Modern Church Architecture*, 34–5.

45 'The Stations of the Cross', in *Our Lady of Fatima, Harlow: Opening Souvenir Booklet* (Harlow New Town: n.p., 1960), 58 (BDA, I3). The sculptor's surname was often written, as here, 'Foord-Kelsey'.

46 *CBRN* (1958), 42–8; attributed to Joseph Nuttgens by Paul Quail, Guild of Catholic Artists and Craftsmen untitled draft news sheet (June 1957) (ASCA, uncatalogued).

47 *CBRS* (1962), 108–13.

48 *CBRS* (1962), 65–6.

49 On this idea, see for example McDannell, *Material Christianity*, 23–4; Victor Turner and Edith Turner, *Image and Pilgrimage in Christian Culture: Anthropological Perspectives* (New York: Columbia University Press, 1978), 193.

50 For example T. Corbishley, letter to the editor, *The Tablet* (27 Jan. 1962), 89; L. L. McReavy and J. B. O'Connell, 'Questions and Answers', *Clergy Review* 51 (1966), 804.

51 Paul VI, 'Indulgentiarum doctrina' (1967), The Holy See, http://www.vatican.va/holy_father/paul_vi/apost_constitutions/documents/hf_p-vi_apc_19670101_indulgentiarum-doctrina_en.html (accessed 31 Oct. 2012).

52 T. J. Hughes (vicar general, diocese of Clifton) to Annibale Bugnini (secretary of the Sacred Congregation for Divine Worship, the Holy See) (12 Feb. 1972); Hughes to Bugnini (19 Oct. 1972); Bugnini to Hughes (20 Nov. 1972) (CDA, Cathedral File, 'Way of the Cross').

53 Typescript text of Stations of the Cross (*c*.1972); W. J. Mitchell (secretary to bishop of Clifton) to members of the Liturgical Commission of the Diocese of Clifton (10 Mar. 1972) (CDA, Cathedral File, 'Way of the Cross').

54 William Mitchell, telephone interview with Robert Proctor (23 Nov. 2012).

55   Ibid.

56   For example Victor Turner, *Dramas, Fields and Metaphors: Symbolic Action in Human Society* (Ithaca, NY: Cornell University Press 1974), 166–230; Turner and Turner, *Image and Pilgrimage*, 27, 29–31.

57   V. Turner, *Dramas, Fields and Metaphors*, 197.

58   Ibid. 223.

59   Robert Maniura, *Pilgrimage to Images in the Fifteenth Century: The Origins of the Cult of Our Lady of Częstochowa* (Woodbridge: Boydell Press, 2004), 88.

60   Ibid. 90.

61   'Friaries: The Carmelite Friars of Aylesford', in William Page (ed.), *A History of the County of Kent*, vol. 2 (London: Archibald Constable, 1926), 201–3, British History Online, http://www.british-history.ac.uk/report.aspx?compid=38223 (accessed 2 Nov. 2012).

62   Joseph Christie, 'English Saints: St Simon Stock – A Sturdy Kentishman – England's First Carmelite Friar', *Catholic Herald* (16 May 1941), 6.

63   Douglas Hyde, 'The Carmelites Kept Vigil at Aylesford: Home at Last', *Catholic Herald* (4 Nov. 1949), 1.

64   'A Great New Shrine of Our Lady', *Catholic Herald* (13 July 1951), 1; 'St Simon Home in Triumph', *Catholic Herald* (20 July 1951), 1.

65   Much of what follows borrows from Rosemary Hill, 'Prior Commitment', *Crafts* 172 (Sept.–Oct. 2001), 28–31; on Kossowski's work, see Pearson, 'Broad Visions', 7.

66   [Michael de la Bédoyère], 'Ancient Stones Guarded Secret', *Catholic Herald* (28 Oct. 1949), 5.

67   'Ancient Stones are Used in New Shrine', *The Universe*, Scottish edn (25 July 1958), 7.

68   'From Our Notebook', *The Tablet* (26 Nov. 1960), 1088.

69   'Carmelites Come Back', *The Tablet* (20 Sept. 1969), 938.

70   'A Great New Shrine of Our Lady'.

71   'Never Tired of Coming', *Catholic Herald* (24 Aug. 1956), 7; 'Inspiration to Great Courage', *Catholic Herald* (4 Dec. 1953), 13.

72   Marian Curd, 'Why Look Abroad for a Building Company?', *Catholic Herald* (6 Feb. 1959), 5.

73   'Shrines of Our Lady', *Catholic Herald* (4 Dec. 1953), 7; 'The Map of the Year', *Catholic Herald* (11 Dec. 1953), 1; Martin Gillett, 'Our Lady's Dowry', letter to the editor, *Catholic Herald* (15 Apr. 1954), 2.

74   John A. W. Bate, 'The Modern Story of Our Lady of the Taper', *Menevia Record* (Feb. 1956), 10 (MDA).

75   Seamus Cunnane, *Our Lady of Cardigan: A History and Memoir* (Cardigan: n.p., 2006), 15–19; O.J.M., 'Our Lady's Triumphal Tour', *Menevia Record* 4 (Aug. 1956), 10–12 (MDA).

76   Seamus Cunnane (parish priest, Our Lady of Sorrows, Cardigan) to John Petit (bishop of Menevia) (23 Mar. 1964), (MDA, parish file for Our Lady of the Taper, Cardigan); Seamus Cunnane, telephone interview with Robert Proctor (29 June 2012).

77   For example parish newsletter for Our Lady of Sorrows, Cardigan (28 May 1967) (MDA, parish file for Our Lady of the Taper).

78   Various correspondence (MDA, parish file for Our Lady of the Taper); Seamus Cunnane, interview with Robert Proctor (29 June 2012).

79   Cunnane, *Our Lady of Cardigan*, 29–31.

9

Ritual and Community

Turner applies the notion of *communitas*, forged in pilgrimage ritual, to show how pilgrimages and their shrines can also lend themselves to the construction of national identities. Catholicism, he argues, often mobilises national sentiments to stimulate religious practice, while nationalism can receive a sacred status through its endorsement within religion.[1] The revived pilgrimages of post-war Britain were overlaid with appeals to communal identities, both Roman Catholic and national. When the faithful engaged in religious rituals in environments overlaid with symbols of national and religious identity, they enacted that shared identity. If this identity-forming aspect of ritual and religious space was true of pilgrimages, it was also true of more everyday religious practices. Benedict Anderson and others argue that the social conformism of ritual lends itself to the imagining of communities: ritual creates a commonality of identity amongst its immediate actors and links them to all those others who share its actions.[2] Rituals surrounding the building of a church and those involving civic space articulated communities of the parish and the city and brought them into being.[3]

Post-war Catholicism in Britain, however, was largely a religion of immigrants and often viewed as un-British. The imaginative geographies of pilgrimage might therefore be seen as attempts to claim a place for the Church within the nation, affirming the identity of a British (or at least a Scottish, English or Welsh) Roman Catholic community in opposition to its perceived foreignness. Meanwhile Irish and other immigrants sometimes sought to display their own national identities in church architecture, sometimes in tension with such British claims. National identities, however, were subsumed into the broader identity of Roman Catholicism, centred on Rome; and communities were also formed around the local centres of the parish and the city. Catholic identity in Britain was fragmented, focused on multiple centres and allegiances and in an uncertain relationship with the modern nation.

PILGRIMAGE AND THE NATION

While Marian pilgrimages such as those at Cardigan and Aylesford comprised locally situated variations on the international cult of the Virgin Mary, pilgrimages were also created around sites considered formative in the Catholic history of the nation. Two case studies illustrate this tendency: the shrine of St Ninian in Whithorn resulted from the revival of a medieval pilgrimage for Scotland, while a pilgrimage in central London manifested the modern cult of the Forty Martyrs of the Reformation in England and Wales. Both promoted the sense of a national Catholic identity through sacred rituals that retold history. One asserted the continuity of modern Catholicism with that of the past, nostalgically eliding the rupture of the Reformation, while the other brought that rupture to consciousness as a point of sacred memorial. Both forms had their place in reconciling Catholics to a nation that had historically rejected them.

At Whithorn on the south-west coast of Scotland a pilgrimage to St Ninian was revived in the early twentieth century under the bishop of Galloway, William Turner, with the encouragement of John Crichton-Stuart, the Marquess of Bute.[4] St Ninian was a fifth-century Christian missionary to the Picts, bishop of a diocese dedicated to St Martin and the subject of a major medieval pilgrimage cult until its prohibition in 1581.[5] The twentieth-century Catholic revival of this pilgrimage attempted to reinstate an element of the lost ritual landscape of medieval Scotland. Its focus was a cave behind a rocky beach four miles from the town, reputed to have been Ninian's chapel, while a ruined Norman priory and cathedral on the town's high street, where the saint was thought to be buried, were further landmarks. On St Ninian's feast day in September, thousands of pilgrims would gather at the mouth of the cave to attend Mass at a temporary altar and to walk in procession through the town. The cave bore few traces of ancient use and was unlikely to have been a feature of the medieval pilgrimage. Its adoption in the twentieth century romantically evoked the hardships of the early Christian missionary. It was literally a liminal place, sited between land and sea, a space without conventional sacred or secular function, at the edge of the nation and, perhaps significantly, also close to the border with England.

The Catholic church of St Martin and St Ninian at Whithorn was used in these pilgrimage celebrations, but its Victorian iron building was too small for the cult's growing popularity. The parish acquired a large plot of land on the high street around 1951, and, with the patronage of Crichton-Stuart's grandson Lord David Stuart, launched a campaign for a pilgrimage church. Stuart commissioned Scottish architect Basil Spence for a design and urged the diocese to embark on a 'National appeal for a National Shrine of St Ninian'.[6] Spence's design alluded to the mythic cave in a modern architecture tinged with historic and national references (Figure 9.1). The church was to be set back from the street and a stone figure of St Ninian placed before it. Pilgrims would pass through a screen, arriving at a cloistered courtyard paved with stones taken from the beach in front of the cave.[7] The church's long nave had cave-like granite walls curving inwards and daylight entered through slits angled towards the sanctuary.[8] Spence's design suggested the atmosphere of Ninian's primitive church, and his building would have complemented the

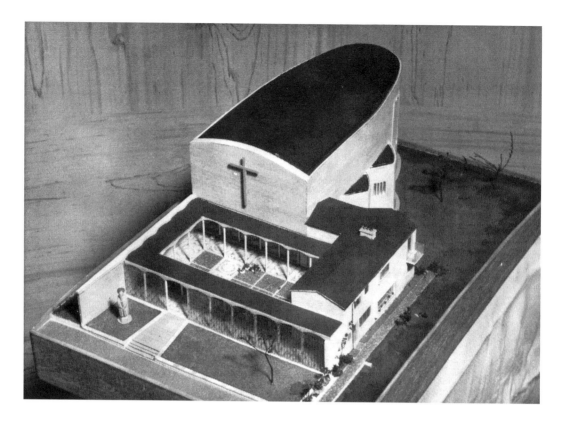

pilgrims' experience of the seashore shrine. It also suggested a Scottish identity in its architecture with a monumental use of masonry and small castle-like windows.

A model was shown at one of the annual pilgrimages to great excitement, but after the bishop's death in 1952 the project was shelved, as his successor Joseph McGee disliked Spence's modernism.[9] Nevertheless McGee asked all the parishes of the diocese of Galloway to contribute to a building fund, arguing it was 'not simply … a matter of supplying the needs of the Catholic community of Whithorn but … one involving the prestige of the Catholic Church in this Diocese and, indeed, in Scotland'.[10] Goodhart-Rendel was commissioned for a modest building seating only 200. His design followed Arts and Crafts principles with a local vernacular style, its plain neo-Gothic windows and harled exterior recalling churches of the seventeenth and eighteenth centuries (Figure 9.2).[11] In that period, Scottish Catholics could rarely worship in churches of this kind. Goodhart-Rendel's design therefore implied a nostalgic reminder of underground Catholicism, while also resembling a typical Scottish parish church, perhaps helping to assert a general national allegiance for Catholicism in Scotland. The church's simplicity avoided competing with the priory opposite, allowing the original medieval structure to retain its authenticity as the real shrine of St Ninian. The new church, opened in 1960, was too small for the crowds of pilgrims, who instead stood on a sloping strip of outdoor space behind it facing a permanent altar built at the church's rear wall.

9.1   Basil Spence, design for St Martin and St Ninian, Whithorn, 1951. Photograph of model. Source: © Courtesy of Royal Commission on the Ancient and Historical Monuments of Scotland, Spence, Glover and Ferguson Collection. Licensor, www.rcahms.gov.uk

9.2   St Martin and
St Ninian, Whithorn,
by H. S. Goodhart-
Rendel, 1955–60.
Photo: Ambrose
Gillick, 2012

In this attempt at reviving a medieval pilgrimage and creating a national shrine the parish and the diocese shaped a ritual that constructed a modern Scottish Catholic identity for its participants through an enactment of historical narrative. The procession between priory, church and cave revived the medieval pilgrimage so that pilgrims could identify themselves with their ancient forebears. In celebrating a saint who helped convert Scotland to Christianity, they confronted a point of origin of their faith in the history of the nation. Yet the pilgrimage was a re-telling rather than a re-enactment of history. The open-air gathering reinforced the absence of an adequate church; the makeshift altar on the beach made the absence of monuments felt; the medieval priory was in ruins. Though the Reformation was elided, it was everywhere present. The procession through the street, led by a priest in vestments and servers in cassocks, further defined the pilgrims as Catholic, distinct from their contemporary Christians who had abandoned such activities. While the pilgrimage asserted a Catholic claim to Scottish history, it also constructed an identity for modern Catholics around the nostalgic longing for an irretrievable past.

While this pilgrimage – and a similar revived cult of St Margaret at Dunfermline – contributed to the creation of a modern Scottish Catholic identity, it countered the identity of the *Gaidhealtachd*, the Gaelic Catholicism of the Highlands and Western Isles of Scotland that had persisted beyond the Reformation. When a 7m high statue of Our Lady of the Isles by Hew Lorimer was erected facing the Atlantic on the coast of South Uist, it was interpreted by the Catholic press and the hierarchy on one hand as marking a distinctively local phenomenon of fidelity to the Virgin

and, on the other, as demonstrating Gaelic Catholicism's continued allegiance to Rome through orthodox devotional practices. Indeed its inauguration on the feast of the Assumption in 1958 linked it to the centenary of Lourdes, celebrated throughout the world.[12] Devotion to St Ninian, on the other hand, constructed a less controversial image of a modern Scottish Catholicism of ancient national origin, allied to prevailing Protestant narratives of Christianity though celebrated in a specifically Catholic manner.

While some pilgrimages bridged the Reformation to evoke medieval Christianity, others sought to celebrate a national Catholic identity as one of defiance and martyrdom by remembering the Reformation itself. The Forty Martyrs of England and Wales, executed for their faith in the sixteenth and seventeenth centuries, became particularly important from 1960 when the bishops of England and Wales decided to press for their canonisation, finally achieved in 1970 under Paul VI. Since canonisation required evidence of miracles, campaigns of prayers and events were organised, including pilgrimages to associated sites.[13] One was an annual pilgrimage in honour of the martyrs in central London. A procession began at the Old Bailey court, the site of Newgate prison where many of the martyrs were held, and traced their journey to martyrdom at Tyburn. The landscape of London had irredeemably changed: not only had Newgate disappeared, but Tyburn itself was merely a road junction. This pilgrimage nostalgically reimagined the contemporary environment, inscribing it through ritual with a hidden historical form, sacralising the banal and secular city and claiming it for a Catholic identity.

9.3   Tyburn Convent, London, by F. G. Broadbent & Partners, 1960–63. Photo: Robert Proctor, 2010

Since 1903, part of a Regency terrace on Bayswater Road had been occupied by a convent of French nuns and named after Tyburn.[14] Bombed during the war, it was planned to rebuild it in the 1950s as a 'national shrine' to over 100 Tyburn martyrs, every diocese in England and Wales claiming at least one of the martyrs as their own. It was speculated that ancient trees in the convent garden might have been used as gibbets, giving them the status of relics, and the foundation stone of the new church, laid in 1961 by Cardinal Godfrey, contained a piece of stone from one of the martyrs' prisons in the Tower of London.[15] The new building was designed by F. G. Broadbent & Partners (Figure 9.3). On the ground floor below the convent chapel was a shrine chapel for pilgrims and visitors containing a life-sized replica of the triangular Tyburn gallows placed as a ciborium over the altar, and reliquaries of the martyrs lined its walls.[16] Outside, a balcony became the focus of pilgrimage devotions:

it was used at the culmination of the procession for a sermon and for Benediction of the Blessed Sacrament to the crowds who gathered in the street below.[17] In 1964, on the traffic island nearby at Marble Arch, assumed to be the site of the Tyburn executions, a stone marker was laid in the pavement, a cross in its centre asserting its religious significance, instantly readable to British Catholics as a place made sacred by the blood of martyrs, consecrating a sacred place in the secular urban landscape (Figure 9.4).

The campaign of fundraising for the shrine created a sense of national Catholic community, including spectacular pageants performed at football stadiums throughout the country and widespread devotions to support the cause of canonisation. Many churches were dedicated to one or all of the Forty Martyrs. At St Thomas More, Knebworth, for example, Broadbent designed another Tyburn gallows as a ciborium over an altar that represented the block on which its patron saint was beheaded, bringing an element of the London shrine to this village church.[18] The cult of the Reformation martyrs celebrated the rupture between the nation and Roman Catholicism, identifying Catholics in Britain with the persecuted saints. The Tyburn pilgrimage could also be adapted to a shared identification with other persecuted Catholics: in 1957, a silent march of 15,000 men from Hyde Park, next to Tyburn, to Westminster Cathedral protested against religious intolerance in eastern Europe, particularly Poland and Hungary, with many exiles taking part in the event. *The Tablet* reported:

> Here, within sight of the spot where so many English martyrs died for the Faith in an earlier century, was being actualised our need to identify ourselves with those members of Our Lord's Mystical Body who are suffering and dying for the Faith now, in the twentieth century, in other parts of the world.[19]

NATIONAL IDENTITY

In these cases of the ritual re-telling of history to assert combined national and religious identities for England and Wales and Scotland, few if any commentators ever mentioned the fact that the majority of Catholics in Britain were of Irish ancestry. The shrines at Aylesford and Cardigan owed their success to the efforts of Irish clergy, yet the new pilgrimage landscape promoted native Catholic identities. This apparent contradiction was also sometimes present in parish church architecture.

The strength of Roman Catholicism in Britain by the twentieth century was largely a result of Irish immigration in the nineteenth century, when Ireland had been part of Britain. Throughout the twentieth century, continued immigration ensured that a significant proportion of Catholics in Britain maintained Irish allegiances and a sense of national identity. Parish churches could often become a site for the construction and display of Irish communities. The Church in Britain, however, particularly at the level of the diocese, preferred instead to emphasise its Britishness. The two movements generally coexisted but occasionally came to confrontation. Post-war immigration from other Catholic countries, particularly

Poland and Italy, could lead to even greater complexity in the church's role as a focus for national identities.[20]

Irish immigration peaked in the mid-twentieth century, becoming increasingly diffuse as new industries and transport attracted migrants to London, Birmingham and Cardiff and to industrial towns such as Coventry and Luton in addition to former strongholds such as Liverpool, Manchester and Glasgow.[21] With Irish workers came Irish priests, recruited by British dioceses to compensate for a shortage of clergy in Britain and to cater for their countrymen: in the diocese of Birmingham in the mid-1950s, every parish had at least one Irish priest; in Leeds two-thirds of the clergy were Irish.[22] Even as Irish identities amongst the descendants of earlier migrants abated, new arrivals sought to sustain a distinctive national culture.

Part of that culture was, for most, an adherence to Roman Catholicism, and the Catholic church was often the hub of immigrants' social lives. Rex and Moore described the Catholic church in Birmingham as 'the biggest Irish immigrant organization of all' alongside lesser urban landmarks such as pubs and cafes. Secular social centres were incorporated into church sites: parish halls often had Irish bars and held Irish-themed events as fundraising ventures, often to fund a church building. Weekly attendance for Mass not only enabled the enactment of a ritual duty exactly as fulfilled in Ireland, but was also a social event.[23] Family rituals such as weddings or funerals further reinforced Irish identity through the extensive kinship networks that became visible at these events. In and around and through the church building, the Irish reproduced and performed their identity.[24]

Church buildings were often given signs of Irish identity. A church's dedication could celebrate a national saint and would be accompanied by an appropriate image. Many churches across Britain were dedicated to St Patrick in the post-war period – at Walsall, Coventry, Leicester, St Helens, Rochdale and many other places. St Finbar, seventh-century bishop of Cork, was commemorated with a parish in Liverpool. Dedications gave a familiar mark to a parish, extending to secular activities such as clubs and bars, sports teams and schools, where they became public bearers of a Catholic, and often a specifically Irish, identity. They were also associated with cult devotional practices that enabled the continued fulfilment of an aspect of national identity. In Ireland, the Sacred Heart had an especially strong following: a picture would be placed in the house over the fireplace, and the parish priest would dedicate the family to Christ, signing a document of consecration and attaching it to the wall with the picture, where a lamp would be kept constantly lit.[25] The Sacred Heart shrine within a church evoked the memory of this family consecration, acting as a site of nostalgic evocation of home. Marian imagery was also prevalent in the home as well as the church in Ireland.[26] The Catholic church building in Britain provided for the Irish immigrant a space with familiar resonances in the unfamiliar city.

Shrines to St Patrick were also common in post-war Catholic churches in Britain, endorsing devotion to the national saint. They were often positioned near the door – a position of lower status than the saints associated with Christ, but significant perhaps in that the figure of Patrick was seen on entering and leaving the church, a reminder of identity for the Irish faithful at the point where the familiar space

of religious custom met the secular and foreign world. At Adrian Gilbert Scott's church of Sts Mary and Joseph in Poplar, for instance, a statue of St Patrick was placed on a permanent pedestal near the door (Figure 9.5); and in a more modern interpretation, the church of St Patrick in Coventry designed by Desmond Williams around 1967 included a stained-glass panel of the saint lit with electric light and placed in the vestibule (Figure 9.6). Both were parishes with especially high concentrations of Irish immigrants.

Decorative building materials could also indicate Irishness: one of the most popular, frequently employed for altars and other liturgical furnishings, was 'Connemara marble', dark green in colour. At D. Plaskett Marshall's church of the Sacred Heart in Camberwell, London, of around 1958, the high altar and communion rails were of 'Irish marble', and the brick piers of this otherwise austere church were later clad in the material (Figure 9.7).[27] Grey-veined Kilkenny marble was also frequently used, at Lionel Prichard's St Agnes, Huyton of 1965, for instance, where altar, font and holy water stoups were all carved from it.[28] Such materials would be proudly listed in opening brochures and newspaper reports for the benefit of parishioners. Sometimes they were specifically requested by the parish priest. At Yeading, the diocese of Westminster hesitated to approve a design for a marble altar and baldachino after finding that the priest had drawn it without the architect Justin Alleyn's knowledge. The priest, Edward (or Eamon) Scanlan, was an Irish immigrant himself and had previously ministered in parishes with large numbers of Irish residents, at Somers Town and Southall.[29] No doubt at his request, Alleyn incorporated broad panels of Irish marble into his otherwise modern design,

9.5   Sts Mary and Joseph, Poplar, London, by Adrian Gilbert Scott, 1951–54. Statue of St Patrick; one of the Stations of the Cross by Peter Watts is also visible. Photo: Robert Proctor, 2010

9.6   St Patrick, Coventry, by Desmond Williams, 1967–71. Stained glass depicting St Patrick in the vestibule, artist unknown. Photo: Robert Proctor, 2009

as reredos-like backdrops for the high altar and Lady chapel (Figure 9.8).[30] Marble, however, could also suggest an Italian source, and indeed Italian marble was also often used: St Louis in Brighton of 1965, for example, had an altar described as of 'green Italian marble with insets of Irish Kellymount'.[31] Thus a dual allegiance, to Ireland and to the universal church centred on Rome, could be declared through the fabric of the building at its most sacred points.

The hierarchy of the Catholic Church in England, Wales and Scotland, while attentive to the desires of its many Irish faithful, did not want the Church to be seen as Irish.[32] Many dedications emphasised connections between Ireland and Britain: St Aidan, for example, a seventh-century Irish missionary who founded the monastery at Lindisfarne as part of the conversion of England to Christianity, was commemorated and celebrated with an external statue at the church at East Acton, an area with strong Irish as well as Polish and Italian communities. Fourmaintraux's stained-glass panels in the sanctuary, meanwhile, depicted saints associated with English Christianity: on one side were St Mellitus, a missionary from Rome; St Thomas of Canterbury; St Hilda; St Edmund and St Erconwald, an Anglo Saxon bishop of London; facing them were Reformation martyrs (including, however, Oliver Plunkett, an Irish martyr who died at Tyburn) (Plate 5). The iconography of the church illustrated a predominantly native English Christianity with connections to Ireland.

Sts Mary and Joseph at Poplar similarly positioned Ireland within a political scheme emphasising Britishness. Most of its parishioners were Irish, employed at the nearby docks. Despite the church's octagonal plan, its arrangement followed

9.7   Sacred Heart, Camberwell, London, by D. Plaskett Marshall, 1959. Connemara
marble cladding added to piers later. Photo: Robert Proctor, 2010

9.8   St Raphael, Yeading, London, by Justin Alleyn, 1961. Reredos of Connemara marble; Lady chapel and Sacred Heart chapel also showing use of marble; *dalle de verre* windows by Pierre Fourmaintraux of Whitefriars Studios. Photo: Robert Proctor, 2010

the familiar pattern, with the traditional layout of shrines, those for the Virgin and St Joseph being most prominent; the Sacred Heart was represented by a window in the sanctuary as well as a statue. St Patrick was depicted not only with a statue but also in a stained-glass window at the base of one of the four piers, but the other three pier windows contained images of Sts Andrew, George and David (Figure 9.9). The building therefore represented Ireland as if it was part of Britain, on an equal footing with the latter's component countries; St George, however, was placed adjacent to the sanctuary, in the position of highest status. The upper-level windows depicted Sts John Fisher, Thomas of Canterbury, Thomas More and Edward: all English martyrs. Further groups of saints in the transept windows included St Augustine, early Christian missionary to England, flanked by St Gregory, the pope who sent him, and the English St Edmund; Roman saints such as St Peter were also present, articulating the ultimate authority of the Church. The iconography of this church was also a symbolic geography: while Irish visitors were permitted to feel a connection to their home, they were simultaneously reoriented towards an English and British identity.

Since so many clergy were Irish, tensions between the parish and the diocese could be played out in church buildings. Such a conflict arose at St Joseph, Wolverhampton, designed by Jennings, Homer & Lynch around 1965, partly serving a nearby Irish workers' hostel.[33] The parish priest by then was a Father Connolly, 'whose political views', complained the auxiliary bishop, 'have alienated a number of people', suggesting he supported Irish Republicanism.[34] Connemara marble was used liberally throughout the church, including for the altar (Figure 9.10). Though officially dedicated to St Joseph, the church's foundation

9.9   Sts Mary and
Joseph, Poplar,
London, by Adrian
Gilbert Scott,
1951–55. Stained
glass by William
Wilson. Photo:
Robert Proctor, 2010

stone attributes its patronage to Sts Joseph and Patrick, the latter name seemingly added without diocesan approval. A statue of St Joseph with rough carving and carpenter's tools depicted St Joseph the Worker, a cult devotion created by Pius XII in the mid-1950s to counter European communism while mimicking some of its forms. In this context, the figure strongly suggests a sympathy with the socialist claims of the Irish nationalist movement at this period. Across the rear of the nave, stained-glass panels depicted St Joseph on one side and St Patrick on the other triumphantly raising a clover leaf (Figure 9.11). In his preface to the booklet accompanying the opening ceremony, Connolly declared a 'CEAD MILE FAILTE to our Archbishop', and praised glassmakers Hardmans for following his instructions.[35] The depictions of these two saints at Wolverhampton promoted a highly politicised Irishness compared to the subdued forms of other churches. Connolly's attitude, however, was unwelcome not only to the hierarchy but also to many of his parishioners, and it was an exceptional case.[36] The prevailing model was one of coexistent narratives of identity, Irishness displayed in parallel with a Catholic Britishness.

Besides the Irish, there were significant congregations of Catholics from other countries in Britain. Poles were the largest group, many having arrived in Britain during the Second World War. Their contribution to church art and architecture was substantial. The Liverpool firm of Weightman & Bullen recruited some from amongst the Polish architecture students who had arrived at Liverpool University during the war, forming a Polish School of Architecture, notably Stanislaus Pater-Lancucki (known as Stan Pater) and Jerzy Faczynski.[37] Adam Kossowski, the ceramicist, had been a notable artist in Poland before the war, teaching at the Warsaw Academy

9.10   St Joseph, Wolverhampton, by Jennings, Homer & Lynch, 1967. Connemara marble
in the sanctuary on the wall behind the altar and for the altar and communion rails;
stained glass of Sts Peter and Paul by Hardman & Co. Photo: Robert Proctor, 2009

9.11   St Joseph, Wolverhampton, by Jennings, Homer & Lynch, 1967. View to rear of
church: stained glass of St Patrick by Hardman & Co. Photo: Robert Proctor, 2009

of Art. He arrived in London in 1943 after being released from a Russian prison camp the year before.[38] Many of Greenhalgh & Williams's churches after 1960 were designed by Tadeusz Lesisz, who had been a lieutenant in the Polish navy when it defected to Britain in 1939. He remained after service to train as an architect at the Oxford School of Architecture, his three brothers having been murdered in Dachau and Katyn.[39] Altogether 160,000 Poles stayed in Britain after the war, and, by 1960, there were about 100 Polish priests with their own parallel hierarchy and parish structure in England and Wales established with the help of Cardinal Griffin in 1948. The Polish Catholic Mission began in 1947 to provide for the religious and social needs of exiles and to sustain a particular vision of Polish national identity, one of its primary functions being the provision of church buildings.[40]

One of Lesisz's first commissions as an architect was for the Polish Church of Divine Mercy in Manchester around 1958. Named after the twentieth-century apparitions of Christ as the Divine Mercy to a Polish nun and the subsequent shrine in Krakow, this church served the Polish community throughout Manchester. It began with the purchase of a Victorian Presbyterian chapel, undoubtedly for reasons of economy but also effectively concealing the presence of a Polish congregation from the outside. The same approach was taken in other cities, most importantly in London, where a former Presbyterian chapel in Shepherd's Bush was bought and converted for use as the Polish church of St Anthony Bobola.[41] Inside, however, these churches were redesigned to evoke a Polish identity tied to Catholicism.[42] St Anthony Bobola in London became a repository of Polish national symbols, architect Aleksander Klecki and artist Tadeusz Zielinski working on alterations and new features continuously from 1961 (Figure 9.12). A basement was excavated to create a Polish social centre and café. Above, a new aisle was added with a chapel to contain a celebrated relief of the Virgin, Our Lady of Victories of Kozielsk, named after the town that became a Russian prison camp where it was secretly made by Polish prisoners; the image was accorded sacred status as a symbol of hope for return to Poland after exile. The church was further enhanced with sculpture and artworks. Stained-glass windows commemorated Polish military organisations, and there was a prominent memorial to the dead of the massacre at Katyn. The interior was a setting for ceremonies with a national focus, gathering the Polish community in London for events associated with the Polish government in exile and the military, as well as being a centre of Polish social activity.[43] The church created an image of Polish identity in relation to wartime experiences, becoming essentially a multi-faceted war memorial. The exterior of the church was undemonstratively adorned with a modern sculptural panel of angled crosses, hinting at this extraordinary role.

Another Polish architect, George Wladyslaw Jarosz, arrived in Britain after being released from a Nazi prison camp and completed his studies at the Polish School of Architecture, after its relocation from Liverpool to London in 1947, subsequently joining the office of notable modernist architect William Crabtree.[44] Jarosz was invited to design the chapel of St Ann at Fawley Court in Buckinghamshire, where a seventeenth-century house had been converted into a school for Polish boys in 1952 by the Congregation of Marian Fathers, a Polish order, under the patronage of exiled Prince Stanislaw Radziwill. The chapel was completed in 1973 for use by the school and the local community, but also served as a memorial to Radziwill's

9.12   St Anthony Bobola Polish Church, London, 1961 onwards, alterations by Aleksander Klecki. Sculpture and stained glass by Aleksander Klecki. Photo: Robert Proctor, 2013

mother Anna, Princess Lubomirska, who had died in 1947 in a Soviet labour camp. Jarosz's design had no overtly Polish allegiances, and aimed rather to be sympathetic to its site in a Capability Brown landscape, following the influence of Scandinavian modernist churches the architect had seen, with a tall pitched roof, pine-boarded inside, perched over a brick podium (Figure 9.13).[45] Devotional objects and memorial panels, however, formed focal points with national resonances, including a shrine to Christ of the Divine Mercy and the tomb of Radziwill himself, placed in the crypt after his death in 1976 and guarded by gates containing bronze panels of the Polish eagle with the arms of the Radziwill family.[46] An external altar allowed for outdoor services for liturgical events involving large-scale gatherings of British Poles. Outside the normal systems of patronage for churches, and indeed outside the city, and therefore in something of a liminal space, this church became one of the most important focal points for Polish exile identity in Britain, a site where its community was created and defined. In 1964, for example, celebrating the millennium of the Polish Christian monarchy and the nation, 7,000 Poles attended a service at Fawley Court. Many wore national dress, and the Mass was followed by traditional songs and dances.[47]

In London two cases stand out as being special types of national church, where the home nation's involvement in their creation made them showcases of their respective religious cultures. Notre Dame de France near Leicester Square had been built in the nineteenth century by Parisian architect Louis-Auguste Boileau, circular in plan because of its site on a former panorama. Hector Corfiato of the Bartlett School of Architecture rebuilt it in 1955 following war damage, maintaining the circular plan and much influenced by modern French architecture (Figure 9.14).

The selection of the architect and the organisation of a scheme of artworks was entrusted by the church's priest, Francisque Deguerry, to the French embassy's cultural advisor, René Varin, who used the church to demonstrate contemporary French religious art. Corfiato himself was an alumnus of the École des Beaux-Arts in Paris. External sculpture was commssioned from distinguished French sculptor Georges Saupique, who had previously worked on churches in France. French decorative arts techniques were demonstrated by a ceramic font and by an Aubusson tapestry depicting a figure of the Virgin by French Benedictine Robert de Chaunac, known as Dom Robert, hung behind the altar. The most daring and original work, however, was commissioned from Jean Cocteau, who in 1960 added a striking figurative fresco to the Lady chapel and its altar.[48] Varin must have been aware of the Art Sacré movement, and Cocteau's commission in London was an act of patronage that brought a taste of this movement to Britain, claiming it as a French national project. Meanwhile the German Catholic church of St Boniface at Stepney was also destroyed by German bombs and was rebuilt with the patronage of the West German government and Catholic hierarchy in 1960 by local Catholic architect D. Plaskett Marshall. German artists Heribert Reul and Gunther Reul created a sgraffito artwork behind the altar depicting Christ and St Boniface, the English Christian missionary to Germany.[49]

9.13   Church of St Anne, Fawley Court, Buckinghamshire, by Crabtree & Jarosz, 1973. Photographer unknown. Source: archive of George W. T. Jarosz, London

9.14   Notre Dame de France, London, by Hector O. Corfiato, 1955. Tapestry by Dom Robert, Tabard Workshop, Aubusson, 1955; chapel with fresco by Jean Cocteau of 1960 visible in the centre of the photograph; fresco © ADAGP, Paris and DACS, London, 2013. By permission of the Rector and Trustees of Notre Dame de France. Photo: Robert Proctor, 2010

PARISH COMMUNITIES

National identities, however, were only one amongst several kinds of identity that could be performed in parallel by Catholics in Britain: the construction of local parish and city communities through the church building and associated rituals also contributed to a sense of belonging and a sense of place within the nation. The construction of a parish church itself served as a means of building a parish community through the performance of a shared identity amongst its members. Despite their administrative dependence on the diocese, in theory Roman Catholic parishes had to be financially independent and self-sufficient. Building a church therefore demanded huge efforts at fundraising within the parish. Since most churches were built through bank loans, the debts incurred by parishes required extensive fundraising long after their buildings were completed. While Roman Catholic churches could be dedicated and used as soon as they were finished, they were not permitted to be formally consecrated until the debt had been paid. Achieving the status of a consecrated church was a landmark in the history of every parish, the result of a collaborative project involving virtually every active parishioner, bringing them together in work and entertainment for the benefit of the Church.

Fundraising brought parishioners together in a common aim. While the parish priest and his curates organised much of the work themselves, some parish affairs were delegated to parishioners: parish priest Patrick Waldron of St Francis de Sales, Hampton Hill, in London created numerous lay committees, including a Finance Committee, Entertainments Committee, Liturgy Committee and an Art and Maintenance Committee, all with a role to play in achieving their new church building.[50] A church was the 'dream' of every parish from its inception, often described as such in parish histories, and it was the product of the whole parish, a manifestation of the parish's social life and a representation of its community. Buildings would often commemorate this community aspect of their production. Sometimes a 'golden book' containing a list of donors would be kept in the church: at the Immaculate Heart of Mary in Hayes, opened in 1961, one such book was kept in a chapel under a plaque listing all the priests who had served in the parish.[51] Donations from parishioners towards schemes of furnishing and decoration could also be rewarded by associating donors' names with objects in the church.

One of the most assiduous of such campaigns took place at St Mary at Failsworth in Manchester, where parishioners collaborated in offering items for the church, listed in the booklet accompanying the church's dedication. The parish branch of the Union of Catholic Mothers paid for the baptistery, and the font was donated by over 70 'ladies of the parish', including the 'infant teachers'. The Stations of the Cross were donated by families and painted by a parishioner. Past parishioners were approached to fund the Lady chapel, including those in America and Ireland; its tabernacle and statue were donated, and each panel of its stained glass windows was ascribed to a family. The communion rails were donated by the men's club. Funds for the sanctuary furnishings were raised by the infants' school. The pulpit, side chapels, altar linen, sanctuary lamp, Missal and candlesticks were all attributed to donors. The mosaic reredos was donated by the parish priest in memory of his parents, who had also been parishioners at Failsworth.[52] This associating of objects in the church with donors was met by overwhelming generosity, as many of the faithful wished to be publicly identified as members of the corporate body of the parish through the embellishment of the church.

The opening or consecration of a church was frequently an occasion for setting out the history of the parish, celebrating the communal achievement of its members, and helping to consolidate the notion of the parish as a social unit. The struggles of parishioners as they forged a Catholic society were vividly described, the new church building represented as the culmination of their efforts. Earlier buildings marked phases in the parish's growth. The souvenir booklet of St Columba, Bolton, celebrating its combined opening and consecration of 1956, is typical. Before 1931, the residents of the new housing estate at Tonge Moor walked miles to their nearest church. Some land was bought closer to the estate, intended for a chapel-of-ease; then, in 1931, the diocese created a new parish, and a priest arrived: 'What a task confronted him! All he had was a field'. Mass was said at the cricket club until a temporary church could be built 'at a cost of £800'. 'The parishioners pulled together and Father O'Dwyer laboured on'. His successor built a new junior and infants' school within months of arriving in 1937. A presbytery followed, its cost meticulously documented. 'With the wholehearted co-operation of the faithful and friends the seemingly impossible was accomplished. The parish was free of debt 20th December, 1942'. Immediately fundraising for a new church began. An architect was chosen: Geoffrey Williams was a parishioner of St Columba and waived his fee. The foundation stone was laid in a ceremony of 1955. As the building rose, parishioners inspected it every week after Sunday Mass: a photograph in the booklet records the construction site. 'At a meeting of the men of the parish, one Sunday morning early in 1956, the one and only topic of discussion was our new church – would it be opened by Christmas to celebrate the Silver Jubilee of the first Mass in the "old" church?' The priest assured them it would. And there was more delight: the possibility that the debt would be paid before it was complete, and the church could be consecrated.[53] The consecration and opening ceremonies followed, and the souvenir booklet concludes with a description and photograph of the completed building. This document gives an impression of a parish literally and metaphorically building itself through saving and work.

It is significant that fundraising was motivated by the parish's history, ensuring that St Columba's new church was opened on the anniversary of the old. In many church buildings the parish's history would be literally incorporated into the architecture by integrating a relic from the past. At John Rochford's church of St Paul at Wood Green, the previous church by Edward Goldie of 1904 was demolished, but its stained-glass windows were kept and inserted into a specially designed entrance corridor (Figure 9.15).[54] At their new church of St Catherine, Horsefair in Birmingham, Harrison & Cox incorporated stained-glass windows from the Victorian church that had been demolished by order of the city. At St Peter-in-Chains, Doncaster, the Victorian church's high altar and reredos, designed by John Francis Bentley, were rebuilt as a Blessed Sacrament chapel in Langtry-Langton's much larger church of 1973. The replacement of a parish church was a trauma, eased by incorporating its fragments within the new church to symbolise the unity of a parish over time.

Ritual celebrations surrounding new buildings were occasions for symbolic enactments of the Catholic parish in its relationships to both the broader Church and to the secular world. The laying of the foundation stone, the dedication and opening ceremony and the consecration, often decades later, were ceremonies normally performed by the bishop, and were often spectacular displays of the local or national hierarchy. The entire parish would participate, often in public processions, encompassing the grounds of the church, extending through surrounding streets, and in some cases accompanying the transfer of the Blessed Sacrament from its previous location to the tabernacle of the new church. The opening of St Mary, Leyland, in 1964 was one of the most dazzling events of this kind: the procession went through the town from the old church in the centre to the new building a mile away (Figure 9.16). The clergy, including the celebrant Bishop Parker of Northampton (whose brother had been a priest at Leyland), Bishop Beck of Liverpool and the monks of the friary, accompanied by the servers, all in their most splendid vestments, followed 2,000 parishioners, divided into ranks according to their membership of parish institutions. Mothers pushing infants in prams formed one cohort, representing the Union of Catholic Mothers; men formed another; boys and white-dressed girls from the schools and older women in old-fashioned hats made up further groups. Also in attendance was a large delegation from Ampleforth, including its abbot, Basil Hume. The local Member of Parliament and town councillors were invited, showing the parish's relationship to its civic community.[55] A brass band accompanied the procession. Crowds of non-Catholic onlookers lined the streets as spectators. The parish performed and effected community through such a display of unity in public view.

9.15   St Paul, Wood Green, London, by John Rochford, 1965–72. Vestibule passageway containing stained glass from former church of 1904. Photo: Robert Proctor, 2010

In several cities, particularly in Lancashire, further public rituals defined Catholics specifically in terms of their civic identity. The Manchester Whit Walk was an event that developed during the mid-nineteenth century as a city-wide ceremony. The week following Whitsun was a holiday in Manchester and its surrounding towns, for which the churches organised religious spectacles. On Monday, the children of all Anglican parishes in the city walked from their churches to the city centre, converging on Albert Square in front of the Town Hall. On Friday, it was the turn of Catholics, who did the same. The boys of each parish wore school uniforms, and the girls wore white dresses and carried lilies; they also held banners bearing the names of their churches. Parish groups also joined in, and each parish had its own band. The procession was most famous for the lavish displays staged by the Italian church at Ancoats: the men walked in procession carrying the church's crucifix and the flower-bedecked statue of the Virgin Mary borrowed from the Lady chapel. Polish and Ukrainian Catholics also participated as distinct groups, many in national dress. The procession filed past the bishop of Salford for over three hours before assembling in Albert Square. In 1949, it was estimated that 20,000 joined in the walk, revived then for the first time after the war.[56]

This ritual presented Roman Catholics to themselves and their neighbours in the context of the city as a civic group rather than as a diocesan or parochial one. Nevertheless it showed the city's Catholics in terms of their parishes. Italians and Poles defined themselves as Catholics through their participation, while celebrating their distinctive identities as settlers in the city.[57] A similar event took place in Bolton, but, in 1968, after several experiences of poor weather,

9.16   St Mary, Leyland. Procession at opening ceremony, 1964. Photo: Tony Hart, 1964. Source: parish archive

there was doubt over its future. Bishop Thomas Holland of Salford noted arguments for its discontinuation, including suggestions that developments in Christian unity might be hindered by displays of Catholic rivalry with other denominations. It was also important to consider the increasing secularisation of society and its preference for confining the sacred to a separate sphere. Against such claims, however, he insisted the event proceed: the procession was important as a 'public witness to our Faith'. 'We strengthen the ties which link us to our parish and the parishes to one another', he argued, and 'we enrich the life of our city'.[58] Through this ritual the streets of the city became a sacred space, activated by a spectacular processional movement that enacted relationships between Catholics, their institutions and the city. A Catholic geography of the city was articulated through the convergence of parishes, united at the central point where the city's corporate identity was embodied. In asserting their 'right to the city' by claiming public space for religion, Roman Catholics demonstrated their presence in civic society and brought their communities into being.[59]

NOTES

1   Turner and Turner, *Image and Pilgrimage*, 63–93, 106–35.

2   Benedict Anderson, *Imagined Communities: Reflections on the Origin and Spread of Nationalism* (London: Verso, 1991), 145; see also for example Judith Butler, 'Performative Acts and Gender Constitution', in Michael Huxley and Noel Witts (eds), *The Twentieth-Century Performance Reader* (London: Routledge, 2002), 120–34.

3   The theoretical framework for this chapter derives from several sources: Émile Durkheim, *The Elementary Forms of Religious Life*, trans. Karen E. Fields (New York: Free Press, 1995); summarised by Catherine Bell, *Ritual: Perspectives and Dimensions* (New York: Oxford University Press, 1997), 24–5; David Parkin, 'Ritual as Spatial Direction and Bodily Division', in Daniel de Coppet (ed.), *Understanding Rituals* (London: Routledge, 1992), 11–25; Roy A. Rappaport, 'Enactments of Meaning', in Michael Lambek (ed.), *A Reader in the Anthropology of Religion* (Oxford: Blackwell, 2008), 410–28; Andrew Parker and Eve Kosofsky Sedgwick, 'Introduction', to eid. (eds), *Performativity and Performance* (London: Routledge, 1995), 1–18.

4   'Pontifical Mass in Scots Cave', *Catholic Herald* (25 Sept. 1953), 1; 'Whithorn Pilgrimage', *St Andrew Annual: The Catholic Church in Scotland* (1960–61), 93.

5   J. Stopford, 'Some Approaches to the Archaeology of Christian Pilgrimage', *World Archaeology* 26 (1994), 57–72 (60–61); Francis Hindes Groome (ed.), *Ordnance Gazetteer of Scotland: A Survey of Scottish Topography, Statistical, Biographical and Historical*, vol. 6 (Edinburgh: T. C. Jack, 1882–85), 484–6.

6   David Stuart to William Mellon (bishop of Galloway) (27 Sept. 1951) (SCA, DG/54/2).

7   Basil Spence to Joseph McGee (bishop of Galloway) (5 Feb. 1954) (SCA, DG/54/2).

8   Design drawings and photographs of model (Royal Commission on the Ancient and Historic Monuments of Scotland, Edinburgh, Spence, Glover and Ferguson Collection, SGF 1950/66/1, SGF 1950/42/1/8); see also Clive Fenton and David Walker, 'The Modern Church', in Louise Campbell, Miles Glendinning and Jane Thomas (eds), *Basil Spence: Buildings & Projects* (London: RIBA Publishing, 2012), 104.

9   McGee, circular letter to diocesan clergy (3 Feb. 1956) (SCA, DG/54/3).

10   McGee, circular letter to diocesan clergy (3 Feb. 1956) (SCA, DG/54/3).

11   H. S. Goodhart-Rendel to McGee (21 Dec. 1955) (SCA, DG/54/2).

12   Ray Burnett, '"The Long Nineteenth Century": Scotland's Catholic Gaidhealtachd', in Raymond Boyle and Peter Lynch (ed.), *Out of the Ghetto? The Catholic Community in Modern Scotland* (Edinburgh: John Donald, 1998), 179, 184.

13   'Joint Pastoral on 40 Martyrs', *Catholic Herald* (1 July 1960), 1.

14   T. F. T. Baker, Diane K. Bolton and Patricia E. C. Croot, *A History of the County of Middlesex*, vol. 9: *Hampstead, Paddington*, ed. C. R. Elrington (Oxford: Oxford University Press, 1989), 259–60, British History Online, http://www.british-history.ac.uk/report.aspx?compid=22675 (accessed 6 Dec. 2012).

15   'Shrine Will Rise on Tyburn Ruins', *Catholic Herald* (4 Jan. 1952), 1; 'From Our Notebook', *The Tablet* (25 Nov. 1961), 1127.

16   'From Our Notebook', *The Tablet* (19 Mar. 1960), 273; 'Tyburn's New Shrine', *Catholic Herald* (25 Mar. 1960), 1; '£25,000 Debt on Shrine', *Catholic Herald* (29 May 1964), 1.

17   Advertisement, 'Annual Tyburn Walk', *The Tablet* (15 Apr. 1961), 367.

18   G. C. Davey, 'A Tyburn Tree for Knebworth', *Catholic Herald* (12 May 1961), 6; *CBRS* (1963), 49–53.

19   'From Our Notebook', *The Tablet* (13 Apr. 1957), 355; see also 'Exiles' Candles Symbolises the Silent Church', *Catholic Herald* (12 Apr. 1957), 1.

20   The framework for the analysis that follows is provided by Anne-Marie Fortier (*Migrant Belongings: Memory, Space, Identity* [Oxford: Berg, 2000]).

21   Enda Delaney, *The Irish in Post-War Britain* (Oxford: Oxford University Press, 2007), 89–109; Jackson, *The Irish in Britain*, 11–19; see also Hornsby-Smith, 'A Transformed Church', 8–9.

22   Delaney, *Irish in Post-War Britain*, 145.

23   See Sharon Lambert, *Irish Women in Lancashire, 1922–1960: Their Story* (Lancaster: Centre for North-West Regional Studies, 2001), 63.

24   This section on Irish national identity is adapted from Robert Proctor, 'Religion and Nation: The Architecture and Symbolism of Irish Identity in the Roman Catholic Church in Britain', in Raymond Quek, Darren Deane and Sarah Butler (eds), *Nationalism and Architecture* (Aldershot: Ashgate, 2012), 39–51.

25   Lambert, *Irish Women in Lancashire*, 46.

26   On the similar role of devotions to the Virgin Mary, see Bronwen Walter, *Outsiders Inside: Whiteness, Place and Irish Women* (London: Routledge, 2001), 18.

27   *CBRS* (1958), 88.

28   *CBRN* (1965), 62–3.

29   'Obituaries: Valuable Participant at Vatican II', *Catholic Herald* (8 Jan. 1993), 3; 'Father's Farewell' [newspaper cutting] (c.1986) (parish archive, St Raphael, Yeading, London).

30   [Derek Worlock] (private secretary to William Godfrey, archbishop of Westminster) to B. Kent (assistant to finance secretary, diocese of Westminster) (30 June 1960) (WDA, Godfrey Papers, Go/2/132).

31   *CBRS* (1965), 88.

32   Hickman, *Religion, Class and Identity*, 12, 204, ch. 5.

33   Visitation Report (7 Feb. 1949) (ARCAB, Parish Files, P316/T5).

34   Joseph F. Cleary (auxiliary bishop), visitation report (1972) (ARCAB, Parish Files, P316/T5).

35   St Joseph, Wolverhampton, opening souvenir brochure (4 Dec. 1967) (ARCAB, uncatalogued).

36   Cleary, visitation report (1972) (ARCAB, Parish Files, P316/T5).

37   Patricia Brown and David John Brown, interview with Ambrose Gillick, York (3 Apr. 2012).

38   Martin Sankey, 'An Interview with Adam Kossowski, 1978', in Read et al., *Adam Kossowski*, 65–80.

39   Michael Dembinski, 'Tadeusz Lesisz: Pole who Sailed with the Royal Navy and Saw Action on D-Day and in the Battle of the Atlantic', *The Independent* (12 Oct. 2009), http://www.independent.co.uk/news/obituaries/tadeusz-lesisz-pole-who-sailed-with-the-royal-navy-and-saw-action-on-dday-and-in-the-battle-of-the-atlantic-1801365.html (accessed 2 Jan. 2013).

40   Nick Gill, 'Pathologies of Migrant Place-Making: The Case of Polish Migrants to the UK', *Environment and Planning A* 42 (2010), 1157–73 (1164).

41   Walker, 'Developments in Catholic Churchbuilding', 345.

42   *CBRN* (1959), 94–7; see also *CBRN* (1968), 79–81.

43   See Andrzej Suchcitz (ed.), *Kronica Kościoła św. Andrzeja Boboli w Londynie, 1961–2011* (London: Polish Catholic Mission Hammersmith, 2012).

44   Wladyslaw Jarosz to Robert Proctor (13 Jan. 2013).

45   Wladyslaw Jarosz, interview with Robert Proctor, London (11 Feb. 2013).

46   'Church of St Anne, Fawley Court' (28 Sept. 2009), English Heritage, http://list.english-heritage.org.uk/resultsingle.aspx?uid=1393459 (accessed 4 Jan. 2013).

47   '7,000 Poles Rally at Henley', *Catholic Herald* (22 May 1964), 3.

48   D. Raabe, P. O'Reilly and G. Dumas, *Notre Dame de France* (London: n.p., 1965), 24.

49   For example 'Destroyed – Rebuilt', *Catholic Herald* (18 Nov. 1960), 5; 'Sleek, Neat and Modern', *Catholic Herald* (26 Aug. 1960), 7.

50   Ann Kimmel, 'Go-Ahead Priest with Go-Ahead Parishioners', *Catholic Herald* (16 Dec. 1966), 3.

51   'Immaculate Heart of Mary Parish, Hayes Middlesex' [parish history] (n.d.), 14–15 (parish archive).

52   'St Mary's, Failsworth: 1845–1964' (parish archive).

53   'Souvenir to Commemorate the Consecration, 12th December, 1956 and Solemn Opening, 16th December 1956, of St Columba's Church, Bolton' (parish archive).

54   A. P. Baggs et al., *A History of the County of Middlesex*, vol. 5: *Hendon, Kingsbury, Great Stanmore, Little Stanmore, Edmonton Enfield, Monken Hadley, South Mimms, Tottenham*, ed. T. F. T. Baker and R. B. Pugh (Oxford: Oxford University Press, 1976), 355–6, British History Online, http://www.british-history.ac.uk/report.aspx?compid=26994 (accessed 31 Jan. 2013); *CBRS* (1970), 72–3.

55   'Mile Long Procession', *Catholic Pictorial* [souvenir supplement] (12 Apr. 1964), 8; *Leyland Guardian* [souvenir supplement] (10 Apr. 1964) (parish archive, St Mary, Leyland).

56   '20,000 Walk in Whit-Friday Procession', *Catholic Herald* (17 June 1949), 7.

57   George Andrew [Beck], draft foreword to programme (16 Apr. 1962) (SDA, Building Office papers, 094).

58   Thomas [Holland], foreword to *Bolton Annual Catholic Procession, 1968, Sunday, June 9th, Official Programme* (archive of Thornleigh Salesian College chapel, Bolton).

59   See Tovi Fenster, 'Non-Secular Cities? Visual and Sound Representations of the Religious-Secular Right to the City in Jerusalem', in Justin Beaumont and Christopher Baker (ed.), *Postsecular Cities: Space, Theory and Practice* (London: Continuum, 2011), 69–86.

10

The Church and the World

The Roman Catholic Church in Britain wanted to claim a civic status, and its architecture contributed to this aim: its embrace of modernism demonstrated its willingness to participate in the modern nation. Yet new theological ideas began to change the Church's conception of its purpose and its relationship to the world, and church architecture changed accordingly. The siting of churches had theological significance: the relationship between the church building and its environment reflected ideas about the nature of the Church, ideas that changed during these decades. The extent of agreement between clergy and town planners over church siting and design is often remarkable: if the Church aspired to a civic status, it accepted the ways in which that status was framed. But influences went both ways: planners accepted the Church's changing views and allowed them expression in their cities.

In the 1950s, the parish church was considered a sacred edifice declaring its noble purpose as a shrine of worship and prayer and was often charged with expressing the fervour of the faithful. In the 1960s, this approach began to be attributed to a 'fortress' Church, intent on creating exclusionary bastions of faith to keep the faithful under surveillance, within its moral and social precincts.[1] These criticisms emerged from the new theology of the Church in the world pronounced at the Second Vatican Council. As early as 1952, Jesuit theologian Hans Urs von Balthasar urged the 'razing of the bastions' and the 'descent of the Church into contact with the world' in a critique of conventional views that influenced the council's thinking.[2] Theologians who invoked the image of the 'fortress' instead supported new models of a 'pilgrim' Church and a Church of 'service'. Monumental churches began to be viewed with suspicion as the symbol of a Church under the delusion of triumph. It was argued that the Church should work more subtly within the world for its salvation, both through liturgy and through more material and social action. The Church had to be open to the world around it rather than confronting it, a view that also implied new attitudes to Christians of other denominations in a growing movement towards Christian unity, or 'ecumenism'. These concepts found expression in new forms of church and new relationships between church and city.

10.1   St Anthony of Padua, Preston, by Giles Gilbert Scott, 1958–59. Photo: Robert Proctor, 2013

CHURCH AS SOCIAL MONUMENT

Whether traditional or modern in style, churches were often considered as monuments – distinguished urban landmarks, symbols of God's transcendent presence and eternity and an expression of the strength of the Catholic community. The figure of the fortress was sometimes used positively to suggest the permanence of the Church through its architecture: St Anthony of Padua at Preston by Giles Gilbert Scott, sited on a major road into the city, was described by the bishop of Lancaster as 'fitted to take its place among the other churches which stood like bastions around the Catholic town of Preston' (Figure 10.1).[3] Yet the design of the parish church was seen as a statement of the presence of the Catholic community within the wider civic body, a contribution to civic space rather than a rejection of it. Monumental churches suggest a desire to Catholicise and sacralise the city, consecrating modern civic endeavour. Town planners strengthened this attitude, encouraging the Church to design prominent landmark buildings.

Churches in new estates and older suburbs were carefully considered to maximise their prominence and visibility. In some cases, sites had been acquired in suburban developments before the war and new post-war churches replaced temporary buildings – at St Theresa, Sheffield, for example, where John Rochford's modern Byzantine church was sited in a valley, overlooked by housing estates on the surrounding hills (Figure 10.2). New sites were acquired on major roads, central to the housing groups the parish served and often facing busy road junctions or roundabouts. Basilican churches presented their entrance gables to the most

10.2   St Theresa, Sheffield, by John Rochford, 1959–60. External sculpture
by Philip Lindsey Clark. Photo: Robert Proctor, 2009

10.3   St Anthony, Wythenshawe, by Adrian Gilbert Scott, 1957–60. The Portway runs alongside the
church; its junction with Rudpark Road is at the centre of the photograph. Photo: Robert Proctor, 2013

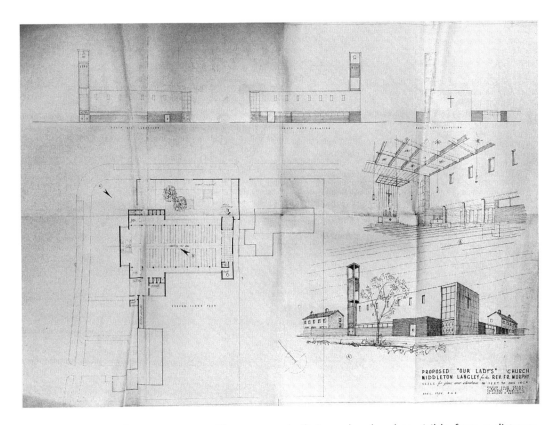

10.4   Our Lady of
the Assumption,
Langley, near
Manchester, by W. &
J. B. Ellis, 1956–61.
Initial design
proposal of
1956. Courtesy
of Ellis Williams
Architects. Source:
parish archive

important street. Towers were built to make churches visible from a distance, often with illuminated crosses – at Reynolds and Scott's church of St Bernard at Burnage in Manchester, for example, incongruous neon lighting meant its gable cross 'can be seen for some considerable distance'.[4] At Wythenshawe in Manchester in the late 1950s, the diocese of Shrewsbury obtained a central site in a post-war extension of this large suburban estate, and commissioned Adrian Gilbert Scott for a substantial statement church dedicated to St Anthony. The bishop, John Murphy, insisted that Scott plan the building 'to dominate the approach from Rudpark Road' and suggested placing the tower on its axis.[5] The building presented its flanking silhouette to this approach so that its west front faced the neighbourhood centre and another junction on the Portway, a major road through the estate (Figure 10.3). Architects and clergy hoped their churches would dominate the urban landscape, representing the Church's centrality in the lives of citizens.

These conventional patterns of siting were maintained in post-war suburban estates, where the urban poor were decanted to garden-city-style housing. Our Lady of the Assumption in Langley, north of Manchester, was typical. Langley was a post-war estate created with new powers granted to city authorities for 'town expansion'.[6] Through its centre ran Wood Street, along which several institutional buildings were planned, including an Anglican parish church, a substantial Catholic school and a neighbourhood shopping centre, while a municipal library and other facilities terminated the road. The provision of such amenities was

intended to prevent the estate from becoming a dormitory suburb, helping a permanent community to develop: as Harold Macmillan, Minister of Housing and Local Government, put it, new residents 'are expected to settle and make a new life, with their industries and employment, their social activities, their churches, their chapels and clubs in the areas to which they are asked to move'.[7] Local authorities planning such estates therefore looked favourably on the clergy's desire to build for their new parishes, allowing churches to become important features.

At Langley the Catholic parish acquired a site at a junction on Wood Street at the centre of the estate and at its highest point. W. & J. B. Ellis were selected as architects, and their initial design of 1956 showed a modern church presenting its flank to Wood Street (Figure 10.4). The diocese of Salford insisted on a revision to enhance the church's presence by turning the gable to this main road, and a revised design followed accordingly; eventually, the new orientation was kept but the style changed to Romanesque (Figure 10.5).[8] The architects proudly explained that their church would 'dominate the new estate', where it was to 'stand on the crest of the hill on the main approach road from the old town centre ... and will be clearly visible from all parts of the estate', an aim enhanced by its lofty campanile.[9]

Of the 22,000 new residents of Langley in around 1960 a third were Catholic. Within 10 years, parish priest John Murphy, with help from Bishop Beck of Salford, arranged for five new schools and two convents of nuns providing household assistance to parents and the aged, besides the church itself costing £100,000 and seating 800.[10] New estates such as Langley had unusually high proportions of young families, who took priority in city re-housing programmes. Church attendance was

10.5   Our Lady of the Assumption, Langley, near Manchester, by W. & J. B. Ellis, 1956–61. In the final design the church's orientation was rotated by 90°, and its tower moved to the road junction; also visible here are a convent on the left and the presbytery on the right. Photo: Robert Proctor, 2013

comparatively high, perhaps partly because Catholic schools required attendance for admission, but also because new residents sought social contacts before other neighbourhood networks had become established. Church buildings therefore seemed urgent for pragmatic as well as symbolic reasons. As in many other places, the parish church was one aspect of a campaign of provision for Catholic settlers – migrants, in a way, however short the distance – helping them adapt to their new situation. The Byzantine-Romanesque style of Ellis's church with its vivid internal mosaics, especially typical of Lancashire, made a reassuring impression for Catholics uprooted from the city and resettled in unfamiliar surroundings, converting the space of modern planning into a place of significance and identity.[11]

While Langley benefited from a range of municipal facilities, other places were less fortunate, and churches provided a civic life where the city had failed. At the pre-war estate of Southmead in Bristol, the central open space of a new housing estate became a religious centre: four churches were constructed around a green immediately behind the shopping area. Bristol's pre-war housing had been sharply criticised by local sociologist Rosamond Jevons, who reported that suburban estates lacked adequate facilities and attributed widespread anti-social behaviour to 'the absence of a social cement'.[12] A decade later, Southmead still lacked any municipal facilities, but the principal Christian denominations had established themselves in temporary buildings around the estate, and their provision of halls and rooms and their organisation of social life compensated for this complete absence of provision by the city.[13]

One of Jevons's criticisms of Bristol's housing was that the central areas were fragmented, and their greens had no purpose: 'some centres have sacrificed the sense of unity through their excessive area of unusable open space', she wrote, 'and by the scattering of public buildings too uniformly around their fringes. The scale is too large for the size of buildings.'[14] If the corporation (as the city council was called) could rarely provide substantial public buildings, it evidently realised that the churches would do so and accorded them prominent sites. The Catholic church of St Vincent de Paul designed by Kenneth Nealon was the first permanent church at Southmead, its site on the highest corner of the green obtained from the corporation, and the other denominations followed, one on each corner. Churches provided estates with the image of a township and of a coherent community that was otherwise lacking: as the Anglican priest of St Stephen phrased it, the churches could 'build up our "Southmead consciousness"'.[15]

In another estate, churches were, unusually, planned from the outset. Richard O'Mahony's church of St Michael and All Angels at Woodchurch outside Birkenhead benefited from its extraordinary siting and responded to it meaningfully. Woodchurch was planned as a 'garden city' housing 10,000 and including two new churches, and Herbert Rowse of Liverpool was appointed architect-planner in 1947.[16] Rowse's scheme was Beaux-Arts in plan, three broad green boulevards radiating down the hill from the existing medieval Anglican church. Community facilities lined the central avenue and the two new churches were sited on a secondary boulevard.[17] In contrast to pre-war estates, Woodchurch was designed with a social infrastructure: 'The Woodchurch Estate', wrote Rowse, 'is ... the architectural setting of a fully developed sociological conception of a community

of people living within a defined neighbourhood, having a conscious identity of its own and equipped for the maximum possibilities of the full social intercourse of such a community'.[18] Rowse's arguments reflected developments in modernist urbanism, the need for a 'heart of the city' being an important aspect of the thinking of CIAM after the war. The realisation of residents' needs for social life prompted the integration into the urban plan of institutional buildings, which included churches.

By 1960, the Roman Catholic parish of St Michael and All Angels was given a broad site at the end of this boulevard of housing, facing along its axis to the Anglican church a mile away at the top of the hill (Plan 7b). O'Mahony inherited the church commission from Velarde, who had already built the presbytery and planned a church off-centre. O'Mahony instead placed the church as close as possible to the axis so that the church terminated the street. Since the medieval church formed the focal point of the estate and the Catholic church took a marginal and opposite position, this urban setting presented an image of the structure of the nation, overseen by the established Church, within which Catholics hoped to take an important part. Lance Wright commented on the Catholic church's siting with wry bemusement, noting that, despite the emerging ecumenical movement, the planners had imposed 'a formidable display of disunity' amongst the faithful: on Sunday mornings Anglicans walked up the hill to church and Catholics walked past them on the way down.[19]

10.6 St Michael and All Angels, Woodchurch, Birkenhead, by F. X. Velarde Partnership, 1962–65. Photographer unknown, c.1965. Source: Architectural Press Archive / RIBA Library Photographs Collection

10.7   St Michael
and All Angels,
Woodchurch,
Birkenhead, by F. X.
Velarde Partnership,
1962–65. Sculpture
of the Virgin and
Child by Norman
Dilworth. By
permission of
Norman Dilworth.
Photographer
unknown,
c.1965. Source:
Architectural Press
Archive / RIBA
Library Photographs
Collection

While the estate was Beaux-Arts in plan, its housing had an Arts and Crafts appearance with pitched-roofed cottage-style terraces. The housing was meant to give the estate 'the general character of a contemporary version of the traditional English village scene', invoked also by the huddling of housing around the medieval church and the linear versions of village greens onto which the avenues' houses faced.[20] O'Mahony's church design reflected the domestic roofs of its neighbours, with a modern twist: their angles were continued in its hipped construction; their gables found a resonance in the lantern that completed the church's aluminium-covered pyramid; and a chimney was implied with a blue-brick pillar that housed the sculpture of the Virgin (Figure 10.6). The church was conspicuous, an unmistakeably religious building type within its housing context, suggesting a conventional understanding of the transcendence of the Church in the world. Yet it was also modest, raising the domestic to a higher plane.[21] The shape of the roof was carried through to the interior, its pine-boarded underside a symbol of shelter unifying the family of worshippers (Figure 10.7). In echoing and transforming the architecture of the house, it suggested the origins of the church in the early Christian house-church commonly evoked by the liturgical movement. O'Mahony's church at Woodchurch marked a beginning of transition in Roman Catholic church design away from a monumental approach.

PERMANENCE AND MODERNISM: NEW TOWN CHURCHES

In the post-war New Towns monumental churches were actively encouraged by planners. Modern architecture was also preferred, and was accepted by clergy as appropriate to the setting: a monumental modernism therefore followed. New Towns had a larger scale and sense of political importance than suburban estates, and planners, architects and clergy all hoped that churches could contribute to the creation of a civic identity and community.

Glenrothes illustrates how clergy and planners negotiated the incorporation of churches into the New Towns. As in most other New Towns, its first master plans of 1949 by architect-planner Peter Tinto contained no church sites at all. When the Church of Scotland requested a site, it was told to collaborate with other denominations through an 'Inter-Churches Committee'.[22] These committees existed throughout Britain after the war: originally tasked with co-ordinating joint applications for building licences, they soon found another purpose in apportioning sites in new developments, and when licensing ended in 1954 this became their primary function. At Glenrothes the inter-churches committee presented the development corporation with a demand for 12 church sites in total, one of which was for Catholics.[23] The 1952 outline plan was then marked up with sites for churches (Figure 10.8). Most proposed locations were at prominent points on main roads, several at roundabouts; some were in the town centre, others in neighbourhood units, a few at the edges of the town as potential landmarks on approach. The Catholic parish was initially offered a prominent site at a corner of the town centre facing a traffic intersection.[24] The diocese was advised to accept it quickly, as it would be in high demand: 'You have been able to get in on a first rate site in the very heart of the Town', wrote their solicitor.[25] Later, however, the archbishop requested a different location, further east and conspicuous within a neighbourhood, placing the Catholic church more centrally in relation to its parishioners, as Glenrothes developed first towards the east.[26] These negotiations between the development corporation and the denominations show a pragmatic rather than principled approach to planning churches, but planners and churches all agreed in wanting landmark sites for both social and visual reasons.

When the archdiocese acquired the site, it came with a condition normally applied by New Town development corporations to private buildings, that a permanent building had to be completed within a fixed time limit. In most cases of New Town churches, this condition made it impossible to build up a site and a parish in stages in the normal way. Glenrothes refused the Catholic diocese's request to build a temporary church, while Archbishop Gray thought that to build a permanent church immediately 'would put an intolerable burden upon the small congregation'.[27] The diocese's request for the alternative neighbourhood site undoubtedly reduced the corporation's expectation of a substantial building, and allowed Gillespie, Kidd & Coia's modest church of St Paul to be completed within the required timeframe. Planners exerted pressure on churches to build quickly and ambitiously, hoping to show rapid progress in building the New Towns, avoiding the criticisms that had been made of suburban estates.

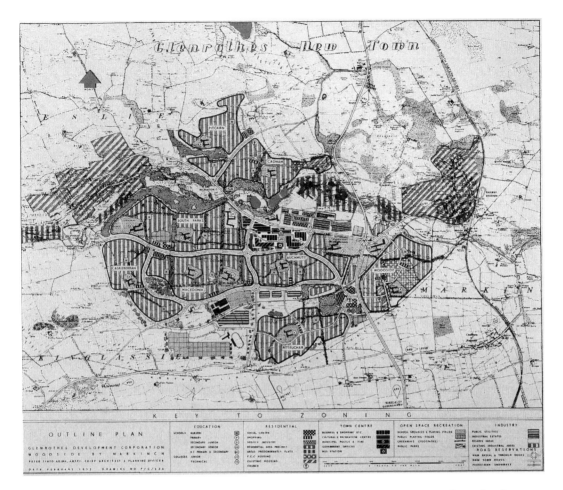

10.8   Glenrothes
New Town Outline
Plan, by the
Glenrothes New
Town Development
Corporation
Architects' Office
under Peter Tinto,
1952, showing sites
for churches. By
permission of Fife
Council Archive
Centre, Glenrothes

Gillespie, Kidd & Coia were probably chosen as architects at Glenrothes because of the New Town location. Reginald Fairlie had originally been commissioned for sketch designs for the central site, but was soon dismissed. The archdiocese briefly considered holding a competition for a new church design, to be judged by the development corporation. They appointed Coia, however, perhaps because he was already involved with St Bride's at East Kilbride.[28] Metzstein and MacMillan explained how they had considered their design for Glenrothes in relation to its context: 'The design of the buildings is intended not only to embody the relatively modest accommodation in striking form, but also to express the adventurous spirit of the New Town', they wrote: the tower, lighting the altar below, would serve as a 'landmark'.[29] When the architects exhibited a model in the town, parish priest Pierce Grace wrote excitedly to Coia that 'the impression made was extremely good. One heard such expressions as: exciting, fascinating, unique etc. The Corporation officials were unreserved in their commendation. Taylor the County Planning Officer expressed his "great pleasure" that it was on show'.[30] The clergy were anxious that the church should be seen as a building worthy of its modern context. Their sensitivity to non-Catholic opinion suggests that they wanted their

church to represent the New Town's Catholic community to others, showing that it was an active and contributing part of the new society that the New Town enterprise sought to create.

In richer and more optimistic dioceses and more confident New Towns, such pressure from planners for early permanent churches was more eagerly accepted by the clergy. At both East Kilbride and Harlow, the Catholic Church undertook substantial modern buildings in harmony with New Town design principles as contributions to their civic environment. At East Kilbride, parish priest John Battel urged the diocese of Motherwell to build a 'commodious and attractive building, something of the dignity and character of a Catholic Town Centre, standing at a focal point'.[31] As early as 1952, Battel agreed a central site for the future permanent church, and a site for a second parish church in the Westwood neighbourhood.[32] The central site offered by the development corporation was prominently located on top of a hill that was to be left as a park, next to a Catholic school already being built, overlooking the main road from Glasgow (Plan 7a). Francis Scott, architect-planner for East Kilbride, praised the site's 'dominating character' and copious open spaces, and Coia advised the diocese that it was 'admirably placed for a church'.[33]

10.9   St Bride, East Kilbride, by Gillespie, Kidd & Coia, 1957–64. Photo: G. Forrest Wilson, c.1964. Source: Glasgow School of Art

10.10   Anglican church of St Paul, Harlow New Town, by Humphrys & Hurst, 1957–59. Photo: Robert Proctor, 2010

Metzstein and MacMillan's design linked church and presbytery across a courtyard to enhance the scale of the building, and the church's sheer brick bulk and modern tower dominated the approach road from the hilltop (Figure 10.9). At its opening in 1964, it was revealed that from the beginning the bishop of Motherwell, James Scanlan, by then Archbishop of Glasgow, 'had set his heart on "the provision of a church of the architectural distinction appropriate to this great venture in town-planning"'.[34]

The site for the second Catholic church at East Kilbride, Our Lady of Lourdes, was also provided by the development corporation and was similarly positioned on an embankment overlooking another main road. This time the development corporation offered to build the church themselves, its chairman, Sir Patrick Dollan, a Catholic and former Provost of Glasgow, noting that 'the site is an excellent one and worthy of the best buildings we can design and construct'.[35] The church was designed by Robert Reid of the development corporation architects' office and opened in the same year as St Bride.[36] Not only was the form of its site similar to that of St Bride, but so was its design, a modern brick and reinforced-concrete rectangular building, its gable and detached tower overlooking the road, though its detailing owed more to Coventry Cathedral than to Metzstein and MacMillan's brutalism. At East Kilbride, planners, clergy and architects collaborated in producing a modern monumental form of church.

The urban situation of Our Lady of Fatima at Harlow New Town was no less important than its liturgical innovations. At Harlow, architect-planner Frederick Gibberd had already proposed a church as a feature of the town's civic centre, and the site was granted to the Church of England for their church of St Paul, a modern building designed by Derrick Humphrys (Figure 10.10). Through the Essex Churches Reconstruction Committee, the equivalent of the inter-churches committee at Glenrothes, the Catholic diocese of Brentwood requested three church sites.[37] Bishop Beck wanted their churches to be close to the Catholic schools, whose siting had been agreed in the early stages of the master plan.[38] The first church site was therefore agreed alongside a school on a main road, close to a roundabout between the town centre and Mark Hall North, one of the earliest neighbourhoods. Clergy and planners both gave careful thought to the treatment of this site.

Initially the Catholic site, which was also to contain a convent and church hall, did not extend to the road junction, but consisted only of a strip along First Avenue. At a meeting between Beck, parish priest Francis Burgess, their architect R. A. Boxall and the development corporation, it was agreed that 'both the Roman Catholics and the Corporation were anxious to secure first-class usage and architectural relationship between the buildings and an impressive frontage to First Avenue'.[39] Clergy and planners agreed to extend the site around the corner onto Howard Way. Eric Adams, General Manager of Harlow Development Corporation, thought 'that by rounding the corner the appearance of their scheme as a whole might benefit from a sense of greater compactness and more effective use of the corner'.[40] The planners expected the Catholic church to provide a monumental landmark facing onto the roundabout, and the clergy and their architects agreed, proposing to place the church in this position and promising completion within five years (Figures 10.11, 10.12).

In contrast to the parish of Our Lady of Fatima, a priest in the south of the town who wanted to build a modest temporary church a few years later was snubbed: 'From a planning point of view we would not wish to see a building of this character in the New Town', the planners complained, noting that their policy was 'to encourage ecclesiastical bodies to put up permanent buildings from the outset', even though all denominations found this difficult.[41] Eventually a permanent church of the Holy Cross was opened in the south of the town, and a further church, St Thomas More, was built by Burles, Newton & Partners in a prominent location in the Little Parndon neighbourhood a few years later. New Town planners prevented the construction of temporary buildings for aesthetic reasons, demanding ambitious permanent churches in return for their allocation of prominent sites.

The selection of Gerard Goalen as architect for Our Lady of Fatima was also related to the New Town context. Goalen was a senior architect for the Harlow New Town Development Corporation under Gibberd designing factories for the town's industrial estate. His final-year thesis project at the University of Liverpool had been a modern pilgrimage church, inspired by Auguste Perret's church at Le Raincy, a design he showed to Burgess.[42] Goalen was also recommended to Burgess by Gibberd:

> He would design a building which would look well and would fit into the overall scheme. I have been a bit worried about the general treatment of your site, in that there is a danger that as different architects have been working on it, it will not hold together as a total design. … Here again Mr. Goalen might be very valuable to you.[43]

10.11   Our Lady of Fatima, Harlow New Town, by Gerard Goalen, 1954–60. Photo:
Ray Stebbings, c.1960. Source: reproduced by courtesy of Essex Record Office, Chelmsford

10.12   Our Lady of Fatima, Harlow New Town, by Gerard Goalen, 1954–60. Photo: Robert Proctor, 2010

Others in the development corporation concurred, and their approbation was an important factor in the parish's choice of architect: the likelihood that he would build a church in keeping with Harlow's design ethos appealed to planners and clergy alike.[44]

Goalen's church was similar to the T-shaped concrete-framed Anglican church of St Paul, though his tall spire and *dalle de verre* windows tempered the building's modernism with historical reminiscences. Goalen wrote in favour of monumental churches: 'A church is the house of God. It should be as fine a building as we can afford, and ... its scale should be generous.'[45] The development corporation, the parish priest and even, as the diocese discovered when it questioned the cost, the parishioners, all shared in this opinion.[46] The building's plan, liturgically innovative as it was, followed logically from the church's urban situation. The T-shaped nave with identical arms and entrance gables was appropriate to the corner site, the church facing each direction from which it would be viewed and approached. The liturgical movement's egalitarian principle of the gathered congregation was also politically allied to the egalitarian ideals of the New Town. Goalen's church embraced the spirit of the New Town, providing the Catholic community with a space that connected their modern social and physical environment with their religious lives.

Some of these buildings might well seem to justify the notion of the inward-looking fortress Church, monumentality and permanence implying isolation from the transitory secular world. St Bride at East Kilbride, lacking any windows and entered from a courtyard, detached from the world around it, could be seen to fit this image. Yet these and many other churches also suggest otherwise. Their prominent siting shows a desire to contribute to each town's identity, participating in the post-war programme of resettlement and the establishment of new communities. Planners, meanwhile, wanted landmark churches to present their towns as balanced and settled places. Catholics adopted modern architecture to show their participation in the modern venture of the New Town: as their worshippers came to reside in modern houses, to shop in modern shopping centres graced with modern art, to work in newly built factories and study in bright modern schools, so they were to worship in churches that expressed the universal faith in the character of the modern town.

CHURCH AS MODERN URBAN LANDMARK: CITY CENTRES

Inner-city areas were also radically transformed by planners, often demanding urgent consideration from the clergy. Here, too, the Church accepted and engaged with the emerging modern city in the architecture of its churches. A comparison between church projects in Birmingham and Edinburgh, however, shows how this ambition began to be questioned. Like many other British cities, Birmingham's centre was broadly redesigned after the war in response to modern ideas in urbanism, including the zoning of urban functions, high-rise housing and new forms of traffic management. Birmingham's City Engineer, Herbert Manzoni, and, from 1952, City Architect Alwyn Sheppard

Fidler, undertook major new road schemes and a massive programme of slum clearances and tower blocks. One of these projects was a ring-road encircling the city centre, originally mooted in the 1930s, planned in 1943, and begun in the late 1950s.[47] Its first section went straight through Dunn and Hansom's substantial late-Victorian Roman Catholic church of St Catherine of Siena at Horsefair. The city set aside a new site for a replacement church in a key position on the outer edge of the ring road, looking across it towards a future shopping centre.

Parish priest Robert Nicholson considered appointing Bower Norris as architect, but a committee of his parishioners changed his mind: 'it was pointed out that this was a grand opportunity for an enthusiastic and able young architect to make a name for himself', he told Archbishop Grimshaw. 'He couldn't have a greater incentive than an important church on a conspicuous site in the centre of the city.'[48] The modernity of the new setting suggested the need for a young modern architect: 'Since the whole area is going to be completely rebuilt over the next few years and our site will be a very prominent one, it would be unwise to wholly ignore the Contemporary environment', wrote Nicholson. Moreover Fidler had declared himself 'very interested in the building we are going to put up', conveying to Nicholson a sense of responsibility towards the modern city.[49] Nicholson then appointed church architects for the diocese Harrison & Cox, who gave the job to a young assistant, Bernard James.[50] James's circular plan may have been inspired by the liturgical movement, but it was also a response to the isolated and prominent site on the ring-road (Figure 10.13). Its simple volumes read well at speed and from a distance; its tower was an instantly comprehensible sign; its circular plan addressed views from around the road junction. St Catherine was substantial in scale and cost partly because of the city's expropriation grant, but also because Birmingham's policy of inner-city high-rise housing meant that this remained one of the diocese's most populous parishes, over 2,500 Catholics attending every Sunday in the mid-1960s.[51]

A similar scheme was proposed for the Roman Catholic Cathedral of St Mary in Edinburgh, but its abandonment marked a change of approach. The cathedral occupied an early Gothic-revival church by James Gillespie Graham, opened in 1814, originally hemmed in amidst Victorian tenements. In 1963, it found itself at the centre of a newly declared Comprehensive Development Area: Edinburgh Corporation planned to demolish swathes of tenements and build new housing; a developer would build a commercial megastructure on the hill behind the cathedral; and the cathedral would face a junction on a newly planned motorway ring-road.[52] The diocese, which also owned a disused theatre on the site, was courted by the city planners, who asked the archbishop if the developers could make proposals affecting, and potentially moving, the cathedral. The archdiocese cagily accepted: 'We would naturally wish to make our development in keeping with the development of the whole area', wrote the Vicar General, James Monaghan, who hoped for 'a Cathedral precinct worthy of the City'.[53] The diocese was eager to participate in the new development but was also concerned that a developer would ignore them, a worry the planners assuaged.[54]

10.13   St Catherine of Siena, Horsefair, Birmingham, by Harrison & Cox, 1961–65. Photo: Robert Proctor, 2009

10.14   Cathedral of
St Mary, Edinburgh.
Sketch proposal
for rebuilding the
cathedral by T. Harley
Haddow & Partners,
1966. Perspective by
Alexander Duncan
Bell showing view
from Leith Walk.
Source: Scottish
Catholic Archives,
Edinburgh

The following year, however, representatives of the diocese were called to a meeting with the Town Planning Officer, who asked whether the diocese would agree to relocate the cathedral altogether if a new site could be found west of the centre to 'give the Cathedral prominence'. The meeting concluded with a demand 'to clear our minds on the image we want the Cathedral to portray in the City'.[55] The diocese decided not to move, but considered a new cathedral inevitable: when the large and complex developments surrounding it were complete, they would not only leave the cathedral outdated and irrelevant, but the road layout would obstruct access to its entrance, so it had to be designed to address a new pedestrian route behind the existing site.[56] The diocese commissioned sketch designs and a model from engineer Tom Harley Haddow, who proposed a giant circular drum inside a reinforced-concrete frame (Plate 16, Figure 10.14). Its form would give it prominence as a unique building in an anticipated setting of rectilinear blocks and meant that it addressed both the road and the pedestrian approach from the future St James Centre. It was well received by the clergy: 'If this scheme were to materialise it would certainly give us a Cathedral and precincts worthy both of the Church and of the City', wrote Archbishop Gray, adding that everyone who had seen it had been 'most impressed'.[57] A combination of anxiety and excitement over the city's transformation inspired a vision of a new cathedral that engaged with the modern city in its own terms.

The construction of the St James Centre proceeded, but neither the motorway nor the new cathedral were built. Pressure from residents halted the ring-road.[58] The St James Centre's precast concrete bulk created a discordant backdrop to the ageing cathedral, but there were several reasons for the diocese to set aside its proposals of 1966. One was that the archbishop consulted Robert Matthew, then Professor of Architecture at the University of Edinburgh, who recommended repairing and extending the cathedral. The excessive cost was another factor; yet the economic argument was also an urban one: 'I should be reluctant to restrict church building where churches are required', wrote Gray, 'simply in order to erect a completely new Cathedral which many of our people might regard as a prestige project'.[59] New and smaller churches in peripheral housing areas to bring the liturgy to the people were accorded a higher priority.

MONUMENTAL QUESTIONS

By the mid-1960s, the NCRG had begun to question the prevailing monumentality in church architecture. Small, temporary, flexible or expandable church buildings, it was argued, were most capable of generating genuine participation in worship and more faithful to the original spirit of the liturgy and to the Church's position in modern society than large, elaborate churches.[60] These conclusions had already been made by Régamey and Couturier in France, and the article by Capellades reprinted in *Churchbuilding* similarly argued that monumental churches for the few sapped resources that would be better spent on supplying the spiritual needs of the many, proposing that modesty and asceticism were morally desirable in church architecture.[61]

Other dioceses besides St Andrews and Edinburgh also turned away from monumental churches in the mid-1960s. When Heenan became archbishop of Westminster, he questioned the prevailing approach in the diocese: 'Where sites can be found for new churches we must create smaller units', he argued. 'The anonymity of the vast city parish makes a true relationship between priest and people impossible.'[62] Other ambitious projects also raised doubts. When the construction of Clifton Cathedral was delayed by financial difficulties, Bishop Rudderham consulted the diocesan clergy over whether to proceed. Many recommended abandoning the project in favour of more pressing priorities. Others doubted the wisdom of extravagance in a period of economic crisis. In Bath, 11 out of 15 priests opposed the building, citing the 'spirit of poverty' advocated by the Second Vatican Council.[63] Construction only began in 1970 because a donor had offered half the cost for a 'place of worship and a monument to Almighty God'.[64] The diocese of Brentwood, meanwhile, was considering building a new cathedral, since its Victorian gothic former parish church had become inadequate for large ceremonies with increasing congregations. A new church accommodating up to a thousand was proposed with a tower and illuminated cross to 'set off the cathedral as the focal point for many miles'.[65] The diocesan financial secretary, however, thought it preferable to build several Mass centres.[66] The secretary of the diocesan senate of priests, Michael Butler, listed his objections in the diocesan newsletter. 'According to the spirit of Vatican II', he wrote, 'the worship of God now seems to be better offered in smaller rather than larger communities', and, given greater awareness of world poverty, the money would be better spent on charitable work.[67] These arguments went to the core of the Church's vision of its role in the world, a vision that underwent reform at the Second Vatican Council.

Firstly, the council's thinking about liturgy motivated a preference for small congregations in intimate churches. Lance Wright, Nigel Melhuish and Peter Evans explored this approach in the three Catholic churches they designed after the council. St Gregory at Alresford was a small square church with a pyramidal roof over a central altar, the congregation seated on three sides. Behind it the architects built a group of houses to fund its construction, amidst which the church, on lower ground, had a modest prominence, its materials and outline deliberately suggestive of domestic architecture (Figure 10.15). Wright had previously argued that small scale was an advantage that would make genuine community possible through liturgy, evoking the primitive worship of early Christianity.[68] The idea of the church as a domestic space was popularised by Belgian Benedictine monk, Frédéric Debuyst, who lectured for the Birmingham Institute for the Study of Worship and Religious Architecture in 1966.[69] His lectures, published as *Modern Architecture and Christian Celebration*, interpreted the liturgy as a celebratory feast, proposing the early Christian house-church as a model for modern church buildings. The faithful, he thought, would then be able to conceive of themselves as a family gathered in a homely space.[70] The church at Alresford captured this ideal of the humble 'Eucharistic room', and was widely published as an exemplar: the *Architectural Review* depicted the church in use, the congregation pressed closely together around the altar under the sheltering roof, visually expressing liturgical movement thought (Figure 10.16).[71]

The other reason for rejecting monumentality came from the Second Vatican Council's statements on the nature of the Church and its role in the world. The 'Dogmatic Constitution on the Church' of 1964 described the structure and purposes of the Church in poetic and far from triumphant language: 'the Church strains toward the consummation of the kingdom', it said, suggesting an unfulfilled project. Until this end was attained, the Church remained 'an exile', 'journeying in a foreign land away from her Lord', 'in pilgrimage upon the earth'.[72] The 'pilgrim Church' was an evocative image that became widely used. It had further implications: the Church, pronounced the council, 'takes on the appearance of this passing world': 'she herself dwells among creatures who groan and travail in pain'.[73] Later, the 'Pastoral Constitution on the Church in the Modern World' developed these images in a discussion of the relationship between the Church and the secular sphere. 'The Church, at once a visible assembly and a spiritual community, goes forward together with humanity and experiences the same earthly lot which the world does', it said. 'She serves as a leaven and as a kind of soul for human society as it is to be renewed in Christ and transformed into God's family'.[74] These documents evoked an image of the Church as different from the world, aiming beyond it and working for its conversion, and yet also permeable to it and inextricably involved in its history.

10.15   St Gregory,
Alresford, by Melhuish,
Wright & Evans, 1968.
Photo: Robert Proctor, 2010

The council summarised recent theology that understood the Church as constituted within its historical situations and that viewed secular history itself as imbued with divinity.[75] By the 1960s, a further influence was the Jesuit Pierre Teilhard de Chardin, whose writing became widely known after his death in 1955. *The Phenomenon of Man*, published in English in 1959, argued that matter and spirit, or consciousness, were intertwined. Biological evolution, thought Teilhard, applied to history and human nature: technical progress would stimulate a global consciousness, ending in a single collective consciousness and a utopian paradise, an evolutionary process directed by God from 'the heart of matter'.[76] The Church, therefore, had to recognise this presence

10.16   St Gregory, Alresford, by Melhuish, Wright & Evans, 1968. Interior during Mass,
as published in *Architectural Review* (1970). Photo: Peter Baistow, 1970.
Source: Architectural Press Archive / RIBA Library Photographs Collection

of God in the world and promote the evolution of consciousness, opening itself to the world to permeate it and concerning itself with humanity's material well-being. These ideas, becoming mainstream in the 1960s, were endorsed in moderation by the council and also chimed with utopian popular youth movements and increasing press interest in the 'third world'. Lance Wright, citing Teilhard, argued that church buildings should express the pilgrim nature of Christianity, as well as a concern with social justice and involvement with the world: churches, he thought, should therefore adopt 'an ordinary secular architecture so as to make the Church one with the secular environment and to give the church building some measure of openness to the outside', adding that 'our generation has come to realize in a special way that the material universe and all that man does are capable of what Teilhard de Chardin calls divinization'.[77]

10.17   St Bernadette, Bristol, by Kenneth Nealon, Tanner & Partners, 1966–68. Photo: Robert Proctor, 2013

SYMBOLIC ENGAGEMENT

One response in church architecture to these new concepts was a symbolic engagement that otherwise retained the conventional model of the parish church. St Bernadette in Bristol, for example, by James Leask of Kenneth Nealon, Tanner & Partners, was designed with a hyperbolic paraboloid roof in thin-shell reinforced concrete forming a pointed canopy over the L-shaped nave, thin supports meeting the ground like tent poles (Figure 10.17).[78] The interior of the canopy roof formed an expressive shelter, a glazed gap around its edges suggesting the provisional

nature of its enclosure. The architecture represented the idea of a pilgrim Church, literally and figuratively encamped on the road. Originally the architects proposed to separate the church from the street with a wall forming an enclosed courtyard around the entrance, but parish priest Joseph Sutton insisted it address the street as a statement of the Church's open relationship to the world.[79] At the entrance brick gave way to glass, revealing the interior. The liturgy could therefore be seen by passers-by, and as the celebrant faced outwards, he looked directly out to the street, symbolically encompassing the world beyond the church in his prayers.[80]

Our Lady of the Wayside at Shirley near Birmingham, designed by Brian Rush of Rush, Granelli & Partners, was similarly open to the busy road outside the church, as glass doors made passing traffic both visible and audible.[81] Inside, Elisabeth Frink contributed a figure of the Risen Christ, life-sized and more human than hieratic, his divinity implied by the gilded bronze material. Placed against the long brick wall over the altar, the figure's arms were outstretched in welcome, its knee bent in action, and its face turned towards the door as if looking out to the world beyond (Figure 10.18).[82] Nearby a wooden sculpture of the Virgin was made by local sculptor Walter Ritchie, once briefly a student of Gill (Figure 10.19). The parish priest Patrick O'Mahony's brief for this figure compared Christ to a poor migrant, 'a displaced person', and required the depiction of the child in this figure to emphasise that, though an outcast, 'he embraces the world'.[83] In Ritchie's interpretation Christ clung to his mother, whose enveloping cloak suggested the flight of a refugee, while the child suggested parallels with photographs of third world children that were then becoming regular features in the news.

Despite its liturgically developed plan and architectural modernism, this church's programme of artworks and external tower retained conventional notions of the church building: Gilbert Cope criticised its 'architectural extravagance'.[84] Yet the novel interpretations in these sculptural figures were part of a culture in this parish of engagement with social concerns beyond its walls: O'Mahony established links to aid projects in India and Africa, sending money and goods from the parish and receiving news in return. This activity was organised in relation to the liturgy: parishioners abstained from luxuries on Fridays, presenting the money they had saved when attending Mass, and O'Mahony read letters from India and addressed issues of development in his sermons.[85] This parish's social action was motivated by an encyclical of Paul VI, 'On the Development of Peoples' of 1967, where a Teilhardian interpretation of progress led the pope to urge a redistribution of wealth to end poverty in the developing world. O'Mahony evoked Teilhard directly in his writing and no doubt also in his sermons. Modern communications and travel, he wrote, made the brotherhood of man a tangible reality: 'Now, suddenly, through an infinite array of communications, and our interconnected biosphere, we are asked to make this belief a reality by our love of this planet in our racial attitudes and in our international outlook.'[86] O'Mahony's church building was intended to encourage his parishioners to adopt this attitude, identifying Christ in the suffering poor and as a model of social action and seeing it as their Christian duty to contribute to the improvement of the world.

THE MULTI-PURPOSE CHURCH

Meanwhile, Cope and others were already arguing for an alternative model of church-building that would make this role of the Church a reality through its physical arrangement and its architectural relationship with the secular world. The multi-purpose church seemed to offer this potential: non-liturgical functions serving the wider neighbourhood would be accommodated in the church building, even in its liturgical spaces. It had long been a common approach in some Nonconformist denominations, and Anglicans began to experiment with such churches several years before Catholics considered them.[87] J. G. Davies of the Birmingham Institute argued in his book *The Secular Use of Church Buildings* that churches throughout history had housed social and civic functions as well as sacred ones. Multi-purpose churches integrated into the social provisions of towns would, he thought, help fulfil the Christian duty towards mankind, potentially as important an aspect of the church building as its liturgical function.[88]

The most influential British building of this type was Sts Philip and James at Hodge Hill in Birmingham, completed in 1968. This was an experimental project in which the Anglican diocese of Birmingham collaborated with the Birmingham Institute and architects Martin Purdy and Denys Hinton of the Birmingham School of Architecture. The church's brief was devised by theologians, sociologists and architects working together, and occupancy studies evaluated it in use. The building centred on two main spaces, a hall and 'worship room', surrounded by subsidiary social spaces including a kitchen, lounge and games room, all accessed from one entrance. Several rooms opened into the nave, and the nave itself was used for social activities presided over by the railed sanctuary. The building was widely published in architectural journals, by the Birmingham Institute and also by the Roman Catholic *Clergy Review*.[89] Catholics soon began to look favourably on such models.

One early Catholic church to adopt the multi-purpose model was the 'parish centre' of St Thomas More in Sheffield, designed by Anthony Tranmer of John Rochford & Partners and completed in 1969. Here the parish priest wanted to provide facilities for the entire neighbourhood regardless of their religious affiliations. The building was sited at the heart of the suburban pre-war municipal housing estate of Parson Cross in Sheffield, in a neighbourhood centre opposite a row of shops. The low, domestic elevations and clustered pitched roofs of the building's exterior gave it continuity with the surrounding housing, while its scale and detailing suggested its role as a community building, only qualified by a small rooftop cross (Figure 10.20). In Tranmer and Rochford's first designs of 1964, a social centre was contained in a separate building from the church, but as the

project developed following the Second Vatican Council the plan became more integrated, with a single building designed for both social and worship use (Plan 6a). At the centre was the church with permanent sanctuary, Blessed Sacrament chapel and a nave for daily use (Figure 10.21). Its sacred purpose was expressed through high-level glazing, a stained-glass window and specially designed liturgical furnishings. All around it and opening into it were rooms for social functions. The largest was a hall, divided from the nave and entrance corridor by curtains and a folding screen: hall and nave could be opened to each other, doubling the size of the nave on Sundays (Figure 10.22). Other facilities included a room for old people, a youth club with dance area and coffee bar and its own entrance, and workshops for training young people. The bishop of Leeds, William Wheeler, wrote that the parish centre was 'an expression of the thought of the Second Vatican Council, with all its pastoral and ecumenical undertones', and auxiliary bishop Gerald Moverley asserted, 'in brief, it is the Church in the Modern World'.[90]

Flexible multi-purpose churches with a range of facilities at least for parish use became increasingly common around 1970. Weightman & Bullen built several. Their scheme for St Helen at Crosby was approved by the archdiocese of Liverpool after some hesitation and an investigation of St Thomas More in Sheffield.[91] The building was square in plan with sliding partitions dividing it into four main sections, capable of being used independently of each other or combined in different configurations. A permanent worship space had a sanctuary at an internal corner; on Sundays its partition walls would be folded back to combine the social areas into an additional large L-shaped nave (Figure 10.23).

10.20 St Thomas More, Sheffield, by John Rochford & Partners, 1964–69. Exterior viewed from main road. Photo: Anthony Tranmer, c.1969

10.21   St Thomas More, Sheffield, by John Rochford & Partners, 1964–69. View of nave: stained-glass crucifix by Patrick Feeny. Photo: Anthony Tranmer, *c.* 1969

10.22   St Thomas More, Sheffield, by John Rochford & Partners, 1964–69. View of hall, open to corridor at the left and the nave partitions beyond. Photo: Anthony Tranmer, *c.*1969

10.23　St Helen's Parochial Centre, Crosby, by Weightman & Bullen, 1973–74. Interior viewed from social room, arranged for Sunday liturgy. Photo: Robert Proctor, 2008

10.24　St Helen's Parochial Centre, Crosby, by Weightman & Bullen, 1973–74. Photo: Robert Proctor, 2008

10.25 St John Stone, Woodvale, Southport, by Richard O'Mahony & Partners, 1970–71. Interior in use at time of opening. Photo: James Hunter, c.1971. Source: archive of OMF Derek Cox Architects, Liverpool

During the week the building was divided into meeting rooms and a hall that could be rented to non-parishioners. The architects explained that the plan visibly integrated social activities into the parish, reducing divisions between secular and sacred functions. What it achieved in plan it also expressed in elevation: 'clear glass is used wherever possible to indicate that the Church must go out to the world and be seen to be living', stated the architects in an appeal to the Second Vatican Council (Figure 10.24).[92] St Helen's was, like St Thomas More, externally modest, eschewing conventional statements of religious identity to reveal its purpose through use. 'Recognition has at last been fully given to the fact that churches are built primarily for congregations not to add beauty to the skyline', wrote parish priest Michael Garvey after its opening in 1974 (though his words seem to have been supplied by the architects). 'A spire topped by an iron cross gives far less witness to Christ than the almost tangible spirituality and vitality that emanates from the new Church and Parochial Centre of St Helen at Crosby.'[93]

The Archdiocese of Liverpool similarly approved Richard O'Mahony's design for St John Stone in Southport, where liturgical space doubled as social space. The church was built for a young congregation who had worshipped for several years in a nearby surgery in the neighbourhood centre and wished to retain the sense of community that had arisen in those expedient circumstances.[94]

10.26   Cathedral of St Mary and St Helen, Brentwood, alteration and extension of church of 1861, by Burles, Newton & Partners, 1974. View from sanctuary showing partitions. Photographer unknown. Source: Brentwood Diocesan Archive

10.27   Cathedral of St Mary and St Helen, Brentwood, alteration and extension of church of 1861, by Burles, Newton & Partners, 1974. View towards new entrance with original spire behind. Photographer unknown. Source: Brentwood Diocesan Archive

O'Mahony thus attempted to capture the qualities of the makeshift liturgical space amidst the secular world. The church was a simple square hall with a small permanent weekday chapel screened by a partition. Unlike St Helen at Crosby, this chapel was not used on Sundays; instead, a wooden platform and timber altar were placed in one corner of the hall and seating was arranged around it to form a nave (Figure 10.25). Rather than an extendable church space, it was a flexible, multi-purpose interior with overlapping sacred and secular functions. Its space-frame ceiling suggested the building's neutrality, intended as neither intrinsically sacred nor secular but simply an envelope for the activities that filled it.[95]

Even Brentwood Cathedral was finally rebuilt as a multi-purpose church. It was decided to extend the Victorian church: Burles, Newton & Partners removed a side wall, rotating the axis to place a new sanctuary against the remaining wall, and built a new square nave in front (Figure 10.26). Newton described the project as an 'expandable cathedral': its core was a permanent worship space that could be enlarged for cathedral ceremonies by opening partitions to rooms on two sides of the nave. These subsidiary spaces included a hall and meeting rooms for social activities.[96] The merging of social and worship spaces was not only economical but also theologically justified: 'The extension of the liturgy into the two social areas flows quite naturally and demonstrates the meaning of "liturgy and life"', wrote Newton.[97] From outside the extension's generic modern architecture, though stone-clad, had little to distinguish it as a church (Figure 10.27). The retention of much of the Victorian church, including its steeple, presented the cathedral as a sacred building, the Victorian section housing the sanctuary; yet it simultaneously undermined this convention, suggesting that the concept of sacred space belonged to the past and was not necessary or possible in the modern world.

CHRISTIAN UNITY: THE ARCHITECTURE OF ECUMENISM

In interpreting the Church as embedded in the world and open to it, the Second Vatican Council also encouraged Christian unity. The council's 'Decree on Ecumenism' of 1964 urged Roman Catholics to engage with other Christians, anticipating a future 'common celebration of the Eucharist' that would restore unity to the Church. This document encouraged joint social action and shared prayer services, though it maintained that only the Roman Catholic Eucharist and priesthood were valid.[98] The late 1960s and early 1970s was a period of increasing warmth between Roman Catholics and Anglicans in Britain. Archbishop Heenan of Westminster, by then a cardinal, advocated Christian unity, accepting the sincerity of Anglicans who claimed continuity with the ancient Church: earlier, in Liverpool, he had founded an office for engagement with other denominations and had become involved in the Vatican's Secretariat for Promoting Christian Unity from 1960, helping to organise a visit of the archbishop of Canterbury, Geoffrey Fisher, to Pope John XXIII and contributing to the Second Vatican Council's documents.[99]

Following the 'Decree on Ecumenism', shared services were promoted and Catholics were permitted to attend non-Catholic liturgies.[100] Increasing collaboration and experimentation led to several significant inter-denominational endeavours in church architecture that also represented an engagement with the secular world.

The first movements towards shared churches were made in chapels for special groups, particularly university chaplaincies. A national campaign to provide Catholic chaplaincies to the burgeoning new universities was undertaken in the 1960s. The new universities of this period were planned with the same optimistic and egalitarian aspirations as the New Towns, but in the smaller, more self-contained environments of their campuses their utopian aims had greater effect: clergy involved in providing for students imbibed the general air of enthusiasm for these projects. The first inter-denominational chaplaincy was at Keele University, where a temporary hut had been provided for Christian denominations to share. Their co-operation made them want to continue sharing a building. Catholics, however, wanted a separate space to reserve the Blessed Sacrament. The new chaplaincy was designed by George Pace to house all groups, 'with the minimum of interference with any one group by another', and opened in 1965.[101] Its central worship space was intended mainly for the Church of England: two protruding apses behind the sanctuary could be screened from the body of the church, one for Nonconformist worship and another furnished with a tabernacle for Roman Catholics, the nave seating turned towards them when needed.[102] Before long, however, the partitions were left unused and all denominations worshipped at the central altar. By 1967, this building was criticised for having calcified a vision of ecumenism that was too conservative.[103]

A Catholic chaplaincy for Lancaster University was seen as an especially important project by the diocese of Lancaster, and architects Cassidy & Ashton were asked to request a site from the university while the campus was being planned in 1964. Later that year, however, the university decided there would be a single chaplaincy centre for all denominations, and accepted Cassidy & Ashton as its architects. The building's construction was funded by the denominations according to the proportions of space they would occupy: the government's University Grants Committee funded the communal areas, and the university took ownership on completion.[104] The Catholic chaplain, John Taylor, supported ecumenism, but the diocese insisted on a separate Catholic chapel in the shared building and so provided nearly half of the cost of the centre.[105] Completed in 1969, the Lancaster Chaplaincy Centre embodied the Catholic view of ecumenism. The two chapels, one for Catholics and one shared by Anglicans and Nonconformists, each occupied a circle on the plan, maintaining the separation of Catholic liturgy. The chapels, however, looked onto a central concourse, glazed walls allowing views into and between them, promoting mutual understanding (Figure 10.28, Plan 6c). The third circle comprised the chaplains' flats and social areas, with rooms for Jewish students, showing the Catholic desire to collaborate in pastoral service.

The building also embodied an aspiration towards future unity. The three spires converged over the central concourse to create a soaring interior, daylight entering at the top, symbolising a trajectory towards unity (Figure 10.29).[106] More practically, the glazed timber panels of the chapels could glide back, opening them into the central space and creating a single large area, and the chapels' furniture

10.28   Lancaster University Chaplaincy Centre, Lancaster, by Cassidy & Ashton, 1966–69. View of central concourse towards Roman Catholic chapel with screens opened. Photo: Robert Proctor, 2011

was moveable for use in combined services. The chapels were frequently opened up for shared inter-denominational non-liturgical events such as carol services. The concourse, meanwhile, became an even more important feature than had been anticipated when Anglicans and Catholics decided to schedule their Sunday liturgies to coincide so that their congregations would meet before and after services, uniting them in an extension of liturgy, not just for secular activity.[107]

Other inter-denominational chapels preceded the development of shared churches. Frederick Gibberd's chapel at Heathrow Airport in London was especially important. Archbishop Godfrey had requested a Catholic chapel at London airport in 1958, mainly to encourage religious observance amongst airport workers. The Ministry of Civil Aviation, however, insisted on a single chapel for all denominations.[108] Gibberd's design was ready in 1964, just as Heenan arrived at Westminster from Liverpool, and shortly before the 'Decree on Ecumenism' was published. St George's Chapel, as it was called, was a three-lobed underground space with Catholic, Anglican and Nonconformist apses looking onto a shared nave, its central seating moveable to face any direction. At first, despite the fact that Heenan was in Rome working on the council's statements on ecumenism,

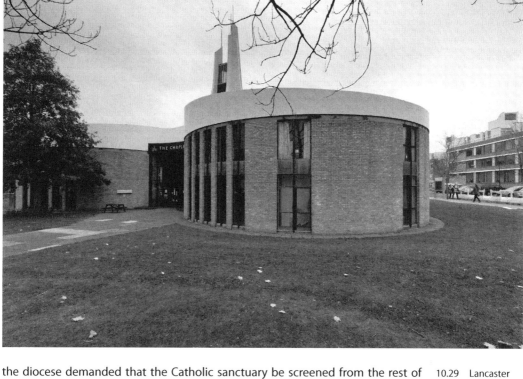

the diocese demanded that the Catholic sanctuary be screened from the rest of the space, much to Gibberd's consternation, mainly because it was felt that the tabernacle should not be exposed to other denominations' services.[109] When the chapel was completed in 1968, however, Catholic confidence in ecumenism had grown, and it was built much as Gibberd had originally proposed, without a screen (Figure 10.30).[110] The chapel at Heathrow was soon also viewed as too conservative: within a few months of opening, all denominations agreed to share a single altar.[111]

As yet there were no purpose-built shared churches for parish use, but that situation changed with the church of St Andrew at Cippenham in Slough, west of London. A major obstacle to shared churches came from the Church of England's rules on church consecration: Anglican churches could only be used for Anglican worship, a position enshrined in British law. In 1968, the first report of the Anglican–Roman Catholic Joint Preparatory Commission, later renamed the Anglican–Roman Catholic International Commission, recommended joint prayer and worship and the sharing of churches wherever desired.[112] Coincidentally, one of the commission's early meetings took place in Cippenham, where Anglican and Roman Catholic congregations had already considered sharing a church. In 1969, the 'Sharing of Church Buildings Act' changed the law to enable the construction of inter-denominational churches, establishing a method of shared ownership and management. St Andrew, Cippenham, was the first project to benefit from this innovation, partly because its congregation had seen early drafts of the Act. It became a model church for the ecumenical movement in Britain, and represented the Catholic view of engagement with other Christians and with the secular world.

10.29   Lancaster University Chaplaincy Centre, Lancaster, by Cassidy & Ashton, 1966–69. Photo: Robert Proctor, 2011

10.30   St George's
Chapel, Heathrow
Airport, London, by
Frederick Gibberd &
Partners, 1964–68.
View from Anglican
apse towards
Roman Catholic
apse. Photographer
unknown, c.1968.
Source: Architectural
Press Archive / RIBA
Library Photographs
Collection

As David Woodard, Cippenham's Catholic priest, explained, the design brief
required a church that reflected the fact that the congregation had already achieved
a 'certain measure of unity'. The building was not to look ' "churchy" or "monumental" '
but had to relate to its surroundings, including a housing estate and factories.[113]
It had to provide for different types and scales of liturgy for both denominations,
with social spaces for use by the congregation and for renting to others.[114]
Designed by parishioner Michael Hattrell, a member of the NCRG, and completed in
1970, the church of St Andrew had an open and flexible interior (Figures 10.31, 10.32,
Plan 6b). Like the exactly contemporary church at Crosby, it was square in plan, sliding
timber partitions enabling different configurations: a small chapel and a series of rooms,
a larger chapel, or a single large space for either secular or sacred use. The steel truss
roof eliminated any sense of hierarchy, though a lantern designated a place for worship.
All furnishings, including altar and font, were of timber and perspex and could be
rearranged as desired. The same worship space and liturgical furnishings – and even the
same vestments – were used by each congregation at different times. At first there was
no tabernacle, but after a year such consensus was reached that a shared tabernacle
was added with separate compartments for Anglican and Catholic reservation.

10.31   St Andrew, Cippenham, Slough, by Michael Hattrell, 1968–70. View from
social areas towards worship space: font in timber and perspex at opening. Photo:
Colin Westwood, c.1970. Source: RIBA Library Photographs Collection

10.32   St Andrew, Cippenham, Slough, by Michael Hattrell, 1968–70. View of worship space: partitions and liturgical furnishings mostly not original. Photo: Robert Proctor, 2010

The flexibility of the interior permitted future developments in unity and also expressed the continuity of liturgy with non-liturgical service spaces. Devotional objects, including the tabernacle, were placed in a recess that could be screened to allow a completely secular function for the building. From outside, the church's low, flat-roofed elevations resembled more a factory than a church, in deference to the industrial neighbourhood (Figure 10.33). Nevertheless its controlled lighting, hard materials and careful detailing led Lance Wright to argue that it retained an ecclesiastical character.[115] Hattrell also applied the emerging principles in modernist architecture of flexibility and interactive systems, popularised by Cedric Price in his 'Fun Palace' project, to embody the joint congregation's aspirations for openness to each other and to the world around them.[116]

Cippenham motivated several similar projects. In Telford New Town, All Saints' church, also called the Stirchley Worship Centre, designed by Peter Bosanquet & Russell Diplock Associates and opened in 1976, had a shared permanent sanctuary, its corners defined by the reinforced-concrete legs of a pyramidal tower, with a Catholic tabernacle placed behind a curtain. Its social spaces could be booked by anyone in the Stirchley neighbourhood and could be opened up with partitions to form a single large church interior.[117] Anglican and Catholic parishes at Stirchley had previously worked together at an ecumenical pastoral centre in 1969 and benefited from the involvement of the Birmingham Institute, which encouraged its integration into the neighbourhood.[118] Telford Development Corporation collaborated with the clergy at Stirchley to site the church within the neighbourhood centre, alongside other social amenities.

10.33   St Andrew, Cippenham, Slough, by Michael Hattrell, 1968–70. Photo: Colin Westwood, c.1970. Source: RIBA Library Photographs Collection

Planners began to encourage shared churches to foster community co-operation in new neighbourhoods. At the Pin Green area of Stevenage New Town, discussions between the development corporation and the churches led to the idea of incorporating a shared church into a community centre. Anglicans and Methodists agreed to co-operate in funding, ownership and worship, and Catholics, led by parish priest Charles Farrell and supported by the Archdiocese of Westminster, later joined the project. The All Saints church and Oval Community Centre formed a single building, designed by the development corporation architects and opened in 1974.[119] Church and centre shared a common entrance in the neighbourhood shopping street, next to a pub (Figures 10.34, 10.35). A door from the centre's interior gave access to the church, in what was perhaps the most integral relationship between sacred and secular space of all church schemes

10.34   All Saints, Pin Green, Stevenage New Town, by Stevenage Development Corporation Architects'
Department, 1970–74. Exterior viewed from within neighbourhood centre. Photo: Robert Proctor, 2013

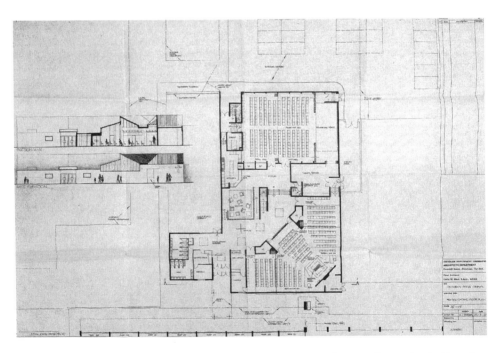

10.35   All Saints, Pin Green, Stevenage New Town, by Stevenage Development Corporation Architects'
Department, 1970–74. Design plan for church and community centre, 1970. Source: parish archive

in which Catholics were involved in this period. Nevertheless the church space remained distinct, and expressed its difference from the secular surroundings through a simple use of exposed brick and laminated timber roof beams with a studied use of natural light (Figure 10.36).

Opposition from a nearby parish priest in Stevenage, Leo Straub, prompted much debate in the local press and amongst Roman Catholics about ecumenism and the nature of the Church. Straub, a traditionalist who rejected the new liturgy, insisted that the shared church would embody a state of unity that did not in reality exist, leading to confusion over the relationships of Catholics to other Christians. Straub and others also argued that Catholics' devotional needs would remain unsatisfied at Pin Green, since it lacked a Lady chapel, Stations of the Cross and other conventional features.[120] When it opened in 1974, the church's modern architecture was viewed by some as inimical to a sense of the sacred, even in liturgical use.[121] Parishioners, however, were enthusiastic about the project and the building, writing of a 'flourishing and genuine interdenominational harmony' and a powerful feeling of community.[122] 'The very fact that a local authority commissioned a church as an essential part of its community centre', wrote George Davey, a canon of the diocese, 'shows that the scandal caused by a divided Christianity is disappearing and that the Church is again being given its rightful place as the centre of community life'.[123] Meanwhile ecumenical practices at Pin Green went further than anywhere else, even including regular joint Eucharistic services in which consecration and communion were enacted simultaneously though separately.[124] Catholics and Anglicans reserved the sacrament in separate tabernacles behind

10.36   All Saints, Pin Green, Stevenage New Town, by Stevenage Development Corporation Architects' Department, 1970–74. Photo: Robert Proctor, 2013

a single veil. Pin Green embodied and brought into being an optimistic vision of the Church, open to future unity with other Christians as an important aspect of its openness to the world. In 1972, a report of the Roman Catholic Ecumenical Commission of England and Wales recommended Pin Green as a model for future churches: 'The whole design reflects an understanding of the relationship of the Church to mankind, both in the distinctiveness of the Christian community, and in its relationship to the wider human community', argued its authors, in a realisation of the full import of the Second Vatican Council.[125]

NOTES

1   For example Hornsby-Smith, *Roman Catholics in England*, 21.

2   Hans Urs von Balthasar, *Razing the Bastions: On the Church in This Age*, trans. Brian McNeil (San Francisco: Ignatius Press, 1993, originally published 1952), 99.

3   *CBRN* (1959), 176.

4   *CBRN* (1959), 78.

5   'Summary of Bishop's Remarks of New Church Project' (c.1957); also Adrian Gilbert Scott to M. B. Kehoe (parish priest, St Anthony, Wythenshawe) (20 Aug. 1957) (parish archive, St Anthony, Wythenshawe).

6   J. B. Cullingworth, 'Overspill in South-East Lancashire: The Salford-Worsley Scheme', *Town Planning Review* 30 (1959), 189–206.

7   Cited ibid. 201.

8   Diocese of Salford Finance Board, minute book no. 6 (14 May 1958), 173 (SDA, C123); W. & J. B. Ellis, drawings (1956, n.d.) (parish archive, Our Lady of the Assumption, Langley).

9   *CBRN* (1958), 98.

10   Michael Morrissey, 'Five Schools in Nine Years', *Catholic Herald* (24 Nov. 1961), 5; 'Souvenir of the Blessing and Dedication of Our Lady of the Assumption, Langley' (1961) (parish archive).

11   My thinking here is broadly influenced by Henri Lefebvre (*The Production of Space*, 33–5, 48–52, 118). See also Simon Naylor and James R. Ryan, 'The Mosque in the Suburbs: Negotiating Religion and Ethnicity in South London', *Social & Cultural Geography* 3 (2002), 39–59; Catherine Brace, Adrian R. Bailey and David C. Harvey, 'Religion, Place and Space: A Framework for Investigating Historical Geographies of Religious Identities and Communities', *Progress in Human Geography* 30 (2006), 28–43.

12   Rosamond Jevons and John Madge, *Housing Estates: A Study of Bristol Corporation Policy and Practice Between the Wars* (Bristol: University of Bristol, 1946), 70.

13   Vigilans, letter to the editor, *Southmead Echo* 6 (Oct. 1956), 4; 'Addresses of Some Organisations on the Estate', *Southmead Echo* (Feb. 1955), 7–8; 'A Letter From the Union of Catholic Mothers (Southmead Branch)', *Southmead Echo* (June–July 1957), 4; Jevons and Madge, *Housing Estates*, 80–83.

14   Jevons and Madge, *Housing Estates*, 23.

15   Michael Mannox, 'Hello, Southmead!', *Southmead Echo* (Feb.–Mar. 1957), 5; this conclusion draws from Louis Althusser, 'Ideology and Ideological State Apparatuses

(Notes Towards an Investigation)', in id., *Lenin and Philosophy and Other Essays*, trans. Ben Brewster (London: Monthly Review Press, 1971), 127–86.

16   First scheme described in 'Layout for the Woodchurch Estate, Birkenhead', *Builder* (24 Nov. 1944), 408–9.

17   'Woodchurch Estate, Birkenhead', *Architect and Building News* (14 Feb. 1947), 132–5; 'The Woodchurch Estate, Birkenhead', *Architect and Building News* (13 Oct. 1950), 406–9.

18   'The Woodchurch Estate', *Architect and Building News* (13 Oct. 1950), 406.

19   'Church at Woodchurch, Birkenhead', *Architects' Journal* (13 Apr. 1966), 941–52.

20   'The Woodchurch Estate', *Architect and Building News* (13 Oct. 1950), 406, 409.

21   'Church at Woodchurch', 946.

22   Minutes of meetings of the Glenrothes Development Corporation Committee (7 Sept. 1949; 16 Nov. 1949) (Fife Council Archives, Glenrothes [FCA], GDC/1); Robert Mackintosh (Church of Scotland Home Board) to Walter J. Glancy (finance secretary, Archdiocese of St Andrews and Edinburgh) (18 Oct. 1949); W[alter] G[lancy] to James Lyons (solicitor) (20 Oct. 1949); Lyons to Glancy (21 Oct. 1949) (SCA, DE/59/222).

23   Minutes of meetings of the Glenrothes Development Corporation Committee (16 Nov. 1949; 18 Jan.; 4 Oct. 1950; 4 June 1952) (FCA, GDC/1).

24   Glenrothes Development Corporation Committee (6 Feb. 1952) (FCA, GDC/1); outline plan of Glenrothes New Town with Roman Catholic church site marked (4 Feb. 1952); preliminary site plan for Roman Catholic Church (14 Feb. 1952) (SCA, DE/59/226); [anon.] to Frank A. B. Preston (Glenrothes Development Corporation) (1 Feb. 1952) (SCA, DE/59/225).

25   Norman C. Grant (Allan McNeil & Son) to Glancy (8 Mar. 1952) (SCA, DE/59/225).

26   Glenrothes Development Corporation Committee (21 Dec. 1955) (FCA, GDC/1).

27   Gordon Joseph Gray (archbishop of St Andrews and Edinburgh) to Pierce Grace (parish priest, Falkland, later of St Paul, Glenrothes) (5 Nov. 1954) (SCA, DE/59/201).

28   Glancy to Grant (21 June 1955) (SCA, DE/59/229).

29   Press releases (n.d.) (GSAA, GKC/CG/1/8).

30   Grace to J. A. Coia (Gillespie, Kidd & Coia) (19 Oct. 1956) (GSAA, GKC/CG/1/1).

31   John Battel (parish priest, East Kilbride) to John Rooney (secretary, Diocese of Motherwell Finance Board) (28 Apr. 1949) (SCA, DM/27/150).

32   'Minutes of Meeting re Sites of Roman Catholic Churches in East Kilbride, Held at Torrance House, East Kilbride' (11 Sept. 1952) (SCA, DM/27/152).

33   [Francis Scott] (Chief Architect and Planning Officer, East Kilbride Development Corporation) to [Charles] Craigen (secretary, Diocese of Motherwell Finance Board) (15 Sept. 1952) (SCA, DM/27/152); Coia to Craigen (31 Oct. 1952) (SCA, DM/27/152).

34   *Solemn Opening: St Bride's Church, East Kilbride* (East Kilbride: n.p., 1964) (SCA, HC/57).

35   Patrick Dollan (chairman, East Kilbride Development Corporation) to [James Scanlon] (bishop of Motherwell) (17 Feb. 1958) (SCA, DM/27/143).

36   *Solemn Opening of the New Church of Our Lady of Lourdes, East Kilbride* (East Kilbride: n.p., 1964) (SCA, HC/57).

37   For example 'Meeting with Representatives of the Essex Churches Reconstruction Committee' (7 Mar. 1949) (Records of Harlow Development Corporation, Essex Record Office, Chelmsford [HDC], 379, 37/1).

38   V. Hamnett (executive architect, Harlow Development Corporation) to Adams (9 July 1952) (HDC, 379, 37/1).

39   'Roman Catholic Site North of First Avenue: Note of Meeting' (8 Sept. 1953) (HDC, 379, 37/5).

40   'Roman Catholic Site North of First Avenue: Note of Meeting' (14 Dec. 1953) (HDC, 379, 37/5).

41   [Ben Hyde Harvey] (general manager, Harlow Development Corporation) to [Hamnett] (15 Feb. 1957); [Hamnett] to [Harvey] (13 Feb. 1957) (HDC, 379, 37/5).

42   Martin Goalen to Robert Proctor [memo] (Mar. 2012).

43   Frederick Gibberd to Burgess (19 Nov. 1953) (BDA, I3).

44   Also Burgess to Beck (24 Nov. 1953) (BDA, I3).

45   Gerard Goalen, 'The House of God', Church Buildings Today (Jan. 1961), 3.

46   Eric H. Goldingay, 'Report on the Public Meeting Held at Fatima Hall, Harlow' (6 Aug. 1957) (BDA, I3).

47   Gold, Practice of Modernism, 74, 82–3.

48   R. H. Nicholson (parish priest, St Catherine, Horsefair) to [Francis Joseph Grimshaw] (archbishop of Birmingham) (9 Nov. 1958) (ARCAB, P10/T8).

49   Nicholson to [Grimshaw] (12 Sept. 1958) (ARCAB, P10/T8).

50   Nicholson to [Grimshaw] (9 Nov. 1958); Herbert Manzoni (City of Birmingham Public Works Department) to Nicholson (2 Apr. 1959) (ARCAB, P10/T8).

51   Parish return, St Catherine of Siena, Horsefair (7 May 1966) (ARCAB, P10/T8).

52   Corporation of Edinburgh, Edinburgh. St James' Square (Leith Street Etc.): Comprehensive Development Area. Developers' Brief [1963] (SCA, DE/58/11).

53   [James Monaghan] (vicar general, Archdiocese of St Andrews and Edinburgh) to Town Clerk (Corporation of Edinburgh) (18 Feb. 1963) (SCA, DE/58/12).

54   Deputy Town Clerk to Monaghan (25 Mar. 1963) (SCA, DE/58/12).

55   'Memo. Meeting between the Town Planning Officer and Monsignor Quille and Father Glancy in the City Chambers on 4th February, 1964' (SCA, DE/58/12).

56   'Draft for Report to the Chapter' (25 Oct. 1965); Allan McNeil & Son (Solicitors) to Town Clerk (Corporation of Edinburgh) (26 Nov. 1965); also T. Harley Haddow, 'Some Personal Notes on St. Mary's Roman Catholic Cathedral Revelopment' (Mar. 1969) (SCA, DE/58/15).

57   Gordon Joseph Gray (archbishop of St Andrews and Edinburgh) to Robert Matthew (10 Jan. 1967) (SCA, DE/58/14).

58   Walter Glancy (finance secretary, Archdiocese of St Andrews and Edinburgh) to Haddow (16 June 1967) (SCA, DE/58/14).

59   Gray to Matthew (11 May 1966) (SCA, DE/58/12).

60   For example H. Benedict Green, 'House of God and Church Centre: The Two Approaches Related', Church Buildings Today (Jan. 1961), 11; George G. Pace, 'Notes and Comment: Temporary Churches', Church Building Today (Apr. 1961), 7–10.

61   Capellades, 'Transparent Poverty', 4, 7; see also Régamey, *Art sacré au XXe siècle*,
     26–7; Rainer Senn, 'The Spirit of Poverty', *Churchbuilding* (Apr. 1963), 23. Paul Walker
     takes a critical view of Senn's paternalistic attitude ('Developments in Catholic
     Churchbuilding', 149–50, 162).

62   John Cardinal Heenan, foreword to *CBRS* (1966), 29.

63   Ciprian Harris (parish priest, St Aldgate's, Oxford) to Joseph Rudderham (bishop of
     Clifton) (29 Dec. [1969]); Leo Delan (Beeches Green, Stroud) to Rudderham (30 Dec.
     [1969]); report of deanery meeting, St Mary's, Bath (14 Dec. 1969) (CDA, Cathedral File).

64   [Name withheld at diocese's request] to Rudderham (18 Feb. 1970) (CDA, Cathedral
     File, 'Miscellaneous Correspondence').

65   Denis Petry (canon, diocese of Brentwood) to Patrick Casey (bishop of Brentwood)
     (9 May 1970) (BDA, N2/a).

66   Eric H. Goldingay (financial secretary, diocese of Brentwood) to Casey (14 May 1970)
     (BDA, N2/a).

67   Quoted in 'From Our Notebook', *The Tablet* (12 Dec. 1970), 1206; newspaper cutting
     from *The Times* (17 Nov. 1970) (BDA, N2/a); see also William E. A. Lockett, 'Some
     Reflections on Cathedral Building in the Twentieth Century', *Churchbuilding* (Jan. 1968),
     3–5.

68   For example Wright, 'Architectural Seriousness', 233–5.

69   J. G. Davies, 'The Establishment of the Institute for the Study of Worship and Religious
     Architecture', in *Institute for the Study of Worship and Religious Architecture: Research
     Bulletin* (1966), 8 (ARCAB, Dwyer Papers, GPD/S/A9).

70   Frédéric Debuyst, *Modern Architecture and Christian Celebration* (London: Lutterworth
     Press, 1968), 29–31; Walker, 'Developments in Catholic Churchbuilding', 222–31.

71   *Manplan 5*, special issue of *Architectural Review* (Mar. 1970); Alresford was also the
     only modern church illustrated in the briefing guide (New Churches Research Group,
     Church Buildings, cover).

72   'Dogmatic Constitution on the Church (*Lumen Gentium*) (1964)', in Abbott (ed.), *The
     Documents of Vatican II*, 18–21, 78; Richard P. McBrien, 'The Church (*Lumen Gentium*)', in
     Hastings (ed.), *Modern Catholicism*, 84–95.

73   'Dogmatic Constitution on the Church', 78–9.

74   'Pastoral Constitution on the Church in the Modern World (*Gaudiam et spes*) (1965)', in
     Abbott, *The Documents of Vatican II*, 239.

75   For example Fergus Kerr, *Twentieth-Century Catholic Theologians: From
     Neoscholasticism to Nuptial Mysticism* (Oxford: Blackwell, 2007), 70–77, 87–99, 146–9;
     Mettepenningen, *Nouvelle Théologie – New Theology*, 96–100; Congar, *Lay People in
     the Church*, 60–91; Henri de Lubac, *Catholicism: Christ and the Common Destiny of Man*,
     trans. Lancelot Sheppard (London: Burns & Oates, 1962; first published 1938); Jean
     Daniélou, 'The Conception of History in the Christian Tradition', *Journal of Religion* 30
     (July 1950), 171–9.

76   Pierre Teilhard de Chardin, *The Phenomenon of Man* (London: Collins, 1959), 294.

77   Wright, 'Architectural Seriousness', 236, 239.

78   J. A. Harding, *The Diocese of Clifton, 1850–2000* (Bristol: Clifton Catholic Diocesan
     Trustees, 1999), 92–3; *CBRS* (1966), 176–7; (1967), 168–9.

79   Bryan Little, 'Review of New Church: St Bernadette's, Bristol', *Clergy Review* 53 (1968),
     749–56 (753).

80   J. A. Harding (former parish priest of St Bernadette), conversation with Robert Proctor, Bristol (21 Jan. 2008).

81   Visible in contemporary plans (parish archive, Our Lady of the Wayside, Shirley, Birmingham).

82   Frederick A. Hall, letters to the editor, *The Tablet* (8 Jan. 1966), 52; (21 Aug. 1965), 940.

83   [Patrick O'Mahony], 'Brief for Sculpture' [Sept. 1965] (ARCAB, P245/T1).

84   Gilbert Cope, 'Some Recent Churches in the East Midlands', *Churchbuilding* (Oct. 1968), 9–12 (9).

85   'Shirley Fasts – Calcutta Eats', *Catholic Herald* (12 Jan. 1968), 10; Patrick J. O'Mahony, 'A Parish and Overseas Project', *Clergy Review* 54 (1969), 536–40; 'From Our Notebook', *The Tablet* (8 Feb. 1969), 138.

86   Patrick O'Mahony, 'One Parish, One World', *The Tablet* (6 Apr. 1974), 343; id., 'Project India', *The Church in Shirley Magazine* (Nov. 1968), 3–5 (ARCAB, P245/T1).

87   For example Michael Farey, 'The Church Centre', *Church Buildings Today* (Jan. 1961), 6–10.

88   J. G. Davies, *The Secular Use of Church Buildings* (London: SCM Press, 1968), 212, 246.

89   *Institute for the Study of Worship and Religious Architecture: Research Bulletin* (1966) (ARCAB, GPD/S/A9); Peter Bridges, 'Review of New Church Centre: SS Philip and James, Hodge Hill, Birmingham', *Clergy Review* 54 (1969), 241–8; 'Building Study: Church and Youth Centre', *Architects' Journal* (8 Oct. 1969), 875–6; Walker, 'Developments in Catholic Churchbuilding', 217–21.

90   St Thomas More, Sheffield, dedication ceremony souvenir booklet (parish archive).

91   Minutes of meetings of the Council of Administration, Archdiocese of Liverpool (21 Apr.; 14 July 1969; 19 Oct. 1970) (LRCAA, Beck Collection, 5/S3/1).

92   *CBRN* (1973), 8.

93   Joseph M. Garvey, 'Church of Saint Helen and Parochial Centre: Appreciation on Behalf of User', *CBRN* (1974), 172–4; *St Helen's Catholic Church: Eighty Years On* (Crosby: n.p., 2010) (parish archive).

94   *CBRN* (1971), 92.

95   Kenneth Nugent, 'Architecture for Eschatologists: Church of St John Stone, Woodvale, Lancashire', *Clergy Review* 56 (1971), 241–7 (242).

96   John Newton, 'The Expandable Cathedral', in *St Helen's Cathedral, Brentwood* (Brentwood: n.p., c.1974) (BDA, N2/a).

97   A. J. Newton, 'The Story of a Cathedral', *CBRS* (1974), 12, 7.

98   'Decree on Ecumenism (1964)', in Abbott (ed.), *The Documents of Vatican II*, 341–66; 'Ecumenism in England: The Hierarchy's Statement', *The Tablet* (12 Dec. 1964), 1421.

99   Heenan, *Crown of Thorns*, 202–3, 209–10, 322–8; Tom Stransky, 'The Secretariat for Promoting Christian Unity', in Hastings (ed.), *Modern Catholicism*, 182–4.

100 'New Rulings on Ecumenism', *The Tablet* (23, 30 Dec. 1967), 1357–8.

101 'A Chapel at Keele: Shared Between the Students of Three Confessions', *The Tablet* (9 July 1960), 660.

102 Pace, *Architecture of George G. Pace*, 188–91.

103 Ralph Tubbs, 'What We Have Learned From Building and Using a University Chapel', in K[athleen] B[liss] (ed.), *The Ecumenical Situation Today and the Responsibility of the*

University Christian Community in It [report on conference at the University of York] (*c.*1967) (LRCDA, Lancaster University Chaplaincy File).

104 Oswald Goodier (Oswald Goodier & Co., solicitors) to Brian Charles Foley (Roman Catholic bishop of Lancaster) (28 Apr. 1965); Charles Carter (vice-chancellor, University of Lancaster), 'The University of Lancaster: Proposed Religious Centre' (May 1965); Carter to Cassidy & Ashton (18 Dec. 1964); [Gerald] Cassidy to Carter (4 Feb. 1965); *The Chaplaincy Centre, Lancaster University: An Illustrated History* (*c.*1989) (LRCDA, Lancaster University Chaplaincy File); see also William E. A. Lockett, 'Some Recent Church Buildings in the North West', *Churchbuilding* (Apr. 1969), 15–20 (18); *CBRN* (1968), 288–90.

105 'Catholic Chaplaincy to Lancaster Appeal Fund' [typescript] and circular letter from Thomas Pearson (auxiliary bishop of Lancaster) to parishes (*c.*1969) (LRCDA, Lancaster University Chaplaincy File).

106 Cassidy & Ashton, 'University of Lancaster Proposed Chaplaincy Centre' [typescript] (n.d.) (LRCDA, Lancaster University Chaplaincy File).

107 *The Chaplaincy Centre, Lancaster* (LRCDA).

108 David Cashman (auxiliary bishop of Westminster) to Hay (19 Oct. 1963); Cashman to David Norris (secretary to archbishop of Westminster) (11 Oct. 1963); Cashman to Derek [Warlock] (secretary to archbishop of Westminster) (19 Oct. 1963) (WDA, He/3/96).

109 Cashman to John C. Heenan (archbishop of Westminster) (19 Sept. 1964); Heenan to Cashman (22 Sept. 1964) (WDA, He/3/96).

110 'Airport Chapel', *Architect and Building News* (9 Oct. 1968), 36–7.

111 'Lessons From Geneva', *Churchbuilding* 29 (Jan. 1970), 11.

112 'Approaches to Catholic–Anglican Unity', *The Tablet* (30 Nov. 1968), 1202.

113 David Woodard, 'The Cippenham Shared Church' [pamphlet] (*c.*1970) (HDC, 379, 37/1); David Woodard, 'Cippenham Shared Church', *One in Christ* 6 (1970), 61; 'The First Joint Church Building', *The Tablet* (28 Oct. 1967), 1129; 'From Our Notebook', *The Tablet* (4 Oct. 1969), 980.

114 David Woodard, 'The Cippenham Shared Church', *Clergy Review* 53 (1968), 381–3.

115 Lance Wright and Michael Hattrell, 'Building Study: Shared Church at Elmshott Lane, Cippenham', *Architects' Journal* (12 May 1971), 1055–66 (1060).

116 For some criticisms of the building in use, see ibid. 1059; David Woodard, 'First Ten Years at Cippenham Shared Church', *One in Christ* 17 (1981), 43–5.

117 *CBRS* (1973), 196–7; Walker, 'Developments in Catholic Churchbuilding', 537.

118 Peter Bridges, 'Recommendations for the Church's Mission in Dawley New Town', *Institute for the Study of Worship and Religious Architecture Research Bulletin* (1966), 45–61; Peter Bridges, 'The Function of the Pastoral Centre', *Institute for the Study of Worship and Religious Architecture Research Bulletin* (1966), 63–8 (ARCAB, GPD/S/A9); also F. C. Price, 'New Towns Inspire Fresh Thinking on Church Building', *Catholic Herald* (20 Feb. 1970), 3; Walker, 'Developments in Catholic Churchbuilding', 274–6.

119 Stevenage Development Corporation, 'A Note on the Development of the Oval Community Centre and All Saints Church' (1974) (parish archive); A. Rivers (finance officer, Archdiocese of Westminster) to Heenan (archbishop of Westminster) (29 Jan. 1971) (WDA, He1/C23(c)); minutes of meeting of the Council of Administration

(12 May 1971); Leo Straub (parish priest, Transfiguration of Our Lord, Stevenage), letter (22 Mar. 1972) (WDA, He4/C2).

120 Straub to Heenan (3 May 1972) (WDA, He4/C2).

121 D. G. Galvin, letter to the editor, *The Tablet* (19 Oct. 1974), 1015.

122 Peter Towers to Heenan (21 Nov. 1971); William Slavin to Heenan (11 Apr. 1972) (WDA, He4/C2).

123 George C. Davey, letter to the editor, *The Tablet* (26 Oct. 1974), 1040.

124 Nigel Dees, 'Shared and Multi-Purpose Church Buildings' [paper given at conference of Liturgy Commission Department of Art and Architecture, Kessington, 1978]; *Forward in Faith: Britain's First Purpose-Built Shared Church and Community Centre* (Stevenage: Shared Churches (Stevenage Pin Green) Ltd., 1976); Charles Farrell, 'United We Serve', *New Life* (Sept.–Oct. 1975), 13–17 (parish archive, All Saints, Pin Green, Stevenage New Town).

125 Peter Hocken and John Coventry, 'The Sharing of Resources', 1972, quoted in 'The Tablet Notebook', *The Tablet* (28 Sept. 1974), 945.

11

Conclusion

Roman Catholic church architecture in post-war Britain was prodigious and creative, testament to the vitality of the Church at the time. It was the product of architects, often in tandem with artists, many with clear and innovative ideas, working with a clergy eager to obtain the best and most appropriate buildings for their people. Congregations, at a historical peak of participation in parishes, equally wanted churches and worked together to achieve them. Town planners enabled and further motivated church-building. Churches were designed to be outward-facing, presenting Catholic communities to contemporary society in order to claim a stake within it. Church architecture represented cultural capital, as economic capital was put to use to elevate the status of the institution and its people. Nevertheless churches were also functioning spaces, housing the distinctive religious practices of an enthusiastic faithful. This was a period characterised by huge changes and upheavals: in the forms of cities and the lives of their inhabitants, which were followed by the Church; in liturgical and devotional worship and in theological conceptions of the Church's place in society; in architectural forms and methods. Yet, at least until the end of this period, the one common conviction was that the church building had an important role to play, above all in bringing the faithful together to constitute a social body, constructing the Church as a reality in all its varied local manifestations.

In completing this book I am acutely aware of the many things I have had to omit. My focus has been on the new urban parish church, and I have had to neglect many important buildings that did not fit this model, including new abbeys and convents and their churches, smaller chapels and shrines, and extensions, remodellings, rebuildings and reorderings of all kinds. Even significant and prolific architects have barely been mentioned. Though this is an overview of a relatively narrow subject, it only scans the surface of a rich and complex culture. Other stories can and should be told.

This culture is now history, and the evidence for it is in decline: many churches have been demolished or altered beyond recognition. While modern church architecture is often criticised for poor-quality construction, often the result of innovations in building techniques or inadequate maintenance, traditionally built churches have not been immune from destruction: indeed Velarde's best post-war church in Liverpool was demolished long ago, and at the time of writing another in Birkenhead is available for purchase, complete with a magnificent mural. The shift towards modernism in church architecture and the liturgical and theological innovations that took place in this period, meanwhile, are increasingly regarded as an aberration, as revisionary interpretations of the Second Vatican Council at its fiftieth anniversary emphasise continuity with tradition and lead to reversals of reform. However much of an aberration it might one day prove to have been, this period's church architecture represents a vitally important aspect of the history of Roman Catholicism, indeed of Christianity, in Britain and internationally, and it is equally significant in the history of British towns and cities, their architecture and their social life.

Colour Plates

1 St John Fisher, West Heath, Birmingham, by Sandy & Norris, 1963–64. *Dalle de verre* windows by Jonah Jones. Photo: Robert Proctor, 2009

2 Holy Trinity, Dockhead, London, by H. S. Goodhart-Rendel, 1958–60. Photo: Matt Clayton, 2013

3　St Luke, Pinner, London, by F.X. Velarde, 1958. Interior with Crucifixion by David John. By permission of David John. The original sanctuary fittings have been altered. Photo: Robert Proctor, 2010

4 St Augustine, Manchester, by Desmond Williams, 1965–68. Reredos sculpture, altar, crucifix and candlesticks by Robert Brumby; *dalle de verre* slot windows by Pierre Fourmaintraux of Whitefriars Studios. By permission of Robert Brumby. Photo: Robert Proctor, 2012

5   St Aidan, East Acton, London, by Burles & Newton, 1959–61. Sanctuary artworks: six of the Forty Martyrs in *dalle de verre* by Pierre Fourmaintraux of Whitefriars Studios and painting of the Crucifixion by Graham Sutherland, c.1964. Courtesy of the Estate of Graham Sutherland. Photo: Robert Proctor, 2009

6   St Bernadette, Lancaster, by Tom Mellor, 1958. Reredos painting by John Piper.
Courtesy of the Estate of John Piper. Photo: Robert Proctor, 2011

7   Metropolitan Cathedral of Christ the King, Liverpool, by Frederick Gibberd,
1960–67. Stained glass by John Piper and Patrick Reyntiens. © Patrick Reyntiens,
all rights reserved, DACS, London, 2013. Photo: Robert Proctor, 2012

8   St Mary, Leyland, by Weightman & Bullen, 1960–64. Frieze of the Last Judgement in ceramic by Adam Kossowski. Photo: Robert Proctor, 2010

9   Cathedral of Sts Peter and Paul, Clifton, Bristol, by Percy Thomas Partnership, 1965–73. The
original doors by William Mitchell have been replaced. Photo: Robert Proctor, 2013

10   Good Shepherd, Nottingham, by Gerard Goalen, 1961–64. Stained glass, 'Tree of the Cross', in *dalle de verre*
by Patrick Reyntiens. © Patrick Reyntiens, all rights reserved, DACS, London, 2013. Photo: Robert Proctor, 2009

11 St Paul, Wood Green, London, by John Rochford, 1967–72. Sculpture by Michael Clark; stained glass by Moira Forsyth; resin and fibreglass painting in nave of the Seven Sacraments by Carmel Cauchi; added c.1980. By permission of Joseph Lindsey-Clark and Carmel Cauchi. Photo: Matt Clayton, 2012

12   Our Lady of Fatima, Harlow New Town, by Gerard Goalen, 1954–60. Stained glass by Charles Norris showing the Mysteries of the Rosary (transepts), Tree of Jesse and Our Lady of Fatima (nave). Photo: Robert Proctor, 2010

13   Votive Shrine of Our Lady of Lourdes, Blackpool, by F. X. Velarde, 1955–57. Sculpture
by David John. By permission of David John. Photo: Robert Proctor, 2011

14   English Martyrs, Horley, by Justin Alleyn, 1959–62. Stations of the Cross in *dalle de verre* by Pierre Fourmaintraux of Whitefriars Studios. Photo: Robert Proctor, 2010

15   St Francis of Assisi, Cardiff, F. R. Bates, Son & Price, 1960. Stations of the Cross in sgraffito and ceramic by Adam Kossowski. Photo: Robert Proctor, 2010

16   Cathedral of St Mary, Edinburgh. Sketch proposal for rebuilding the cathedral by T. Harley Haddow & Partners, 1966. Perspective by Alexander Duncan Bell showing view from within the St James Centre. By permission of Alexander Duncan Bell and Harley Haddow. Source: Scottish Catholic Archives, Edinburgh

Plans

All plans are by Ambrose Gillick, 2012–13, and depict the buildings as completed and with liturgical arrangements at the time of opening, as far as can be deduced.

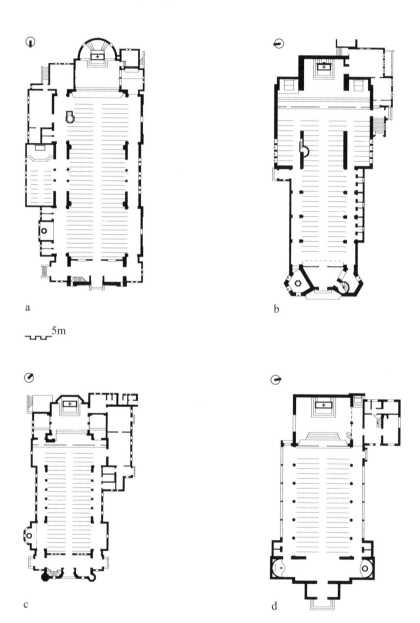

a

⌐_⌐5m

b

c

d

1a   St Joseph, Wembley, London, by Reynolds & Scott, 1956–58

1b   Holy Trinity, Dockhead, London, by H. S. Goodhart-Rendel, 1958–60

1c   St Bernard, Burnage, Manchester, by Reynolds & Scott, 1957–59

1d   St Luke, Pinner, London, by F. X. Velarde, 1958. By permission of OMF Derek Cox Architects, Liverpool

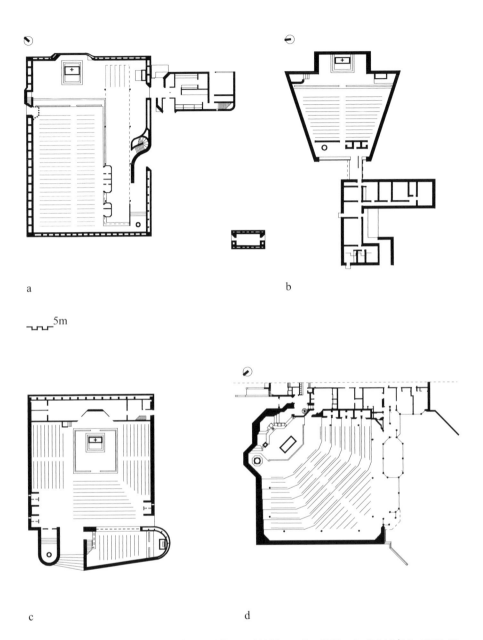

a

b

⌐⌐_5m

c

d

2a   St Bride, East Kilbride, by Andy MacMillan and Isi Metzstein of Gillespie, Kidd & Coia, 1957–64
2b   St Paul, Glenrothes, by Andy MacMillan and Isi Metzstein of Gillespie, Kidd & Coia, 1956–58
2c   St Joseph, Faifley, Glasgow, by Andy MacMillan and Isi Metzstein of Gillespie, Kidd & Coia, 1960–63
2d   St Margaret, Clydebank, Glasgow, by Andy MacMillan and Isi Metzstein of Gillespie, Kidd & Coia, 1970–72

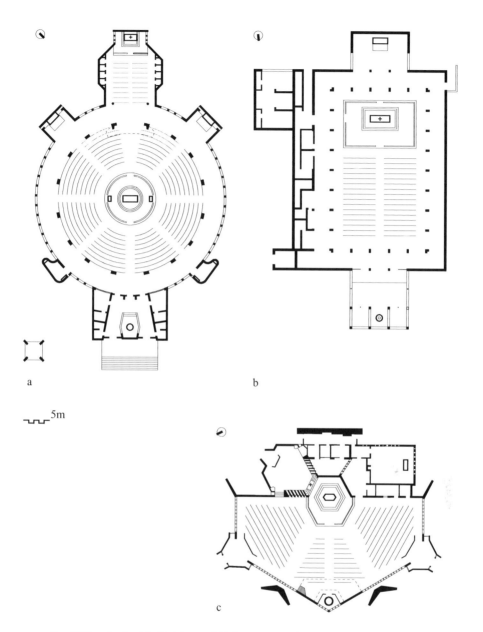

3a   St Mary, Leyland, by Weightman & Bullen, 1960–64. Courtesy of the Trustees of the Roman Catholic Archdiocese of Liverpool and Weightman & Bullen Architects

3b   St Ambrose, Speke, Liverpool, by Weightman & Bullen, 1958–61. Courtesy of the Trustees of the Roman Catholic Archdiocese of Liverpool and Weightman & Bullen Architects

3c   St Agnes, Huyton, Liverpool, by Lionel A. G. Prichard & Son, 1959–65

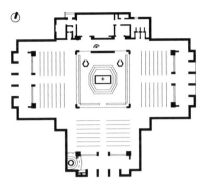

a

5m

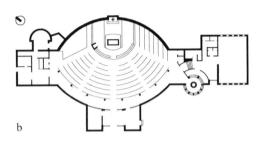

b

c

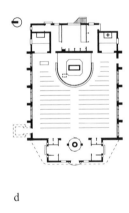

d

4a   Our Lady of Fatima, Harlow, by Gerard Goalen, 1954–60

4b   St Gregory, South Ruislip, London, by Gerard Goalen, 1965–67

4c   St Michael and All Angels, Woodchurch, Birkenhead, by F. X. Velarde Partnership, 1962–65. Courtesy of OMF Derek Cox Architects, Liverpool

4d   Holy Redeemer, Pershore, by Hugh Bankart, 1957–59

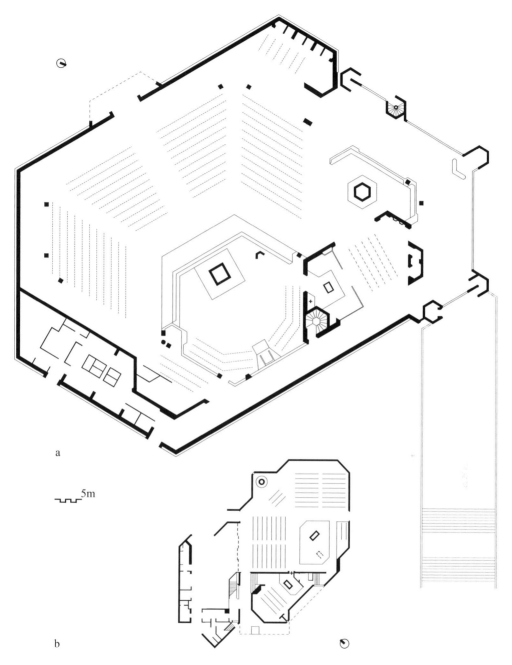

a

—5m

b

5a   Cathedral of Sts Peter and Paul, Clifton, Bristol, by Percy Thomas Partnership, 1965–73

5b   St Margaret, Twickenham, London, by Williams & Winkley, 1964–69.
Courtesy of Austin Winkley & Associates, London

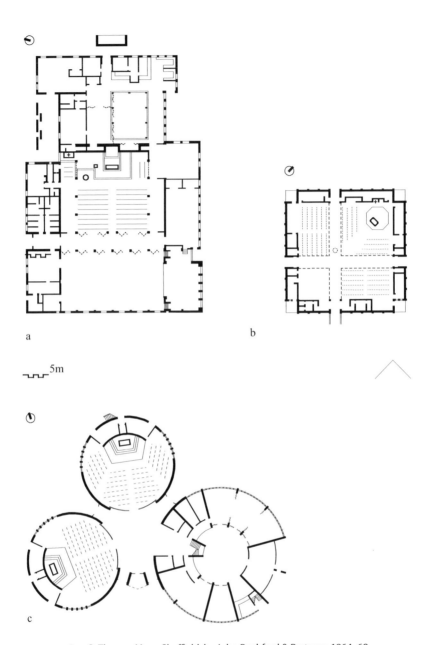

a

b

5m

c

6a   St Thomas More, Sheffield, by John Rochford & Partners, 1964–69

6b   St Andrew, Cippenham, Slough, by Michael Hattrell, 1968–70

6c   Lancaster University Chaplaincy Centre, Lancaster, by Cassidy &
        Ashton, 1966–69. © Cassidy + Ashton, Preston

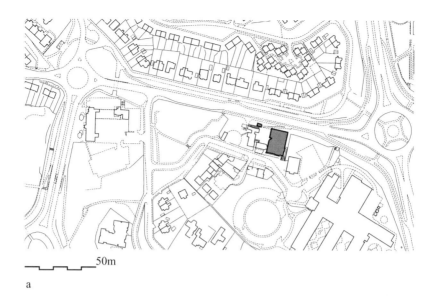

a

b

7a St Bride, East Kilbride, by Andy MacMillan and Isi Metzstein of Gillespie, Kidd & Coia, 1957–64.
Map reproduced by permission of Ordnance Survey on behalf of HMSO.
© Crown Copyright 2013. All rights reserved. Ordnance Survey licence number 100013973

7b St Michael and All Angels, Woodchurch, Birkenhead, by F. X. Velarde Partnership, 1962–65.
Map reproduced by permission of Ordnance Survey on behalf of HMSO.
© Crown Copyright 2013. All rights reserved. Ordnance Survey licence number 100013973

Bibliography

PRINCIPAL ARCHIVES

ARCAB	Archives of the Roman Catholic Archdiocese of Birmingham
ASCA	Archive of the Society of Catholic Artists, London
BDA	Brentwood Diocesan Archives
CDA	Clifton Diocesan Archive, Bristol
HDC	Records of Harlow Development Corporation, Essex Record Office, Chelmsford
FCA	Fife Council Archives, Glenrothes
GRCAA	Glasgow Roman Catholic Archdiocesan Archives
GSAA	Glasgow School of Art Archives
LDA	Leeds Diocesan Archives
LRCAA	Liverpool Metropolitan Cathedral and Roman Catholic Archdiocesan Archives
LRCDA	Lancaster Roman Catholic Diocesan Archives
MDA	Menevia Diocesan Archives, Swansea
RIBA	Royal Institute of British Architects Library, London
SCA	Scottish Catholic Archives, Edinburgh
SDA	Salford Diocesan Archive, Manchester
WDA	Westminster Diocesan Archives, London

PRINCIPAL CONTEMPORARY PERIODICALS

Architect
Architect and Building News
Architects' Journal
Architectural Design
Architectural Review
L'Art sacré
Catholic Herald. http://archive.catholicherald.co.uk (accessed 2010–13)
CBRN – Catholic Building Review, northern edn
CBRS – Catholic Building Review, southern edn
Churchbuilding [published as *Church Buildings Today* until 1961]
Clergy Review
RIBA Journal

St Andrew Annual: The Catholic Church in Scotland
The Tablet
The Universe

BOOKS AND ARTICLES

'7 New Churches'. *Architectural Review* (Oct. 1965): 246–58.

'7,000 Poles Rally at Henley'. *Catholic Herald* (22 May 1964): 3.

'20,000 Walk in Whit-Friday Procession'. *Catholic Herald* (17 June 1949): 7.

'£25,000 Debt on Shrine'. *Catholic Herald* (29 May 1964): 1.

Abbott, Walter M. (ed.) *The Documents of Vatican II*. New York: Geoffrey Chapman, 1966.

Abercrombie, Nigel J. 'The Approach to English Local Authorities, 1963–1978'. In John Pick (ed.), *The State and the Arts*, 63–75. Eastbourne: John Offord, 1980.

Adler, Gerald. *Robert Maguire & Keith Murray*. London: RIBA Publishing, 2012.

'Airport Chapel'. *Architect and Building News* (9 Oct. 1968): 36–7.

Allan, Kenneth. 'Obviously Post-Vatican II'. *Catholic Herald* (3 Mar. 1967): 6.

Althusser, Louis. 'Ideology and Ideological State Apparatuses (Notes Towards an Investigation)'. In id., *Lenin and Philosophy and Other Essays*, trans. Ben Brewster, 127–86. London: Monthly Review Press, 1971.

'Ancient Stones are Used in New Shrine'. *The Universe*, Scottish edn (25 July 1958): 7.

Anderson, Benedict. *Imagined Communities: Reflections on the Origin and Spread of Nationalism*. London: Verso, 1991.

'Anglican Church in Stepney'. *Churchbuilding* (Oct. 1962): 14–23.

'Approaches to Catholic-Anglican Unity'. *The Tablet* (30 Nov. 1968): 1202.

'Archbishop Opens New City Church of St Alexander', *Liverpool Daily Post* (29 July 1957), Liverpool History Projects, http://www.liverpoolhistoryprojects.co.uk/stalexander/news.htm (accessed 4 Nov. 2011).

Architectural Competition for the Metropolitan Cathedral of Christ the King, Liverpool: Conditions and Instructions to Competing Architects. Liverpool: Roman Catholic Archdiocese of Liverpool, 1959.

'Architecture and the Artist'. *The Tablet* (28 June 1969): 648–9.

Baggs, A. P., et al. *A History of the County of Middlesex*, vol. 5: *Hendon, Kingsbury, Great Stanmore, Little Stanmore, Edmonton Enfield, Monken Hadley, South Mimms, Tottenham*, ed. T. F. T. Baker and R. B. Pugh. Oxford: Oxford University Press, 1976. British History Online, http://www.british-history.ac.uk/source.aspx?pubid=87 (accessed 31 Jan. 2013).

Baker, T. F. T., Diane K. Bolton and Patricia E. C. Croot. *A History of the County of Middlesex*, vol. 9: *Hampstead, Paddington*, ed. C. R. Elrington. Oxford: Oxford University Press, 1989. British History Online, http://www.british-history.ac.uk/report.aspx?compid=22675 (accessed 6 Dec. 2012).

Banham, Reyner. 'The New Brutalism'. *Architectural Review* (Dec. 1955): 355–61.

—— *The New Brutalism: Ethic or Aesthetic?* London: Architectural Press, 1966.

Bate, John A. W. 'The Modern Story of Our Lady of the Taper'. *Menevia Record* (Feb. 1956): 10.

Beck, George Andrew, 'Buildings and Costs', *CBRN* (1964): 162.

——— 'Design, Price and Value'. *CBRN* (1960): 171–6.

——— 'Liturgy and Church Building'. *CBRN* (1962): 159–64.

——— 'Plans and Prices'. *CBRN* (1959): 215–24.

——— 'Value for Money'. *CBRN* (1958): 193–9.

[Bédoyère, Michael de la]. 'Ancient Stones Guarded Secret'. *Catholic Herald* (28 Oct. 1949): 5.

Bell, Catherine. *Ritual: Perspectives and Dimensions*. New York: Oxford University Press, 1997.

'Benediction in the Market Place'. *Catholic Herald* (12 June 1953): 7.

Blakeman, Charles. 'The Problem of Church Art'. *Clergy Review* 40 (1955): 22–33.

Bolton, Diane K., et al. *A History of the County of Middlesex*, vol. 4: *Harmondsworth, Hayes, Norwood with Southall, Hillingdon with Uxbridge, Ickenham, Northolt, Perivale, Ruislip, Edgware, Harrow with Pinner*, ed. T. F. T. Baker, J. S. Cockburn and R. B. Pugh. Victoria County History. London: Oxford University Press, 1971. British History Online, http://www.british-history.ac.uk/source.aspx?pubid=86 (accessed 29 June 2011).

Bourdieu, Pierre. *Distinction: A Social Critique of the Judgement of Taste*. London: Routledge, 1984.

——— *Outline of a Theory of Practice*, trans. Richard Nice. Cambridge: Cambridge University Press, 1977.

Bouyer, Louis. *Liturgy and Architecture*. Notre Dame, IN: University of Notre Dame Press, 1967.

Brace, Catherine, Adrian R. Bailey and David C. Harvey. 'Religion, Place and Space: A Framework for Investigating Historical Geographies of Religious Identities and Communities'. *Progress in Human Geography* 30 (2006): 28–43.

Breuer, Marcel and Hamilton Smith. 'The Buildings at St John's Abbey, Collegeville, Minnesota'. *Design Quarterly* 53 (1961): 1–31.

Bridges, Peter. 'Review of New Church Centre: SS Philip and James, Hodge Hill, Birmingham'. *Clergy Review* 54 (1969): 241–8.

Brown, Callum G. *Religion and Society in Twentieth-Century Britain*. Harlow: Pearson, 2006.

Buckley, Joseph C. 'The Parish and the Future'. *Clergy Review* 50 (1965): 931–40.

'Building Study: Church and Youth Centre'. *Architects' Journal* (8 Oct. 1969), 875–6.

Bullen, J. B. *Byzantium Rediscovered: The Byzantine Revival in Europe and America*. Oxford: Phaidon, 2003.

Bullock, Nicholas. *Building the Post-War World: Modern Architecture and Reconstruction in Britain*. London: Routledge, 2002.

Butcher, Harold. 'Dom Vernacular Tours the United States'. *Catholic Herald* (28 Aug. 1959), 5.

Burnett, Ray. ' "The Long Nineteenth Century": Scotland's Catholic Gaidhealtachd'. In Raymond Boyle and Peter Lynch (eds), *Out of the Ghetto? The Catholic Community in Modern Scotland*, 163–92. Edinburgh: John Donald, 1998.

Butler, Judith. 'Performative Acts and Gender Constitution'. In Michael Huxley and Noel Witts (eds), *The Twentieth-Century Performance Reader*, 120–34. London: Routledge, 2002.

Caldwell, Simon. 'One Man's Passion'. *The Universe*, English edn (26 Nov. 1995): 7.

Campbell, Louise. *Coventry Cathedral: Art and Architecture in Post-War Britain*. Oxford: Clarendon Press, 1996.

Capellades, M.-R. 'Transparent Poverty', trans. Keith Harrison. *Churchbuilding* (Oct. 1962), 4–8.

'Carmelites Come Back'. *The Tablet* (20 Sept. 1969): 938.

Casel, Odo. *The Mystery of Christian Worship and Other Writings*, ed. Burkehard Neunheusen. London: Darton, Longman & Todd, 1962.

Catt, John, et al. 'Design for Coventry Cathedral 1951'. *Churchbuilding* (Jan. 1963): 5–17.

' "A Centre of Spiritual Life": Pope Paul'. *The Universe*, Scottish edn (4 Dec. 1964): 5.

'A Chapel at Keele: Shared Between the Students of Three Confessions'. *The Tablet* (9 July 1960): 660.

Christ-Janer, Albert, and Mary Mix Foley. *Modern Church Architecture: A Guide to the Form and Spirit of 20th Century Religious Buildings*. New York: McGraw-Hill, 1962.

Christie, Joseph. 'English Saints: St Simon Stock – A Sturdy Kentishman – England's First Carmelite Friar'. *Catholic Herald* (16 May 1941): 6.

'Church and Presbytery at Glenrothes New Town'. *Architects' Journal* (5 Feb. 1959): 231–8.

'Church and Presbytery of St. Mary and St. Joseph, Canton Street, Poplar'. *Architect and Building News* (24 Dec. 1953): 774.

'Church at Bow Common, London'. *Architectural Review* (Dec. 1960): 400–405.

'Church at Woodchurch, Birkenhead'. *Architects' Journal* (13 Apr. 1966): 941–52.

'Church Building: A Great Challenge'. *The Universe*, Scottish edn (4 Sept. 1964): 4.

'Church is Built on "Raft" '. *Catholic Guardian* (18 Oct. 1957): 7.

'Church, Nottingham'. *Architect and Building News* (23 Sept. 1964): 583–9.

'Church of St. Francis, Duston'. *Churchbuilding* (Jan. 1967): 8–10.

'Church of St Gregory the Great'. *Building* (Mar. 1968): 95–8.

Clausen, Meredith L. *Spiritual Space: The Religious Architecture of Pietro Belluschi*. Seattle: University of Washington Press, 1992.

Collins, Peter. *Concrete: The Vision of a New Architecture: A Study of Auguste Perret and His Precursors*. London: Faber & Faber, 1959.

'Comment on the Liverpool Catholic Cathedral Competition'. *Architectural Design* (Oct. 1960): 425–6.

'Competition: Metropolitan Cathedral of Christ the King, Liverpool'. *Architects' Journal* (1 Sept. 1960): 313–33.

Congar, Yves M. J. *Lay People in the Church: A Study for a Theology of Laity*, trans. Donald Attwater. London: Geoffrey Chapman, 1963.

Conlay, Iris. 'Patronage the Only Answer'. *Catholic Herald* (9 Dec. 1960): 5.

Cope, Gilbert. 'Some Recent Churches in the East Midlands'. *Churchbuilding* (Oct. 1968): 9–12.

—— and Giles Blomfield. 'A Survey of Six Continental Churches'. *Church Buildings Today* (Oct. 1961): 3–11.

Corbould, Edward. 'St Mary's Priory Church, Leyland'. *Churchbuilding* (Oct. 1964): 3–9.

Crichton, J. D. 'Art at the Service of the Liturgy'. In id. (ed.), *The Liturgy and the Future*, 164–73. Tenbury Wells: Fowler Wright Books, 1966.

—— 'A Dream-Church'. *Music and Liturgy* (June 1943): 71–5.

—— 'The Liturgical Movement from 1940 to Vatican II'. In J. D. Crichton, H. E. Winstone, and J. R. Ainslie (eds), *English Catholic Worship: Liturgical Renewal in England Since 1900*, 60–78. London: Geoffrey Chapman, 1979.

—— 'The New Rite and Baptism'. *The Tablet* (18 July 1970): 702–3.

—— H. E. Winstone and J. R. Ainslie (eds). *English Catholic Worship: Liturgical Renewal in England Since 1900*. London: Geoffrey Chapman, 1979.

Crinson, Mark and Claire Zimmerman (eds). *Neo-Avant-Garde and Postmodern: Postwar Architecture in Britain and Beyond*. New Haven: Yale University Press, 2010.

Cronshaw, Jonathan. '"This Work Has Never Been Commissioned At All": Jacob Epstein's Madonna and Child'. *Art and Christianity* 66 (Summer 2011): 5–7.

Croot, Patricia E. C. (ed.) *A History of the County of Middlesex*, vol. 12: *Chelsea*. London: Institute for Historical Research, 2004. British History Online, http://www.british-history.ac.uk/report.aspx?compid=28726 (accessed Oct.–Dec. 2012).

Crozier, Mary. 'A Dialogue Mass'. *The Tablet* (14 Mar. 1958): 249.

Cullingworth, J. B. 'Overspill in South-East Lancashire: The Salford-Worsley Scheme'. *Town Planning Review* 30 (1959): 189–206.

Cunnane, Seamus. *Our Lady of Cardigan: A History and Memoir*. Cardigan: n.p., 2006.

Curd, Marian. 'Why Look Abroad for a Building Company?' *Catholic Herald* (6 Feb. 1959): 5.

Daniélou, Jean. 'The Conception of History in the Christian Tradition'. *Journal of Religion* 30 (July 1950): 171–9.

Davey, G. C. 'A Tyburn Tree for Knebworth'. *Catholic Herald* (12 May 1961): 6.

Davies, J. G. *The Architectural Setting of Baptism*. London: Barrie and Rockliff, 1962.

—— *The Secular Use of Church Buildings*. London: SCM Press, 1968.

Davis, Charles. 'The Christian Altar'. In William Lockett (ed.), *The Modern Architectural Setting of the Liturgy*, 13–31. London: SPCK, 1964.

—— 'Church Architecture and the Liturgy'. In Peter Hammond (ed.), *Towards a Church Architecture*, 107–27. London: Architectural Press, 1962.

Dayer, Peter. 'Philip Richard Dayer, 1912–2005: A Tribute by his Brother' (2005). St Gregory the Great, South Ruislip. http://stgregory.all-catholic.net/philipdayer.html (accessed 29 June 2011).

Debuyst, Frédéric. *Modern Architecture and Christian Celebration*. London: Lutterworth Press, 1968.

Deiss, Lucien. 'The Gradual Psalm'. In Lancelot Sheppard (ed.), *The New Liturgy*, 73–91. London: Darton, Longman & Todd, 1970.

Delaney, Enda. *The Irish in Post-War Britain*. Oxford: Oxford University Press, 2007.

Dembinski, Michael. 'Tadeusz Lesisz: Pole who Sailed with the Royal Navy and Saw Action on D-Day and in the Battle of the Atlantic'. *The Independent* (12 Oct. 2009). http://www.independent.co.uk/news/obituaries/tadeusz-lesisz-pole-who-sailed-with-the-royal-navy-and-saw-action-on-dday-and-in-the-battle-of-the-atlantic-1801365.html (accessed 2 Jan. 2013).

'Destroyed – Rebuilt'. *Catholic Herald* (18 Nov. 1960): 5.

Dix, Gregory. *The Shape of the Liturgy*. London: Dacre Press, 1945.

Doak, A. M. 'Buildings in Prospect'. *Architectural Prospect* (Summer 1959): 10–13.

Donovan, Kevin. 'Influences on the English Liturgical Scene'. In J. D. Crichton, H. E. Winstone and J. R. Ainslie (eds), *English Catholic Worship: Liturgical Renewal in England Since 1900*, 110–23. London: Geoffrey Chapman, 1979.

Doorly, Moyra. *No Place for God: The Denial of the Transcendent in Modern Church Architecture*. San Francisco: Ignatius Press, 2007.

'Dunbar Church Re-Opened'. *St Andrew Annual: The Catholic Church in Scotland* (1960–61): 56.

Durkheim, Émile. *The Elementary Forms of Religious Life*, trans. Karen E. Fields. New York: Free Press, 1995.

'E-Day is Nov. 29'. *The Universe*, Scottish edn (31 July 1964): 1.

'Ecumenism in England: The Hierarchy's Statement'. *The Tablet* (12 Dec. 1964): 1421.

Edwards, Arthur Trystan. *Good and Bad Manners in Architecture*. London: P. Allan, 1924.

English Heritage. 'Church of St Anne, Fawley Court' (28 Sept. 2009). http://list.english-heritage.org.uk/resultsingle.aspx?uid=1393459 (accessed 4 Jan. 2013).

——— 'Thanksgiving Shrine of Our Lady of Lourdes' (30 June 1999). http://list.english-heritage.org.uk/resultsingle.aspx?uid=1387319 (accessed 23 Oct. 2012).

Epstein, Jacob. *Epstein: An Autobiography*. London: Hulton Press, 1955.

Ethrington, James. 'The Church of St Aidan, East Acton, London, W3'. In James Ethrington and Terence Mullally, *St Aidan's, East Acton: The Church and Its Art*, unpaginated. London: n.p., *c*.1964.

Evans, Peter Ansdell, 'Clifton's Catholic Cathedral'. *Architects' Journal* (11 July 1973): 70–72.

——— 'Six Churches: Part 1'. *Architects' Journal* (12 Dec. 1973): 1459–73.

Evinson, Denis. *Catholic Churches of London*. Sheffield: Sheffield Academic Press, 1998.

'Exiles' Candles Symbolises the Silent Church'. *Catholic Herald* (12 Apr. 1957): 1.

Fair, Alistair. ' "A New Image of the Living Theatre": The Genesis and Design of the Belgrade Theatre, Coventry, 1948–58'. *Architectural History* 54 (2011): 347–82.

Farey, Michael. 'The Church Centre'. *Church Buildings Today* (Jan. 1961): 6–10.

'Farnworth's New Church Opened'. *Catholic Guardian* (18 Oct. 1957): 6.

Farrell, Charles. 'United We Serve'. *New Life* (Sept.–Oct. 1975): 13–17.

Fenster, Tovi. 'Non-Secular Cities? Visual and Sound Representations of the Religious-Secular Right to the City in Jerusalem'. In Justin Beaumont and Christopher Baker (eds), *Postsecular Cities: Space, Theory and Practice*, 69–86. London: Continuum, 2011.

Fenton, Clive, and David Walker. 'The Modern Church'. In Louise Campbell, Miles Glendinning and Jane Thomas (eds), *Basil Spence: Buildings & Projects*, 104–17. London: RIBA Publishing, 2012.

Fenwick, John and Bryan Spinks. *Worship in Transition: The Twentieth Century Liturgical Movement*. Edinburgh: T.&T. Clark, 1995.

'The First Joint Church Building'. *The Tablet* (28 Oct. 1967): 1129.

Flanagan, Kieran. *Sociology and Liturgy: Re-Presentations of the Holy*. Basingstoke: Macmillan, 1991.

Flannery, Austin (ed.) *Liturgy: Renewal and Adaptation*. Dublin: Scepter, 1968.

—— (ed.) *Vatican Council II: More Postconciliar Documents*. Leominster: Fowler Wright Books, 1982.

'Flats at Ham Common'. *Architectural Review* (Oct. 1958): 218–25.

Fleetwood-Walker, C. 'Review of New Church: St Michael and All Angels, Woodchurch, Birkenhead'. *Clergy Review* 51 (1966): 825–32.

Fortescue, Adrian. *The Ceremonies of the Roman Rite Described*, revd J. B. O'Connell. London: Burns Oates and Washbourne, 1948.

Fortier, Anne-Marie. *Migrant Belongings: Memory, Space, Identity*. Oxford: Berg, 2000.

Forward in Faith: Britain's First Purpose-Built Shared Church and Community Centre. Stevenage: Shared Churches (Stevenage Pin Green) Ltd., 1976.

Foster, Stewart M. *A History of the Diocese of Brentwood, 1917–1992*. Brentwood: Diocese of Brentwood, 1994.

Foucault, Michel. *Archaeology of Knowledge*, trans. A. M. Sheridan Smith. London: Routledge, 2002.

Fraser, Murray, and Joe Kerr. *Architecture and the 'Special Relationship': The American Influence on Post-War British Architecture*. London: Routledge, 2007.

Gaine, Michael. 'Beck, George Andrew (1904–1978)'. In *Oxford Dictionary of National Biography*. Oxford: Oxford University Press, 2004. http://www.oxforddnb.com/view/article/65084 (accessed 5 June 2013).

Garner, Stephen. 'St Peter's Church and Presbytery, Dumbarton'. *Clergy Review* 59 (1974): 237–43.

Garvey, Joseph M. 'Church of Saint Helen and Parochial Centre: Appreciation on Behalf of User'. *CBRN* (1974): 172–4.

Gibberd, Frederick. 'The Liverpool Metropolitan Cathedral'. In William Lockett (ed.), *The Modern Architectural Setting of the Liturgy*, 55–69. London: SPCK, 1964.

—— *Metropolitan Cathedral of Christ the King, Liverpool*. London: Architectural Press, 1968.

Giedion, Siegfried. *Space, Time and Architecture: The Growth of a New Tradition*. Cambridge, MA: Harvard University Press, 1982.

Gifford, John, and Frank Arneil Walker. *Stirling and Central Scotland*. Buildings of Scotland. London: Yale University Press, 2002.

Gill, Eric. 'Mass for the Masses'. In *Sacred and Secular &c.*, 143–55. London: J. M. Dent & Sons, 1940.

—— 'The Problem of Parish Church Architecture'. In *Art Nonsense and Other Essays*, 124–30. London: Cassell, 1929.

—— 'Westminster Cathedral'. *New Blackfriars* 1 (1920): 148–53.

Gill, Nick. 'Pathologies of Migrant Place-Making: The Case of Polish Migrants to the UK'. *Environment and Planning A* 42 (2010): 1157–73.

Glendinning, Miles. 'Teamwork or Masterwork? The Design and Reception of the Royal Festival Hall'. *Architectural History* 46 (2003): 277–319.

Goalen, Gerard. 'The House of God'. *Church Buildings Today* (Jan. 1961): 3.

Godin, Henri, and Yvan Daniel. 'France A Missionary Land?'. In Maisie Ward, *France Pagan? The Mission of Abbé Godin*, 65–191. London: Sheed and Ward, 1949.

Gold, John R. *The Practice of Modernism: Modern Architects and Urban Transformation, 1954–1972*. London: Routledge, 2007.

Goldhagen, Sarah Williams. 'Coda: Reconceptualizing the Modern'. In Sarah Williams Goldhagen and Réjean Legault (eds), *Anxious Modernisms: Experimentation in Postwar Architectural Culture*, 301–23. Cambridge, MA: MIT Press, 2000.

——— 'Something to Talk About: Modernism, Discourse, Style', *Journal of the Society of Architectural Historians* 64 (2005), 144–67.

'The Good Church Guide: St Aidan's, Coulsdon'. *Clergy Review* 58 (1974): 552–4.

Goodhart-Rendel, H. S. *Commonsense Churchplanning*. London: Incorporated Church Building Society, n.d.

——— *English Architecture Since the Regency: An Interpretation*. London: Constable, 1953.

Gray, Joseph. 'Modern Church Building'. *CBRN* (1970): 273–6.

'A Great New Shrine of Our Lady'. *Catholic Herald* (13 July 1951): 1.

Green, H. Benedict. 'House of God and Church Centre. The Two Approaches Related'. *Church Buildings Today* (Jan. 1961): 11–12.

Groome, Francis Hindes (ed.) *Ordnance Gazetteer of Scotland: A Survey of Scottish Topography, Statistical, Biographical and Historical*, vol. 6. Edinburgh: T. C. Jack, 1882–85.

Guardini, Romano. *The Spirit of the Liturgy*, trans. Ada Lane. London: Sheed & Ward, 1930.

Gy, Pierre Marie. 'The Constitution in the Making'. In Austin Flannery (ed), *Liturgy: Renewal and Adaptation*, 9–18. Dublin: Scepter, 1968.

Hammond, Peter. 'A Liturgical Brief'. *Architectural Review* (Apr. 1958): 240–55.

——— *Liturgy and Architecture*. London: Barrie and Rockliff, 1960.

——— 'A Radical Approach to Church Architecture'. In Peter Hammond (ed.), *Towards a Church Architecture*, 15–37. London: Architectural Press, 1962.

——— (ed.) *Towards a Church Architecture*. London: Architectural Press, 1962.

Harding, J. A. *The Diocese of Clifton, 1850–2000*. Bristol: Clifton Catholic Diocesan Trustees, 1999.

Harris, Ruth. *Lourdes: Body and Spirit in the Secular Age*. London: Allen Lane, 1999.

Harrison, Bernard A. *St Luke's Catholic Church, Pinner: The Story of a Parish*. London: n.p., 2007.

Harrison, Frank. *St Mary's, Leyland: The History of a Catholic Community*. Preston: n.p., 1995.

Harrod, Tanya. 'Obituary: Steven Sykes'. *The Independent* (24 Feb. 1999). http://www.independent.co.uk/arts-entertainment/obituary-steven-sykes-1072852.html (accessed 11 July 2011).

Hartwell, Clare, Matthew Hyde and Nikolaus Pevsner. *Lancashire: Manchester and the South-East*. London: Yale University Press, 2004.

Harwood, Elain. 'Liturgy and Architecture: The Development of the Centralised Eucharistic Space'. *Twentieth Century Architecture 3: The Twentieth Century Church* (1998): 51–74.

Hastings, Adrian (ed.) *Modern Catholicism: Vatican II and After*. London: SPCK, 1991.

Hebblethwaite, Margaret. 'Devotion'. In Adrian Hastings (ed.), *Modern Catholicism: Vatican II and After*, 240–45. London: SPCK, 1991.

Heenan, John C. *Council and Clergy*. London: Geoffrey Chapman, 1966.

—— *A Crown of Thorns: An Autobiography, 1951–1963*. London: Hodder & Stoughton, 1974.

Henze, Anton. 'The Potentialities of Modern Church Art and Its Position in History'. In Anton Henze and Theodor Filthaut (eds), *Contemporary Church Art*, trans. Cecily Hastings, 15–48. New York: Sheed & Ward, 1956.

Heynen, Hilde. *Architecture and Modernity: A Critique*. Cambridge, MA: MIT Press, 2009.

Hickman, Mary J. *Religion, Class and Identity: The State, the Catholic Church and the Education of the Irish in Britain*. Avebury: Ashgate, 1995.

Higgott, Andrew. *Mediating Modernism: Architectural Cultures in Britain*. London: Routledge, 2007.

Hill, Rosemary. 'Prior Commitment'. *Crafts* 172 (Sept.–Oct. 2001): 28–31.

Hilton, J. A. *The Artifice of Eternity: The Byzantine-Romanesque Revival in Catholic Lancashire*. Wigan: North West Catholic History Society, 2008.

Hitchcock, Henry Russell. *Architecture: Nineteenth and Twentieth Centuries*. New Haven: Yale University Press, 1977.

Hobhouse, Hermione, and Stephen Porter (eds). *Survey of London*, vol. 43: *Poplar, Blackwall and Isle of Dogs*. London: Athlone, 1994. British History Online, http://www.british-history.ac.uk/source.aspx?pubid=369 (accessed 3 May 2013).

Hobsbawm, Eric. 'Introduction: Inventing Traditions'. In Eric Hobsbawm and Terence Ranger (eds), *The Invention of Tradition*, 1–14. Cambridge: Cambridge University Press, 1983.

Horner, Libby. 'Patrick Reyntiens' Autonomous Panels: Myth, Music and Theatre'. *Decorative Arts Society Journal* 35 (2011): 63–80.

Hornsby-Smith, Michael P. (ed.), *Catholics in England 1950–2000*. London: Cassell, 1999.

—— *The Changing Parish: A Study of Parishes, Priests and Parishioners after Vatican II*. London: Routledge, 1989.

—— *Roman Catholics in England: Studies in Social Structure Since the Second World War*. Cambridge: Cambridge University Press, 1987.

—— 'A Transformed Church'. In Michael P. Hornsby-Smith (ed.), *Catholics in England, 1950–2000: Historical and Sociological Perspectives*, 3–25. London: Cassell, 1999.

'House in Soho, London: Alison and Peter Smithson'. *Architectural Design* (Dec. 1953): 342.

Howell, Clifford. *The Work of Our Redemption*. Oxford: Catholic Social Guild, 1953.

Howell, Peter. 'Letters from J. F. Bentley to Charles Hadfield: Part II'. *Architectural History* 25 (1982): 65–97, 156–61.

Hughes, Rosemary. 'La Musique sacrée'. In D. Mathew et al., *Catholicisme Anglais*, 283–90. Paris: Éditions du Cerf, 1958.

Hurley, Richard. *Irish Church Architecture in the Era of Vatican II*. Dublin: Dominican Publications, 2001.

—— and Wilfrid Cantwell. *Contemporary Irish Church Architecture*. Dublin: Gill & Macmillan, 1985.

Hyde, Douglas. 'The Carmelites Kept Vigil at Aylesford: Home at Last'. *Catholic Herald* (4 Nov. 1949): 1.

'Infant Baptism: The New Rite'. *The Tablet* (28 June 1969): 655.

'Inspiration to Great Courage'. *Catholic Herald* (4 Dec. 1953): 13.

' "It Was to Have Been Church of Our Times" '. *The Universe*, Scottish edn (27 Nov. 1964): 11.

Jackson, John Archer. *The Irish in Britain*. London: Routledge & Kegan Paul, 1963.

James-Chakraborty, Kathleen. *German Architecture for a Mass Audience*. London: Routledge, 2000.

Jevons, Rosamond, and John Madge. *Housing Estates: A Study of Bristol Corporation Policy and Practice Between the Wars*. Bristol: University of Bristol, 1946.

'Joint Pastoral on 40 Martyrs', *Catholic Herald* (1 July 1960), 1.

Jones, Peter. *Jonah Jones: An Artist's Life*. Bridgend: Seren, 2011.

Judge, Urban. 'Erection of the Stations of the Cross', *Clergy Review* 44 (1959), 682–5.

Jungmann, Joseph A. *The Mass of the Roman Rite: Its Origins and Development*, trans. Francis A. Brunner, ed. Charles K. Riepe. Westminster, MD: Christian Classics, 1980.

Kerr, Fergus. *Twentieth-Century Catholic Theologians: From Neoscholasticism to Nuptial Mysticism*. Oxford: Blackwell, 2007.

Kidder Smith, G. E. *The New Churches of Europe*. London: Architectural Press, 1964.

Kieckhefer, Richard. *Theology in Stone: Church Architecture From Byzantium to Berkeley*. Oxford: Oxford University Press, 2004.

Kimmel, Ann. 'Go-Ahead Priest with Go-Ahead Parishioners'. *Catholic Herald* (16 Dec. 1966): 3.

Kirwin, Anthony P. 'A Way Through the Weeds: Graham Sutherland's "Crucifixion" in East Acton'. *The Tablet* (11 Jan. 1964): 181–2.

Kite, Stephen. 'Softs and Hards: Colin St. John Wilson and the Contested Visions of 1950s London'. In Mark Crinson and Claire Zimmerman (eds), *Neo-Avant-Garde and Postmodern: Postwar Architecture in Britain and Beyond*, 55–77. New Haven: Yale University Press, 2010.

Koenker, Ernst B. *The Liturgical Renaissance in the Roman Catholic Church*. Chicago: Chicago University Press, 1954.

——'Objectives and Achievements of the Liturgical Movement in the Roman Catholic Church since World War II'. *Church History* 20 (June 1951): 14–27.

Lambert, Sharon. *Irish Women in Lancashire, 1922–1960: Their Story*. Lancaster: Centre for North-West Regional Studies, 2001.

'Lansbury Neighbourhood'. *Architects' Journal* (15 June 1950): 737–51.

Larmour, Paul, and Shane O'Toole (eds). *North by Northwest: The Life and Work of Liam McCormick*. Kinsale: Gandon Editions, 2008.

'Layout for the Woodchurch Estate, Birkenhead'. *Builder* (24 Nov. 1944): 408–9.

Leach, Kenneth. 'Obituary: Father Gresham Kirkby', *The Guardian* (22 Aug. 2006). http://www.guardian.co.uk/news/2006/aug/22/guardianobituaries.religion (accessed 13 July 2012).

'Leeds Diocese'. *CBRN* (1957): 146–7.

Lefebvre, Gaspar. *The New Liturgy of Holy Week: Supplement to the Saint Andrew Daily Missal*. Bruges: Liturgical Apostolate, Abbey of Saint André, 1956.

Lefebvre, Henri. *The Production of Space*, trans. Donald Nicholson-Smith. Oxford: Blackwell, 2001.

Leo XIII. 'On the Recitation of the Rosary'. 1884. http://www.vatican.va/holy_father/leo_xiii/encyclicals/documents/hf_l-xiii_enc_30081884_superiore-anno_en.html (accessed 10 Aug. 2012).

'Lessons From Geneva'. *Churchbuilding* (Jan. 1970): 11.

Lethaby, W.R., and Harold Swainson. *The Church of Sancta Sophia, Constantinople: A Study of Byzantine Building*. London: Macmillan, 1894.

'A Letter From the Union of Catholic Mothers (Southmead Branch)'. *Southmead Echo* (June–July 1957): 4.

Little, Bryan. *Catholic Churches Since 1623: A Study of Roman Catholic Churches in England and Wales from Penal Times to the Present Decade*. London: Robert Hale, 1966.

—— 'Four New Birmingham Churches'. *Clergy Review* 55 (1970): 1009–14.

—— 'Review of New Church: St Bernadette's, Bristol'. *Clergy Review* 53 (1968): 749–56.

'Liturgical Reform: An International Conference at Mont Sainte-Odile'. *The Tablet* (1 Nov. 1952): 365.

Llewellyn, Robert. 'The Congregation Shares in the Prayer of the President'. In Lancelot Sheppard (ed.), *The New Liturgy*, 103–12. London: Darton, Longman & Todd, 1970.

Lockett, William E. A. (ed.) *The Modern Architectural Setting of the Liturgy*. London: SPCK, 1964.

—— 'Some Recent Church Buildings in the North West'. *Churchbuilding* (Apr. 1969): 15–20.

—— 'Some Reflections on Cathedral Building in the Twentieth Century'. *Churchbuilding* (Jan. 1968): 3–5.

Longhi, Andrea, and Carlo Tosco. *Architettura, chiesa e società in Italia (1948–1978)*. Rome: Edizioni Studium, 2010.

'Low Cost Church the Shape of a House'. *Catholic Herald* (3 June 1966): 3.

Lubac, Henri de. *Catholicism: Christ and the Common Destiny of Man*, trans. Lancelot Sheppard. London: Burns & Oates, 1962.

McBrien, Richard P. 'The Church (*Lumen Gentium*)'. In Adrian Hastings (ed.), *Modern Catholicism: Vatican II and After*, 84–95. London: SPCK, 1991.

MacCarthy, Fiona. 'Obituary: Patrick Nuttgens'. *The Guardian* (17 Mar. 2004). http://www.guardian.co.uk/news/2004/mar/17/guardianobituaries.highereducation (accessed 18 June 2012).

McDannell, Colleen. *Material Christianity: Religion and Popular Culture in America*. New Haven: Yale University Press, 1995.

McGarry, J. G. 'Holy Week 1956'. *Furrow* 7 (1956): 323–32.

McRoberts, David (ed.) *Modern Scottish Catholicism, 1878-1978*. Glasgow: Scottish Catholic Historical Association, 1978.

Maguire, Robert. 'Church Design Since 1950'. *Ecclesiology Today* 27 (Jan. 2002): 2–14.

—— and Keith Murray. 'The Architect Must Ask Questions'. *Church Buildings Today* (Oct. 1960): 3–4.

—— *Modern Churches of the World*. London: Studio Vista, 1965.

Maniura, Robert. *Pilgrimage to Images in the Fifteenth Century: The Origins of the Cult of Our Lady of Częstochowa*. Woodbridge: Boydell Press, 2004.

Mannox, Michael. 'Hello, Southmead!'. *Southmead Echo* (Feb.–Mar. 1957): 5.

'The Map of the Year'. *Catholic Herald* (11 Dec. 1953): 1.

Maritain, Jacques. *Art and Scholasticism, with Other Essays*, trans. J. F. Scanlan. London: Sheed & Ward, 1930.

Martin, Christopher, and Alex Ramsay. *A Glimpse of Heaven: Catholic Churches of England and Wales*. Swindon: English Heritage, 2009.

Mathew, D., et al. *Catholicisme Anglais*. Paris: Editions du Cerf, 1958.

Melville, Robert. 'Personnages in Iron'. *Architectural Review* (Sept. 1950): 147–51.

Mercier, George. *L'Art abstrait dans l'art sacré: La Tendance non-figurative dans l'art sacré chrétien contemporain*. Paris: Éditions E. De Boccard, 1964.

Mettepenningen, Jürgen. *Nouvelle Théologie – New Theology: Inheritor of Modernism, Precursor of Vatican II*. London: T. & T. Clark International, 2010.

Michonneau, G. *Revolution in a City Parish*. London: Blackfriars, 1949.

'Mile Long Procession'. *Catholic Pictorial* [souvenir supplement] (12 Apr. 1964): 8.

Mills, Edward D., and William E. A. Lockett. 'Plans of Churches Here and Abroad'. *Church Buildings Today* (Oct. 1960): 9–13.

Minchin, Basil. 'Review of *Phoenix at Coventry*, by Basil Spence'. *Churchbuilding* (Jan. 1963): 26–7.

Ministry of Education. *The Story of Post-War School Building*. London: HMSO, 1957.

Mitchell, Dolores. 'Art Patronage by the London County Council (L.C.C.), 1948–1965'. *Leonardo* 10 (1977), 207–12.

'A Moment of Reverence'. *The Universe*, Scottish edn (13 June 1958): 16.

Morgan, David. *The Sacred Gaze: Religious Visual Culture in Theory and Practice*. Berkeley: University of California Press, 2005.

Morris, Dorothy. *The Catholic Church in Rainham, 1921–2000*. Rainham: n.p., 2000.

Morrissey, Michael. 'Five Schools in Nine Years'. *Catholic Herald* (24 Nov. 1961): 5.

Mullaly, Terence. 'Art at St Aidan's'. In James Ethrington and Terence Mullaly, *St Aidan's, East Acton: The Church and Its Art*, unpaginated. London: n.p., c.1964.

Mumford, Eric. *The CIAM Discourse on Urbanism, 1928–1960*. Cambridge, MA: MIT Press, 2000.

Murray, Gregory. *A People's Mass*. London: Cary & Co., n.d.

Murray, Keith, and Esther de Waal. 'Obituary: Canon Peter Hammond'. *The Independent* (24 Mar. 1999). http://www.independent.co.uk/arts-entertainment/obituary-canon-peter-hammond-1082634.html (accessed 27 June 2012).

Nairn, Ian. 'Criticism: Lansbury Centrepiece'. *Architectural Review* (Oct. 1954): 263–4.

National Liturgical Commission of England and Wales. *Pastoral Directory for Church Building*. London: Burnes & Oates, 1968.

Naylor, Simon, and James R. Ryan. 'The Mosque in the Suburbs: Negotiating Religion and Ethnicity in South London'. *Social and Cultural Geography* 3 (2002): 39–59.

'Never Tired of Coming'. *Catholic Herald* (24 Aug. 1956): 7.

'The New Brutalism'. *Architectural Design* (Jan. 1955): 1.

'The New Brutalism'. *Architectural Review* (Apr. 1954): 274–5.

'New Chapel on Site of Saint's Home'. *The Universe*, Scottish edn (14 Nov. 1958): 9.

'New Church a Challenge'. *The Universe*, Scottish edn (4 Dec. 1964): 5.

'The New Church at Poplar'. *The Tablet* (31 July 1954): 118.

'New Church of Our Lady of Good Counsel, Dennistoun'. *St Andrew Annual: The Catholic Church in Scotland* (1964–65): 41.

'The New Church of St John, Rochdale, Lancs.' *Architects' Journal* (29 July 1925): 162–9.

New Churches Research Group. *Church Buildings: A Guide to Planning and Design*. London, Architects' Journal, 1967.

'New Liturgy in Centre'. *The Tablet* (20 Dec. 1969): 1278–9.

'New Rulings on Ecumenism'. *The Tablet* (23, 30 Dec. 1967): 1357–8.

Newman, John Henry. *An Essay on the Development of Christian Doctrine*. London: James Toovey, 1845.

Newton, A. J. 'The Story of a Cathedral'. *CBRS* (1974): 8–19.

Nugent, Kenneth. 'Architecture for Eschatologists: Church of St John Stone, Woodvale, Lancashire'. *Clergy Review* 56 (1971): 241–7.

——— 'Clifton Cathedral Church of SS Peter and Paul'. *Clergy Review* 58 (1973): 737–44.

——— 'Review of New Church: Our Lady of the Rosary, Donnington, Shropshire'. *Clergy Review* 52 (1952): 1001–8.

O'Brien, Susan. 'Making Catholic Spaces: Women, Décor, and Devotion in the English Catholic Church, 1840-1900'. In Diana Wood (ed.), *The Church and the Arts: Papers Read at the 1990 Summer Meeting and the 1991 Winter Meeting of the Ecclesiastical History Society*, 449–64. Studies in Church History 28. Oxford: Blackwell, 1992.

O'Connell, J. B. 'The Care of the Blessed Sacrament'. *Clergy Review* 43 (1958): 11–18.

——— *Church Building and Furnishing: The Church's Way*. London: Burns & Oates, 1955.

——— 'The International Liturgical Congress at Assisi'. *Clergy Review* 41 (1956): 641–9.

——— 'The New Instruction of the Congregation of Rites'. *Clergy Review* 44 (1959): 90–99.

O. J. M. 'Our Lady's Triumphal Tour'. *Menevia Record* (Aug. 1956): 10–12.

O'Mahony, Patrick. 'One Parish, One World'. *The Tablet* (6 Apr. 1974): 343.

——— 'A Parish and Overseas Project'. *Clergy Review* 54 (1969): 536–40.

O'Mahony, Richard, and William E. A. Lockett. 'The Metropolitan Cathedral of Christ the King'. *Clergy Review* 52 (1967): 753–60.

O'Neill, Colman. 'General Principles'. In Austin Flannery (ed.), *Liturgy: Renewal and Adaptation*, 19–32. Dublin: Scepter, 1968.

'Opening of St Columba's Church, Cupar, Fife'. *St Andrew Annual: The Catholic Church in Scotland* (1964–65): 43.

Orenduff, Lai-Kent Chew. *The Transformation of Catholic Religious Art in the Twentieth Century: Father Marie-Alain Couturier and the Church at Assy, France*. Lewiston, NY: Edwin Mellen Press, 2008.

Orsi, Robert Anthony. *The Madonna of 115th Street: Faith and Community in Italian Harlem, 1880–1950*. New Haven: Yale University Press, 1985.

Osborne, June. *John Piper and Stained Glass*. Stroud: Sutton Publishing, 1997.

'Out on a High Note'. *Catholic Herald* (24 Jan. 1992): 1.

Pace, George G. 'Notes and Comment: Temporary Churches'. *Church Building Today* (Apr. 1961): 7–10.

——— 'Review of New Church: St Mary's Priory, Leyland'. *Clergy Review* 50 (1965): 81–8.

Pace, Peter. *The Architecture of George G. Pace, 1915–75*. London: Batsford, 1990.

Page, William (ed.) *A History of the County of Kent*, vol. 2. London: Archibald Constable, 1926. British History Online, http://www.british-history.ac.uk/source.aspx?pubid=198 (accessed 2 Nov. 2012).

'Parish of 50 has its Procession'. *Catholic Herald* (1 June 1951): 5.

Parker, Andrew, and Eve Kosofsky Sedgwick. 'Introduction', in eid. (eds), *Performativity and Performance*, 1–18. London: Routledge, 1995.

Parkin, David. 'Ritual as Spatial Direction and Bodily Division'. In Daniel de Coppet (ed.), *Understanding Rituals*, 11–25. London: Routledge, 1992.

'Pastoral Liturgy: British Delegates to Assisi Congress'. *Catholic Herald* (11 May 1956): 1.

Paul VI. *Apostolic Constitution (Missale Romanum) and General Instruction on the Roman Missal*, trans. Clifford Howell. London: Catholic Truth Society, 1973.

——— 'Indulgentiarum doctrina'. 1967. The Holy See, http://www.vatican.va/holy_father/paul_vi/apost_constitutions/documents/hf_p-vi_apc_19670101_indulgentiarum-doctrina_en.html (accessed 31 Oct. 2012).

Pearson, Lynn. 'Broad Visions: Ceramics in the Twentieth Century Church'. Paper presented at conference of the Tiles and Architectural Ceramics Society, 'Church Ceramics: Decorative Tiles, Mosaic and Terracotta During and After the Gothic Revival', Coalbrookdale, 2006. http://www.lynnpearson.co.uk/Broad%20Visions.pdf (accessed 4 May 2012).

——— 'To Brighten the Environment: Ceramic Tile Murals in Britain, 1950–70'. *Journal of the Tiles and Architectural Ceramics Society* 10 (2004): 12–17.

Pevsner, Nikolaus. *Lancashire: The Industrial and Commercial South*. Buildings of England. Harmondsworth: Penguin, 1969.

Pichard, Joseph. *L'Art sacré moderne*. Paris: B. Arthaud, 1953.

Pick, John. 'Introduction: The Best for the Most'. In John Pick (ed.), *The State and the Arts*, 9–19. Eastbourne: John Offord, 1980.

Pilloton, Franck (ed.) *Églises de France reconstruites*. Paris: Musée d'Art Moderne, 1956.

Pius X. *Tra le sollecitudini: sulla musica sacra*. 1903. The Holy See, http://www.vatican.va/holy_father/pius_x/motu_proprio/documents/hf_p-x_motu-proprio_19031122_sollecitudini_it.html (accessed 18 July 2012).

Pius XII. '*Mediator Dei*: On the Sacred Liturgy'. 1947. The Holy See, http://www.vatican.va/holy_father/pius_xii/encyclicals/documents/hf_p-xii_enc_20111947_mediator-dei_en.html (accessed 19 July 2012).

Pollard, Richard, Nikolaus Pevsner and Joseph Sharples. *Lancashire: Liverpool and the South West*. London: Yale University Press, 2006.

'Pontifical Mass in Scots Cave'. *Catholic Herald* (25 Sept. 1953): 1.

Powers, Alan. *Francis Pollen: Architect, 1926–1987*. Oxford: Robert Dugdale, 1999.

—— (ed.) *H. S. Goodhart-Rendel, 1887–1959*. London: Architectural Association, 1987.

Price, F. C. 'New Towns Inspire Fresh Thinking on Church Building'. *Catholic Herald* (20 Feb. 1970): 3.

Price, Jay M. *Temples for a Modern God: Religious Architecture in Postwar America*. New York: Oxford University Press, 2013.

Proctor, Robert. 'Churches for a Changing Liturgy: Gillespie, Kidd & Coia and the Second Vatican Council'. *Architectural History* 48 (2005): 291–322.

—— 'Modern Church Architect as Ritual Anthropologist: Architecture and Liturgy at Clifton Cathedral'. *Architectural Research Quarterly* 15 (2011): 359–72.

—— 'Religion and Nation: The Architecture and Symbolism of Irish Identity in the Roman Catholic Church in Britain'. In Raymond Quek, Darren Deane and Sarah Butler (eds), *Nationalism and Architecture*, 39–51. Aldershot: Ashgate, 2012.

Raabe, D., P. O'Reilly and G. Dumas. *Notre Dame de France*. London: n.p., 1965.

Rappaport, Roy A. 'Enactments of Meaning'. In Michael Lambek (ed.), *A Reader in the Anthropology of Religion*, 410–28. Oxford: Blackwell, 2008.

Read, Benedict, et al. *Adam Kossowski: Murals and Paintings*. London: Armelle Press, 1990.

Régamey, P.-R. *Art sacré au XXe siècle?* Paris: Éditions du Cerf, 1952.

Reilly, C. H. *Some Architectural Problems of To-Day*. London: Hodder & Stoughton, 1924.

'Review of New Church: Our Lady of Fatima, Harlow New Town: Architect: Gerard Goalen'. *Clergy Review* 48 (1963): 69–72.

Rex, John, and Robert Moore. *Race, Community, and Conflict: A Study of Sparkbrook*. London: Oxford University Press, 1967.

Richards, J. M. and Eric de Maré. *The Functional Tradition in Early Industrial Buildings*. London: Architectural Press, 1958.

Risselada, Max, and Dirk van den Heuvel (eds). *Team 10, 1953–1981: In Search of a Utopia of the Present*. Rotterdam: NAi, 2005.

Robin, Suzanne. *Églises modernes: Évolution des édifices réligieux en France*. Paris: Hermann, 1980.

Robinson, Paul, and Robert Robinson. *Fanfare for a Church: The Story of the Church of the Blessed Sacrament, Gorseinon*. Talybont, Gwynedd: Y Lolfa, 2010.

Rodger, Johnny (ed.) *Gillespie, Kidd & Coia: Architecture, 1956–1987*. Glasgow: Lighthouse, 2007.

Rogerson, Robert W. K. C., *Jack Coia: His Life and Work*. Glasgow: n.p., 1986.

Rose, Michael. *Ugly as Sin: Why They Changed our Churches from Sacred Places to Meeting Spaces, and How We Can Change them Back Again*. Manchester, NH: Sophia Institute Press, 2001.

Roulin, E. *Modern Church Architecture*, trans. C. Cornelia Craigie and John A. Southwell. St Louis: B. Herder, 1947.

Rowe, Colin. 'Dominican Monastery of La Tourette, Eveux-sur-Arbresle, Lyons'. *Architectural Review* (June 1961): 400–410.

Rowley, Ellen. 'Transitional Modernism: The Case of 1950s Church Architecture in Dublin'. In Edwina Keown and Carol Taffe (eds), *Irish Modernism: Origins, Contexts, Publics*, 195–216. Bern: Peter Lang, 2009.

Rubin, William S. *Modern Sacred Art and the Church of Assy*. New York: Columbia University Press, 1961.

Rykwert, Joseph. 'The Churches We Deserve?' *New Blackfriars* 37 (1956): 171–5.

—— 'Passé récent et problèmes actuels de l'art sacré'. In D. Mathew et al., *Catholicisme Anglais*, 291–8. Paris: Éditions du Cerf, 1958.

Sacerdos. 'May Queen Unsuitable Customs'. *Catholic Herald* (31 May 1957): 2.

Sacred Congregation of Rites. 'Instruction on Worship of the Eucharistic Mystery' (1967). *The Catholic Liturgical Library*. http://www.catholicliturgy.com/index.cfm/FuseAction/ DocumentContents/Index/2/SubIndex/11/DocumentIndex/338 (accessed 12 Sept. 2012).

Saint, Andrew. 'Some Thoughts About the Architectural Use of Concrete'. *AA Files* 22 (Autumn 1991): 3–16.

—— *Towards a Social Architecture: The Role of School-Building in Post-War England* (London: Yale University Press, 1987).

'St Andrew's Day, 1964, in Dumfries'. *St Andrew Annual: The Catholic Church in Scotland* (1964–65): 10.

'St Bride's: An Appraisal'. *RIBA Journal* (Apr. 1966): 170–79.

'St Simon Home in Triumph'. *Catholic Herald* (20 July 1951): 1.

Sanders, John. 'Pugin & Pugin and the Diocese of Glasgow'. *Architectural Heritage* 8 (1997): 89–107.

Schloeder, Stephen J. *Architecture in Communion: Implementing the Second Vatican Council Through Liturgy and Architecture*. San Francisco: Ignatius Press, 1998.

Schnell, Hugo. *Twentieth Century Church Architecture in Germany*. Munich: Schnell & Steiner, 1974.

Schotz, Benno. *Bronze in My Blood: The Memoirs of Benno Schotz*. Edinburgh: Gordon Wright, 1981.

Schreggenburger, Thomas, and Claude Lichtenstein (eds). *As Found: The Discovery of the Ordinary*. Zurich: Lars Muller, 2001.

Schwarz, Rudolf. *The Church Incarnate: The Sacred Function of Christian Architecture*, trans. Cynthia Harris. Chicago: Henry Regnery, 1958.

—— *Kirchenbau: Welt vor der Schwelle*. Heidelberg: F. H. Kerle, 1960.

Scott, George. *The R.Cs: A Report on Roman Catholics in Britain Today*. London: Hutchinson, 1967.

Scully, Vincent. *Louis I. Kahn*. London: Prentice-Hall, 1962.

Senn, Rainer. 'The Spirit of Poverty'. *Churchbuilding* (Apr. 1963): 23.

Sheppard, Lancelot. 'L'Assemblée liturgique'. In D. Mathew et al., *Catholicisme Anglais*, 226–35. Paris: Éditions du Cerf, 1958.

—— 'The Changing Liturgy II: The People's Role in Public Worship'. *The Tablet* (4 July 1964): 742–4.

—— (ed.) *The New Liturgy*. London: Darton, Longman & Todd, 1970.

—— 'The New "Ordo Missae"'. In Lancelot Sheppard (ed.), *The New Liturgy*, 19–37. London: Darton, Longman & Todd, 1970.

—— 'Reforming the Liturgy'. *The Tablet* (15 Jan. 1955): 57–8; (22 Jan. 1955): 81–2; (29 Jan. 1955): 104–5.

'Shirley Fasts – Calcutta Eats'. *Catholic Herald* (12 Jan. 1968): 10.

'Shrine Will Rise on Tyburn Ruins'. *Catholic Herald* (4 Jan. 1952): 1.

'Shrines of Our Lady'. *Catholic Herald* (4 Dec. 1953): 7.

Silber, Evelyn. *The Sculpture of Epstein*. Oxford: Phaidon, 1986.

'The Sinking Church is Now "Refloated"'. *The Universe*, Scottish edn (30 Jan. 1970): 14.

'Sleek, Neat and Modern'. *Catholic Herald* (26 Aug. 1960): 7.

Smithson, Alison (ed.) *Team 10 Meetings, 1953–1984*. Delft: Publikatieburo Bouwkunde, 1991.

—— (ed.) *Team 10 Primer*. London: n.p., c.1963.

—— and Peter Smithson. 'The Function of Architecture in Cultures-in-Change'. *Architectural Design* (Apr. 1960): 149–50.

'Some New Ecclesiastical Structures'. *Concrete and Constructional Engineering* (Jan. 1964): 38–9.

'Some Interesting Liverpool Development Information Supplied by Lanner Ltd of Wakefield'. *CBRN* (1971): 176–80.

Spence, Basil. *Phoenix at Coventry: The Building of a Cathedral*. London: Geoffrey Bles, 1962.

Stamp, Gavin. 'Adrian Gilbert Scott'. In Geoffrey Fisher, Gavin Stamp and Joanna Heseltine, *Catalogue of the Drawings Collection of the Royal Institute of British Architects*, vol. 14 *The Scott Family*, 184–5. Amersham: Gregg, 1981.

—— ' "A Catholic Church in Which Everything is Genuine and Good": The Roman Catholic Parish Churches of Sir Giles Gilbert Scott'. *Ecclesiology Today* 38 (2007): 63–80.

—— 'The Myth of Gillespie Kidd & Coia'. *Architectural Heritage* 11 (2000): 68–79.

—— 'Victorian Survival of Revival? The Case of H. S. Goodhart-Rendel'. *AA Files* 15 (1987): 60–66.

Stirling, James. 'Garches to Jaoul: Le Corbusier as Domestic Architect in 1927 and 1953'. *Architectural Review* (Sept. 1955): 145–51.

—— 'Ronchamp: Le Corbusier's Chapel and the Crisis of Rationalism'. *Architectural Review* (Mar. 1956): 155–61.

Stock, Wolfgang Jean. *European Church Architecture, 1950–2000*. Munich: Prestel, 2002.

Stopford, J. 'Some Approaches to the Archaeology of Christian Pilgrimage'. *World Archaeology* 26 (1994): 57–72.

Stransky, Tom. 'The Secretariat for Promoting Christian Unity'. In Adrian Hastings (ed.), *Modern Catholicism: Vatican II and After*, 182–4. London: SPCK, 1991.

Suchcitz, Andrzej (ed.) *Kronica Kościoła św. Andrzeja Boboli w Londynie, 1961–2011*. London: Polish Catholic Mission Hammersmith, 2012.

Summerson, John. 'William Butterfield: Or, the Glory of Ugliness'. In John Summerson, *Heavenly Mansions*, 159–76. London: Cresset, 1949.

Teilhard de Chardin, Pierre. *The Phenomenon of Man*. London: Collins, 1959.

T. F. B. 'Obituary: Lancelot Sheppard'. *The Tablet* (3 Apr. 1971): 343.

Thomas, Brian, and Eileen Richardson (eds). *Directory of Master Glass-Painters*. London: Oriel Press, 1972.

Turner, Garth. ' "Aesthete, Impresario, and Indomitable Persuader": Walter Hussey at St Matthew's, Northampton, and Chichester Cathedral'. In Diana Wood (ed.), *The Church and the Arts: Papers Read at the 1990 Summer Meeting and the 1991 Winter Meeting of the Ecclesiastical History Society*, 523–35. Studies in Church History 28. Oxford: Blackwell, 1992.

Turner, Victor. *Dramas, Fields, and Metaphors: Symbolic Action in Human Society*. Ithaca, NY: Cornell University Press, 1974.

—— and Edith Turner. *Image and Pilgrimage in Christian Culture: Anthropological Perspectives*. New York: Columbia University Press, 1978.

'Tyburn's New Shrine'. *Catholic Herald* (25 Mar. 1960): 1.

Tyrwhitt, Jacqueline, Josep Luis Sert and Ernesto Rogers (eds). *The Heart of the City: Towards the Humanisation of Urban Life*. London: Lund Humphries, 1952.

'U.S. Priests Coming to Leicester'. *Catholic Herald* (24 Aug. 1951): 5.

Velarde, R., and F. X. Velarde. 'Modern Church Architecture and Some of its Problems'. *Clergy Review* 38 (1953): 513–26.

Von Balthasar, Hans Urs. *Razing the Bastions: On the Church in This Age*, trans. Brian McNeil. San Francisco: Ignatius Press, 1993.

Walker, Paul D. 'Developments in Catholic Churchbuilding in the British Isles, 1945–1980'. PhD diss., University of Sheffield, 1985.

—— 'Liturgy and Architecture: Catholic Church Building in the Twentieth Century'. *Ecclesiology Today* 38 (2007): 43–51.

—— 'Prophetic or Premature? The Metropolitan Cathedral of Christ the King, Liverpool'. *Theology* 105 (2002): 185–93.

Walsh, Christopher J. 'Initiation'. In Harold Winstone (ed.), *Pastoral Liturgy: A Symposium*, 159–88. London: Collins, 1975.

Walsh, Michael. 'Michael Shaw Obituary'. *The Guardian* (13 Sept. 2012). http://www.guardian.co.uk/music/2012/sep/13/michael-shaw-obituary (accessed 4 Oct. 2012).

—— 'Pius XII'. In Adrian Hastings (ed.), *Modern Catholicism: Vatican II and After*, 20–26. London: SPCK, 1991.

Walter, Bronwen. *Outsiders Inside: Whiteness, Place and Irish Women*. London: Routledge, 2001.

Ward, Fiona. 'Merseyside Churches in a Modern Idiom: Francis Xavier Velarde and Bernard Miller'. *Twentieth Century Architecture* 3: *The Twentieth Century Church* (1998): 95–102.

Watters, Diane. *Cardross Seminary: Gillespie, Kidd & Coia and the Architecture of Postwar Catholicism*. Edinburgh: Royal Commission on the Ancient and Historical Monuments of Scotland, 1997.

—— 'Post-War Church Patronage in the West of Scotland: The Ecclesiastical Architecture of Gillespie, Kidd & Coia'. *Journal of the Scottish Society for Art History* 3 (1998): 44–51.

Webb, Michael. *Architecture in Britain Today*. London: Country Life, 1969.

Weeks, Ronald. 'The Design and Construction of the Cathedral Church of SS. Peter and Paul, Clifton'. *Pax* 63 (Autumn–Winter 1973): 60–69.

Wells-Thorpe, John A. 'Church Building and New Construction Techniques'. *Churchbuilding* (Jan. 1965): 11–13.

—— 'Relevance in Church Building'. *Clergy Review* 55 (1970): 81–8.

'Westminster Centre's Task is Liturgical Renewal'. *Catholic Herald* (19 Dec. 1969): 2.

Wharton, Kate, 'Genesis of a Cathedral'. *Architect and Building News* (1, 15 Jan. 1969): 22–9.

—— and Ronald Weeks. 'Architectural Heritage Year 2075 … ? Clifton Cathedral'. *Architect* (May 1975): 24–5.

'Whithorn Pilgrimage'. *St Andrew Annual: The Catholic Church in Scotland* (1960–61): 93.

Winkley, Austin S. 'The Place of Celebration'. In Harold Winstone (ed.), *Pastoral Liturgy: A Symposium*, 45–54. London: Collins, 1975.

—— 'Review of New Church: St Gabriel's, Holloway, London'. *Clergy Review* 53 (1968): 997–1004.

—— 'Some Changes in Existing Churches: Westminster Cathedral and Waxwell Farm Chapel'. *Clergy Review* 50 (1965): 817–24.

Winstone, Harold (ed.) *Pastoral Liturgy: A Symposium*. London: Collins, 1975.

Wolff, Janet. *The Social Production of Art*. London: Macmillan, 1981.

'Wombwell: St. Michael and All Angels'. *Churchbuilding* (Jan. 1968): 21.

Woodard, David. 'The Cippenham Shared Church'. *Clergy Review* 53 (1968): 381–3.

—— 'Cippenham Shared Church'. *One in Christ* 6 (1970): 59–65.

—— 'First Ten Years at Cippenham Shared Church'. *One in Christ* 17 (1981): 43–5.

'Woodchurch Estate, Birkenhead'. *Architect and Building News* (14 Feb. 1947): 132–5.

'The Woodchurch Estate, Birkenhead'. *Architect and Building News* (13 Oct. 1950): 406–9.

Wright, Lance. 'Architectural Seriousness'. In Peter Hammond (ed.), *Towards a Church Architecture*, 220–44. London: Architectural Press, 1962.

—— 'Evolution of the Multi-Cell Church: Appraisal of St Margaret's, Twickenham'. *Clergy Review* 55 (1970): 497–504.

—— 'Liverpool Cathedral: An Architectural Appraisal'. *The Tablet* (13 May 1967): 520–22.

—— and Michael Hattrell. 'Building Study: Shared Church at Elmshott Lane, Cippenham'. *Architects' Journal* (12 May 1971) 1055–66.

Zeidler, Cordula. 'Die Einheit des Raumes: Kirchenbauten des britischen Architekten Gerard Goalen'. *Kunst und Kirche* 3 (2003): 136–8.

Index

Illustrations are indicated by page numbers in **bold**.

Aachen 136
acoustics 7, 73, 180, 206
active participation, see participation
Adams, Eric 289
Aidan, St 260
All Saints, Stevenage 315–18, **316**, **317**
All Saints, Telford 314
Allan, Kenneth 204–5, 220
Alleyn, Justin 235, 259-60, **262**, **Plate 14**
altar rails 73, 142, 144, 146, 173, 176, 192,
    193, 208, 259, 269
altars
    design 5, 71, 73, 87, 111, 136, 148–9,
        152, 186–93, 199–200, 204, 207–8,
        212–3, 262
    directionality (for Mass) 4, 5, 140, 144,
        148–9, 154, 174, 180, 196, 199–200,
        204, 223
    positioning 6, 75, 80, 135, 138, 142–4,
        147–9, 152–4, 162–3, 173–4, 179–80,
        200, 207–8, 223
    purpose 144, 160, 193
Alresford 134, 296, **297–8**
ambos 144, 148, 160, 163, 200, 204,
    205–6, 207, 210
Ampleforth Abbey 22, 36, 123, 149, 270
Ancoats 71, 271
Anderson, Benedict 251
Anwyll, George 242
Archard, Albert 57–8
Archard & Partners 27, 41
Architects' Journal 51, 133, 134
Architectural Association School of
    Architecture 29, 48, 156
Architectural Design 86
Architectural Prospect 51

Architectural Review 60, 69, 89, 109, 180,
    296, **298**
Armstrong, Timothy 95, **96**
art 6, 7, 17–18, 47–8, 54–5, 60-61, 75–6,
    91, 109–27, 135, 226, 231–7, 239,
    265, 267, 300–301
Art and Scholasticism (Maritain) 29
art deco 21, 31, 187
L'Art d'église 51
L'Art sacré 51, 55, 84, 91, 94–5, 110, 119,
    127
Art Sacré movement 111, 113, 119, 267
Arts and Crafts 109, 126–7, 253, 284
Arts Council 110, 117
Arup, Ove 78
Aspinall, Christopher 116
Assisi Congress 143, 144, 148, 186
Assy 18, 54, 110, 113, 114
Audincourt 54, 110–13, **112**, 123
Aylesford Priory 76, 238–42, **240–41**, 257

B. Stevens & Partners 84
Bagshawe, John 58
baldachinos 123, 186, 187, 193
Balthasar, Hans Urs von 277
Banham, Reyner 78, 86
Bankart, Hugh 144, **146**, **332**
baptism 4, 139, 144, 160, 195, 207, 213
baptisteries 92, 111, 113, 144, 148, 149,
    150, 160–63, 186, 195–6, 207, 269
Barnsley **100**, 126, **128**
Bartlett School of Architecture 266
Bate, Stanley Kerr 36
Battel, John 287
Bazaine, Jean 111, **112**, 113
Beare Green, Surrey 134

Beck, George Andrew 55–6, 69, 70, 78, 84, 89, 99, 120–23, 140, 148, 204, 222, 270, 281, 289
Belgrade Theatre, Coventry 70
Bellalta, Jaime 157
Bellot, Paul 89
Belluschi, Pietro 149
Benedictine Abbey church, Ealing 36
Benediction 223, 225, 239, 257
Bentley, J.F. 19, **20**, 29
Bernard of Clairvaux, St 94
Beyer, Ralph 7, **9**
Birkdale 41
Birkenhead 32, **32**, 200, 282–4, **283–4**, 326, **332**, **335**
Birmingham 22, **26**, 27, 63, **64**, 174, **176**, 199–200, **201**, **202**, 207–8, **230**, 258, 270, 291–2, **293**, 300–302, **300–301**, **Plate 1**
Birmingham Institute for the Study of Worship and Religious Architecture, 134, 136, 139, 149, 296, 302, 314
Birmingham School of Architecture 302
bishops' thrones 160, 199, 204
Black, John 208
Blackley 73, **221**, 221
Blackpool 21, 41, 230, **232**, **Plate 13**
Blakeman, Charles 111
Blessed Sacrament, Braunstone 21, 225
Blessed Sacrament, Gorseinon 152
Blessed Sacrament chapels 120–23, 144, 149, 150, 152, 157, 160, 162–3, 196, 199, 200, 204, 207, 223, 225, 270, 303
Blessed Sacrament Fathers 225
Blomfield, Giles 136
Böhm, Dominikus 138
Boileau, Louis-Auguste 266
Bolland, Sydney 221
Bolton, Lancashire 48, 70–71, **71**, **72**, 73, **74**, 83, 84, 181, 269–70, 271–2
Bootle 31, 32, **33**, 62, **102**, 102, 223, 235
Borehamwood 32, **192**, 193
Bosham 101
Bouyer, Louis 127
Bow Common 92–4, **94**, 133, 138–40, **139**, 141
Boyson, Alan **28**
Boxall, R.A. 289
Bradford **100**, 100–101, 142, **143**, 208
Braunstone 21, 225
Brentwood Cathedral 295–6, 308, **307**
Breuer, Marcel 79

brick 6, 7, 15, 18–19, 21–2, 27, 29, 31–2, 35, 36, 51, 58, 61, 70, 73, 75, 79, 84, 86–7, 89, 91–5, 144, 176, 210, 211, 317
Brighton 101, 260
Bristol 27, 52, 159–66, **161–5**, 182, 236–7, **237**, 282, 295, 299, 299–300, **333**, **Plate 9**; *see also* Clifton Cathedral
British Empire Exhibition, Glasgow 49
Broadbent, Francis 30, **30–31**, 223, **255**, 256–7; *see also* Broadbent, Hastings, Reid & Todd; F. G. Broadbent & Partners
Broadbent, Hastings, Reid & Todd, 41
Brown, David 100–101, 187; *see also* Weightman & Bullen
Brown, Patricia 100–101, 149–52, 187; *see also* Weightman & Bullen
Brumby, Robert 91, 120, **121**, 223, **224**, **Plate 4**
brutalism 7, 49, 84–98, 136, 139; *see also* New Brutalism
Bugnini, Annibale 236
Buckfast Abbey 116
Buckley, Joseph 160
building companies 101–2
building licences 3, 285
Bullen, Alfred 51, 99, 127; *see also* Weightman & Bullen
Burgess, Francis 147–8, 227, 289
Burles, Newton & Partners 63, **114**, 114, 133, 182, **184**, **205**, **213**, 219, **220**, 289, **307**, 308, **Plate 5**
Burnage 21, **25**, 280, **329**
Burwash 101
Butler, Michael 296
Butler, Rab 117
Butterfield, William 29
Byzantine revival architecture 18–28, 31–2, 35, 40, 89, 91, 225, 278, 282

Cachemaille-Day, N.F. 38
Camberwell 259, **261**
Cambridge, Mass. 80
Camelon 186
campaniles 16, 21, 58, 73, 150, 230, 281; *see also* towers
Candela, Felix 80
candlesticks 148, 185, 186, 193, 196, 200, 207, 269
canon law 185–94, 198, 204
Cantley, Doncaster 208
Capellades, Marie-Robert 94–5, 103, 295

Cardiff 235, 258, **Plate 15**
Cardigan 242–5, **244**, 257
Cardross 181, **182**
Carfin 230
Carpender's Park 57–8
Carson, Fred 233
Casabella 54
Casel, Odo 140
Cashman, David 63
Cassidy & Ashton 309–10, **310–11, 334**
Castlemilk 233–5, **235**
Catherine Labouré, St 226
Catholic Action movement 141
Catholic Building Review 16–17, 55–6
Catholic Churches Since 1623 (Little) 10
Catholic Herald 225, 242, **243**
Catholic identity 251, 254–5, 257, 270–72
Catt, John 134
Cauchi, Carmel **Plate 11**
celebrants' chairs 157, 196, 199, 200, 207, 208
Centre de Pastorale Liturgique 140–41
Chagall, Marc 110
Chandigarh 95
Chaunac, Robert de 267, **268**
Chelsea 225
Chichester 28
    Cathedral 115, 127
Childs, Charles Wilfrid 98
choir galleries 27, 71, 73, 142, 196
choirs 27, 141, 142, 144, 149, 157, 196
Chrestien, John **202**
Christ Church, Heald Green 235
Christ Our Hope, Beare Green 134
Christ the King, Plymouth 35, **37**
Christian unity 272, 277, 283, 303, 308–18
'Church Building and Art' exhibition 127
Church Building and Furnishing (O'Connell) 17, 185–6, 193
Church Buildings Today, see Churchbuilding
Church Incarnate (Schwarz) 94, 137
Churchbuilding 51, 80, 92–5, 99, 123, 134, 135, 295
ciboria 27, 70–71, 92, 138, 186, 187, 256
Cippenham 311–14, **313–15, 334**
circular plans 56, 89, 138, **144**, 149, 152–5, 174, 207–8, 230, 266, 292, 294
city centre churches 291–5
Clark, Kenneth 117
Clark, Michael **60**, 114, 126, 233, **234**, 239, **240, Plate 11**

Clark, Philip Lindsey 115, 126, 127, **279**
Clarke, Geoffrey 116, 123
CLASP building system 98, 100–101
Clergy Review 111, 134, 143, 148–9, 154, 185, 200, 232, 302
Clifton Cathedral, Bristol 52, 159–66, **161–5**, 182, 236–7, **237**, 295, **333, Plate 9**
Clinkham Wood 91–3, **92, 93**
Clubmoor 31
Clydebank 84, 210, **330**
Cocagnac, Maurice 127
Coia, Jack 49–51, 52, 53, 78, 86, 87, 119, 180, 286–7; *see also* Gillespie, Kidd & Coia
Cocteau, Jean 267, **268**
Collegeville, MN 79
Collins, Peter 78
Cologne 95, 136, **137**
Commonwealth Institute, London 80
communion 73, 138, 139, 141, 193, 196, 206
communion rails 73, 142, 144, 146, 173, 176, 192, 193, 208, 259, 269
community 136, 138, 140, 238, 251, 257, 268–72, 315
Comper, J.S. 41
concelebration 181–2
concrete, reinforced 6–7, 30, 61, 78–83, 85–6, 101–3, 138, 149, 150, 207, 210, 299, 314
Congar, Yves 141, 142
Congrès Internationaux d'Architecture Moderne (CIAM) 86, 109, 283
consecration 269–70, 311
'Constitution on the Sacred Liturgy' 5, 55, 111, 141–2, 157, 180, 182, 196–8, 204, 207, 219
Cope, Gilbert 134, 136, 139, 301, 302
Cordiner, Thomas 53, 84
Corfiato, Hector 187, **188**, 225, 266, **268**
Cornford, Christopher 127
coronas 187, 208
Corpus Christi, Aachen 136
Corpus Christi, feast of 225
Corpus Christi, Stechford 207–8
Costantini, Celso 54
Coulsdon 204, **205**, 219–20, **220**
Council of Trent 4, 17
Counter Reformation 73, 173, 225
Couturier, Marie-Alain 51, 54, 84, 110, 111, 295
Coventry 70, 258, 259, **260**
    Cathedral 6, 7, 15, 78, 80, 113–19, 124, 135

Cowderoy, Cyril 239–42
Cox, Oliver 110
Crabtree, William 265, **267**
Craze, Romilly 36
Crichton, J.D. 111, 123, 142–4, **145**, 146, 149, 233
Crichton-Stuart, John 252
Crosby 303–6, **305**
crucifixes 32, 110, 119, 123, 124, 186, 187, 196, 200, 219
crucifixion images 113, 114–15, 124, 127
Cudworth 126, **128**
Cumbernauld 187, **190**, 210, 235
Cunnane, Seamus 242
Cupar 154, **155**

dalle de verre 22, 27–8, 91, 113, 116, 124, 149, 227, 235, 239, 291
Dapré, Vincent 242
Davey, George 317
Davies, John Gordon 134, 139, 302
Davis, Charles 134, 154, 193
Dayer, Philip 1, 2, 3, 5
De La Salle Training College, Middleton 52, **53**
de Maistre, Roy 115
de Maré, Eric 89
Debuyst, Frédéric 51, 296
'Decree on Ecumenism' 308–9, 310
Deguerry, Francisque 267
Dennistoun 49, 196, **198**, 200, **203**
Denton, Manchester 80–83, **83**
devotions 213, 219–45
dialogue Mass 4, 140, 141, 146, 174
Didsbury 41
Dilworth, Norman 200, **284**
Dinan, Timothy 63
Dix, Gregory 135
Dockhead, London 29–30, **329**, **Plate 2–3**
Dodds, Eduardo 75–6, **77**
'Dogmatic Constitution on the Church' 296
Dollan, Sir Patrick 288
Dommerson, Sydney 156
Doncaster 57, 208, 270
Donnington, Shropshire 95, **96**
Dooley, Arthur 125, **126**
Douai Abbey, Berkshire 52
Droylsden 176, **178**, 187, 227–9, **229**
Drumchapel 83, 200
Dumbarton 95, **97**
Dumfries 199
Dunfermline 254

Dunstable 174, **175**
Duston, Northamptonshire 100
Dwyer, George 142, 222–3

E. & J. Blackwell 226, **228**
Ealing 36
East Acton 61, **114**, 114–15, 126, 182, 235, 260, **Plate 5**
East Kilbride 51, 86–7, **88**, 91, 180, 187, 196, **197**, 286–8, **287**, 291, **330**, **335**
Easton & Robertson 80
economy 21, 22, 30, 35, 36, 62–4, 98–103
Ecumenical Commission 318
ecumenism 272, 277, 283, 303, 308–18
Edge, Richard 99
Edinburgh 174, 233, 292–5, **294**, **Plate 16**
Edinburgh College of Art 116
Ellis, J.B. 187, **189**, **280–81**, 281–2
Ellis, William 187, **189**, **280–81**, 281–2
Eltham 38
Elwès, Simon 60–61
English Martyrs, Horley 235, **Plate 14**
English Martyrs, Wallasey 32
Entwistle, Clive 232
Epstein, Jacob 91, 117, **118**
Ethrington, James 115
Eucharistic devotions 222–5
Evans, Illtud 116
Evans, Peter Ansdell 134, 165, 296; *see also* Melhuish, Wright & Evans
Eyre, Charles 35

F.G. Broadbent & Partners **30–31**, 255, 256; *see also* Broadbent, Hastings, Reid & Todd; Broadbent, Francis
F.R. Bates, Son & Price 207, **210**, 235, **Plate 15**
F.X. Velarde Partnership **92–3**, **192**, **283–4**, **332**, **335**; *see also* Velarde, F.X.; O'Mahony, Richard
Faczynski, Jerzy 123–4, **125**, 149, **184**, 263; *see also* Weightman & Bullen
Faifley 180, **181**, **330**
Failsworth 226, **227**, **228**, 269
Fairlie, Reginald 58, 286
Falkirk 186
Falmer House, University of Sussex 95
Farebrother, Arthur 27, 41, 48
Farnworth, Lancashire 73, **74**
Farrell, Charles 315
Fawley Court 265–6, **267**
Festival of Britain 15, 70, 71, 75, 109
Fidler, Alwyn Sheppard 291–2

Filthaut, Theodor 113
Filton 27
financing 3–4, 62–4, 268–70, 295
First Unitarian Church, Rochester, NY 86
Fischer, Theodor 29
Fisher, Geoffrey 308
Fitzsimons, Edmund 123, 125, 149
Fleischmann, Arthur **114**, 115, 235
flexible churches 211–13, 295, 302–18
Flood, Bernard 99
Flynn, Anthony 186
Flynn, Thomas 231
fonts 1, 92, 93, 139, 144, 148, 157, 160,
     163, 195–6, 207, 267, 269
Foord-Kelcey, Irene 233, **234**
Forrest, Jack 204
Forsyth, Moira **Plate 11**
'fortress' churches 277, 278, 291
Forty Martyrs of England and Wales 252,
     255–7
Fourmaintraux, Pierre 27–8, **28**, 235, 260,
     262, **Plates 4–5**, **Plate 14**
French immigrants 266–7
French, Neal **28**
Frink, Elisabeth 123, **124**, 299, **300**
furnishings 6, 27, 126–7, 141, 144, 148,
     185–94, 199–207, 212–13, 312; *see also*
     altars; baldachinos; candlesticks;
     ciboria; crucifixes; tabernacles

Gaelic identity 254–5
garden cities 280–81, 282–3
Garforth 101
Garner, Preston & Strebel 95, **97**
Garvey, Michael 306
Gaudin, Jean 22
'General Instruction on the Roman Missal'
     206, 207
German immigrants 267
Gibberd, Frederick 6, 15, 52, **53**, 55–6,
     56–7, 58, 116–17, 120–23, **121–2**,
     124, 127, 149, 153–5, **154**, 204,
     232–3, 288, 289, 310–11, **312**, **Plate 7**
Giedion, Siegfried 51, 136
Gilbey, Peter 133
Gill, Eric 126–7, 142, 233
Gillespie, Kidd & Coia 49, **50**, 52–3, 58, 63,
     78–9, **79**, 84, 86–7, **88**, 91, 101,
     117–19, **119–20**, 179–81, 186–7,
     190, 195–6, **197–8**, 200, **203**, 210,
     233–5, **235**, 285–6, **287**, **330**, **335**
Gillett, Martin 242, 245
Gipton 187–92, **191**

Glasgow 35, 49, 53, 58, 78–9, **79**, 83, 84,
     117–19, **119**, 174, 180, **181**, 187–92,
     196, **198**, 200, **203**, 210, 233–5, **235**,
     258, **330**
Glasgow School of Architecture 49
Glasgow School of Art 119
Glenrothes 49, **50**, 51, 63–4, 119, **120**,
     179, **179**, 180, 186, 285–6, **286**, **330**
Gnosspelius, Janet 32; *see also* Velarde, F.X.
Goalen, Gerard 3, **5**, 5–7, **8–9**, 48, 127,
     147, 147–9, 152, 155, **156**, 193, **194**,
     207, 226–7, **234**, 289–91, **290**, **332**,
     Plate 10, **Plate 12**
Godfrey, William 1, 16–18, 55, 57–8, 61,
     63, 182, 186, 256, 310
Godin, Henri 141
Godward, Brian 102
Golden Lane estate, London 27
Goldie, Edward 270
Good Shepherd, Nottingham 193, **194**,
     Plate 10
Goodhart-Rendel, Harry Stuart 29–30,
     30–31, 42, 35, 36, 41, 47, 58, 62, 127,
     253, **254**, **329**, **Plate 2**
Gorleston-on-Sea 142
Gorseinon 152–3
Gorton 174, **177**
Gothic revival architecture 6, 35–40, 53, 58
Gowan, James 7, 86, 89, 91
Grace, Pierce 119, 286
Graham, James Gillespie 292
Gray, Charles 230
Gray, Gordon 87, 119, 186, 199, 233, 285,
     294–5
Gray, Nicolete 60
Greenford 61, **61**, 79, **81**, 186
Greenhalgh & Williams 48, 70, **71–2**, 73,
     74, 84, 98, 103, 156, 176, 181, 226,
     227–9, 265
Gregorian chant 141, 142, 144, 160
Griffin, Bernard 58, 242, 265
Grimshaw, Francis 63, 143, 212, 292
grottos 229–30
Guardini, Romano 111, 138, 219
Guild of Catholic Artists and Craftsmen 127
Guildford Cathedral 36
Gwilliam & Armstrong **96**

Hackenthorpe 38, **38**, 174
Hackney 41
Haddow, Tom Harley 294, **294**, **Plate 16**
Hadfield, Cawkwell & Davidson 192
Hagia Sophia, Istanbul 19, 22

Haig, Henry 163, **165**
Ham Common flats 86
Hammond, Peter 133–6, 139, 140, 142, 149, 184, 193
Hampton Hill 182–4, **184**, 268–9
Handisyde, Cecil 15, **16**
Hanwell 39, **39**, **40**
Hardman & Co. 263, **264**
Harlow 116, **147**, 147–8, 152, 155, 193, 226–7, 233, **234**, 288–91, **288**, **291**, **332**, **Plate 12**
Harris, Augustine 120
Harrison & Cox 27, 73–5, **75–6**, **176**, **230**, 270, 292, **293**
Harwood, Elain 10
Hattrell, Michael 312–14, **313–15**, **334**
Hayes 182, **183**, 204, 269
Heald Green, Manchester 235
Heathrow Airport Chapel 310–11, **312**
Heenan, John C. 3, 5, 52, 55–7, 58, 99, 101, 116, 120, 134, 142, 152, 154–5, 157, 225, 295, 308, 310
Hellmuth, Obata & Kassabaum 149, **150**
Henze, Anton 113
Herwegen, Ildefons 140
Heston 182, **183**
hexagonal plans 73, 80, 100, 150, 163
Hickson, Peter 57
Hinton, Denys 302
Hiscoe, Gerald 152–3
Hobsbawm, Eric 18
Hodge Hill, Birmingham 302
Holland, Thomas 272
Holloway, Antony 110
Holy Apostles, Pimlico 127, 192
Holy Child Jesus convent, Cavendish Square 117, **118**
Holy Cross, Birkenhead **32**, 32
Holy Cross, Harlow 289
Holy Cross, Hucknall 38
Holy Family, Pontefract 222–3, **224**
Holy Family, Southampton 84, **85**
Holy Family, Thurnscoe 101
Holy Ghost, Bootle 235
Holy Ghost, St Leonards-on-Sea 84
Holy Redeemer, Pershore 144–6, **146**, 149, **332**
Holy Trinity, Dockhead 29–30, **329**, **Plate 2**
Holy Week liturgies 157, 195, 200
Horley 235, **Plate 14**
Hornsby-Smith, Michael 10
housing 2, 47, 48, 70, 86, 98, 110, 278–84, 291, 292

Howell, Clifford 142
Hucknall 38
Hudson, John 222
Hughes, John 87
Hughes, Thomas 160
Hume, Basil 270
Humphrys, Derrick **288**, 289
Hunslet 208, **211**, 235
Hussey, Walter 113, 115
Huyton 80, **82**, 84, 259, **331**
hyperbolic paraboloid structures 80–83, 84, 299–300

Immaculate Conception, Leeds 176
Immaculate Conception, Maryhill 84
Immaculate Heart of Mary, Hayes 182, **183**, 204, 269
immigration 2, 251, 257–67
Independent Group 86, 91, 233
indulgences 236
Institute for the Study of Worship and Religious Architecture, *see* Birmingham Institute
Institute of Contemporary Arts 86
'Instruction on Sacred Art' 18, 54, 60–61, 111, 115
'Instruction on the Worship of the Eucharistic Mystery' 196, 199, 222
International Congress on Liturgy, Lugano 143
International Congress on the Pastoral Liturgy, Assisi 143, 148, 186
International Style 49, 69, 84
Irish identity 257–63
Irish immigrants 2, 109, 174, 238, 251, 257–63
Isle of Wight 89
Italian immigrants 258, 260, 271
Ivor Day & O'Brien 207

Jacobsen, Arne 6
James, Bernard 292; *see also* Harrison & Cox
Jarosz, George Wladyslaw 265, **267**
Jennett, Frederick 159–66; *see also* Sir Percy Thomas & Son
Jennings, Homer & Lynch 262–3, **264**
Jevons, Rosamond 282
John, David **34**, 35, 123, 127, **128**, **221**, **232**, 233, **Plate 3**, **Plate 13**
John XXIII, Pope 141, 308
John Rochford & Partners 52, 126, **128**, 210, 233, **234**, 270, **271**, 278, **279**, 302–3, **303–4**, **334**, **Plate 11**

Jones, Jonah 22, **25**, 27, **Plate 1**
Jordan, Robert Furneaux 117
Jungmann, Josef 135, 140, 148

Kahn, Louis 49, 86, 89, 95
Keele University Chaplaincy 309
Kelvinside 78–9, **79**, 117–19, **119**, 187–92
Kennedy, T. Warnett 49
Kensington 35–6, **37**, 58–61, **59**, **60**, 62, 80
Kilpatrick, James 87
Kilsyth 49, **50**, 87, 101
Kirkby, Gresham 138, 141
Kirkby Lonsdale 236
Klecki, Aleksander 265, **266**
Knebworth 257
Knightswood 35
Kossowski, Adam 75–6, **77**, 115, 123–4,
    125, 126, 127, 187, 235–6, 239,
    240–41, 263–5, **Plate 8**, **Plate 15**
Kresge Auditorium, Cambridge, MA 80

La Tourette 84–6
Lady chapels 220, 226, 227, 267, 269
Lancaster 114, 115–16, **116**, 117, 126,
    128, 230–31, **231**, **Plate 6**
Lancaster University Chaplaincy Centre
    309–10, **310–11**, **334**
Langley 280–82, **280–81**
Langtry-Langton, J.H. 142, **143**, 208, **210**,
    270
Langtry-Langton, Peter 48–9, **143**, 208,
    210, 235
Lanner Limited 101–2, **102**
Lansbury Estate, London 15, **16**, **17**
Lasdun, Denys 127, 155, **155**
Latin 4, 174, 180, 198
lay participation, *see* participation
Lay People in the Church (Congar) 141
lay readings 205
Le Corbusier 7, 49, 51, 69, 84–6, 87, 91, 95,
    134, 136
Le Raincy 7, 35, 78, 123, 149, 289
Leask, James 299, **299**
Leeds 101, 176, 187–92, **191**, 208, **211**,
    222–3, **224**, 235, 258
Lefebvre, Henri 10
Léger, Fernand 54, 111, 113, 119
Leicester 21, 22, **23**, **25**, 27, 181, 225
Leo XIII, Pope 174
Lesisz, Tadeusz 226, 265
Lethaby, William 19
Levenshume 179
Leversbach 136

Lewerentz, Sigurd 91
Leyland 116, 123–6, **125**, **126**, 149, 152,
    187, 195, 223, 270, **272**, **331**, **Plate 7**
Lichfield 95, **96**
Lionel A.G. Prichard & Son 41, 48, 80, **82**,
    223, 225, 259, **331**
Lipchitz, Jacques 110
Little, Bryan 10
liturgical movement 5, 7, 48, 52, 70, 133,
    138, 140–66, 173–85, 187, 194, 196,
    200, 213, 219, 226, 233, 237, 292
liturgical reform 4–5, 55, 73, 135, 138,
    140–52, 160, 173–85, 194–213
Liturgy 142
Liturgy and Architecture (Hammond) 133,
    139
Liturgy Commission 204, 212
Liverpool 21, 31, **32**, 35, 48–9, 51, 52,
    57, 62, 80, **82**, 84, 99, **102**, 102,
    149–50, **151**, 186–7, 195, 204–5,
    221, 223, 225, 235, 258, 259, 282,
    308, 326, **331–2**; *see also* Liverpool
    Metropolitan Cathedral
Liverpool Cathedral 35
Liverpool Metropolitan Cathedral 6, 52,
    55–6, **57**, 62, 116–17, 120–23, **121**,
    122, **124**, 125, 127, 134, 152, 153–5,
    154, **155**, **156**, 181, 195, 204, 207,
    232–3, **Plate 7**
Liverpool School of Architecture 19, 147, 263
Locket, William 154, 179
Loire, Gabriel 28
London 1–7, **5**, **8**, **9**, 15, **16**, **17**, 18–19, **20**,
    21, **24**, 27, 29–30, **29**, **30**, 32, **34**,
    35–6, **37**, 38–9, **39**, **40**, 41, 48, 53,
    57–61, **59**, **60**, **61**, 62–3, 70, 76,
    79–80, **81**, 86, 92–4, **94**, 101, **114**,
    114–15, 117, **118**, 127, 133, 138–40,
    139, 156–9, **158**, **159**, 182–4, **183**,
    184, 186–7, **188**, **192**, 192–3, 195,
    199, 204–5, **205**, 207, **209**, 210,
    212–3, **212**, **213**, 219–20, **220**, 223,
    225, 233, **234**, 235, **255**, 255–7, **256**,
    258–62, **259**, **261–3**, 265–70, **266**,
    268, **271**, 310–11, **329**, **332–3**,
    Plate 2, **Plate 5**; *see also* Westminster
    Cathedral; St George's Cathedral,
    Southwark; entries for individual
    churches and districts
London County Council Architects'
    Department 70, 109–10
Lorimer, Huw 253
Lourdes 226, 229–31, 255

Lowton 150–52, **151**, 186–7, 192
Lugano 143
Lurçat, André 110, 113
Luton 258
Lutyens, Edwin 56
Lynch, Malachy 239, 242

McAnally, Alexander 53, 58
MacCallum, Charles 49
McCormick, Liam 84, **85**
McGee, Joseph 253
Machynlleth 159, 225
Mackintosh, Donald 49
McLellan, Sadie **190**, 235
MacMillan, Andy 49, 78, 86–7, 91, 119,
    180, 233, 286, 288; *see also* Gillespie,
    Kidd & Coia
Macmillan, Harold 281
McShane, Joseph 101
Madden, Tim 242, **243**
Maguire, Robert 92, 94, **94**, 127, 133, 134,
    136, 138–9, **139**, 146, 149, 154, 156, 184
Maison Dieu, La 141
Maisons Jaoul 86
Manchester 21, **25**, 27–8, **28**, 41, 48, 52,
    53, **53**, 71, 73, 80–83, **83**, 89, 91, 99,
    102, 174, 176, **177**, **178**, 179, 187,
    221, 221, 226–9, **227**, **228**, **229**, 235,
    258, 265, 269, 271, **279**, 280–82,
    280–81, **329**, **Plate 4**
Mangan, Wilfrid 27, 230
Maniura, Robert 238
Manor House, London 212–13, **213**
Manzoni, Herbert 291
marble 19, 21, 71, 87, 119, 149, 187, 192,
    200, 204, 207, 259–60, 262
Maria Laach Abbey, Germany 140
Marian devotions 225–31, **229–30**, 242,
    244, 252, 254
Maritain, Jacques 29, 94, 110
Marshall, D. Plaskett 259, **261**, 267
Martin, George Mayer **221**
Martin, Leslie 70
Maryhill 84
Marylebone 29–30, **30**, **31**, 62
Mass 4, 140, 141, 142, 143, 144, 146, 148,
    160, 173–4, 180–82, 196–206, 239
Massey, Edward J. 27–8, **28**
Massey & Massey 27–8, **28**, 187
Matisse, Henri 54, 110, 113
Matthew, Robert 100, 295; *see also* Robert
    Matthew, Johnson-Marshall & Partners
Maufe, Edward 36

Mediator Dei 17–18, 54, 58, 141, 147–8
Meistermann, Georg **137**
Melhuish, Nigel 134, 296; *see also*
    Melhuish, Wright & Evans
Melhuish, Wright & Evans **297–8**
Mellor, Tom 114, 116, **116**, **128**, 230, **231**,
    Plate 6
Metzstein, Isi 49, 53, 78, 86–7, 91, 180,
    233, 286, 288; *see also* Gillespie,
    Kidd & Coia
Middlesborough 225
Middleton, Lancashire 52, **53**, 280–82,
    280–81
Mies van der Rohe, Ludwig 84
Milan 138
Mills, Edward 179
Minchin, Basil 135
Miraculous Medal 226
Mission de Paris 141
Mitchell, William **57**, 110, 163, 236–7, **237**
Modern Church Architecture (Roulin) 22
modernism 6, 15–18, 41, 47–52, 54–64,
    69–103, 133–66, 277, 283, 285, 291
Monaghan, James 292
monstrance thrones 223–5
monstrances 153, 222, 223–5
monumental churches 277, 278–95
Mooney, Brian 41
Moore, Henry 123
Moore, Robert 174, 176, 258
Moore, Temple 29
Moreton 36
Morgan, David 222
mosaics 19, 22, 27, 31–2, 187, 195, 223,
    226, 231, 235, 269, 282
Moverley, Gerald 303
Mullaly, Terence 115
multi-purpose churches 211–13, 295,
    302–18
municipal modernism 69–78
murals 70, 75, 91, 326
Murphy, John 280
Murray, Gregory 160
Murray, Keith 92, **94**, 133, 134, 136,
    138–9, **139**
music 4, 110, 141, 142, 144, 160, 163, 205,
    212
Musicae sacrae disciplina 110
Mystici corporis Christi 141

Nairn, Ian 15, 60
National Council for the Lay Apostolate
    156

national identity 251, 253–5, 257–67
Naylor, Ben 80
Nealon, Kenneth 282, 299, **299**
Neasden 101
Nervi, Pier Luigi 79, 149, **150**
New Brutalism 51, 86, 87, 93, 134, 138;
     see also brutalism
New Churches Research Group (NCRG)
     133–6, 142, 146, 149, 152, 153,
     156–7, 165, 173, 179–80, 182,
     193, 213, 226, 295, 312
New Empiricism 69–70, 86, 87, 95, 98,
     109, 113
New Malden, London 223
New Monumentality 51
new towns 2, 47, 285–91, 314–7
Newman, John Henry 18
Newton, John 61, 63, 133, 182–4, 199,
     204, 212, 308; *see also* Burles,
     Newton & Partners
Nicholson, Robert 292
Ninian, St 252
Nolan, B. **227**
Norris, Charles **5**, 116, 117, 123, **147**, 227,
     239, **240–41**, **Plate 12**
Norris, Ernest Bower 21, 22–7, **25–6**, 41,
     89, 225, 292, **Plate 1**; *see also*
     Sandy & Norris
North Peckham Civic Centre 76
Northampton 113, 115
nostalgia 219, 238, 252, 253, 254, 255, 258
Notre Dame de France, London 266–7, **268**
Notre Dame de Toute Grâce, Assy 18, 54,
     110, 111, 113, 114
Notre Dame du Haut, Ronchamp 52, 84,
     91, 123, 136
Notre Dame du Raincy 7, 35, 78, 123, 149,
     289
Nottingham 38, 52, 193, **194**, **Plate 10**
Novarina, Maurice 54, 110, **112**
Nuttgens, Joseph 116, 235
Nuttgens, Patrick 100, 133, 134, 180

O'Brien, Morris & McCullough 27
O'Connell, Joseph 17–18, 54, 111, 143,
     160, 185–6, 193, 195, 199
O'Connor, John 142
octagonal plans 102, 142, 149, 260
O'Mahony, Patrick 300–302
O'Mahony, Richard 32, 41, 51, 84, 91–5,
     92–3, **96**, 154, 195, 200, 207, 282–4,
     283–4, **306**, 306–8, **332**, **335**
'On Implementing the Constitution on
     the Sacred Liturgy' 157, 196

'On the Development of Peoples' 301
opening ceremonies 269–70, **272**
Osman, Louis 117, **118**
Ottaviani, Alfredo 143
Our Lady, Thurcroft 101
Our Lady and St Joseph, Hanwell **39**, **40**
Our Lady and St Peter, Wimbledon 210, **212**
Our Lady and the First Martyrs, Bradford
     142, **143**
Our Lady and the Welsh Martyrs, Overton
     101
Our Lady Help of Christians, Tile Cross 63,
     64, 199–200, **201**, **202**
Our Lady of Fatima, Harlow 116–17, **147**,
     147–9, 152, 186, 193, 199, 226–7,
     233, **234**, 288–91, **290**, **332**, **Plate 12**
Our Lady of Good Counsel, Dennistoun
     196, **198**, 200, **203**
Our Lady of Lourdes, Birkdale 41
Our Lady of Lourdes, Blackpool (shrine)
     126, 231, **232**, **Plate 13**
Our Lady of Lourdes, Bolton 181
Our Lady of Lourdes, East Kilbride 288
Our Lady of Lourdes, Farnworth 73, **74**
Our Lady of Lourdes, Hackenthorpe 38,
     38, 174
Our Lady of Mount Carmel and St Simon
     Stock, Kensington 35–6, **37**
Our Lady of the Assumption, Blackpool 41
Our Lady of the Assumption, Langley
     280–82, **281**
Our Lady of the Assumption, Stainforth 57
Our Lady of the Rosary, Donnington 95, **96**
Our Lady of the Rosary, Marylebone
     29–30, **30**, **31**, 62
Our Lady of the Taper, Cardigan (shrine)
     242–5, **244**, 257
Our Lady of the Victories, Kensington
     58–61, **59**, **60**, 62, 64, 117
Our Lady of the Visitation, Greenford **61**,
     61, 79–80, **81**, 186
Our Lady of the Wayside, Shirley 300–302,
     300, **301**
Our Lady of Walsingham, Bootle 102, **102**
Our Lady Queen of Apostles, Heston 182,
     183
Overton 101
Oxford 6
Oxford School of Architecture 265

Pace, George 133, 309
Palace of Assembly, Chandigarh 95
Paolozzi, Eduardo 86

Paris 140-41
parish communities 268–72
Parson Cross, Sheffield 302–3, **303–4, 334**
participation 4, 71, 73, 75, 135, 141, 143, 149–52, 154, 160, 163, 173–4, 196, 204–6, 226, 295
partitions 179, 211, 212, 223, 302–3, 308, 312, 314
'Pastoral Constitution on the Church in the Modern World' 296
Pastoral Directory for Church Building 206
pastoral liturgy 140–41, 143
Pater, Stanislaus 149–50, 263; *see also* Weightman & Bullen
Patrick, St 258–9, 262–3
Paul VI, Pope 141, 236, 255, 301
People's Mass, A (Murray) 160
Pepler, Conrad 127
Percy Thomas Partnership **161–5, 333**; *see also* Sir Percy Thomas & Son
Perret, Auguste 7, 35, 78, 149, 225, 289
Pershore 142–6, **145, 146**, 149, **332**
Peter Bosanquet & Russell Diplock Associates 314
Petit, John 242
pews, *see* seating
Phenomenon of Man (Teilhard de Chardin) 297–9
Picasso, Pablo 54
'Pilgrim' Church 83, 277, 296, 300
pilgrimage shrines 10, 229–30, 238–45, 251, 252–7
pilgrimages 229–30, 238–45, **244**, 252–7
Pimlico 127, 192
Pin Green, Stevenage 315–18, **316–17**
Pinner 32, **34, 329, Plate 3**
Piper, John 113, 114, 115–17, **116, 124, 154, Plates 6–7**
Pius IX, Pope 226
Pius X, Pope 73, 141, 142
Pius XII, Pope 17-18, 60, 75, 110, 141, 143, 147–8, 150, 186, 195, 226, 227, 242, 263
Plymouth 35–6, **37**
Polish Church of Divine Mercy, Manchester 265
Polish identity 265–6
Polish immigrants 51, 258, 262, 263–6, 271
Polish School of Architecture 263, 265
Pollen, Francis 127
Pollitt, Kimball 101

Pontefract, Leeds 222–3, **224**
Poplar 15, **16, 17**, 18–19, 62, 223, **259**, 259, 260–62, **263**
Poremba, Anthony 159–66; *see also* Sir Percy Thomas & Son
Port Talbot 207, **210**
Portsmouth Priory, RI 149
Powell, Sebastian Pugin 35
prefabrication 47, 83, 98, 100–103
Preston 27, 36, 278, **278**; *see also* Leyland
Prestonpans 233
Price, Cedric 314
Prichard, Francis 48, 80; *see also* Lionel A.G. Prichard & Son
Prichard, Lionel 41, 80, **82**, 223, 225, 259; *see also* Lionel A.G. Prichard & Son
processional aisles 138, 144, 149, 150, 157, 163, 195
processions 4, 138, 144, 150, 163, 195, 205, 223, 225, 227, 232, 236, **244**, 245, 252, 254, 257, 270–72, **272**
Production of Space (Lefebvre) 10
proscenium arches 176–9
Pruden, Dunstan 219
Pugin, A.W.N. 35, 36
Pugin & Pugin 35
pulpits 86, 144, 148, 152, 180, 230, 269
Purcell, Charles 35
Purdy, Martin 302

Quail, Paul 127
Quarant'Ore 223
Quarr Abbey, Isle of Wight 89
quarry tiles 7, 91–2, 95

Radziwill, Prince Stanislaw 265
Rainham, Kent 75–6, **77**
Ratcliffe College, Leicester 22, **25**, 27, 181
rationalised building systems 98–103
Ravenna 19, 22, 193
readings 4, 140, 144, 148, 157, 205
Reformation 238, 252, 254, 255
Forty Martyrs of 239, 252, 255–7
Régamey, Pie-Raymond 51, 295
Reid, D.A. **30–31**; *see also* F.G. Broadbent & Partners
Reid, Robert 288
Reilly, Charles 19
reinforced concrete 6–7, 30, 61, 78–83, 84–6, 101, 103, 138, 149, 150, 163–5, 207, 210, 299, 314
relics 186, 238–9, 256
Renaissance revival architecture 49

Reul, Gunther 267
Reul, Heribert 267
Rex, John 174, 176, 258
Reynolds, Francis 21, 41
Reynolds & Scott 21–2, **23–5**, 27, 28,
    36–40, **38–40**, 52, 53, **53**, 78, 83, 174,
    195, 235, 280, **329**
Reyntiens, Patrick **5**, 7, **9**, 113, 115,
    116–17, **122**, 123–4, **124–6**, 127, 133,
    154, **158–9**, **194**, **Plate 7**, **Plate 10**
Richards, Ceri 120–23, **122**
Richards, J.M. 89, 109
Richier, Germaine 114
Ritchie, Walter 300, **301**
ritual 4, 162–3, 194–6, 211, 213, 231–2,
    236, 251, 252, 255, 258, 270–72
Robert Matthew, Johnson-Marshall &
    Partners 80, 98
Robinson, Robert 152
Rochdale 22, 89, **89**, **90**
Rochester, NY 86
Rochford, Alan **304**
Rochford, John 52–3, 126, **128**, 233, **234**,
    270, **271**, 278, **279**, 302, **303–4**, **334**,
    Plate 11; *see also* John Rochford &
    Partners
Roman Missal 185, 198, 206
Romanesque revival architecture 6, 18–
    35, 40–41, 49, 53, 225, 226, 281, 282
Ronchamp 51, 84–6, 91, 123, 136
Ronchetti, R.S. 27, 176
rosary 174, 226, 227, 239
Rothenfels 138
Rotherfield 101
Rouault, Georges 54
Roulin, Eugène Auguste 22
Rowe, Colin 127
Rowse, Herbert 282–3
Royal Festival Hall, London 70
Royal Fine Art Commission 58
Royal Horticultural Hall, Kensington 80
Royal Institute of British Architects (RIBA)
    49, 52, 79, 159
Ruckstuhl, Xaver 220, **220**
Rudderham, Joseph 159–60, 295
Rudolph, Paul 95
Ruislip 1–3, **5**, 5–7, **8**, **9**
Rush, Brian 300
Rush, Granelli & Partners 300, **300–301**
Rykwert, Joseph 115, 127, 138, 185

Saarinen, Eliel 80
Sacré-Coeur, Audincourt 54, 110, 111–12,
    112, 113, 119, 123

Sacred Congregation of Rites 186
Sacred Heart 221, 226, 258, 262
Sacred Heart, Camberwell 259, **261**
Sacred Heart, Cumbernauld 187, **190**,
    210, 235
Sacred Heart, Gorton 174, **177**
Sacred Heart, Moreton 36
St Agnes, Huyton 80, **82**, 84, 259, **331**
St Aidan, Coulsdon 204, **205**, 219–20, **220**
St Aidan, East Acton 61, **114**, 114–15, 116,
    126, 182, 235, 260, **Plate 5**
St Albert, Leversbach 136
St Alexander, Bootle 32, **33**, 62, 223
St Aloysius, Somers Town 62–3, 199
St Ambrose, Speke 149–50, **151**, 186–7,
    195, **331**
St Andrew, Cippenham 311–14, **313**, **314**,
    315, **334**
St Andrew, Dumfries 199
St Ann, Fawley Court 265–6, **267**
St Anne, Dennistoun 49
St Anselm, Southall 204
St Anthony, Wythenshawe **279**, 280
St Anthony Bobola, Shepherd's Bush 265,
    266
St Anthony of Padua, Preston **278**, 278
St Augustine, Manchester 91, **Plate 4**
St Benedict, Drumchapel 83, 200
St Benedict, Garforth 101
St Bernadette, Bristol **299**, 299–300
St Bernadette, Lancaster 114, 115–16,
    116, 117, 126, **128**, 230, **231**, **Plate 6**
St Bernadette, Liverpool 21
St Bernard, Burnage 21, **25**, 280, **329**
St Boniface, Salford 187
St Boniface, Stepney 267
St Bride, East Kilbride 51, 86–7, **88**, 91,
    180, 187, 196, **197**, 286–7, **287**, 288,
    291, **330**, **335**
St Catherine, Didsbury 41
St Catherine of Siena, Horsefair 174, **176**,
    230, 270, 291–2, **293**
St Catherine of Siena, Lowton 150–52,
    151, 186–7, 192
St Catherine's College, Oxford 6
St Cecilia, Trimley 134
St Charles Borromeo, Kelvinside 78–9, **79**,
    117–19, **119**, 187, 192
St Christophorus, Cologne-Niehl 95, 136,
    137
St Clare, Blackley **221**, 221
St Columba, Bolton 70–71, **71**, **72**, 83, 84,
    181, 269–70

St Columba, Cupar 152, **153**
St Elphege, Wallington 207, **209**
St Francis, Duston 100
St Francis de Sales, Hampton Hill 182–4, **184**, 268–9
St Francis of Assisi, Cardiff 235–6, **Plate 15**
St Gabriel, Prestonpans 233
St George's Cathedral, Southwark 36
St George's Chapel, Heathrow Airport 310–11, **312**
St Gregory, Alresford 134, 296, **297**, **298**
St Gregory the Great, Portsmouth, RI 149
St Gregory the Great, South Ruislip 1–3, **5**, 5–8, **8**, **9**, **332**
St Helen, Crosby 303–6, **305**
St Helens 91–3, **92**, **93**, 187, **189**, 195, 199, 200
St John, Hackney 41
St John Bosco junior school, Blackley 73
St John Fisher, West Heath 22, **26**, 27, **Plate 1**
St John Stone, Woodvale 84, **306**, 306–7
St John the Baptist, Rochdale 22, 89
St John Vianney, Blackpool 21
St John's Abbey Church, Collegeville, MN 79, 142
St Joseph, Faifley 180, **181**, **330**
St Joseph, Hunslet 208, **211**, 235
St Joseph, Wembley 21, 22, **24**, 195, **329**
St Joseph, Wolverhampton 262–3, **264**
St Joseph the Worker, Sutton-in-Ashfield 21
St Leonards-on-Sea 84
St Louis, Brighton 260
St Louis Priory, MO 149, **150**
St Luke, Pinner 32, **34**, 126, **329**, **Plate 3**
St Margaret, Clydebank 84, 210, **330**
St Margaret Clitherow, Threshfield 208
St Margaret Mary, Liverpool 99, 195
St Margaret of Scotland, Twickenham 156–9, **158**, **159**, **333**
S. Maria Nascente, Milan 138
Sainte Marie de La Tourette, Éveux 84–6
St Mark's Cathedral, Venice 19
St Martin, Castlemilk 233, **235**
St Martin and St Ninian, Whithorn 252–4, **254**
St Mary, Denton 80–83, **83**
St Mary, Dunstable 174, **175**
St Mary, Edinburgh 292–5, **294**, **Plate 16**
St Mary, Failsworth 226, **227**, **228**, 269
St Mary, Leyland 116–17, 123–5, **125**, 126, 127, 149–52, 187, 195, 223, 270, **272**, **331**, **Plate 8**

St Mary and the Angels, Camelon 186
St Mary Magdalene, Cudworth 126, **128**
St Matthew, Clubmoor 31
St Matthew, Northampton 113, 115
St Michael, Ancoats 71, 271
St Michael, Wolverhampton 207, **208**
St Michael and All Angels, Wombwell 100–101, **100**
St Michael and All Angels, Woodchurch 200, 282–4, **283**, **284**, **332**, **335**
St Monica, Bootle 31
St Nicholas, Gipton 187, **191**, 192
St Ninian, Knightswood 35
St Ninian, Whithorn (shrine) 252–4, **254**
St Paschal Baylon, Liverpool 221
St Patrick, Coventry 258, 259, **260**
St Patrick, Kilsyth 49, **50**, 87, 101
St Patrick, Leicester 21, **23**
St Patrick, Rochdale **89**, 89, **90**
St Patrick, St Helens 91–3, **92**, **93**, 195, 200
St Patrick, Walsall 73–5, **75**, **76**
St Paul, Bow Common 92–4, **94**, 133, 138–40, **139**, 141
St Paul, Glenrothes 49, **50**, 51, 63–4, 119, **120**, **179**, 179, 180, 186, 285–7, **330**
St Paul, Harlow **288**, 288–9
St Paul, Shettleston 49
St Paul, Wood Green 210, 233, **234**, 270, **271**, **Plate 11**
St Peter, Dumbarton 95, **97**
St Peter, Gorleston-on-Sea 142
St Peter-in-Chains, Doncaster 208, 270
St Peter's College, Cardross 181, **182**
St Pius X, New Malden 223
St Raphael, Stalybridge 27–8, **28**, 187
St Raphael, Yeading 259–60, **262**
St Richard, Chichester 28
St Saviour, Eltham 38
St Simon Stock, Aylesford Priory (shrine) 76, 238–42, **240–41**, 257
St Stephen, Droylsden 176, **178**, 187, 227, **229**
St Teresa, Filton 27
St Teresa, Upholland 31
St Teresa of Avila, St Helens 187, **189**, 199
St Theresa, Sheffield 278, **279**
St Theresa of Lisieux, Borehamwood 32, **192**, 193
St Thérèse of Lisieux, Sandfields 207, **210**
St Thomas More, Harlow 289
St Thomas More, Knebworth 257
St Thomas More, Manor House 212–13, **213**

St Thomas More, Sheffield 302–3, **303**, **304**, **334**
St Thomas of Canterbury, Rainham 75–6, **77**
St Vincent de Paul, Southmead 282
St William of York, Stanmore 187, **188**
Sts Mary and Joseph, Poplar 15, **17**, 18, 19, 60, 62, 223, **259**, 259, 260–62, **263**
Sts Peter and Paul, Lichfield 95, **96**
Sts Philip and James, Hodge Hill 302
Salford 187; see also Manchester
Samuely, Felix 30
Sandfields, Port Talbot 207, **210**
Sandy & Norris 21–7, **25–6**, 181, **Plate 1**
Saupique, Georges 267
Scanlan, Edward 259
Scanlan, James 180, 288
schools 15, 21, 48, 51, 69, 70, 73, 91, 98–9, 100, 109–10, 181, 222, 258, 265, 269–70, 280–82, 287, 289, 291
Schotz, Benno 117–19, **119–20**, 192
Schwarz, Rudolf 94, 95, 136–8, **137**, 149, 159, 210
Scott, Adrian Gilbert 15, **17**, 18, 19, 21, 41, 56, 58, **59–60**, 60–63, 204, 223, 239, **240–41**, 259, **259**, **263**, **279**, 280
Scott, Francis 287
Scott, Sir Giles Gilbert 35–6, **37**, 41, 278, **278**
Scott, Richard Gilbert 41, 48, 63, **64**, 199–200, **201–2**
Scott, William 21; see also Reynolds & Scott
Scottish identity 253–5
sculpture 6, 7, 32, 75–6, 91, 114, 117–27, 192, 200, 219–20, 226, 239, 265, 267, 300–301
seating 6, 27, 73, 75, 80, 138, 142, 144, 149–50, 152, 155, 157, 162–3, 180, 206, 210–11
Secretariat for Promoting Christian Unity 308
Second Vatican Council 4–5, 54–5, 63, 83, 111, 141–2, 144, 157, 160, 174, 180–81, 185–6, 194, 196, 204, 219, 222, 225, 236, 277, 295–7, 302–3, 306, 308, 318, 326
Secular Use of Church Buildings (Davies) 302
sermons 84, 87, 174, 206, 239–40, 257, 301
Sharing of Church Buildings Act 311
Sheedy, Gilbert **184**
Sheffield 38, **38**, 52, 174, 278, **279**, 302–3, **303–4**, **334**

Shepherd's Bush, London 265, **266**
Sheppard, Lancelot 160, 194, 206
Shettleston 49
Shirley 300–302, **300–301**
shrines 10, 227–31, 238–45, 221, 251, 252–7, 258–9, 260–62, 266
side altars 180–82, 186, 196, 221
side chapels 21, 63, 144, 149, 152, 155, 180–82, 195, 200, 204, 207, 220–21, 269; see also Blessed Sacrament chapels; Lady chapels
singing 4, 141, 142, 144, 160, 163, 205
Sir Percy Thomas & Son 52, 159–66, **161–5**, **237**, **333**, **Plate 9**
Sisters of the Adoration Réparatrice 225, 231
siting 278–95
Sloan, Merrick 242
Slough 311–14, **313–15**, **334**
Smithson, Alison 7, 80, 86, 91, 93, 136
Smithson, Peter 7, 80, 86, 91, 93, 134, 136, 156
socialism 70–73, 138, 263
Society of Saint Gregory 142, 143
Soho House project 86
Somers Town 62–3, 199, 259
Soukop, Willi 6, **9**
South Uist 254–5
Southall 204, 259
Southampton 84, **85**
Southmead, Bristol 282
Southport 41, 84, **306**, 306–8
Southwark 36
space frames 83–4, 210, 308
Speke 149–50, **151**, 186–7, 195, **331**
Spence, Sir Basil 6, 15, 49, 78–9, 95, 113, 117, 155, 252–3, **253**
spires 16, 80, 291, 309; see also towers
Spirit of the Liturgy (Guardini) 111, 137
Spode House, Staffordshire 127–8
square plans 80, 83, 91, 144, 157, 204, 207, 208–10, 296, 303, 308, 312
Stafford, 21
stained glass 6, 7, 22, 27–8, 113, 116–17, 120–23, 124, 163, 235, 259, 262–3, 265, 269–70, 303; see also dalle de verre
Stainforth 57
Stalybridge 27–8, **28**, 187
Stanmore 187, **188**
Stark, D. Rogers 15, **16**
Stations of the Cross 115, 117, 123, 125, 126–7, 149, 184, 200, 219, 221, 226, 231–7, 239, 269

statuary 219–21, 225–6, 227, 254, 259,
    263, 269; *see also* sculpture
statue shrines 221, 242–5
Stechford 207–8
steel 21, 29, 35, 47, 71, 73, 83–4, 92–3, 98,
    114, 144, 182, 210, 312
Steffan, Emil 138
Stepney 267
Stevenage 315–18, **316–17**
Stirchley 314
Stirling, James 7, 86, 89, 91
Stoke-on-Trent, 21
Stokes, David **61**, 61, 79, **81**, 154–5, 186
Straub, Leo 317
Stuart, Ian **125**
Stuart, Lord David 252
Stüflesser 111
suburbs 2, 69, 70, 95, 115, 242, 278–84, 302
Summerson, John 29, 36
Sutherland, Dickie & Partners 199
Sutherland, Graham 113, **114**, 114–15,
    124, 126–7, 135, **Plate 5**
Sutton, Joseph 300
Sutton-in-Ashfield 21
Swansea 152–3
Sykes, Steven 7, **8**
symbolism 17–18, 73, 78, 111, 120, 123,
    124, 135, 151–4, 160, 299–302

tabernacles 5, 91, 120, 144, 148–50, 157,
    160–3, 180, 186–7, 193, 195–6,
    199–204, 207–8, 210, 212, 222–3,
    269–70, 309, 311–12, 314, 317–18
tapestries 110, 113, 114, 124, 135, 267
Tablet, The 60–61, 115, 133, 144–6, 257
Taylor, John 309
Taylor, Thomas 230
Team 10 86, 91, 93, 136
Teilhard de Chardin, Pierre 297–9, 301
Telford 314
temporary churches 138, 174, 176–9, 269,
    285, 289
Thornleigh Salesian School, Bolton 181
Thornton, Leslie 123
Threshfield, Yorkshire 208
thrones, *see* bishops' thrones; monstrance
    thrones
Thurcroft 101
Thurnscoe 101
Tile Cross 63, **64**, 199–200, **201**, **202**
timber 22, 32, 36, 63, 70–71, 84–7, 91, 95,
    212–13
    laminated 70, 83–4, 101–2, 103, 317

Tinto, Peter 285, **286**
Tomei, Mackley & Pound 210, **212**
Towards a Church Architecture
    (Hammond) 134
towers 15, 17, 22, 29–32, 36, 36–9, 61, 63,
    70, 75, 79–80, 86, 135, 152, 163, 200,
    230, 236, 239, 280, 292, 301, 314; *see
    also* campaniles; spires
town planning 2–3, 8, 277, 278–95, 315, 325
tradition 15–18, 28–9, 40–41, 57–8, 62,
    185–6
Traherne, Margaret **121**
Tranmer, Anthony 302; *see also* John
    Rochford & Partners
Trimley 134
Trinity Congregational church, Poplar
    15, **16**
Turner, Victor 238, 251
Turner, William 252
Twickenham 156–9, **158**, **159**, **333**
Tyburn, London 255–7, **256**
Tyburn Convent, London **255**, 256–7

Ukrainian immigrants 271
Ulm 29
universities 70, 91, 95, 98, 100, 309–10
Upholland 31
urban planning 2–3, 8, 277, 278–95, 315,
    325
urbanism 8, 47, 86, 93, 291

Varin, René 267
Vatican 3, 17–18, 54–5, 60–61, 110–11,
    115, 141–2, 157, 174, 181, 186,
    196–9, 222, 225, 308; *see also* Second
    Vatican Council
Vatican II, *see* Second Vatican Council
vaulting 21, 27, 29, 30, 63, 78, 79–80, 83,
    95, 138, 149, 182, 193, 207
Velarde, Francis Xavier 19, 21, 29, 31–5,
    32–34, 41, 47, 49, 62, 126, **192**, 193,
    223, 231, **232**, 283, 326, **329**, **Plate 3**,
    Plate 13
Velarde, Julian 32
Vence 54
Venice 19
vernacular language (Mass) 4, 160, 198,
    205
Viollet-le-Duc, Eugène 35
visibility 6, 21–2, 71, 73, 148, 155, 162,
    173, 206, 223
'Visual Arts Weeks' (Guild of Catholic
    Artists and Craftsmen) 100, 127

Wakefield 101
Waldron, Patrick 268
Walker, Derek 101, 222, **224**
Walker, Paul 10, 204
Walker, Thomas 142
Walkinshaw, Robert 49; *see also* Gillespie,
   Kidd & Coia
Wall, Bernard Patrick 148
Wallasey 32
Wallington 207, **209**
Walsall 73–5, **75**, **76**
Walter Stirrup & Son 80, **83**
Walters, F.A. 36
Warrington 27
Watts, Peter 114, 117, 126, **128**, **259**
Weeks, Ronald 159–66; *see also* Sir Percy
   Thomas & Son
Weightman & Bullen 49, 51, 52, 57, 99–
   100, **100**, 101, 103, 116, 123, **125–6**,
   126–7, 149–50, **151**, 152, 186–7, **191**,
   192, 195, 221, **221**, 235, 242, **244**,
   263, 303, **305**, **331**, **Plate 8**
Welch & Lander 38
welfare state 2, 48, 70, 98, 109–10
Welland, Arthur 62–3
Wells-Thorpe, John 99–100, 103
Wembley 21, **24**, 195, **329**
West Heath 22, **26**, 27, **Plate 1**
Westminster Cathedral 19–21, **20**, 27,
   115, 126, 199, 233, 242, 257
Wheeler, William 208, 303
Whiston, Peter 52, 58, 152–3, **153**
Whit Walk, Manchester 271–2
White, K.C. **77**
Whithorn 252–4, **252**, **254**
Widnes 223
Williams, Desmond 48, **89–90**, 89–91,
   174, **175**, 207, **208**, 259, **260**, **Plate 4**

Williams, Geoffrey 70–73, 98, 269; *see also*
   Greenhalgh & Williams
Williams, John 156
Williams, Reg 100
Williams & Winkley **158–9**, **209**, **333**;
   see also Winkley, Austin
Wilson, Colin St John 7, 91
Wilson, William **263**
Wimbledon 210, **212**
Winkley, Austin 48, 51, 133, 134, 146,
   156–7, **158–9**, 162, 180, 207, **208**,
   211, **333**
Winstone, Harold 212
Wolverhampton 207, **208**, 262–3, **264**
Wombwell **100**, 100–101
Wood Green, London 210, 233, **234**, 270,
   271, **Plate 11**
Woodard, David 312
Woodchurch, Birkenhead 200, 282–4,
   283–4, **332**, **335**
Woodvale, Southport 84, **306**, 306–8
Work of Our Redemption (Howell) 142
worker-priest movement 141
Worship 142
Wright, Lance 61, 117, 127, 133, 134, 159,
   283, 296, 299, 314; *see also* Melhuish,
   Wright & Evans
Wythenshawe **279**, 280–82, **280–81**

Yeading 259–60, **262**
York 100
York University 98, 100
Young Christian Workers 156

Zielinski, Tadeusz 265